THE
JIM CROW
NORTH

THE JIM CROW NORTH

THE STRUGGLE FOR CIVIL RIGHTS IN POTTSTOWN, PENNSYLVANIA

MATTHEW GEORGE WASHINGTON

Copyright © 2024 by The University Press of Kentucky

Scholarly publisher for the Commonwealth,
serving Bellarmine University, Berea College, Centre
College of Kentucky, Eastern Kentucky University,
The Filson Historical Society, Georgetown College,
Kentucky Historical Society, Kentucky State University,
Morehead State University, Murray State University,
Northern Kentucky University, Spalding University,
Transylvania University, University of Kentucky,
University of Louisville, University of Pikeville,
and Western Kentucky University.
All rights reserved.

Editorial and Sales Offices: The University Press of Kentucky
663 South Limestone Street, Lexington, Kentucky 40508-4008
www.kentuckypress.com

Library of Congress Cataloging-in-Publication Data

Names: Washington, Matthew George, author.
Title: The Jim Crow north : the struggle for civil rights in Pottstown,
    Pennsylvania / Matthew George Washington.
Other titles: Struggle for civil rights in Pottstown, Pennsylvania
Description: Lexington, Kentucky : University Press of Kentucky, [2024] |
    Includes bibliographical references and index.
Identifiers: LCCN 2023048953 | ISBN 9781985900233 (hardcover) | ISBN
    9781985900240 (paperback) | ISBN 9781985900264 (pdf) | ISBN
    9781985900257 (epub)
Subjects: LCSH: African Americans—Civil rights—Pennsylvania—Pottstown—
    History—20th century. | Civil rights movements—Pennsylvania—Pottstown—
    History—20th century. | African American civil rights workers—Pennsylvania—
    Pottstown—History—20th century. | Civil rights workers—Pennsylvania—
    Pottstown—History—20th century. | Segregation—Pennsylvania—Pottstown—
    History—20th century. | Pottstown (Pa.)—Race relations—History—20th
    century. | Pottstown (Pa.)—Social conditions—20th century. | Pottstown Mercury.
Classification: LCC F159.P8 W37 2024 | DDC
    323.1196/073074812—dc23/eng/20231025
LC record available at https://lccn.loc.gov/2023048953

This book is printed on acid-free paper meeting
the requirements of the American National Standard
for Permanence in Paper for Printed Library Materials.

Manufactured in the United States of America.

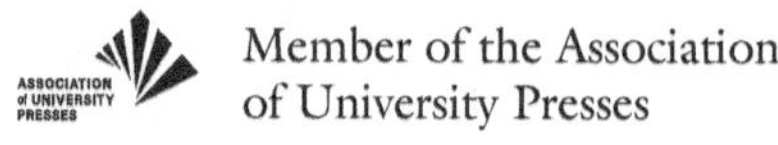

To God Almighty Jesus Christ; my precious wife,
Hannah Kristine; and our beautiful daughter,
Madelyn Grace

Contents

Illustrations follow page 146

Abbreviations

African Methodist Episcopal	(AME)
American Bowling Congress	(ABC)
American Civil Liberties Union	(ACLU)
American Friends Service Committee	(AFSC)
Anti-Defamation League of B'nai B'rith	(ADL)
Associated Press	(AP)
Congress of Industrial Organizations	(CIO)
Congress of Racial Equality	(CORE)
Federal Bureau of Investigation	(FBI)
Frankford Improvement Association	(FIA)
Human Relations Commission	(HRC)
Ku Klux Klan	(KKK)
Maryland Congress of Parents and Teachers	(MCPT)
Mayor's Friendly Relations Committee	(MFRC)
Montgomery County Housing Authority	(MCHA)
National Association for the Advancement of Colored People	(NAACP)
National Association of Intergroup Relations Officials	(NAIRO)
National Conference of Christians and Jews	(NCCJ)
National Council of the Churches of Christ in the United States of America	(NCCCUSA)
Pottstown Bowling Association	(PBA)
Pottstown Civic League	(PCL)
Pottstown Committee on Human Relations	(PCHR)
Pottstown Human Relations Council	(PHRC)
Pottstown Junior High School	(PJHS)
rhythm and blues	(R&B)
Seventh-day Adventist	(SDA)
Teenagers Organization for a Productive Summer	(TOPS)

United Steelworkers	(USW)
Valley Improvement Association	(VIA)
Young Men's Christian Association	(YMCA)
Young People's Interracial Fellowship	(YPIF)
Young Women's Christian Association	(YWCA)

1

Pottstown, Pennsylvania, a Center of Civil Rights Significance

In late January 2015, southern African American transplant Newstell Marable, who made southeastern Pennsylvania his home for roughly sixty years, passed away. Born in Birmingham, Alabama, in 1930, Marable was a veteran of the United States Army (1953–1955) and graduated from one of his native state's historically Black institutions of higher education, Alabama A&M University (Huntsville). Eventually, Marable made his way to Pennsylvania during the Great Migration, the massive exodus of millions of southern-born African Americans between approximately 1915 and 1970 to the Northeast, Midwest, and West. Settling in Pottstown and later nearby Douglassville, both located in southeastern Pennsylvania, he wedded Pottstown African American Millicent Corum during the 1950s, following his military service.[1]

By marrying Millicent, Marable became a part of an active and involved local African American family, especially when it came to fellowship within Black Pottstown and the borough's civil rights struggle. For example, prior to World War II, Marable's father-in-law, James H. Corum, not only was active with local labor but also was a member of Pottstown's Second Baptist Church. Yet beginning in World War II and continuing well into the postwar era, Corum became largely involved in racial justice work as well. In addition to his union activism with Local 2326 of the United Steelworkers (USW)—an affiliate of the Congress of Industrial Organizations (CIO)—Corum played a pivotal role in civil rights work with organizations in the borough such as the Pottstown branch of the National Association for the Advancement of Colored People (NAACP), the Pottstown Civic League (PCL), and the Pottstown Committee on Human Relations (PCHR).[2]

Two of James's younger brothers, William D. and Thomas W. Corum, were also heavily engaged in the local Black community and civil rights activism. Both congregated at Pottstown's Bethel African Methodist Episcopal (AME), a local church representative of Black Pottstown.[3] The Corum brothers were additionally active with the local all-Black musical group, "the Keystone State quartet," and Pottstown's "Colored Community Hospital auxiliary."[4] Moreover, starting during World War II, William spearheaded "Negro Extension Work" activism with the Pottstown branch of the Young Men's Christian Association (YMCA), and he, like his elder brother James, labored with both the PCL and the PCHR during the postwar years.[5] In collaboration with the local white-owned advocacy newspaper, the *Pottstown Mercury*, Thomas struggled passionately during World War II so that the borough government authorized an African American "special police officer" as the global war raged. In sum, his activism led him to becoming the first Black cop of Pottstown's local police force.[6]

Likewise, soon after his arrival in southeastern Pennsylvania, it did not take Marable long at all to immerse himself directly in the local African American community and civil rights causes indigenous to the region. Like William and Thomas Corum, their niece's southern-born husband was a faithful congregant of Pottstown's Bethel AME. In fact, it was there where Marable and Millicent initially encountered one another. Yet Marable's civil rights work had the greatest historical mark in and around Pottstown. In addition to his activism with the Pottstown Human Relations Council—another appellation of the PCHR—Marable was an integral laborer of the local NAACP, especially during his reign as branch president, which lasted from the early 1960s to his death in the mid-2010s.[7] Overall, so paramount was the Alabama-born activist's connection to Pottstown's Black freedom struggle that in early May 2019, the Pennsylvania government even lionized his lasting civil rights legacy publicly by "unveil[ing] a new sign" denoting "the bridge on a portion of Route 100 . . . in Pottstown as the Newstell Marable Sr. Memorial Bridge."[8]

The illustrations of Marable and the Corum family are only a few examples of many active participants connected to Black Pottstown and the civil rights struggle in and around the borough. However, from World War II through the late 1960s, both African Americans and whites played chief roles in combating local manifestations of white supremacy and anti-Black discrimination. Through their important work, they sought to radically alter unequal and exclusionary conditions locally and thereby actualize a freer and more inclusive America.

The Jim Crow North: The Struggle for Civil Rights in Pottstown, Pennsylvania chronicles the history of Pottstown's Black freedom struggle from World War II through the late 1960s and the ways in which it played out in southeastern Pennsylvania and beyond. To be sure, when thinking about civil rights history in the United States and its centers of geographical importance during the twentieth century, the small, working-class borough of Pottstown, Pennsylvania, located in Montgomery County and approximately forty miles northwest of Philadelphia, does not usually come to mind. But the location was a significant hub of civil rights activism. With an interracial movement conceived during World War II, Pottstown activists launched multiple civil rights campaigns to improve the conditions of local African Americans well into the late 1960s.[9]

Yet even with having this interracial component from inception, it was African Americans themselves who were at the forefront of the local civil rights struggle.[10] During World War II and the postwar era, Black-led activist groups—such as the Pottstown NAACP, the "Negro Extension Work" program of the local YMCA, and the PCL—led the fight. Utilizing Black community spaces like Second Baptist Church, such entities provided local civil rights work with both effective African American leadership and grassroots activists in their fervent quest for racial justice and equitability. Moreover, their resistance strategies for civil rights advancement, especially during World War II, incorporated "equalization" and other traditional Black internal improvement practices.[11] However, during the war and subsequent years, activists also advocated "a liberal interracialist" strategy. Regarding this latter scheme, local activists' plan of action coincided with the national struggle.[12] On the other hand, African American–led organizations in Pottstown during World War II served as important early proving grounds for local Black leadership, so much so that several of these African American leaders went on to have great success in future civil rights struggles.[13]

While African Americans were at the foreground of democratic racial change in and around Pottstown, they too received direct support, assistance, and collaboration from local whites. Organized only months following the United States Supreme Court's decision in *Brown v. Board of*

Education (May 1954), which annulled racially segregating Black and white pupils lawfully within public schooling, the PCHR, an interracial organization of advocates and activists, for instance, had great impact, leading particularly to many inquiries and discussions across the nation that were germane to local civil rights struggle and Black freedom work. In short, the PCHR was a by-product of both national and local civil rights activism. Whereas local civil rights discourses and *Brown* influenced the *Pottstown Mercury* to begin publishing reports that exposed discrimination that targeted African Americans on the local front, the newspaper's reporting, in turn, served as the impetus to the creation of the PCHR. Moreover, the activism of PCHR members and the impact of its programs were further buttressed by the Pottstown group's connections to another, larger reform organization located in nearby Philadelphia.[14]

Starting in the early 1940s, Fellowship House not only fought for policies of interracialism and integration consistently but also promoted egalitarian values in the world. Beyond its headquarters in Philadelphia, Fellowship House also owned and operated a farm near Pottstown in Fagleysville, Pennsylvania.[15] Fellowship House and Farm enjoyed a number of affiliated organizations across the United States and had the support of an extensive web of civil rights activists with national clout. In the end, Fellowship House and Farm activists would utilize this expansive web to promote the PCHR, especially its "Pottstown Plan," throughout the country.[16]

Yet as significant as the Fellowship House organization was in the promotion of African American civil rights struggle in Pottstown and beyond, the most consistent local, white-led institution that championed the causes of Black equality and racial inclusion was the *Pottstown Mercury*. The positive impact of the newspaper on the efforts of local civil rights activists cannot be overstated. More than simply reporting news of developments within the borough's Black freedom struggle, or even voicing support for racial reforms, through its editorials, opinion columns, and publications of many letters to the editor correspondences, the *Pottstown Mercury* continually advocated the causes of Black equality and freedom.

Established during the Great Depression, the *Pottstown Mercury* additionally gave important visibility to civil rights activists and racial reformers in and around Pottstown, especially during the critical years between World War II and the late 1960s. In short, the newspaper used its advocacy reporting work at a number of important and crucial historical junctures in time. Moreover, not only the press applied direct media pressure on initiatives and practices it saw as local forces of racism, bigotry, and exclusion at work, but its rationality in doing so was also both morally and philosophically based. Specifically, the ethos of the Pottstown newspaper's civil rights advocacy work rested in sincere and honest attempts at curbing such undemocratic practices across the borough, which, to be sure, had long been historically implemented and entrenched. At the same time, some of the newspaper's efforts even went beyond Pottstown, influencing not only regional civil rights activism but also national developments congruent to the larger Black freedom struggle of World War II and postwar America.[17]

Yet notwithstanding the interracial—and at times regional and national—nature of some of the most critical civil rights work done in the name of racial progress across Pottstown and beyond, the indubitable fact that local Blacks consistently spearheaded such work should not be ignored. From World War II through the late 1960s, Pottstown African Americans played instrumental roles in the local Black freedom struggle, carrying out and initiating most of the activism by themselves. Despite the small size of the African American community, Black Pottstown activists were generally the vanguard of local civil rights leadership and development efforts.[18] While some of them were natives of Pennsylvania, others relocated from the American South both before and during the Great Migration. Whatever their origins, these Black freedom fighters helped bring about tangible change locally for themselves and the larger African American community during World War II and subsequent postwar decades.[19]

"A Northern Style Jim Crow System"

By the time Pottstown activists began waging their important civil rights struggles during World War II, the plight of local Blacks and the racial prejudices they encountered on a daily basis were indicative of the larger African American experience throughout the industrialized North. To be sure, northern African Americans, like those residing in Pottstown and adjacent locales, were already well accustomed and all too familiar with the ways in which white supremacy and anti-Black racism permeated a variety of spaces. Undergirded by the covert yet pervasive inequitable structure of "'de facto' segregation," these discriminatory initiatives engendered an atmosphere throughout the North that both informally and ubiquitously relegated African Americans to a second-class status.[20]

In Pottstown and nearby areas specifically, local African Americans experienced firsthand the harsh reality of de facto segregation through the spheres of employment, housing, interment, recreation, entertainment, leisure, and educational structures in both private and public institutions. For example, in employment, white bosses assigned local Blacks to working-class jobs of the lowest pay and skill set—rarely did borough African Americans find themselves in positions of leadership and authority. In housing, even well before World War II, they not only endured living within poor and dilapidated residential structures and housing discrimination; they also faced harsh and strident racial exclusionary policies within predominately white neighborhoods. These white residential locations were usually more modern and had updated buildings as well. In interment, African Americans found themselves having to collaborate with local whites who were, in fact, maintaining a de facto segregated space; thus, Black congregants implemented a graveyard initiative with the objective of serving the larger local African American population's burial needs. In recreation, entertainment, and leisure establishments and programming, African Americans in and around the borough dealt directly and particularly with embarrassing policies of complete and outright racial separation or banning alongside selective segregation initiatives. Regarding these latter policies from the majority white community, they were arguably as humiliating and psychologically mortifying to local Blacks. And finally, in the arena of education, while schools in Pottstown and nearby had long been integrated, de facto segregation still did manifest itself on several notable occasions in which local whites in the region tried excluding—whether purposefully or incidentally—African Americans from these learning spaces.[21]

Other instances of de facto segregation also came about where local African Americans were not receiving the same educational privileges afforded to their white counterparts, so much so that in one particular illustration when local Black activists sought educational reforms, regional whites responded by pushing back against and countering their righteous and racially inclusive "demands."[22] In the end, whether passively, implicitly, or even ambiguously, local whites fully embraced and supported the de facto structure in and around Pottstown. By doing so, they also played active and definitive roles in both sustaining and maintaining its pervasive discriminatory philosophies, exclusionary schemes, and subterfuge.

Unlike the American South, which legally codified race bigotry—known as Jim Crow segregation—more informally, Blacks residing in Pottstown, adjacent areas, and other locales above the Mason-Dixon Line between World War II and the postwar era also came face to face with "a northern style Jim Crow system." This "system," which the present study interchangeably identifies as de facto separation, was "an informal" yet "airtight" pattern "of segregation." Indeed, this "northern style Jim Crow system" was arguably as pervasive and ubiquitous as its southern counterpart structure, which formally utilized legal means—that is, "'de jure' segregation"—as a central and evident vehicle of racial separation and oppression, alongside the furtherance and promulgation of regional exclusionary customs germane to Dixie.[23]

Yet while southern Jim Crow was legally visible and overt, the ways in which whites in Pottstown and surrounding areas of the North enforced, supported, and maintained their regional Jim Crow structure was through more clandestine and covert policies and practices. To put it more directly, Pottstown, like many other urban locations above the Mason-Dixon Line, had both "informal" and "subtle methods" that governed the local racial landscape and power structure.[24] In turn, the borough fully accommodated camouflaged white supremacy and unobtrusive anti-Black racism. Thus, de facto "discriminations" were "long embedded in the fabric of the [Pottstown] community."[25] They also both underhandedly and pervadingly targeted local African Americans during the decades of this "northern style Jim Crow system."

Approximately nine months after the announcement of *Brown v. Board of Education*, the New Jersey–based newspaper, the *Plainfield Courier-News*, provided further corroborative remarks that demonstrated the informality of de facto segregation—the North's own Jim Crow structure—and how it inextricably permeated the small borough. According to the Garden State press, "Pottstown is not different from most Northern small towns. They all think the Supreme Court decision was aimed only at the South. There are no Jim Crow laws up here." However, the *Plainfield Courier-News* went on, such white racism was pervasively "disguised."[26] Born in 1954, Jewish Pottstown native Lawrence Cohen made remarks that also demonstrate the ways in which Jim Crow manifested across the small northern borough. Recalling his formative days as a child residing within the borough during the 1950s and 1960s, Cohen recalls that "while Pottstown at the time was not palpably racist, it remained rigidly segregated." He additionally asserts, "I grew up with no African-American friends and attended a 100% white elementary school." To be sure, although local residential or educational spaces were not legally practicing segregation, as was the case of the codified de jure structure below the Mason-Dixon Line, Cohen's comments speak further to more covert and clandestine policies of race bigotry and exclusion across Pottstown in his reflections on the postwar era.[27]

In the end, like the entrenchment of southern Jim Crow, which was clearly manifested, African Americans residing within this "informal," "subtle," yet wide-reaching de facto racial caste structure of Jim Crow above the Mason-Dixon Line in places such as Pottstown found it just as dehumanizing and racially unjust, even characterizing the "system" on a par with the South. At times, Pottstown Blacks even argued that the "northern style Jim Crow system" was far worse.[28] For example, local African American Frances Young Williams, who juxtaposed Pottstown with Dixie in late July 1954, declared, "Let me say that there were times during my childhood that lead me to believe that conditions for Negroes in Pottstown were not half as good as they were for Negroes in the South." Moreover, Williams added, "at least in the South a Negro knew where he stood and he did not have to face embarrassment by attempting to seek social life, entertainment or jobs above a certain level or field."[29]

In addition, while commenting on Pottstown in the aftermath of *Brown*, white *Pottstown Mercury* journalist Normand Poirier demonstrated how the borough "might be called an average Northern community."[30] By Poirier identifying Pottstown as such, he affirmed that the Pennsylvania locale's "informal" yet "airtight" Jim Crow structure of de facto segregation that oppressed borough Blacks was likewise identical to additional seemingly normal northern locales. At the same time, the white journalist constructed arguments in which he utilized the American South as his comparison point or barometer.[31] However, in order to support one argument in which he centers on the fact that both systems equally and extensively oppressed African Americans, Poirier additionally declared, "Segregation, whether brought about with Jim Crow signs in buses and restaurants" like the de jure structure "or . . . the more polite, subtle methods" regarding de facto separation locally across Pottstown, as well as the North more broadly, "is exactly the same thing."[32]

White army soldier David Chaplin, when remarking on how de facto segregation permeated the locale, analogously correlated Pottstown's racial struggles with his alma mater, Amherst College (Amherst, Massachusetts), even recalling how "race relations" there were similar to all northern small communities. Specifically, Chaplin added, these locations were "governed by a subtle Jim Crow line . . . as fixed as the obvious one down South." Indeed, like Chaplin, *The Jim Crow North* stresses both the informality and the ubiquity of how the traditions of racial bigotry in Pottstown and nearby locales both clandestinely and epidemically manifested across the de facto structure vis-à-vis Jim Crow in the North during World War II and the postwar period.[33]

Naturally, *The Jim Crow North* is not the first study to interpret manifestations of racial prejudice in the American North through the analytical framing of de facto segregation. In fact, from a traditional standpoint, scholars have, more broadly, even understood civil rights history as it relates to practices of white racism above and below the Mason-Dixon Line within the theoretical dichotomy of de facto segregation in the North and the de jure legal structure across the South. Even though recently academics like Matthew Lassiter and Jeanne Theoharis sharply criticize the de facto/de jure juxtaposition, *The Jim Crow North* nevertheless emphasizes its utility. Specifically, when Pottstown activists talked about racial injustices, multiple times they contrasted the more covert discriminatory conditions that permeated the area with the de jure, or legally mandated and apparent, racialized system throughout Dixie. Moreover, much of the contemporary evidence utilized throughout this book speaks about exclusionary racial policies within the ethos of de facto segregation—the pervading structure of Jim Crow in the North. Consequently, when interpreting the ways in which the far-reaching manifestations of racial exclusion rested across Pottstown and nearby locales of civil rights struggle in the North from World War II through the late 1960s, this book also identifies the discriminatory schemes within the orthodox structuring of de facto and de jure racism.[34]

Of course, there can most certainly be limitations to interpreting civil rights history through this traditional theoretical dichotomy, as historian Jason Sokol demonstrates in his more nuanced assessment examining the ways in which racial interactions played out above the Mason-Dixon Line. "The cities of the Northeast were simultaneously beacons of interracial democracy and strongholds of racial segregation." Sokol adds, "Both stories—seemingly contradictory stories—unfolded side by side, at the same moments, in the same places."[35] Nevertheless, even though *The Jim Crow North* recognizes some of the analytical shortcomings of the conventional de facto/de jure comparative model, the book underscores both its practicality and its intellectual usefulness when evaluating and assessing Pottstown's Black freedom struggle from World War II throughout the 1960s, as well as its historical connections to the Jim Crow regions both above and below the Mason-Dixon Line.[36]

Finally, a note on phrases used to describe civil rights struggles in Pottstown, adjacent areas, and beyond is essential. Phrases such as *Black freedom struggle, civil rights struggle, civil rights work, civil rights activism, Black freedom activism,* and *Black freedom work* are all interchangeable terms. Moreover, the words *civil rights advocacy work* and *civil rights advocacy* are utilized as well, especially when talking about the *Pottstown Mercury* and its involvement in local civil rights activism. In the end, these various phrases are used to both capture and identify the critical civil rights struggles connected to the small northern borough of Pottstown, Pennsylvania—a central hub of Black freedom activism, beginning during World War II and continuing well into the postwar era.[37]

Pottstown, PA: A Locus of Civil Rights Importance in Historical Context

As indicated prior, *The Jim Crow North* interprets de facto segregation correspondingly as the "informal," "subtle," yet ubiquitous Jim Crow structure above the Mason-Dixon Line.[38] However, the book also contributes particularly to the growing body of scholarly literature on the history of northern civil rights (and beyond). Since the early 2000s, this subfield of the study of the Black freedom struggle has benefited, evolved, and progressed, especially because of the important work of scholars such as Jeanne Theoharis, Komozi Woodard, Thomas J. Sugrue, Martha Biondi, Randal Maurice Jelks, Jack Dougherty, Beth T. Bates, Brian Purnell, Peter B. Levy, and Jason Sokol.[39] In many ways, the expansive development, beyond mere inquiry, into this subtopic is a response to the dominance of the southern narrative—so much so that to this day, the American South remains the most captured space in the study of the Black freedom struggle and the popular understanding of the same history of civil rights activism more broadly.[40]

Yet while scholarship centering on northern civil rights has largely increased the past twenty or so years, it has also generally excluded a specific type of industrial location above the Mason-Dixon Line. To be sure, smaller northern spaces such as Pottstown, which never exceeded twenty-seven thousand residents between 1940 and 1970, are most certainly in direct contrast to similar important battlegrounds of civil rights struggle in the South like Cambridge, Maryland, and Monroe, North Carolina. In particular, scholars have paid the latter southern spaces, which had very minute populations, a decent amount of intellectual attention and space.[41]

To understand this historiographical conundrum, one must note how scholars have generally excluded Pottstown and similar-size northern locales because they are outside the two main geographical spaces highlighted within both traditional and recent civil rights scholarship. Not surprisingly, the first area is the American South—the geographical space, as indicated before, overwhelmingly associated with the conventional perspective. As political scientist Jeanne Theoharis writes, "the dominant civil rights story remains that of a nonviolent movement born in the South during the 1950s," which appeared "triumphant in the early 1960s." However, she continues, such an interpretation goes on by stressing that "the twin forces of Black Power and white backlash" thwarted civil rights activism "when it sought to move North after 1965."[42]

The second geographical region targets vast northern cities. Such recent works even go directly against the traditional interpretation of civil rights history on two levels. First, the scholarship reveals conclusively that the South was not the sole place and space where activists conducted civil rights work. Indeed, northern civil rights activists fought Black discrimination throughout metropolitan centers such as Detroit and Philadelphia and even as far west as Oakland and Seattle.[43] Second, more recent northern-centered scholarship also challenges the traditional time span of the modern civil rights movement, which generally centers on the period from 1954 to 1968 and is primarily associated with the South.[44] However, to reconsider these fourteen years, the literature builds typically on the time period argument laid out in historian Jacquelyn Dowd Hall's significant essay, "The Long Civil Rights Movement and the Political Uses of the Past."[45] Employing Hall's "long civil rights movement" model, the scholarship expands civil rights activism before and after the orthodox time frame on both ends of the spatial continuum.[46]

In the end, while civil rights historians such as Thomas J. Sugrue, Peter B. Levy, and Jill Ogline Titus have in more recent years begun reconsidering the large city emphasis by capturing tinier locations above the Mason-Dixon Line, the fact remains that densely populated spaces in the North have been the main focus of the newer scholarship.[47] "The battle for racial equality in the North played out with special intensity in the major cities that were home to nearly four-fifths of the black population outside Dixie," Sugrue observes. However, he continues, "struggles for civil rights also reshaped small towns and suburbs—a part of the northern story that has been almost completely overlooked."[48] Levy echoes Sugrue's keen analysis, writing, "The traditional narrative of the civil rights years has paid little attention to either the state of race relations or the struggles against inequality in small and medium size cities, particularly those north of the Mason-Dixon line."[49] Finally, and most recently in her monograph on Gettysburg (Pennsylvania)—a location relatively nearby Pottstown yet drastically smaller—Titus (as well as Levy) makes similar historiographical observations as this book, remarking how the central vantage point from scholarship above the Mason-Dixon Line examines "large urban centers where sizable Black populations facilitated the creation of sophisticated organizing networks and mass campaigns." Nevertheless, she continues, "not all northern Blacks lived in large cities, and segregation and discrimination limited opportunities and crushed dreams in small towns and minor urban centers as well," Pottstown being one among them.[50]

Overall, *The Jim Crow North* aligns itself with the more recent scholarship on northern civil rights, placing Pottstown at center stage of the local Black freedom struggle drama in southeastern Pennsylvania, which had both regional and national impact. However, the book also builds on theoretical models and themes already prevalent in the field. For example, the study structures Pottstown's Black freedom struggle by incorporating "the 'freedom North'" and "long civil rights movement" theoretical models. These two "frameworks," which have been utilized by multiple histories on northern civil rights and which historian Brian Purnell has so aptly categorized, originated largely from the scholarship of Theoharis and historian Komozi Woodward as well as that of Hall. As Purnell observes, works employing the freedom North model demonstrate how protestors fervently battled "local forms of racial discrimination outside the South before, during, and after civil rights movements emerged in southern cities and towns." By utilizing the long civil rights movement model, which Purnell additionally describes, this book also reassesses the accepted time frame of twentieth-century civil rights. In short, the chronology of working-class Pottstown and local civil rights work expands on the long-established time frame found in the historiography, mainly because it begins the analysis during World War II and concludes the historical narrative in 1969.[51]

Nevertheless, while this book situates the history of Pottstown within the analytical conceptualization of Hall's "long civil rights movement," it also acknowledges both the shortcomings and the limitations of the generalized archetype. As historian Jeffrey Helgeson notes in his short yet poignant article reviewing two scholarly compilations, "Beyond a Long Civil Rights Movement," the fact is, without question, that "there was no long uninterrupted civil rights movement in the 20th century." Instead, Helgeson points out, the same Black freedom struggle was, conversely, many noncontinuous—and, rather, fractured, splintered, and varied—civil rights initiatives that launched at specific moments in historical time and space. As such, the ethos behind activists' intentions, functions, and civil rights operations were in direct concert and tailored to particular historical events across the twentieth century in the United States.

Similarly, *The Jim Crow North* demonstrates a more nuanced structuring of Hall's "long civil rights movement" perspective in the sense that civil rights organizing and activism both germane and indigenous to Pottstown manifested neither monolithically nor continuously. But rather the emergence and genesis of specific instances of racial injustice and exclusion on the local front as a result of precise and unique moments in historical time thereby led to the commencement of such Black freedom activism in and around Pottstown. At the same time, while their activism was not one monolithic or even "long uninterrupted" linear work, to borrow language from Helgeson, the fact does remain that between World War II and throughout the late 1960s, African Americans and whites both conducted and orchestrated relatively consistent, albeit fractured and splintered civil rights projects, in relationship to the local Black freedom struggle.

In short, local civil rights activists, sensitive to the particular circumstances of African American inequality and injustice occurring from World War II throughout the late 1960s, began launching important Black freedom work. In doing so, they were able to directly address the general issues of the day brought on by the de facto segregation structure. Overall, because local activists tackled the concerns head-on, the problems also had the real and tangible possibility of being rectified, coupled with the end goal of them being completely revamped so that the overall betterment and amelioration of local African Americans transpired.[52]

The Jim Crow North also expands on the traditional analytical framing of northern civil rights scholarship because it specifies Pottstown as a Pennsylvania borough—a generally tinier classification when compared to a city.[53] For example, while Levy considers urban populaces like Pottstown to be "midsize cities," which range from 25,000 to 150,000 inhabitants, this study stresses the category of borough.[54] Yet even though it categorizes Pottstown as such, the small northern locale still shared a meaningful historiographical connection to midsize cities between World War II and the late 1960s. In short, and in points similar to Titus's observations, both spaces contrast from the massive cities located above the Mason-Dixon Line since they have drastically smaller Black populations juxtaposed to their white counterparts. Noting multiple examples from 1963 to 1972 relating to midsize cities, Levy additionally reveals how these regions had Black populations that were significantly low.[55] Conversely, large northern cities, such as Philadelphia and Brooklyn, had sizable African American populaces that even rivaled the same cities' white populaces, which totaled in the thousands as well as hundreds of thousands.[56]

Moreover, while more diminutive than most large northern cities, Pottstown still resembled many of them. For instance, the small northern locale was heavily industrialized, especially by World War II. As historian Paul Chancellor writes, Pottstown was never purely "an industrial town." Rather, the borough was "a center of highly important industry." By the early 1950s, Chancellor additionally notes, Pottstown's central commodities encompassed "metal products; textiles; food products, and building materials."[57] During this time, establishments such as Stanley G. Flagg & Company, Doehler-Jarvis Corporation, Mrs. Smith's Pies, Bethlehem Steel Company, and more resided in and around Pottstown too.[58] Likewise, another assessment brags how by the mid-1960s, more than seventy "major industries" on the local front had payrolls approximating twenty thousand laborers.[59] Historian Michael T. Snyder additionally supports the prefatory remarks on extensive industrialism. In short, he writes that the borough had "scores of plants" working twenty-four-seven as World War II raged. As a result, Snyder continues, they contributed immensely to the United States' war effort.[60]

Like the general Black urban experience of the North during the twentieth century, especially in locations where civil rights activism fervently mounted, African American relocation from the South both before and during the Great Migration had also significantly impacted Pottstown. For example, between 1900 and 1915, historian Charles L. Blockson estimates six locales within Montgomery County, including Pottstown, represented the main destinations; overall, approximately one thousand made the trek. Blockson also notes multiple factors that inspired many Dixie-born African Americans in making the Pennsylvania County their home. They included "job opportunities, desire for higher wages and job protection, unsatisfactory living conditions, sentimental factors, interest in better education, injustice from southern courts, escape from the Ku Klux Klan [KKK], the wish to be close to their relatives, and the wish to establish their own business."[61] In addition, Blockson mentions how

Montgomery County civil rights groups zealously fought toward improving African American conditions.[62] As such, this book paints an even more comprehensive picture of civil rights activism launched from Pottstown—another crucial hub in Montgomery County Pennsylvania during early, mid, and late twentieth-century America.

As indicated previously, similar to the civil rights work that manifested across the industrialized North, activism launched from Pottstown additionally benefited because of the ongoing commitment of local African Americans and whites. However, to truly comprehend the ways in which these activists specifically battled practices of anti-Black racism ubiquitous to the local de facto segregated structure between World War II and the late 1960s, one must note the ethos behind their general resistance strategies, with the liberal interracialist tactic being one. In this context, the liberal interracialist strategy relates specifically to the actions, procedures, and methods by which Black and white local activists collaborated on multiple occasions to advance integration and true racial equitability. By doing so, they simultaneously sought to ameliorate the discrimination faced by local African Americans. Moreover, those guided by the liberal interracialist philosophy on the local front had sincere motives when it came to such Black-centered activism. In other words, they believed fully in integration and equality among African Americans and whites.

At the same time, this study suggests that the biracial makeup of local civil rights work directly correlated to the small size of Pottstown's Black community. Indeed, for African Americans to gain more significant social, economic, and political opportunities in and around Pottstown—because they were overwhelmingly the demographic minority—they understood clearly the importance of collaborating with borough whites. As historian Jason Sokol observes, "African Americans' ability to achieve equality all too often depended upon white northerners."[63] Nevertheless, because local Blacks comprehended how their small population size was a handicap, they also sought the assistance of Pottstown liberal whites willing to cooperate with them in both promoting and improving local African Americans conditions.

Thus, the history of Pottstown and its connection to civil rights stresses the relationship between the location's small Black populace—a population that remained much smaller than most northern locales already noted in civil rights scholarship—and its cooperation in interracial civil rights work germane to the local front. Not having a large community essentially made local Black freedom work near impossible without interracial collaboration. In other words, if Pottstown African Americans could find white allies and fellow participants in fruitful civil rights initiatives, then they could ultimately empower and better the conditions of local Blacks throughout the region.

Yet even with Pottstown having this historical connection between the Black minority and the white majority, it also speaks to another important point—that is, just because the two groups had such a relationship for civil rights work does not mean local African Americans never exhibited consternation about racial violence ultimately manifesting from the dominant white population. In support of this latter interpretive statement, historian Randal Maurice Jelks has examined Grand Rapids and its own civil rights history. However, Jelks makes the argument that the Michigan location had interracial peace prior to the mid-twentieth century; his rationale hinges on the fact that the city's Black populace was tiny.

As such, *The Jim Crow North* expands on Jelks's historiographical observation.[64] From the 1940s through the late 1960s, it argues that civil rights work launched from Pottstown was able to have the interracial success that it did precisely because borough Blacks never became numerically significant. The study also asserts that the lack of large-scale racial turmoil is related specifically to the fact that Pottstown's African American population never expanded extensively. In short, Pottstown's African American populace, its smaller composition, and its relative stability only helped ease tensions among local Blacks and whites. Thus, racial violence and antagonisms infamously known throughout the twentieth-century industrialized North are not central components of Pottstown's Black freedom struggle. While in the late 1960s the Pottstown NAACP would take part in soothing racial tensions in nearby Phoenixville, Pennsylvania (Chester County), following violent clashes between African Americans and whites there, the theme of racial violence, as captured by historians such as Levy and Patrick D. Jones, is not central to this mostly localized story of northern civil rights.[65]

At the same time, however, even though Pottstown escaped such ubiquitous violence inextricably linked to race between World War II and the late 1960s, it is worth noting the fact that Pottstown itself did share a historical connection to one of the most infamous white supremacist groups in United States history: the KKK. Indeed, similar to other locations throughout the North (as well as the South and beyond), the KKK also had a localized presence in Pottstown. And when, during the 1920s, the bigoted organization "gained strongholds" within many locales above the Mason-Dixon Line, Sugrue observes, the local KKK, known as Pottstown's "Kurtesy Klub," held public demonstrations continually. Moreover, the white supremacist entity utilized the small northern borough's main drag High Street for such public demonstrations.[66]

Not surprisingly, the local KKK terrorized Pottstown African Americans too. Specifically, they perpetrated "cross burnings on 'Chicken Hill,'" a region that longtime white *Pottstown Mercury* editor Shandy Hill described as being "tightly segregated" and overwhelmingly where Pottstown Blacks resided; moreover, only a "few Negroes left" the residential region "to mingle with whites."[67] The same Pottstown KKK ignited wooden objects "in the flats off West High street when the first Negroes moved to Hemlock row," another predominately Black residential space nearby Pottstown in Stowe, Pennsylvania.[68] Reflecting on the year 1924, historian Gordon P. Griffiths even recalled how frequently the borough KKK enflamed such articles of timber.[69] Griffiths also revealed that the local KKK was heavily involved across "the community's social and religious" existence during the same decade.[70] Last, Pennsylvania-level law enforcement, wrote the *Philadelphia Inquirer* during the mid-1960s, condemned "young rowdies . . . for burning crosses in the Pottstown area." According to this account, the borough KKK, particularly its celebrity from 1928, possibly influenced the ruffians.[71]

While the KKK had a pervasive impact in Pottstown during the 1920s, the same was not the case across World War II and the postwar era. Perhaps, then, the local KKK's failure to gain large-scale power and influence was directly correlated to both the consistent presence and the activism of local civil rights workers. At the same time, although the liberal interracial strategy was primarily the main philosophy engendered and employed by freedom fighters in and around Pottstown, the fact is also true that local African American activists additionally utilized resistance strategies relating to the general philosophy of traditional Black internal improvement work (as previously noted too). Yet spearheaded mainly by Pottstown African Americans during World War II and the early postwar period, such tactics even shared striking similarities to the ways in which southern Blacks battled racial prejudice below the Mason-Dixon Line, especially before World War II. In particular, one notable strategy utilized by local activists worth mentioning, which stemmed largely from the essence of traditional Black internal improvement work, was equalization.

Commenting on Black NAACP attorney Charles Hamilton Houston, specifically how he changed "the NAACP's legal strategy" into something emphatically unique to him, historian John A. Kirk notes that the lawyer specified "the focus of [the organization's] attack to concentrate on gaining more resources for African Americans in 'separate and unequal' public education." Kirk continues writing, therefore, how the Black attorney implemented "a strategy for the equalization of conditions" juxtaposed with swift and speedy integration throughout "public" spaces.[72] While not dealing precisely with educational inequality, Black civil rights activists in and around Pottstown pursued an equalization strategy—alongside other traditional Black internal improvement initiatives—to rectify localized discriminatory practices during World War II and the early postwar years.

However, just because these local African American activists worked with white-led organizations that otherwise practiced discrimination, that did not mean the same Blacks surrendered or yielded to an endorsement of such blatant white racism. Instead, when interpreting local Black activists' partnership, they should only be conceptualized as them pursuing what they understood as necessary collaborations that advanced the immediate African American condition. In short, their cooperation with white Pottstown, especially within the tradition of equalization strategy, rested mainly in pragmatism rather than local Blacks openly or willingly capitulating to a second-class status. Furthermore, even as Pottstown African Americans employed the tactic of equalization, they still believed themselves empowered—so much so that the resistance strategy enabled them to demonstrate Black agency, autonomy, and control over both the well-being and the advancement of local African American conditions.[73]

Major Historiographical Contributions and Book's Outline

"There are many unfortunate gaps in the full story of Pottstown," historian Paul Chancellor observed in the early 1950s, "many uncertain points to clarify, and many changes to record year by year."[74] While *The Jim Crow North* demonstrates that Pottstown was an essential center of civil rights activism—just as significant as other regions throughout the urban North, including those with larger populations—it also incorporates several fresh interpretive perspectives relating to the historiography of the northern Black freedom struggle. First, the book examines the liberal interracialist strategy during World War II (and the postwar years)—a concept already documented within the scholarship of northern civil rights. However, the study also interprets activism within the same Black freedom struggle as the war raged (and at times during the initial postwar) through the tactic of equalization as well as other African American internal improvement strategies. Thus far, civil rights scholarship mainly associates equalization with work below and not above the Mason-Dixon Line.

Second, in capturing the overall civil rights advocacy work of the *Pottstown Mercury* from World War II throughout the late 1960s, this book's interpretation of the local press pushes back against the consensus narrative of the media as it relates to the Black freedom struggle in the North. Specifically, the dominant perspective argues that media outlets with nationwide reach above the Mason-Dixon Line had ironically handicapped northern civil rights work. While Pottstown's main newspaper, the *Pottstown Mercury*, did not have nationwide circulation, its coverage of local civil rights issues contrasts this vantage point sharply. In fact, the *Pottstown Mercury* was the most consistent white cooperator when it came to local civil rights. Another point to note about the Pottstown newspaper was its portrayal of local Blacks involved in civil rights work. In a consistent fashion, the *Pottstown Mercury* humanized the largely Black activists for a mostly white readership, a characteristic that distinguishes the *Pottstown Mercury* from the dominant narrative.[75]

Yet while the role of the *Pottstown Mercury* in advocating civil rights contributed to many successes on the local front, this study, unequivocally, privileges the part played by African American activists in their own liberation. To be sure, the *Pottstown Mercury* was able to have the reporting successes it had, precisely because there was a local activist-driven Black community. From the early 1940s throughout the late 1960s, local African Americans continually provided the newspaper with information on the discrimination and challenges they faced in seeking first-class citizenship. Many times, Pottstown Blacks even let their names be printed by the newspaper. By doing so, they most certainly risked social, economic, and political repercussions from the dominant white population. Nevertheless, they put aside such tangible threats and advocated their and their community's struggle for true racial equality and citizenship. By doing so, they also simultaneously and publicly lambasted local manifestations of white supremacy and anti-Black racism that permeated the borough.

The third important contribution of *The Jim Crow North* to the academic literature is how it captures the initial aftermath of *Brown*, a time period largely ignored within the historiography of northern civil rights. Specifically, this study reveals how quickly the court case launched local activism developments, catapulting them to even the national sphere of the Black freedom struggle. In sum, the civil rights activism that initially percolates from Pottstown, might, in fact, be one of the earliest responses across the industrialized North, if not the country, to the monumental US Supreme Court ruling in *Brown*.[76] This book's fourth and last significant addition to both enhancing and improving intellectual discourse on northern civil rights history is the fact that Pottstown did not experience any large-scale racial violence, unrest, or police brutality from the dominant white populace. In short, the lack of such antagonisms in Pottstown makes the small borough an outlier to most of the northern urban locales already explored within the scholarly literature thus far.

Painting a richer and more in-depth historical narrative, *The Jim Crow North* critically analyzes civil rights work catapulted from Pottstown starting in World War II and continuing into the late 1960s. When applicable, the book frames Pottstown within the larger historical context of the Black freedom struggle. It also engages some of the historiography germane to civil rights topics both above and below the Mason-Dixon Line when relevant.

To begin, chapter 2 starts by examining the genesis of the local Black freedom struggle in Pottstown. Aligning with historian Richard M. Dalfiume's assessment of World War II as a "watershed" in civil rights history, it explores the resistance strategy of equalization and other traditional Black internal improvement tactics.[77] Yet when exploring these strategies, chapter 2 interprets them through three local civil rights projects that simultaneously launched during World War II. The first relates to the establishment of Pottstown Second Baptist Church Cemetery. Beginning the same month that imperial Japan launched its surprise assault on the United States' Pearl Harbor military base, which springboarded American military involvement in World War II, the civil rights activism in Pottstown partnered the historically Black church and white-owned Edgewood Cemetery Company. The same section also highlights other traditional Black internal improvement initiatives conducted by Second Baptist Church, particularly under the pastorate of Virginia-born African American minister Heywood L. Butler.

In addition to Second Baptist Church, chapter 2 evaluates the civil rights activism spearheaded by the "Negro Extension Work" program of the Pottstown YMCA. Starting only a few months before the conclusion of World War II, Pottstown African American and blue-collar worker William D. Corum led the YMCA work. In short, "Negro Extension Work" activists incorporated similar traditional Black internal improvement and equalization strategies as the Second Baptist graveyard initiative.[78] Over time, however, the local Black YMCA program disbanded when the Pottstown organization desegregated in 1949. From there, chapter 2 goes on to illuminate the Black freedom activism of the Pottstown NAACP during World War II. Started in late November 1942, which coincided with the establishment of many other NAACP branches throughout the United States during the war years, the Pottstown branch began its impactful Black freedom work under the leadership of William D. Corum's older brother and fellow working-class African American, James H. Corum. While the Pottstown NAACP utilized traditional Black internal improvement and equalization methods, the local branch, too, embraced the emerging liberal interracialist plan of action, just like its mother organization, stationed in New York City. In further regard to the liberal interracialist resistance strategy, chapter 2 highlights the activism of the older Corum and his important role in leading Local 2326, a CIO-affiliated labor union that represented blue-collar workers, African American and white, who labored at the Stanley G. Flagg factory in nearby Stowe, Pennsylvania.

Next, chapter 3 highlights the ways in which the *Pottstown Mercury* conducted civil rights advocacy work, which expanded from World War II across the postwar period. It does so, however, with four case studies. First, chapter 3 spotlights the partnership of the local newspaper and African American Thomas W. Corum, the middle brother of James H. and William D. Corum, who became Pottstown's pioneering Black police officer. The second micro study documents the all-Black Allegheny Conference of the Seventh-day Adventist Church buying land nearby Pottstown in Pine Forge, Pennsylvania. Early on in Pine Forge, the Allegheny Conference met fervent northern "white pushback" or resistance from the all-white entity known as the Valley Improvement Association.[79] The third case study of chapter 3, in turn, evaluates the *Pottstown Mercury*'s civil rights advocacy regarding the Pottstown Bowling Association (PBA), the borough associate of the American Bowling Congress (ABC). Locally, the PBA aligned with the ABC and its discriminatory practice, which excluded African Americans from membership rolls. From there, chapter 3 ends by capturing the fourth and final micro account of a housing dilemma that almost took away many residential properties from local working-class African Americans residing within Hemlock and Cottage Rows in nearby Stowe, Pennsylvania. This latter residential issue additionally inspired the establishment of the PCL. In short, a central figure involved with the PCL was Georgia-born African American and Pottstown doctor Daniel Lee. Overall, the four events received important coverage and civil rights advocacy work from the *Pottstown Mercury*.

Chapters 4 and 5 focus particularly on the early aftermath of *Brown* in late May 1954 and how the breakthrough US Supreme Court case galvanized and inspired a community-wide liberal interracialist response from locals in Pottstown, adjacent communities, and beyond. Historians have largely ignored this initial period and how it helped influence direct developments within the Black freedom struggle above the Mason-Dixon

Line. To be sure, while they have examined at length white southerners "massive resistance" to integrated schooling soon after the decision, especially in Dixie, *Brown*'s subsequent influence and reach in the North has almost fully alluded them.[80]

Nevertheless, in his examination of African American school reform in Milwaukee (WI), historian Jack Dougherty argues that locals in the northern city tailored the meaning/purpose of *Brown* specifically for their own struggles in seeking first-class citizenship. Thus, Dougherty demonstrates that local African Americans in Milwaukee used the larger premise of the *Brown* ruling as an avenue to ultimately advocate for more Black public school teachers employed in the city. Eventually, the strategy worked.

As such, chapters 4 and 5 build on Dougherty's theoretical framework for the ways in which activists in Milwaukee custom-fitted *Brown*'s meaning/purpose for their own activism for first-class citizenship. However, these two chapters about Pottstown also demonstrate a more nuanced assessment of Dougherty's interpretation.[81] In particular, because the impact of *Brown* transcended multiple areas locally in Pottstown, chapters 4 and 5 reveal how activists fervently committed to equality called out the practice of racial injustice in both public and private employment sectors as well as other spaces pertaining to recreation, entertainment, leisure, and education, with the ultimate objective of both fully and totally integrating these spheres.

Thus, chapter 4 documents the earliest reactions from locals, African American and white, to *Brown*. In short, the reactions occurred only days after the ruling, starting with local leadership. Chapter 4 also examines multiple letter-to-the-editor writers' criticisms of local manifestations of racial injustice as a result of the de facto segregation structure, followed by the *Pottstown Mercury* itself contemplating such unequal practices and fervently lambasting them. However, most forceful in calling out local manifestations of white supremacy and anti-Black racism was the civil rights advocacy work of white *Pottstown Mercury* journalist Normand Poirier.

In fact, chapter 5 shows when interracial civil rights activism in Pottstown had its greatest national impact. A little over a month following *Brown*, the *Pottstown Mercury* started publishing Poirier's reports, which shed direct light on Black inequality throughout the borough and how Jim Crow particularly manifested. In short, the articles eventually gained national attention, with even being discussed and reflected on by individuals across the United States. Moreover, as the local civil rights discourses and *Brown* influenced Poirier's reporting, his journalistic advocacy served as the impetus for establishment of the PCHR, another Pottstown-based civil rights group that ultimately obtained national exposure. The PCHR also brought together seasoned activists—Black and white—in Pottstown as well as outside civil rights workers, particularly from Fellowship House, located in Philadelphia. They included white activists A. Herbert Haslam, Marjorie Penney, and Mitzi R. Jacoby. Last, chapter 5 captures the PCHR's greatest civil rights initiative, "the Pottstown Plan," as well as its involvement in the development of the pioneering artistic endeavor entitled *Count Me In*.[82] Here, the local civil rights initiatives reached the national arena, leading to many individuals as well as progressive organizations wanting to know more, provide direct commentary, and also study and try and incorporate the activism from Pottstown in some way, shape, or form. The chapter then also goes over honors and recognitions relating to both the *Pottstown Mercury* series and work spearheaded by the PCHR. In short, such honors further demonstrate the national impact and acknowledgment of the Black freedom activism catapulted from Pottstown in the aftermath of *Brown*.

Although the Pottstown NAACP disbanded around the time that World War II ended, it was reestablished in late 1951. As such, chapter 6 turns attention back to the borough NAACP and its involvement in the local Black freedom struggle during the 1950s and 1960s. Yet shortly before the group's revitalization, a local issue arose. In sum, the issue focused on an African American suspected perpetrator and gun-carrying whites in nearby Stowe who teamed up with local law enforcement. The notion of white vigilantism became a concern that eventually inspired the national NAACP in New York City to act directly. From there, chapter 6 spotlights local leadership and activism of the Pottstown NAACP.

During the early 1950s through the late 1960s, local African Americans Charles Prince, James H. Corum, and Newstell Marable primarily led the Pottstown NAACP branch. While this chapter analyzes the tenures of these activists and the civil rights work they conducted, it largely spotlights Marable's tenure.[83] Under Marable's leadership the Pottstown NAACP labored fervently in combating racial inequality on the local front in places such as a private swimming club as well as the ways in which the civil rights group conducted activism efforts in nearby Phoenixville, Pennsylvania. There, the Pottstown NAACP coordinated a mass sit-in at the local high school.[84] Chapter 6 also pays special attention to how the Pottstown NAACP softened racial tensions during a race riot in Phoenixville. Last, the chapter highlights the emergence of local northern white resistance or pushback to the liberal interracialist efforts spearheaded by the Pottstown NAACP—the central civil rights entity of the area—particularly during the turbulent 1960s.

Finally, chapter 7 summarizes the main findings of this study and talks about how a close review of the history of Pottstown's Black freedom struggle has the potential to assist modern-day advocates interested in promoting racial justice, equality, and inclusion. The final chapter also highlights the ways in which the interracial civil rights work spearheaded from Pottstown can, in fact, serve as a model for scholars interested in capturing identical smaller locales throughout the United States. On the other hand, for individuals interested in promoting a more inclusive and equal democracy, specifically through racial justice, then they must, in turn, clearly understand that discrimination that fully permeates the modern-day structures of oppression is the result of de facto societal constructs, not of de jure ones.[85]

Chapter 7 also documents some recent organizations in Pottstown, like the local NAACP and its advocacy for civil rights change in early twenty-first-century America. In sum, *The Jim Crow North* hopes to demonstrate the historical significance of the small northern working-class borough of Pottstown, local activists who operated in and around the locale, and their direct contribution to the larger Black freedom struggle of World War II and postwar America. Indeed, their activism can still hold relevance to individuals diligently laboring in the modern day toward creating an even more level playing field—socially, economically, and politically—in the realms of racial and ethnic justice in not only the United States but also possibly the world.

2

The Genesis of the Local Black Freedom Struggle in World War II–Era Pottstown

In his autobiography, *Dear Sir: You Cur* (1969), Shandy Hill, longtime editor of the *Pottstown Mercury*, reflected on the state of race relations at the beginning of the 1940s in Pottstown. Specifically, Hill pondered two points. First, whether "the 'Negro problem'" was an issue in the northern working-class borough. And second, how pervasive was local "discrimination." When referencing "the 'Negro problem,'" the white editor was most likely comparing the status of Pottstown African Americans to their southern Black counterparts, who endured the decades-old practice of de jure segregation, more informally known as Jim Crow, upheld by the United States Supreme Court's ruling in *Plessy v. Ferguson* (1896). Moreover, Hill's analysis examining "discrimination" probably related to the more inconspicuous yet pervasive brand of racial segregation prevalent outside the American South: de facto segregation—which was Pottstown's own "northern style Jim Crow system."[1] In short, Hill found "the 'Negro problem'" across Pottstown as being not discernible outright. Yet he saw "discrimination" as a ubiquitous dilemma—one that then plagued the borough.

Not surprisingly, local African Americans corroborated Hill's "discrimination" argument. Like Blacks across the American North, they experienced racism on multiple fronts. Pottstown African American Oscar Carter even publicly testified in early January 1943 to such clandestine yet entrenched racial inequality that he and his fellow Blacks endured in the small Jim Crow borough of the North.[2]

Captured in the *Pottstown Mercury*'s "Readers Say"/letter-to-the-editor section, while Carter acknowledged "that there are a lot of good white people in this town," his final remarks were less flattering as he expressed bluntly how "the majority is not." From there, the local African American man demonstrated that white racism truly penetrated multiple facets of life for Pottstown Blacks. Regarding employment, Carter argued that white bosses usually gave Pottstown African Americans two options. They were either, on the one hand, "'Sorry, but we don't hire colored', or," on the other hand, "if they do hire you," Carter complained, "it is at some menial task anyone with the mentality of a child can do."

Next, Carter addressed Pottstown white-owned eating establishments and their treatment of potential Black patrons. The first part of his analysis went hand in glove with his overall assessment of white employers in the borough. That is, white restaurateurs blatantly refused service to Pottstown African Americans. Yet their second strategy of bigotry was indeed more covert. According to Carter, Pottstown whites would allow African Americans access to their food establishments. However, when the time came to order something, whites simply ignored them, making Blacks "wait so long until you realize that you are not wanted and leave of your own accord." Finally, Carter touched on Pottstown African Americans' living situation. Put simply, he described it as horrendous. "Where can we rent a place to live?" he asked. "In some shack down along the river," Carter lamented, "that isn't fit for a human being to live in or out in the country somewhere?" As far as Pottstown Blacks residing nearby whites, Carter additionally observed that they vigorously protested such practice.

Carter's transparent remarks, corroborated by other evidence, paints a bleak picture of the racial landscape in Pottstown at the beginning of the 1940s. Yet while racial exclusion permeated a variety of aspects in the borough, Pottstown African Americans would not give in and totally capitulate to such practices of normalized inequality. In cooperation with sympathetic local whites, Pottstown Blacks instead took the offensive, mounting multiple civil rights campaigns to combat the subtle yet pervasive structure of de facto segregation across the small locale of the Jim Crow North. In the end, Pottstown African Americans' activism was clearly intentional. And it was in the context of World War II on the American home front that they began fighting for a level socioeconomic playing field, equitability, and the same access to resources overwhelmingly privileged to the borough's majority white population. Indeed, the genesis of the local Black freedom struggle was upon them.[3]

World War II–Era Pottstown—A Civil Rights Watershed

As on the national landscape, the World War II era proved historically significant to Pottstown and the maturation of developments within the borough's own Black freedom struggle. Specifically, the period related to the launching point of such local civil rights efforts. As the war raged, activists—especially African Americans and sympathetic whites—not only established newfound organizations but also worked within the confines of existing institutions in Pottstown so that the activism was ultimately completed.

Although World War II served as a catalyst to civil rights developments across the broader Black freedom struggle, more recently, scholars have countered historian Richard M. Dalfiume's World War II "watershed" premise.[4] "The search for a 'watershed' in recent Negro history ends at the years that comprised World War II, 1939–1945," Dalfiume argues. "These years of transition in American race relations comprise the 'forgotten years' of the Negro revolution." In the end, whatever appraisals recent scholars have made, Dalfiume's vantage point is still beneficial in understanding that the impetus of civil rights developments in working-class Pottstown occurred during World War II.[5] Such activism, in turn, also laid the foundation for interracial civil rights efforts throughout the postwar period not only in Pottstown but also beyond, even reaching the national sphere.

While the field of northern civil rights history has expanded tremendously since the early 2000s, scholars examining the region have failed to identify a consensus to when such twentieth-century activism originated. However, they have demonstrated conclusively that the traditional 1954 to 1968 time frame is not fully adequate in explaining the launching point of civil rights activism in the North.[6] Their scholarship can also be broken down into mainly three sequential eras. First, a group of northern civil rights historians illuminate "the pre–World War II years" concerning in twentieth-century America as the outset.[7] The second batch of historians such as Dalfiume and this author stress the significance of the World

War II era in spearheading and advancing civil rights progress.[8] Not surprisingly, the third group of historians capture the postwar era as the inception period to the Black freedom struggle above the Mason-Dixon Line.[9]

Yet even though all three categories of historians disagree with the specific time period of the northern Black freedom struggle, they basically employ the historian Jacquelyn Dowd Hall's "long civil rights movement" perspective. In doing so, they challenge the traditional 1954 to 1968 analytical time frame. These same historians also largely push back against the interpretations that emphasize the southern states as primary to fully understanding the history of civil rights struggle across twentieth-century America.[10]

Black Pottstown before and during World War II

Prior to World War II, small locales like Pottstown differed from their larger northern city counterparts because civil rights work was virtually nonexistent there. While civil rights work was almost completely absent, nevertheless, the borough still had a long-standing African American presence. And like the remainder of the American North, Pottstown also shared in the region's history of anti-Black discrimination fully undergirded by the de facto segregation structure.[11]

For example, as indicated by Pottstown Black Oscar Carter's criticism of the inconspicuous yet entrenched bigotry permeating local occupational sectors, food service, and access to efficient housing during the early 1940s, African Americans faced exclusionary circumstances inextricably linked to their racial background. "How would you feel if you were denied the right to work, live, dine or play at a lot of places in this town because you are colored?" Carter straightway opened his early January 1943, *Pottstown Mercury* "Readers Say" correspondence. Indeed, because Carter conveyed generalized points in his opening statements about racial exclusion throughout the local front, then, in fact, they also possibly speak to how widespread and embedded de facto segregation was in the region.[12] Moreover, as this chapter reveals, during World War II and the early postwar period, activists combated and addressed racial prejudice and inequalities across the local Jim Crow structure, specifically regarding access to Black interment space, housing, recreational and leisure activities, and employment.

Commenced in December 1941, Pottstown activists' civil rights work encapsulated the methods, procedures, and ways in which they addressed inequalities throughout and nearby the locale. In effect, their rationality in conducting such activism was to improve the quality of everyday life for the local African American collective. At the same time, local activists orchestrated civil rights activism by implementing a variety of strategies. They included meetings and public gatherings, formulating projects that catered specifically toward local Blacks, canvassing for memberships and accumulating capital while even publicly challenging—if not lambasting—anti-Black sentiments and Jim Crow segregation indigenous to the northern borough and close by areas. Finally, local activists would also go on and apply these same civil rights strategies and methods to their important Black freedom work in Pottstown and beyond during the postwar years.[13]

Yet several other factors also help explain why effective and sustainable civil rights work did not emerge in Pottstown prior to World War II. First, the borough lacked a strong presence of interracial coalitions. This was, of course, less of a handicap in large northern cities such as nearby Philadelphia. In his analysis of interracial activism in Philadelphia, historian Stanley Keith Arnold, for example, highlights Black and white cooperation in improving the conditions of city African Americans through groups like the Young People's Interracial Fellowship, among others, before World War II. However, when Pottstown locals did make some sincere attempts in establishing such interracial coalitions prior to the war years, they proved not only limited in scope but also short lived in duration.[14]

The second factor contributing to the lack of consistent civil rights activism in previous years related to the nature of local leadership among African Americans. To be sure, from a historical standpoint Pottstown Blacks had an organized and vibrant community that well predated the global conflict. Yet African American leadership before World War II worked mainly to build and strengthen internal community institutions like churches. It also generally labored within Black-led organizations constrained by the exclusionary practices of the larger society, mainly brought about by the broader structure of de facto segregation in the Jim Crow North. As such, African American leaders' primary mission was to cater and specifically serve their Black-only constituencies. Indeed, Black leaders in Pottstown understood plainly that their most effective leadership capability pertained to their ability to assist the local African American collective, which was predominantly in the working-class socioeconomic bracket. Overall, Black leadership aimed to ensure that local African Americans had greater chances in obtaining not only material equality and equitability but also the same opportunities and privileges that were afforded to their white counterparts in the small northern borough.

To put it another way, directly challenging the long-standing pervasive practices of local anti-Black prejudices, as well as other exclusionary policies germane to northern Jim Crow, was not necessarily the central objective of most of Pottstown's Black working-class leadership. In fact, these leaders found such activism prior to World War II as not ostensibly promising. Instead, they sought practical Black-centered, traditional internal improvement initiatives. And by seeking such pragmatic solutions, Black leaders believed that they were bettering the social, economic, political, and psychological well-being of the local African American community.[15]

However, these traditional internal improvement initiatives before 1941 would not totally be forgotten during World War II (and beyond). In fact, although also incorporating new strategies within the Black freedom struggle in Pottstown, especially the emerging liberal interracialist scheme, the leadership still utilized those aforementioned methods. And by doing so, the local Black vanguard during World War II (and beyond) was able to implement traditional internal improvement work across the town's minority populace. For example, coinciding with the cataclysmic events of the global war, Black leadership in and around the small northern borough addressed African American interment activism with Second Baptist Church; recreation, leisure and entertainment work through the "Negro Extension Work" programming of the Young Men's Christian Association (YMCA); and instances of similar recreational work and openings of employment opportunities that involved the Pottstown NAACP.[16]

The third factor contributing directly to the lack of Black freedom activism in prewar Pottstown involved the size of the local African American population. Without question, the lack of interracial coalitions and Black leadership promoting more radical external civil rights work in the years before World War II was not helped by the fact that Pottstown's African American population only reached 3 percent of the total population in 1940. Nevertheless, while this percentage was drastically lower to the national Black average of 9.8 percent in 1940, it did reflect substantial local growth. In fact, between 1910 and 1940, Pottstown's African American populace expanded from 341 to 608 or an approximate 78 percent increase.

During the thirty-year period from 1910 to 1940, Pottstown's Black population experienced its greatest spikes between 1910 and 1920, and 1930 and 1940. From 1910 to 1920, the population added 109 African Americans, or almost 32 percent. In the decade between 1920 and 1930, the borough only added four Blacks, or less than a 1 percent increase. However, from 1930 to 1940, Pottstown's Black community grew by 154 African Americans, which was close to a 34 percent rise. Finally, it is worth revealing that beginning in 1940 and concluding in 1970, Pottstown's Black populace grew even more explosively. In fact, within this thirty-year time frame, the population expansively catapulted from 608 to 2,235. In percentage terms, the drastic jump was an enormous 267.6 percent increase over the previous three decades.[17]

According to the 1940 United States census, Pottstown's African American population was mostly Pennsylvania-born. Like other locales across the industrial urban North, however, a substantial amount claimed southern origins. By far, Virginia was the state that had the greatest representation of southern-born African Americans in Pottstown, numerically followed by Georgia and then North Carolina. Smaller pockets of southern-born Blacks who moved to the borough were from Maryland, Alabama, and South Carolina. Moreover, 1940 US census records indicate that several southern Blacks residing in Pottstown came as far as from Tennessee, Kentucky, and even Texas.[18] To be sure, one way to interpret Pottstown's increased African American population by World War II reflects the expanding job opportunities available on the local scene. While Pottstown was relatively close to "Philadelphia . . . the center of

Pennsylvania's wartime activity," historian Merl E. Reed writes, manufacturing in the small northern borough also played its impactful part in war production.[19]

During World War II, industrial powerhouse organizations, including Stanley G. Flagg & Company, Doehler-Jarvis Corporation, Mrs. Smith's Pies, Bethlehem Steel Company, and more, were found in not only Pottstown but also adjacent areas. Of course, local companies like these played significant roles in the larger wartime production efforts spearheaded by the federal government.[20] At the same time, because local African Americans worked at the factories in and around the borough, it should not be surprising that evidence reveals their paramount function within Pottstown's wartime labor force as World War II raged. In late June 1944, commenting on Pottstown Blacks residing "in the community bounded by Beech, Grant, Jefferson and Sheridan streets," the *Pottstown Mercury* noted how African Americans "there are working day and night, employed in local war plants," assisting "to the best of their ability to produce the weapons of war that will" eventually clobber "the Axis dictators."[21]

Like many Americans during World War II, Pottstown Blacks were also fervently committed to the war effort, sacrificing in numerous ways for the cause of total Allied victory in both the European and the Pacific theaters of the global conflict. In late February 1944, for instance, the *Pottstown Mercury* reported how "there will be no meeting of the [borough] NAACP until further notice" because "many of the members are now working on night shifts in local war plants."[22] Yet the conditions relating to the growth of Pottstown's Black community, buttressed by its access to industrial employment opportunities in the borough's wartime economy, also help further explain why the local Black freedom struggle began mushrooming during World War II.

The antiracist and inclusive language included in American wartime propaganda also helps reveal how the war assisted in cultivating an atmosphere for the emergence of Pottstown's Black freedom struggle. Indeed, across the United States during World War II, both the *Pittsburgh Courier*'s "Double 'V' for a Double Victory Campaign" and Franklin D. Roosevelt's "Four Freedoms" address played specific roles in galvanizing African Americans not only in service to their country and patriotism but also for them to expose long-standing exclusionary and oppressive practices of anti-Black racism relating to Jim Crow above and below the Mason-Dixon Line.[23] Like the historically Black Pennsylvania newspaper's "Double Victory Campaign," Dalfiume even notes how, nationally, Blacks' main viewpoint while World War II raged concerned battling "for democracy on two fronts," stateside and overseas.

Not surprisingly, that same "two fronts," activism-centered consciousness manifested locally among Pottstown Blacks.[24] More broadly, of course, such local African American perspectives too aligned with the *Pittsburgh Courier*'s "Double 'V' War Cry." According to the Black newspaper, "Double 'V'" desired "victory over our enemies at home." In other words, it sought the total defeat of white supremacist ideologies and long-standing discriminatory practices pervasive to the racial landscape of both northern and southern Jim Crow in the United States. To be more precise, the *Pittsburgh Courier* demanded the complete destruction of the exclusionary structures of de facto and de jure segregations, which, without question, had many African Americans oppressed throughout the North and South. Moreover, the Black newspaper's international point relating to "victory over our enemies on the battlefields abroad" both illuminated and spoke to the overall patriotic atmosphere of the American home front during World War II. Simply put, to win overseas meant the destruction of the adversaries, the Axis powers. And like the majority white population, Black America was fervently supportive of winning the war effort against the Axis belligerents of World War II. In sum, when it came specifically to both existential adversaries—nationally and internationally—the *Pittsburgh Courier* zealously demanded "a two-pronged" assault.[25]

Interestingly enough, in July 1943, local discourses relating to the "Double 'V,'" "two fronts" consciousness even appeared in the *Pottstown Mercury*'s "Readers Say"/letter-to-the-editor section. While mostly centered on the recent Detroit Race Riot from late June 1943 that resulted in thirty-four fatalities, historian Beth T. Bates reveals, the "Readers Say" writers also made assessments in the vein of "Double 'V.'" For example, the *Pottstown Mercury* printed a correspondence on July 19 from a local African American who signed the piece with the initials "H. C. W." In short, the Black contributor echoed other local African Americans, lamenting his disgust "when we pick up the [news]paper and read articles" on "the race riots and other mobster acts" that targeted Blacks. Such instances of racial bigotry, the author continued, fervently angered African Americans—even himself. Nevertheless, he continued by stressing the importance of Pottstown African Americans staying diligent in their equality missions stateside as well as abroad.[26]

To be sure, these Black Pottstown writers were also fully supportive of "Double 'V'" as it related to the US war against fascist tyranny. They also advocated passionately for African American soldiers' direct involvement in securing democratic liberty and peace throughout the globe. In her letter published on July 20, Pottstown Black Mary Ellen Means stressed that African American males were currently warring "on battle fronts to help maintain freedom and democracy."[27] Another "Readers Say" letter published on July 15 from a local African American who identified as "A Proud Negro" mirrored the prior comments. Echoing his fellow Pottstown African Americans, the writer noted that Blacks were "doing a fine job of fighting for this freedom." Finally, H. C. W. emphasized the imperativeness of local African Americans organizing to improve the Black community's own conditions in Pottstown. His rationale in doing so, he argued, was in supporting local African Americans' "sons and husbands" outside the United States "who are fighting for this entire nation in the four corners of the world."[28]

Pottstown African American Dorothy Gibson made comparable assertions in her July 14 letter as the previous local Blacks. However, Gibson's analysis, which also aligned with the "Double 'V'" Black consciousness perspective, was perhaps the most pronounced among the entirety of the letters to the editors published by the *Pottstown Mercury* in July 1943. Writing in a lamenting tone, Gibson sorrowfully expressed, "It is heartbreaking to know our boys are dying on the battlefront and on the home front by vicious attacks from the white man."[29] Finally, while not commenting specifically on the Detroit Race Riot, Pottstown Black Oscar Carter in his early January 1943 "Readers Say" letter finished his correspondence within a similar conceptualization as "Double 'V.'" Proclaiming emphatically, Carter wrote, "We are all fighting this war to free all peoples of the world from enslavement." However, he boldly asked Pottstown white readership, as well as white America more broadly, "How can we do this for people abroad when you [whites] are doing the same thing to us [Blacks] here."[30]

Yet while articulating points that fell in line with the "Double 'V'" ethos, H. C. W. also invoked language from his commander in chief, FDR, in his letter. By doing so, he further illuminated Black America's desire for true democratic inclusion and first-class citizenship. According to the local African American, the racial injustices perpetrated by whites in Detroit did not deter him. Conveying the message primarily to his targeted local Black audience, he announced zealously the importance of continuously laboring "and fight[ing] for the four freedoms" that America was currently battling diligently toward preserving.[31]

Concerning the last points, Pottstown Blacks not only contributed patriotically to the local defense industry while simultaneously expressing points coinciding with both a "Double 'V'" and "four freedoms" consciousness but also served honorably in the United States military during World War II. The *Pottstown Mercury* even spotlights the names of local African Americans who were drafted and those who volunteered for military duty.[32] Born in Maryland in 1921, local African American Milton Simms, an army private in the Thirteenth Infantry Regiment and Purple Heart recipient, even gave the ultimate sacrifice. Although Simms was the sole Pottstown African American killed in action, another eighty-nine borough soldiers were slain during World War II.[33]

Like his fallen Pottstown comrades in arms, Simms's ultimate sacrifice was not in vain. Nor was his death forgotten. Upon finding out about Simms's death, the Needle-Eye Social Club, a local African American organization, recognized his honorable service.[34] In early 1948, local Blacks, including Milton's brother Eugene Simms, also honored their deceased soldier in arms. They did so, however, in a much grander way, establishing "the first all-Negro veterans group in Pottstown": Milton Simms Post 955 of the American Legion.[35]

During the early postwar period, the Milton Simms Post would play an active role in not only Pottstown's African American community but also the local Black freedom struggle. Yet the very fact that it catered specifically to local African Americans further demonstrated the pervasive exclusionary conditions that Pottstown Blacks endured throughout World War II and the postwar era.[36] For example, in 1954, about six years following the Milton Simms Post's inception, the *Pottstown Mercury* even reported on local white veterans' associations such as the Veterans of Foreign Wars and the American Legion and how they still excluded African Americans from their rank-and-file membership rolls.[37] Nine years later (1963) the local newspaper found that these same ex-servicemen groups continued excluding borough Blacks.[38]

As such, it was this lingering northern Jim Crow climate leading up to and during the World War II era in Pottstown that made the borough a place ripe for the outset of the local Black freedom struggle. Responding to the needs of the time, local activists began their important Black-centered activism. Starting in December 1941, local activists' first civil rights project coincided the same month as imperial Japan launched its surprise military assault on the United States' Pearl Harbor naval base, which springboarded America's military involvement in World War II. Yet it was during this same winter month that Pottstown Blacks and the local white-led Edgewood Cemetery Company began contemplating how to address "the scarcity of allocated space" the business had "remaining for Negro burials."[39]

Pottstown's Second Baptist Church and Black Interment Activism

In *Jones v. Alfred H. Mayer Co.* (1968), the United States Supreme Court struck a mighty blow toward graveyard exclusion that targeted African Americans. Even citing "an 1866 civil rights law," *Jones v. Alfred H. Mayer Co.* announced the racist practice as unconstitutional.[40] To be sure, well before the late 1960s ruling, white-owned cemeteries overtly discriminated against Blacks when it came to interment and entombment.[41] Yet while northern civil rights scholarship has largely ignored such activism, historian Angelika Krüger-Kahloula captures multiple illustrations of Black freedom work across the North that addressed admittance within formerly "all-white" cemeteries.[42] Krüger-Kahloula also reveals discrimination found within graveyards that buried both African Americans and whites. In short, the exclusionary practices reveal how Blacks could not get away from racial prejudice—even when it came to their final resting places.[43]

Similarly, the *Pottstown Mercury* printed a "Readers Say"/letter to the editor in July 1954, showcasing local African Americans' sad reality: even in death, they, too, endured discrimination. "After living as a second rate citizen, paying first rate taxes etc.," wrote Pottstown Black Mary V. Reid, an African American goes on to eternity. Local Blacks, she added, did not have many options when acquiring a mortician—especially finding "one of the few who give colored patrons courteous service." Reid additionally stated that Black interment was even more discriminatory. In essence, she aligned local Black burial with the American South. "The funeral is over and the citizen who resided in Pottstown, Pennsylvania, not Alabama," Reid remarked, "is buried in the one colored cemetery." To further call out the inconspicuous yet entrenched practice of de facto racial exclusion—the Jim Crow structure of the North inextricably alive and well within Pottstown—Reid sarcastically wrote, "I understand the others (white) are filled to capacity when a colored resident tries to purchase a lot."

There are several points to take away from Reid's sobering yet honest analysis of the state of Black burial in Pottstown during the early 1950s. First, by Reid coupling Pottstown with the South, she associated the small northern locale with the conspicuous, legally codified de jure structure of Jim Crow there. At the same time, her remarks essentially lambasted Pottstown as a place not committed to first-class citizenship for its African American population. Her comments also suggest that because the small northern borough practiced racial discrimination when it came to Black burial, then certainly some form of Jim Crow prejudice permeated Pottstown, thereby categorizing the racist structure as not solely southern. Second, when Reid mockingly expressed how white graveyards were "filled to capacity," she was, in fact, demonstrating how local de facto segregation manifested itself within the northern Jim Crow structure in more inconspicuous ways. To be sure, while racism was not lawfully pronounced in Pottstown, nevertheless, it was still an ever-present part of local customs and practices associated with white supremacist beliefs. The third and final point to note from Reid's sharp critique of the African American graveyard plight in Pottstown related more so to providing further clarity to a statement she made rather than her interpretive view of the local racial landscape. In particular, the Black burial space she referenced was Pottstown Second Baptist Church Cemetery.

It is certainly interesting to note that the *Pottstown Mercury* printed Reid's remarks during the summer of 1954.[44] Yet the origins of the historically Black Second Baptist Church Cemetery dated back to the same month the United States officially entered World War II. At this time, Pottstown's white-owned Edgewood Cemetery served the burial needs of both African Americans and whites. On the surface, it appeared seemingly that Edgewood had not only an integrated cemetery but that the white-led business catered unbiasedly to both races. When digging a little deeper, however, the ways in which the company discriminated against African Americans comes to life. In short, Edgewood only accorded Blacks (and whites) a finite number of plots. And beginning in December 1941, the company faced a growing challenge. Specifically, it concerned the precise number of Black-designated space on its cemetery grounds, coupled with the availability of said room being in short supply to potential African American clientele.

Yet instead of making more room, or even removing restrictions altogether, Edgewood proceeded in another direction. Put simply, it decided to contact Pottstown's Second Baptist Church about an initiative for a new cemetery that catered exclusively to African Americans and their graveyard needs. One of several local Black congregations, Second Baptist had been a fixture in Pottstown's African American community since 1895. Edgewood Cemetery, which predated Second Baptist by some thirty-four years (1861), also informed the Black church early on that it would even provide economic assistance toward the cemetery project.

In response, Second Baptist congregants named an internal group of churchgoers by March 1942 whose sole purpose was to act on Edgewood Cemetery's proposal. On June 18, 1942, following months of detailed planning, the Black congregation acquired roughly "four-and-a-half acres" in Douglass Township (Berks County, Pennsylvania), just to the north of Pottstown. Cooperating with Edgewood Cemetery along the lines of equalization and traditional Black internal improvement strategies, it was there in nearby Douglass Township that Second Baptist congregants established their graveyard. At the same time, and holding to its side of the bargain, white-led Edgewood Cemetery Company provided Second Baptist the capital previously vowed in the sum of $200.

Edgewood's response to the graveyard situation in Pottstown emulated older approaches of racial reform, which partnered numerous African Americans and whites, especially outside the South. Indeed, while not overtly hostile to African Americans or the idea of traditional Black internal improvement efforts, whites, nonetheless, protected the inconspicuous yet pervasive structure of de facto segregation—northern Jim Crow—particularly because it fully undergirded white privilege and Black inequality, specifically when it came to access and resources. Consequently, these same whites could seldom envision circumstances of true equality, inclusion, and equitability between the races. Understanding these perspectives embraced by whites, Blacks, in turn, often sought practical solutions that provided some measure of equalization or the best outcomes possible for themselves and the greater African American community, even if such interracial collaborations fell in line with the tenets of anti-Black discrimination. Thus, when Edgewood Cemetery Company approached Second Baptist with pledges of financial and other support necessary to acquire the land for an otherwise separate cemetery for African Americans, the church accepted the offer as no capitulation to racial subordination or a second-class status. In contrast—and as with other demands of an era in which only equalization seemed feasible to Pottstown African Americans—both the conditions and the circumstances seemed a pragmatic necessity for not only such traditional Black internal improvement work among borough African Americans but also the collective betterment of the local minority population.[45]

It should come as no surprise that African Americans native of Pennsylvania were not only an integral part of the history of Second Baptist Church, as will be shown, but that they were also paramount to the local Black freedom struggle during World War II (and beyond). Yet the ways in which southern African Americans chiefly utilized traditional internal improvement and equalization strategies for local Black freedom activism can also not be overstated. For example, Black Virginians "from rural parts" helped organize Second Baptist Church. Moreover, their relocation to obtain employment available throughout Pottstown's growing industrial economy also coincided with others migrating into the locale.[46]

In addition to aiding in the establishment of Second Baptist, Virginia Blacks worked diligently in the planning and materialization phases of the local congregation's cemetery. One of them was Pottstown African American Willis H. Strawther. Strawther chaired the "committee" responsible for the planning stages behind the local Second Baptist Church Cemetery and its creation.[47] Born in Fairfax County Virginia (1882), he left the South for Pottstown in the early 1890s, some two decades before the Great Migration.[48]

While in Pottstown, Strawther began working with the prestigious Hill School, an exclusive boarding school within the borough. "Few men are as beloved as Willis Strawther," wrote the *Philadelphia Inquirer* in early October 1952, "the most famous doorman and major domo at the Hill School in Pottstown."[49] Serving as "doorman" of the institution's central structure on campus—"the Headmaster's house"—the Black Virginian by birth worked faithfully at the Hill School from 1901 to 1955.[50]

In addition to laboring for more than a half century with the prestigious Hill School, Strawther had arguably just as long a connection (if not longer), let alone commitment, to Second Baptist Church. This can probably be attributed to Strawther's dad, John William Strawther, who was also from Virginia, born in 1858.[51] His *Pottstown Mercury* obituary additionally noted that John Strawther was "one of the first Negro Settlers" to the small northern borough.[52] However, historian Linda McCurdy suggests that enslaved African Americans were already residing in the region during the eighteenth century, well before even the official "borough" classification of Pottstown in the mid-1810s.[53] Foreign policy scholar and historian Lawrence Cohen, a native of the small northern borough, on the other hand, notes that "Pottstown's significant African American population dated to the Civil War."[54] Whatever the case, Strawther's obituary estimated that he migrated to Pottstown, leaving his former residence, Culpepper (Virginia), around 1886.[55]

Yet many southern African American transplants would soon find out, as expressed sorrowfully in the following century by Black civil rights activist and Alabama native Rosa Parks, when referencing her transplanted home Detroit, how this region above the Mason-Dixon Line represented "the 'Northern promised land that wasn't.'"[56] In other words, outside the South, Blacks more broadly confronted another Jim Crow structure that lingered and festered throughout the social, economic, and political atmospheres of the North. While more covert than the South's de jure practice, the North's de facto structure was truly just as entrenched. Shortly after *Brown v. Board of Education* (May 1954), which made legal (de jure) separation among Blacks and whites in public schooling as unlawful, the *Pottstown Mercury* even identified this inconspicuous yet engrained structure as "Mister James P. Crow, Esquire," when speaking about how such racism permeated Pottstown.[57] Another description the *Pottstown Mercury* utilized in its study of white bigotry and Black inequality in and around Pottstown was more plainly phrased "Jim Crow, Yankee Style," which, for instance, the *Plainfield Courier-News* (New Jersey) identified "as a Northern style Jim Crow system and an informal—but airtight—form of segregation." In 1963, the *Pottstown Mercury* still echoed the same local Jim Crow arguments made in the aftermath of the US Supreme Court's *Brown* ruling.[58] Overall, by throwing greater light on de facto segregation practices ubiquitous to Pottstown and nearby areas, the *Pottstown Mercury* writings in both 1954 and 1963 argued that such prejudices impacted a variety of local spheres and spaces, including employment, housing, recreation, entertainment, leisure, and education in some way, shape, or form.[59]

While John Strawther was a blue-collar worker like his son Willis, evidence also highlights the elder's firsthand connection to Second Baptist, revealing that he not only assisted in establishing the Black congregation in the mid-1890s but also ministered there.[60] Likewise, Willis's *Pottstown Mercury* obituary revealed his own commitment to Second Baptist. In short, the younger Strawther served with the church's "deacon board," was a part of its "Willing Workers club," as well as its "senior choir." However, missing from the obituary was his chief involvement in spearheading the Second Baptist cemetery project.[61]

Another Virginia native involved in the Pottstown Second Baptist Church Cemetery project was Black minister Heywood L. Butler. Reverend Butler was about three years into his thirty-three-year pastorate of Second Baptist (1938–1971) when Edgewood Cemetery initially contacted his congregation that winter 1941. Born (1907) in Luray, the African American minister graduated from the historically Black Storer College in Harpers Ferry, West Virginia, before studying at the Philadelphia School of Bible. As Butler studied with the Philadelphia School of Bible, the African American Virginian by birth, who relocated to the City of Brotherly Love during the Great Migration, worked for Philadelphia's International Shoe Company as well. In fact, Butler labored there for over a decade (1923–1934).

Prior to his arrival in Pottstown at Second Baptist in 1938, Butler had additionally served in ministry in Virginia, New Jersey, and elsewhere in Pennsylvania, including time as an associate minister with another congregation, this one in the Frankford neighborhood in Philadelphia. Moreover, while pastoring in Pottstown, especially between the late 1930s and the early 1950s, Butler simultaneously resided in Philadelphia.[62]

Assuming the leadership at Second Baptist of Pottstown, Butler did much to help ameliorate the church's overall circumstance. As he found it, Second Baptist's congregation was tiny. Yet during the Black minister's first decade there, Second Baptist enlarged significantly. In 1938, when Butler started pastoring, 37 congregants formed Second Baptist. Before mid-July 1949, however, the number drastically catapulted, claiming 367 churchgoers then. This astronomic spike was about an 892 percent increase.[63]

Clearly the explosive growth of the Second Baptist congregation is a testament to Butler's ability to lead, organize, and get things done for the betterment of his people. His abilities, however, were not just noticed throughout Black Pottstown. In fact, Butler had a general appeal that touched many, African American and white, from diverse backgrounds as well as socioeconomic positions. His *Pottstown Mercury* obituary even categorized him as an "Ecumenical Force." One commentator interviewed in the same obituary additionally pointed out that Butler profoundly helped in linking dissimilarities among peoples, "whether religious, racial or cultural." As the interviewee saw the matter, such opposing views occasionally disconnected people. At the same time, the commentator emphasized the deceased minister's "great leadership qualities" throughout Black Pottstown, alongside the borough's white populace.[64]

Finally, Thomas B. Carter, a local African American also from the Old Dominion State, is worth mentioning in connection to the graveyard activism that helped create the Pottstown Second Baptist Church Cemetery. Carter, who was from Plains (Virginia), arrived on the local front three years before (1892) locals established Second Baptist Church, as well as approximately three years following his own birth, which was around 1889. Because he arrived so young into the region, most likely family, perhaps his father, of whom Carter had the same name, was the one responsible for initially bringing him locally during the early 1890s.

In addition to serving as a deacon at Second Baptist, Carter labored faithfully with Stanley G. Flagg Company, which expanded a little more than three decades from 1925 to 1956. As far as his activism relating to the Pottstown Second Baptist Cemetery went, however, the Black southerner was on its "committee" that Strawther headed.[65] On the other hand, the Second Baptist cemetery project was not the only civil rights committee activism that Carter took part in during World War II. Rather, the Black Virginia transplant additionally participated as an "executive committee" worker with the Pottstown NAACP, which originally launched in late November 1942.[66]

Without question, the Strawthers and Butler, for instance, had to have had a clear and personal understanding of the overt practices of racial oppression and terror associated with Jim Crow in Virginia (if not, generally speaking, the entire segregated South), precisely because they were natives of the Old Dominion State. Moreover, like other southern Blacks, they certainly had to have learned to cope and survive everyday life within such an atmosphere of blatant bigotry, intolerance, and extreme trepidation. In a similar vein, prominent African Americans like Booker T. Washington generally sought internal improvements of the Black community within the philosophical framework of "accommodation" rather than directly advocating for so-called equality with their white counterparts, particularly because of the pervasiveness of the legally codified structure of Jim Crow segregation in the South. This strategy, of course, was especially prevalent in the late nineteenth and early twentieth centuries, decades before the ubiquitous rise of the liberal interracialist strategy of post–World War II America.[67]

Yet during the 1930s southern Blacks began having civil rights success with another stratagem that demanded "equalization" of schoolteachers pay. A legal tactic administered in federal courts, historian John A. Kirk shows that equalization was the brainchild of Black NAACP law activist Charles Hamilton Houston. Like the accommodation initiatives that Booker T. Washington supported, equalization sought internal economic improvement and growth within the Black community. Where equalization differentiated from Washington's "accommodation" perspective, however, concerned a desire for a level financial playing field between African American and white educators in the South. In fact, by southern Blacks demanding that whites capitulated to their long-standing practice of paying African American teachers less than their white associates, they began directly challenging more of the outward/mainstream structure of de jure segregation and the engrained ethos of white supremacy within it rather than entirely stressing internal improvement initiatives in Black America. At this time, moreover, one must note that the majority Black population resided below and not above the Mason-Dixon Line. Finally, while the equalization approach bared its earliest fruit in Maryland during the late 1930s, Black activists would then apply the same civil rights method soon after in neighboring Virginia.[68]

Although there is no evidence directly linking Willis Strawther or Heywood Butler to the equalization work in Virginia, they were most certainly well steeped in the tradition and other Black internal improvement strategies, a fact that becomes evident in their civil rights activism in Pottstown. In addition to the local graveyard initiative, during Butler's pastorate Second Baptist owned "a large grocery store." Bought in 1949, the congregation not only ran the establishment but also catered largely to the Black community.[69]

Interestingly enough, in *Dear Sir*, Shandy Hill noted that historically, local Blacks resided "tightly segregated into one small hilly section of the borough," which was disrespectfully called "Chicken Hill." Outside Blacks traveling for employment, not many Pottstown African Americans made their way from this "restricted area" for purposes in socializing "with whites." In a vein similar to this last argument, it makes complete sense that Second Baptist mainly served the local Black populace, not only because it was historically a predominant African American congregation but also because the food outlet business was geographically nestled in the heart of Black Pottstown, that is, "Chicken Hill."[70] As such, the Black-owned business's location made it directly visible to the small minority community as well as pragmatically functional in servicing its consumption and consumer appetites.

A picture accompanying the July 16, 1949, *Pottstown Mercury* article entitled "Church Goes into Business for Financing New Edifice" further demonstrates the latter points. Captured in the illustration are three Black adults and four African American children. Two of the African American adults, Lillian Williams and Charles Rose, attended Second Baptist and worked at "the new store." Moreover, at the business Williams labored "full-time"; Rose did not, however. The remaining Blacks photographed were shoppers.

In July 1949, the *Pottstown Mercury* also revealed that the graveyard and food business owned by Second Baptist were in operation with the precise hopes of the congregation obtaining enough capital to acquire a bigger church building. At this time, Second Baptist had already outgrown its current house of worship, as evident by the church's explosive growth under Butler's earlier tenure. Finally, it is also interesting to note that the *Pottstown Mercury* labeled Second Baptist's funding initiative as "an unusual self-help" strategy.[71] Continuing in a similar spirit of traditional Black internal improvement and equalization strategies, Butler's congregation additionally had launched "a business and professional week" the previous month (June 1949) as well that included both African American and white professionals scheduled to speak.[72] One esteemed individual from outside the borough who spoke was Black Norristown lawyer Herbert C. Nelson. Later in life, Nelson went on to work as Montgomery County Pennsylvania's pioneering African American assistant district attorney.[73]

Under Butler's strong leadership, Second Baptist's commitment to traditional internal improvement and equalization strategies for the betterment of the local African American community were also on full display in the local housing work he spearheaded. A God-fearing man, Butler cared profoundly about Second Baptist congregants "spiritual" health, but he also prioritized churchgoers "physical" welfare. In other words, Butler wanted his congregants' quality/standard of life to also enhance. Thus, the Black cleric directed a church-based organization in Pottstown, the Frankford Improvement Association (FIA). Named for an organization he most likely had originally established during his time in Philadelphia, the Pottstown FIA helped African Americans acquire houses that they would own outright. In July 1949, the *Pottstown Mercury* reported that Second Baptist had helped African Americans buy seven standing houses locally. The same housing organization, which at the end of the 1940s Second Baptist congregants possessed "the controlling interest" over, likewise had acquired twenty-seven additional building areas as well.[74]

To be sure, Butler and the Pottstown FIA's activism using equalization and traditional Black internal improvement strategies during the 1940s was indicative of local housing needs within the African American community. Indeed, for quite some time, local Blacks had lived in deplorable residences. For example, the Pottstown Chamber of Commerce even reported in 1941 how local African Americans—over 75 percent—resided in structures classified as "sub-standard" in relationship "to their physical condition or over-crowding."[75] Similarly, historian Peter B. Levy notes comparable residential conditions among African Americans throughout York, Pennsylvania, a nearby small town, although bigger than Pottstown, during the postwar years.[76]

As shown in his Pottstown FIA work—as well as other traditional Black internal improvement and equalization activism—the secular aspects of Butler's leadership at Second Baptist thus concerned the material needs of Pottstown African Americans. Ostensibly, his vision in this way even contemplated burial needs. In July 1949, Butler reflected on this important want among local Blacks from earlier that same decade. Specifically, he revealed, "a cemetery in which members of Pottstown's Negro community could bury their dead" was a high priority. Before the Second Baptist graveyard, it was also common place that Pottstown Blacks would journey "great distances" so their deceased could receive proper burial. In effect, Butler viewed the Black graveyard plight throughout Pottstown as unacceptable. A pragmatist committed to traditional internal improvement and equalization work across Black Pottstown because most local whites would not fully yet yield to true racial equality, Butler guided his congregants with the Pottstown Second Baptist Cemetery project.

Yet Butler's perception of this burial need also helps contextualize Second Baptist's receptiveness to the Edgewood offer in December 1941. From the beginning, therefore, Second Baptist understood the graveyard project as practically meeting a local Black necessity.[77] While this cooperation between whites and African Americans did not challenge the norms of northern Jim Crow, it was also not an aberration during the late nineteenth and early twentieth centuries, as historian Nina Mjagkij reveals. On the other hand, even locally a few years before World War I, Pottstown's white-led First Baptist Church assisted Second

Baptist in acquiring a vacant church on Hale Street for use as its new church.[78]

At the same time, while Pottstown Blacks fervently rejected the ideology and structures of de facto segregation that manifested on the local front, they were simultaneously compelled by practical necessity to work within the exclusionary framework of anti-Black discrimination. In forcing the circumstances to yield what they could, the equalization strategy—as well as other traditional Black internal improvement activism—provided African Americans like those in Pottstown the opportunity to exercise agency, control, and autonomy so much so that it was even conducted within a vein similar to the NAACP and its legal strategy of equalization during the 1930s and 1940s, which coaxed greater assets for southern Black schoolteachers, as Kirk reveals. Therefore, equalization strategy—along with other Black internal improvement work initiatives—empowered Pottstown African Americans to further cultivate, foster, and ultimately tailor their own local Black freedom struggle as they specifically saw fit.[79]

Outside of the South in places like Pottstown, although discrimination was not legally enforced, the ways in which northern Jim Crow evidenced there was still just as oppressive, unjust, and dehumanizing. As this de facto structure of inconspicuous yet pervasive racism permeated the region, however, Blacks consciously chose to involve themselves in exclusionary alliances and schemes that partnered them with local white organizations. In doing so, local African Americans collaborations allowed them resources and platforms that they could otherwise not generally access. By developing these relationships with whites, even if based on exclusionary exchanges, they also empowered African Americans to earnestly control and operate traditional internal improvement and equalization work that was not only Black centered but also Black focused.

Thus, it is precisely in this aforementioned context of equalization and other traditional Black internal improvement activism that one must interpret the partnership between Second Baptist and Edgewood Cemetery. For example, when initially contacted by Edgewood Cemetery, Second Baptist did not demand that the white-owned company simply make available more interment spots to African Americans. Rather, the church voluntarily entered into the interracial association with a local business that upheld the inconspicuous yet entrenched practice of de facto segregation. Moreover, the actions of Second Baptist Blacks should not be interpreted as them capitulating to a subjugated status or as individuals overtly accepting the exclusionary business policy of white-owned Edgewood Cemetery. Instead, their decision was one based on pragmatism, with the end goal of internal improvement and equalization work that would both benefit and ameliorate greater opportunities and access to Black Pottstown as a whole, specifically when it came to help mitigating the minority community's burial plight.

Furthermore, the strategies of equalization and traditional internal improvement gave local African Americans the opportunity in the Pottstown Second Baptist Church Cemetery project to demonstrate autonomy, if not control, of their own space during this age of northern Jim Crow. In fact, because Second Baptist congregants sought out "a plot of ground for a separate cemetery" so that the grave site started formulating, they showed their power of choice as well as integral authority over the entire local civil rights project. "After several sites had been inspected," congregants established their internal group, which culminated in the June 18, 1942, property acquisition in nearby Douglass Township.[80] Moreover, Second Baptist membership illustrated control over Black space because the group virtually conducted "all the work on the hilly, wooded site." In short, since congregants own labor drove the physical building and beautifying of the Second Baptist grave site, it, therefore, gave them the ultimate power to create and structure the cemetery as they saw fit.[81]

Finally, because Butler and fellow Second Baptist congregants largely took part in the spatial creation and building of the church's graveyard, they additionally demonstrated a keen sense of Black agency. Indeed, while Edgewood Cemetery provided Second Baptist administrative and economic assistance, the Black congregation was the one that spearheaded the building and beautification project. As noted by the *Pottstown Mercury*, physical labor on the property commenced August 30, 1942, about eight months after Edgewood initially reached out to Second Baptist.[82] "With the Rev. Butler at their side," Second Baptist congregants "hacked a clearing out of the wilderness of brush and trees," chopped "down the top of the hill," reinforced "shoulders to prevent erosion" while simultaneously manufacturing "a cement block wall along a driveway they cut through the plot." Regarding Butler's personal role, the Black minister additionally operated "a bulldozer, mix[ed] cement," while tilling run-off trenches. He also constructed cemented structures direly needed for the grave site.[83]

The Pottstown YMCA and "Negro Extension Work" Activism

Another example of white efforts to assist local African Americans through equalization and other traditional internal improvement strategies but maintain white supremacist policies indicative of the covert yet pervasive structure of de facto racial segregation involves the work of the Pottstown branch of the Young Men's Christian Association (YMCA). Moreover, this illustration represents Black efforts to extract practical equalization, not merely internal improvement work, from ubiquitous discriminatory circumstances apparent throughout the Jim Crow landscape. Organized in Europe in the 1840s, the YMCA initially started operating in the United States the following decade (the 1850s). Not surprisingly, as historian Nina Mjagkij points out, the American YMCA adhered to US traditions of racial segregation in its branch affiliates both above and below the Mason-Dixon Line.[84]

Around the mid-1920s, YMCA operations in many large US cities often offered services to Black clientele through "Colored YMCA" subsidiaries.[85] In smaller locations like Pottstown, however, while the YMCA provided services to whites, racist traditions prohibited equal and fully integrated facility usage to African Americans. Moreover, locations such as Pottstown had African American population numbers that prohibited the full-scale development of permanent Black YMCA facilities. Thus, the YMCA offered services to African Americans through "Negro Extension Work" programs and other programming designated to racially separate the races along the customs and traditions of de facto segregation.[86] Launched in January 1945, the Pottstown initiative, which the Extension Division of the YMCA Boys' Department administered, catered specifically toward local African Americans. "The purpose of the Extension YMCA," the *Pottstown Mercury* reported in early January 1946, "is to provide YMCA services in Character Education to the Negro Community."[87]

Pottstown's history of YMCA activism dated back to the latter half of the nineteenth century. Yet when Negro Extension Work commenced in Pottstown, the YMCA had a structure that was about thirty years old (1913), situated on King and Evans Streets in the borough. The local YMCA, historian Paul Chancellor additionally writes, provided residents initiatives that encompassed "recreation, education, sociability, and character" training.[88] While Black YMCA extension workers would go on to offer similar services to Pottstown's African American collective, their activism conversely started under discriminatory circumstances. In fact, the *Philadelphia Tribune* reported that when these Black workers started their labor, the Pottstown YMCA did not grant them complete access to its entire campus.[89]

As historian Thomas J. Sugrue observes, when an African American populace above the Mason-Dixon Line "was large enough, its Negro Y," played important functions toward giving "social services, housing and food, and education for urban blacks."[90] Although a drastically small Black minority when juxtaposed with vast northern cities like nearby Philadelphia and its enormous African American population, Pottstown YMCA activists, nevertheless, offered Negro Extension Work programs and similar racial exclusion activism in changing, ad hoc locations—whatever facilities they could secure. For example, the *Pottstown Mercury* remarked in late December 1946 about how YMCA Negro Extension Work activism was initially facilitated within the local "Jefferson school." Yet when Pottstown's Recreation Commission—the public agency governing public recreational space—intervened during latter times, local activists implemented and coordinated YMCA Negro Extension Work somewhere else, which ended up being "Bethany center." In the end, these illustrations shed light and speak further on the challenges local Black activists endured in not having a stable and permanent physical space for YMCA Negro Extension Work in Pottstown.[91]

In addition to no permanent facilities, YMCA Negro Extension Work programs like the Pottstown branch early on had only part-time staff. Nevertheless, as with their perspectives on other aspects of institutional discrimination and entrenched inequality during the equalization era, rather than reject separate YMCA services, Blacks, it appears safe to suggest, took pragmatic views of Colored YMCA and Negro Extension programming. Thus, they utilized the work and similar Black internal improvement strategies from these segregated spaces as opportunities to meet immediate needs within African American communities.[92]

Like Willis Strawther, Reverend Butler, and Thomas Carter's roles in the Second Baptist graveyard project, YMCA Negro Extension Work activism advanced because of effective Black leadership. Most notable was African American William D. Corum, who led the program at its inception.[93] A Pottstown native born in 1916, like Carter, Corum worked at Stanley G. Flagg & Company in nearby Stowe, Pennsylvania.[94] Corum was also an active and involved member of the Pottstown Black community. For example, he involved himself in local sporting competition, playing baseball for both "Neville's All-Stars" and the "Pottstown Colored All-Stars."[95] Additionally, Corum managed Pottstown athletic teams comprised entirely of local Blacks. One was even a softball club affiliated with his local congregation, Pottstown's Bethel African Methodist Episcopal (AME). In addition to the Black YMCA activist's athletic work at Bethel AME, Corum involved himself in general church activism there.[96] Yet outside of church, William associated with not only the borough's "Colored Community Hospital auxiliary" but also the local all-Black Keystone Lodge of Masons, where, among other duties, he sang with the "Keystone State quartet."[97]

Although a native of Pottstown, William's father, Benjamin F. Corum Sr. (1868–1928), was from Virginia. Born in 1868, Benjamin relocated to Pottstown well before the twentieth-century Great Migration.[98] And like southern Blacks who made their way to the North during the Great Migration, arguably, what most likely motivated Benjamin F. Corum, as well as other African Americans born in the South who relocated before the mass twentieth-century exodus, was the financial component. Moreover, while most Blacks resided in Dixie between 1860 and 1900, African Americans living above the Mason-Dixon Line expanded exponentially during this forty-year period, going from 344,719 to 911,025.[99] Writing in May 1906 about southern African American relocation over the last almost half century, Black scholar Richard R. Wright Jr., a Georgia transplant himself who obtained a doctorate five years later (1911) from the

University of Pennsylvania, additionally argued "that the chief cause for the movement northward is economic—and is seen from the migrants' point of view in the higher wages offered in the North."[100] In short, this same monetary rationality surely had to have directly inspired native southern Blacks like Benjamin Corum Sr. and others who willingly made the trek to Pottstown and similar locales above the Mason-Dixon Line during the late nineteenth and early twentieth centuries.[101]

Northern civil rights activists like William D. Corum demonstrate both the generational and the peripheral effects of southern Black migration, in particular, on the Black freedom struggle in the North. Indeed, even if his father was not active in local civil rights, the very fact that Benjamin F. Corum Sr. relocated from the American South to Pottstown eventually allowed William—and, as is seen later, other Corum siblings—to directly partake in civil rights work in the small northern borough. While William was a first-generation African American in the North, his life and work, nevertheless, represented peripheral origins from the American South because his father was originally from there. In short, when interpreting the involvement of William Corum and other local African Americans in the Black freedom struggle in Pottstown, one must directly acknowledge the ways in which southern African American migration facilitated and ultimately allowed such work to materialize. And in a vein similar to historian James N. Gregory's keen analysis of the far-reaching impact of Black southerners who made the trek to locales above the Mason-Dixon Line during the twentieth century, the arguments elucidated in this chapter about the Corums can most certainly be applicable to other northern Blacks of the time who had identical familial and generational connections to Dixie.[102]

While other local African Americans assisted throughout the duration of YMCA Negro Extension Work in Pottstown, another notable activist was Black minister Isaiah E. Glenn. Like the Strawthers, Butler, Corum, and Carter, Glenn was a native son of Virginia. Born in 1906, Isaiah grew up in Chincoteague, Accomack County. Eventually, he too relocated from the Old Dominion State to Pottstown during the Great Migration. Evidence even places Isaiah in Pottstown as early as late August 1925, when he wedded Edith Louise Clifton Glenn, a native of Chester, South Carolina.[103]

Like his fellow Black activists in Pottstown, Glenn was a member of its working-class community. According to the 1940 US census, he was a "Laborer" in "Public Work." Moreover, evidence from 1975 reveals that Glenn worked formerly with Bethlehem Steel Corporation. His tenure with Bethlehem Steel, however, began afterward. Outside of his commitment to work, and like the other aforementioned local Blacks, Glenn was a congregant of Second Baptist Church, where he even ministered under Butler's pastorate. In addition to his ministerial duties at Second Baptist, Glenn held the vice presidency with the inaugural Pottstown NAACP chapter, which, again, initially launched in late November 1942.[104]

In addition to Corum and Glenn, African American women participated directly in local YMCA Negro Extension Work. One example was Frances Young. A teenager when the YMCA labor commenced in January 1945, Frances served the Black-centered activism from early on, even well past her graduation from Pottstown Senior High School that June.[105] As noted in the school's yearbook *The Troiad 1945: A Publication Presented Annually by the Graduating Class of Pottstown High School*, it is also worth mentioning that Young was an athlete for the Trojans, playing not only "Basketball" but also "Softball"; she was also a part of the "Glee Club."[106] Regarding the career path she desired, Young additionally confessed that she planned on being a "*Junior typist.*"[107] Moreover, she involved herself with Second Baptist Church.[108]

Young also conveyed an astute civil rights consciousness that was indeed evident in the "Readers Say"/letter-to-the-editor correspondence she wrote to the *Pottstown Mercury* in late July 1954, during the subsequent aftermath of *Brown v. Board*. In the correspondence, Young even talked about her experience with "schooling in Pottstown." Here, her reflections aligned with the inconspicuous yet engrained de facto segregation structure that permeated the small northern borough. For example, sharply lambasting the false sense of racial equality, particularly in that while borough Blacks attended local educational institutions with intentions of obtaining training in white-collar-related work, Pottstown whites, Young ostensibly suggested, instead only desired that African Americans remained working within "a labor, factory or domestic type" occupation. Finally, it is also worth noting that Young came from a family of local civil rights activists such as her parents, Joseph and Geraldine Young. Joseph, an African American Bethlehem Steel worker who was originally from Maryland, and Geraldine, a native of Pottstown, both labored with the Pottstown NAACP. Like Frances, her parents were also active Second Baptist congregants.[109]

YMCA Negro Extension Work, under William D. Corum's tenure, consistently advocated for local Blacks. One pressing concern that Corum identified in early May 1946, even stressed that the local, Black-centered activism needed a place to call its own. As Corum saw the matter, "Our greatest problem is that of procuring a building in which to conduct club meetings, recreational programs, and counselling services to carry on a character building program for our young people." Precisely since Negro Extension Work had no such facilities, Corum continued, its workers could only implement the activism by relying on "the kindness of other social organizations," which made their spaces available to the Black-focused work. Consequently, Corum, a first-generation northern African American, declared, "We need a building in our own community."

Put differently, both to align with the strategies of equalization and other traditional Black internal improvement efforts and because the dominant white population continually insisted on perpetuating its racist power structure of de facto segregation, Pottstown's African American populace, although small, nonetheless still desired its own space. Such space, in turn, would provide local Blacks like Corum, Glenn, Young, and others associated with YMCA Negro Extension Work in Pottstown the opportunity to control the ways in which they ran and operated their own institution. As was the case with the Pottstown Second Baptist graveyard project, by having their own space, local Black YMCA activists could demonstrate agency and autonomy. At the same time, by having this YMCA space, local African Americans would not have to suffer the undignified and exclusionary practices that the Pottstown branch had in place since shortly before World War I. Furthermore, if the Pottstown YMCA was to have segregated programming, then the African American population should not only have its own institution but also have that institution be placed in Black Pottstown. In doing so, it would be isolated from the larger white community and thereby separated existentially from its long-standing racist and unjust practices of ubiquitous de facto segregation, which forcefully permeated the small northern borough at the time.

It also appears safe to argue that the aim of local Black activists at this early postwar juncture, when it came to whites stomaching racial advancement in Pottstown, was not the full breaking down of exclusionary roadblocks held firmly in place by the central YMCA facility on the local front or its white-only power structure but to provide an equal space for the Black population. Thus, the equalization strategy, especially relating to owning and operating facilities, proved most effective and pragmatic to local Black activists associated with YMCA Negro Extension Work. However, because Pottstown African Americans utilized the strategies of equalization and traditional Black internal improvement to facilitate said activism locally, their work, in turn, should not convey that they had an outright hostile professional relationship with the local, main, white-led YMCA. In fact, local Blacks' employing the strategies as a pragmatic solution should not be interpreted as them directly challenging manifestations of local Jim Crow and traditions of perpetual racial exclusion and separation.[110] For instance, local Black YMCA activists often connected with white Pottstown clubs like Rotary, Lions, and American Business. However, their rationale behind doing so was only informal and educative, particularly designed to garner financial support of YMCA Negro Extension Work in Pottstown.[111]

YMCA Negro Extension Work also attracted the service of many borough Blacks, who were passionately committed to serving local African Americans. From a structural and organizational standpoint, however, Negro Extension Work had an all-Black advisory "council . . . composed of 12 leaders of the Negro community and each year six members" were "elected to serve a two year term beginning May 1."[112] Moreover, African American YMCA activists themselves named the all-Black council, further conveying the ways in which they demonstrated both agency and autonomy over their programming. Further, the all-Black council oversaw the YMCA Negro Extension Work activism program. And underneath it was an organizational structure of unpaid, part-time Black workers. Alongside the African American council, these laborers were also principally the ones implementing YMCA Negro Extension Work activism into Black Pottstown.

Consequently, the following examples capture some initiatives orchestrated under YMCA Negro Extension Work activism. They included interracial outreach at both secular and clerical locations, alongside internal fundraising to sustain the Black-centered endeavor.[113] Further initiatives included "the organization of six educational club groups, the organization of the Adult Y club, the planning and carrying out of a recreational program including Teen Age dances, basketball, softball, indoor programs, and special trips for young people, and participation in youth study courses and forums."[114] As indicated earlier, moreover, both local Black men and women were directly involved in Negro Extension Work activism overall.

While Glenn was not the central leader of YMCA Negro Extension Work in Pottstown, he still labored in important leadership capacities within the local, Black-centered programming. For example, Glenn not only sat on the all-Black council but also essentially served on it from the inception of YMCA Negro Extension Work in early January 1945. Moreover, Black YMCA workers went on and appointed Glenn again in late April 1946.[115] Alongside Glenn's general council activism, he also chaired YMCA Extension Work's "committee on church relations."

Corum was a hands-on type of leader with YMCA Negro Extension Work, and so too was the case when it came to other local Blacks like Isaiah E. Glenn. For example, as far as Glenn chairing Negro Extension Work's "committee on church relations," he was directly involved in the facilitation of said activism. As reported by the *Pottstown Mercury* in mid-February 1945, Negro Extension Work had presentations to local Black churches arranged, which Glenn himself organized. Yet for the projected gatherings, while Glenn headed the church committee, Corum was the one tentatively scheduled as the principal speaker. White YMCA Boys Work affiliate Harry Edward Moore Jr. was also booked to accompany them. Finally, the *Pottstown Mercury* revealed the times and dates of the projected gatherings, as well as the Black churches hosting them. They included Pottstown's Mount Herman Baptist, Second Baptist, Bethel AME, in addition to the House of God, which was in nearby Stowe, Pennsylvania.[116]

To demonstrate further the fact that Glenn was not solely a leader by name but action, he served as a ministerial liaison with YMCA Negro Extension Work in Pottstown as well. In this capacity, Glenn frequently participated in the Black-centered activism on the local front.[117] In one event from late November 1945, which occurred in conjunction with Second Baptist's "jubilee banquet" that celebrated its founding fifty years earlier, Glenn was "master of ceremonies." With over one hundred individuals attending, the Black minister introduced YMCA Negro Extension Work chair William D. Corum (as well as others), who made comments. While Corum's statements probably celebrated the establishment of Second Baptist during the mid-1890s, precisely because that was what the event centered on, the Black leader most likely plugged the local YMCA program that he headed within the same remarks as well.[118]

Like Corum and Glenn, Frances Young also demonstrated effective leadership as an activist with local YMCA Negro Extension Work. Indeed, from early on, Young labored diligently,[119] so much so that later in the YMCA programming, she also took on a leadership role as an officer with "the Tri-Hi-Y club."[120] Similarly, Young's athletic background proved beneficial to YMCA Negro Extension Work in that she assisted within an authority capacity in its sports-related programming.[121]

Without question, because of effective leaders like Corum, Glenn, and Young, undergirded by Black boots-on-the-ground activists, YMCA Negro Extension Work got many local African Americans directly involved in participating throughout its programs. For example, in September 1946, YMCA Negro Extension Work activists reported 1,092 served in Pottstown's Bethany Recreation Center. The monthly total, however, broke down into 323 participating in sports-related programming, 220 in club-related activity, 120 for films, and 429 in recreational activity.[122] Moreover, that December, the Negro Extension Work initiative served 2,648 in sum, which, once again broke down into several specific categories, including those pertaining to athletics generally, "social games," and "club events."[123] By late December 1946, YMCA Negro Extension Work activists also had "$1365 in cash and pledges."

Local YMCA workers gathered these resources, the *Pottstown Mercury* added, so that the Negro Extension Work program could ultimately acquire its own housing facility to better serve the African American population in and around the borough.[124]

To be sure, Pottstown's YMCA Negro Extension Work programming was not only multilayered but also popular, assisting large segments of the small Black population.[125] In fact, the *Pottstown Mercury* reported in late December 1946 that under William D. Corum's tenure at the time, Negro Extension Work activism was "serving the character education needs of 262 Negro families in Pottstown with a population of more than 1,500." Ostensibly, because the estimate given by the *Pottstown Mercury* is somewhat high—especially since Pottstown only had 608 African Americans in 1940 and 844 in 1950 according to US census records—the approximation suggests that Negro Extension Work activism had an appeal that transcended the small northern borough. The estimation also shows that Negro Extension Work aided and assisted numerous African Americans.[126]

Yet Negro Extension Work and its traditional Black internal improvement and equalization activism would exist in Pottstown for only a few more years. By the summer of 1949, the Pottstown YMCA was fully desegregated. Thus, local African Americans had complete access to the Pottstown YMCA's total amenities.[127]

Reflecting on the activism in Pottstown, this chapter has shown that equalization strategy appears to complicate what historian Nina Mjagkij suggests was a consensus of Black leadership, for example, inside the YMCA as well as outside. Before World War II, Blacks connected with the YMCA essentially pursued equalization strategies, which some contemporaries have dismissed as little more than "accommodationism and gradualism."[128] Yet the global conflict proved landmark "for African Americans in the United States and in the YMCA," Mjagkij argues. Additionally, she stresses that Black YMCA heads were chiefly influenced by the widespread civil rights activism of African Americans, generally, which sought true racial equitability. As such, Black YMCA heads too denounced greater attempts within the YMCA at "further interracial cooperation without the elimination of segregation."[129] Adamant, they even collaborated alongside civil rights groups such as the National Negro Congress and the NAACP. Ultimately, Black YMCA activists' labor during World War II pressured the YMCA into beginning the dismantling process of its almost century-old discriminatory protocols.[130]

Ostensibly, therefore, Black YMCA leadership in the World War II era dismissed the old model of equalization, or "interracial cooperation without the elimination of segregation."[131] Yet Negro Extension Work, like Colored YMCAs, were well-used, well-regarded pillars of urban Black communities throughout the country. "The Negro Y" additionally represented "one of the most visible manifestations of a politics of respectability and racial uplift," Sugrue contends, even well before World War II.

On the other hand, like the Pottstown Second Baptist Cemetery project, the pragmatism of equalization strategies, as well as similar Black internal improvement activism, represented in YMCA Negro Extension Work also allowed African Americans in and around the borough to experience a real sense of autonomy, agency, and control of a vital community service entity. Moreover, despite the pragmatic attention to immediate needs and services represented by the Negro Extension Work program, local activists concurrently pressed forth and desired for the complete elimination of race discrimination in the local programming, which operated within the structure and parameters of de facto segregation. At the same time, while Black Negro Extension Work activists partnered with the white-led segregated local YMCA, that did not mean they surrendered any sense of moral authority, especially in relationship to conducting future civil rights activist initiatives that battled manifestations and other evidences of anti-Black discrimination and prejudice germane to the area.[132]

Last, YMCA Negro Extension Work activists in Pottstown were "helping produce programs on race relations," William Corum revealed in early February 1946, and were "supplying speakers to churches and clubs and doing an all around race education program." Corum also informed the all-Black council of Negro Extension Work, "We intend to keep moving out in this field."[133] To be sure, under Corum Negro Extension Work activists participated in initiatives that sought to foster better relationships among local Blacks and whites. Some examples of the activism seeking to build greater interracial relationships concerned its involvement in "Race Relations Sunday and Brotherhood Week," both of which promulgated egalitarianism among peoples of diverse backgrounds and ethnicities.[134] Corum even joined an "Inter-Racial Commission" as a main representative of Black Pottstown.[135] While not associated with YMCA Negro Extension Work, Glenn, in his capacity as a minister, partook in similar regional activism that supported harmonious pursuits among Blacks and whites in early postwar America.[136]

The Pottstown NAACP and the Fight for Local Black Advancement

A third perspective on a local organization grappling with changes brought by the World War II era was the Pottstown chapter of the National Association for the Advancement of Colored People (NAACP). Founded in November 1942, the Pottstown NAACP advocated the same civil rights platform as its mother organization, established in 1909 and based in New York City. In particular, the Pottstown NAACP desired that both African Americans' overall livelihood—economic as well as social—and their relationship with the dominant white population would drastically improve. Furthermore, the local NAACP came about so that it could protest the de facto segregation structure and its manifestations of racial inequality directed at African Americans throughout and nearby the small northern borough.[137]

In January 1943, one hundred individuals flocked into Second Baptist in honor of the local branch's launch. During the gathering, white Pottstown lawyer Joseph L. Prince spoke. In short, Prince articulated points that aligned with the NAACP's civil rights platform. For example, structuring his remarks around scripture found in the book of Malachi, "Have we not all one Father," Prince gave an exposition on "equality." In his view, equality had dire importance specifically because of World War II. Yet the white attorney also argued the need of Black self-help and self-improvement. "Any group," Prince announced, "to earn respect of others, must first come to respect its own members." Paradoxically, the white attorney's emphasis on Black self-help and development seemed to favor that local African American activists continue their traditional strategies of equalization and internal improvement work. In other words, rather than argue that the Pottstown NAACP should begin fully challenging conspicuous and apparent manifestations of racial inequality via the northern Jim Crow structure on the local front, Prince, instead, stressed the importance of Pottstown African Americans examining the Black community, and thereby fixing conditions within it. Only then, Prince alluded, would acceptance from those outside Black Pottstown sincerely and honestly manifest.[138]

Whereas Blacks and whites had jointly established the National NAACP decades earlier, the organization's branches across the nation were organized, supported, and led by African Americans.[139] While World War II raged, the organization additionally experienced exponential growth, scholar Charles Radford Lawrence writes, as "an increasing number of communities throughout the nation were being exposed directly to the work of the Association [NAACP]."[140] Between 1941 and 1945, the number of NAACP branches enlarged from 383 to 894. In these same years, NAACP membership additionally expanded from 72,021 to 351,131.[141] During the 1940s, the Pennsylvania State Conference of NAACP Branches desired too that an NAACP "youth council" started inside Pottstown, even as early as 1941.[142]

However, by November 1942 momentum for a full NAACP branch in Pottstown initiated. "We are indeed happy to learn of the fine success you are having in the campaign to organize the Pottstown unit and we shall look forward to receiving the Charter application at an early date," wrote African American NAACP Department of Branches executive assistant Lucille Black in early November 1942 to Pottstown African American James H. Corum.[143] Black sent Corum, who was the older brother of William D. Corum, another letter the following month in late December, which conveyed that the Pottstown NAACP was now "a full member of the Association and we are happy to welcome you into the ranks of full-fledged branches."[144] Nevertheless, this growth would eventually cease around World War II's conclusion.[145]

Like the Second Baptist graveyard project and YMCA Negro Extension Work, without any question, the Pottstown NAACP only existed because of effective and committed Black leadership. Most notable was James H. Corum, another first-generation northern Black. Like his younger sibling William, James, the pioneering president of the local NAACP, was a native of Pottstown, born in 1902.[146] Moreover, James Corum worked for Stanley G. Flagg and Co. in nearby Stowe (Pennsylvania). His tenure, however, started there prior to his younger brother William's; he started working with the company consistently in 1925.

Thus, James Corum labored regularly with Flagg's across five decades, retiring in the late 1960s. Yet well before his retirement, Corum was also directly involved within labor leadership there.[147] While his history with Flagg unionism dated back to 1936—"the old independent union"—the Black laborer played a crucial part establishing Flagg Union Local 2326 of the United Steel Workers (USW), an affiliate of the Congress of Industrial Organizations (CIO), in the early 1940s as well.[148]

Similar to William, James H. Corum was also heavily involved in the Black community of Pottstown. In addition to being one of the main organizers of the Pottstown Second Baptist Church Cemetery, he served administratively with the same local congregation.[149] An affiliate with local Black Boy Scouts, Corum additionally managed his younger brother's local baseball teams, "Neville's All-Stars" and "the Pottstown Colored All-Stars."[150] Altogether, because of his highly esteemed standing within Pottstown's African American community, it should come as no surprise that local Blacks had chosen James Corum to lead and guide their NAACP chapter.

Another local Black who played both direct and active roles in the work of the Pottstown NAACP during World War II was Frank W. Thomas Sr. Born in 1916 in Pennsylvania, Thomas was the inaugural secretary of the local chapter. Similar to his fellow working-class African Americans in Pottstown, Thomas, according to the 1940 US census, labored as a "grinder" in the "pipefitting" industry. This census record, corroborated by a letter Thomas wrote, possibly suggests that he not only worked at Stanley G. Flagg but also was a rank-and-file member of its industrial union, Local 2326.[151] In early March 1944, the *Pottstown Mercury* also revealed that the "Pottstown draft board" changed Thomas and many others' "selective service" classification to "deferred" because of their essentiality to wartime manufacturing. By this time, the newspaper remarked, the board gave over 950 local males of military age postponement from compulsory service in the armed forces.[152] In early February 1943, the local newspaper once again provided additional biographical information on Thomas. Specifically, the Black worker, and over one hundred others, finished training, which associated them with the locale's "Auxiliary Police corps."[153] Evidence also suggests that Thomas attended Second Baptist Church, just like many of the aforementioned local Blacks, such as NAACP President James Corum, Willis Strawther, Reverend Butler, Isaiah Glenn, Frances Young and her family, and Thomas Carter.[154]

Just as African American men across the United States played definitive parts in civil rights activism with the NAACP, so too was the case with Black women. For example, in his keen analysis of NAACP leader

Carolyn Davenport Moore, historian James Wolfinger spotlights the African American activist's impactful role in both promulgating and maintaining civil rights activism throughout nearby Philadelphia as World War II raged.[155] Yet while not working within the same leadership capacity as Moore, local Black women, as they had done for the YMCA Negro Extension Work program, labored early on with the Pottstown NAACP, with borough African American Jennie Thornton being one.

In addition to Corum and Thomas, however, Thornton served with the Pottstown NAACP as an "executive committee" member; in total, the local branch had nine.[156] A native of Pottstown born in 1893, Thornton's maiden name was Green. Like Benjamin F. Corum Sr. (James H. Corum's father), Jennie's father, Jacob Green, who labored at three local companies throughout his lifetime (McClintic Marshall Construction, Pottstown Iron, and George B. Lessig) was originally from Virginia—Rectortown's in particular.[157]

According to the 1940 US census, Thornton conducted "housework" for a "private home." Thornton's occupation status, of course, was indicative of many other working-class Black women across the United States during the twentieth century, as historians such as John S. Portlock and Sugrue demonstrate.[158] At the same time, while Thornton had a peripheral and generational connection to the Great Migration because of her father—similar to the Corum siblings William and James with their father Benjamin—so too was the case with her relationship to her husband, Richard T. Thornton. An African American from nearby Maryland who initially arrived in Pottstown a year before (1913) the official start of World War I, Richard not only worked locally with Bethlehem Steel but was also on "the [Second Baptist Church Cemetery] committee" with Corum, alongside Willis Strawther, who headed it.[159] Moreover, just like Strawther, Corum, and Thomas, both Richard and Jennie Thornton were actively involved in ministry at Second Baptist. Jennie—according to the Black female NAACP activist's *Pottstown Mercury* obituary—even established "the Pastor's Aid Club," and during her time there participated directly as "a . . . member of the senior choir" while also serving as "a member of the Helping Hand Club."[160]

Similar to the YMCA Negro Extension Work in Pottstown, which lacked its own location, the Pottstown NAACP branch, once established, had no physical office space either. For example, Corum and Thomas worked out of their respective residences, both on the 700 block of Beech Street in Pottstown.[161] Moreover, Second Baptist Church served as an occasional meeting space. The Pottstown NAACP also utilized Bethany Recreation Center.[162]

While local NAACP membership numbers paled in comparison to large northern city chapters like Philadelphia and Detroit during World War II, the Pottstown group, nevertheless, did experience growth, particularly in its beginning phase. "We have had a fairly successful campaign here as the number shows as compared to our total population of about 600 colored residents," noted James Corum in a correspondence from late November 1942.[163] Indeed, membership grew steadily, so much so that by January 1943, the local NAACP had 175 enrolled members, which equated to approximately 29 percent of the local African American population during World War II.[164] Yet although a small group, from a percentage standpoint Pottstown had a more extensive representation of NAACP membership from its Black community than Philadelphia or Detroit.[165]

Like Black communities in highly industrialized zones across the wartime United States, Pottstown NAACP membership was generally from the laboring class. This marks a break from the earlier middle-class dominance of chapter NAACPs in places like Detroit and Philadelphia.[166] It additionally demonstrates a signal of shift toward mass membership and mass concerns in war years.[167] Indeed, Corum described Pottstown to the national office, in his late November 1942 correspondence, that it was "a working man's town as most [members] are on defense work."[168]

Furthermore, the class homogeneity of the Pottstown NAACP bears mention, as its leadership conducted similar labor as the rank-and-file membership. This fact set Pottstown apart from many chapter profiles in larger northern cities like Detroit and Philadelphia during the war years, where even as working-class Blacks joined the membership, leadership was still in the hands of professionals and elites. To be sure, during World War II, Pottstown NAACP leadership had no dominant representation from the Black professional classes. Nor did it have any full-time employees on the branch staff who earned their living from the civil rights organization, as demonstrated, for instance, in prior remarks on African American blue-collar workers like Corum, Glenn, Thomas, and Jennie Thornton.[169] Similarly, historian Todd E. Robinson writes that the Grand Rapid's (Michigan) NAACP before World War II had Black leadership from identical working-class employment positions. However, the Grand Rapids branch also had representations from African American "professionals."[170]

Nevertheless, even though the Pottstown NAACP had this intrinsic laboring-class composition among its leadership as well as its rank-and-file, organizational records prove that chapter membership would be faithful, at least in terms of monetary obligations, throughout the war years. On November 9, 1942, James Corum reported that "there were 100 signed paid [membership] cards turned in."[171] Several weeks later, branch secretary Frank W. Thomas sent the NAACP Board of Directors in New York City $79.25 "as payment for 146 adult members and 3 junior members."[172] In mid-January the following year, Thomas shipped funds relating to 12 adult and 4 junior memberships.[173] Finally, within a document stamped June 17, 1943, Thomas proudly announced that the borough NAACP was "still making progress."[174]

Yet despite the national organization's ideological commitments to racial integration, the Pottstown branch still worked within aspects of equalization and traditional internal improvement strategies when pragmatically useful for delivering services otherwise unavailable to Black constituents. For example, the small borough chapter worked with both the Pottstown Recreation Commission and Bethany Recreation Center in search of solutions that ultimately did not challenge the local inconspicuous yet engrained structure of Jim Crow in the North, otherwise known as de facto segregation, especially when seeking to gain better access to recreational space for the local African American collective. Specifically, the local NAACP asked the Pottstown Recreation Commission "that a playground be established for use of the colored, with a colored leader." In response, the recreational group authorized the Pottstown NAACP's inquiry.[175] The following February, in turn, the Pottstown NAACP demonstrated its approval of the Pottstown Recreation Commission's assistance in promoting equalization and traditional Black internal improvement activism by donating $100 toward the NAACP's utilization of Bethany Recreation Center.[176]

Moreover, in reflection on Bethany Recreation Center, "a two-story frame structure with a large gym, five social rooms, a chapel and showers in the basement," one should note the ways in which locals facilitated programming there.[177] In fact, such facilitation further demonstrates how pervasive de facto segregation was in Pottstown, especially during the World War II era. For example, as the global conflict raged, Bethany Recreation Center scheduled enrollment times separately for "White" and "Colored" locals.[178] Likewise, a newspaper advertisement posted by Bethany Recreation Center in early October 1943 highlighted enrollment and upcoming events. It captioned, "Registration: White group, Oct. 13, 4–7 p.m.; colored group, 4–7 p.m., Oct. 15. Free social and square dance instruction, crafts, dramatics, play hours, etc."[179] Finally, it is worth noting that Pottstown formally acquired Bethany Recreation Center from the prestigious Hill School in early February 1943. At this time, the *Pottstown Mercury* identified Bethany Recreation Center as Bethany Chapel. Yet although the Hill School gave the facility to Pottstown, one of the institution's conditions for the small northern borough was "that there be no racial limits" placed on individuals who used it. Ostensibly, while Bethany Recreation Center did not totally exclude African Americans, as underscored in its newspaper enrollment advertisements, its use of separate enrollment times for Blacks and whites demonstrates—without question—the more inconspicuous yet far-reaching structure of de facto segregation.[180]

Nevertheless, while Bethany Recreation Center employed such discriminatory practices, the Pottstown NAACP still used the space. In doing so, however, local African American chapter activists were not capitulating to the cultivation or promulgation of white supremacy and anti-Black racism, which the localized structure of de facto segregation both covertly and pervasively maintained and supported. For example, like African Americans associated with the Second Baptist graveyard project as well as local YMCA Negro Extension Work, Black activists with the Pottstown NAACP were rather essentially seeking pragmatic ways to fully use such spaces to provide services to local African Americans. At the same time, by employing the strategies of traditional internal improvement and equalization, they were able to have greater control over programming within the Black community and thereby further demonstrate autonomy and agency. It seems reasonable to assume that rather than challenge Black exclusion—at the risk of being rebuffed and turned down—the local NAACP (like the YMCA Negro Extension Work program and the cemetery project previously mentioned) sought some approximation of equality as the pragmatic and best solution available in the moment.[181]

The Advent of the Liberal Interracialist Strategy

To be sure, one challenge connecting the Second Baptist graveyard project, Negro Extension Work activism through the YMCA, and the small borough NAACP concerned economics and Pottstown's working-class composition. While not stated explicitly, the fact that Second Baptist willingly accepted monetary assistance from Edgewood Cemetery, which practiced racial discrimination with its quota/spatial allocation system, seemingly suggests that the Black church had trouble acquiring enough capital on its own to obtain the property without help from a better-financed organization like the white-led Edgewood Cemetery. It also suggests that such an inability was characteristic of the broader Black community in Pottstown (and, perhaps, other similarly situated smaller Black populations), who might have otherwise extended financial assistance to the Black church for such a community-beneficial project as a cemetery.[182]

Negro Extension Work activism, like most other iterations of the equalization and traditional internal improvement strategies, endured the challenge of acquiring the necessary capital to conduct YMCA programs sufficiently. While governments collected tax monies in a color-blind fashion, they often discriminated against Black citizens access to the resources those government-funded dollars supported. In the case of private entities (like the YMCA), citizens and charitable interests likewise donated money in support of programs in the public interest. However, racism curtailed the full benefit of this benevolence for Blacks in need. For these reasons, equalization and traditional Black internal improvement strategies seldom yielded sufficient resources. For instance, though part of the YMCA, the all-Black board of Negro Extension Work programs often performed their own fundraising and financing.[183]

On the other hand, under African American William S. Carden (William Corum's successor as head of Negro Extension Work in Pottstown), the leadership of the YMCA program was accorded full-time status. Now, it was able to direct more time and YMCA resources to programs before the Pottstown YMCA dropped the entire biracial system in 1949.[184] As the *Philadelphia Tribune* observed, "service and programs increased when a full-time extension division secretary [Carden] was appointed in February [1947]."[185] "It was mainly through his [Carden's] influence," the newspaper unequivocally argued, "that colored men and boys may belong to the YMCA in Pottstown [on a desegregated basis]."[186]

While the *Philadelphia Tribune* is correct in its point that during Carden's tenure the Pottstown YMCA ultimately desegregated, one cannot lessen the crucial part played by William D. Corum. Corum not only headed Negro Extension Work activism into Black Pottstown for its beginning years, but it was also during this time that the Black-centered initiative established its base. Thus, when Carden replaced Corum, he came into a situation where the activism's foundation had already been framed. Corum must also receive credit for his direct contribution to the dismantling of segregation at the Pottstown YMCA because he was in fact hands on—just like Glenn and Young—and intimately involved with Negro Extension Work activism. For instance, during Corum's tenure, he stayed busy attending Negro Extension Work gatherings. He also frequently visited local outside groups—African American and white—to not only spread the word about what Black-focused activism was but also raise the monetary support to sustain it, provide internal encouragement and motivation for extension work activists themselves, and to seek out the Black volunteers needed to ultimately advance the Black-centered activism.[187]

Moreover, of all the activists involved in the launch of the Pottstown NAACP branch, James H. Corum's brief time as its president (1942–1944) would hold significance for several reasons.[188] First, under Corum, when the Pottstown NAACP established working-class and labor relations footings, it helped African Americans obtain employment in the war industry.[189] As he quickly built up Pottstown's membership (and thus revenues to New York), his talents were also appreciated by the national office, which sheds light on an interesting historiographical point about the national NAACP's connection with subordinate branches.[190] Historian Patrick Flack reveals that the Detroit chapter constantly clashed with NAACP headquarters over "priorities" in the Motor City. Such conflict, he argues, was essentially there from around the time that the Detroit NAACP formulated.[191]

Conversely, in its early organizational conduct and activism, the Pottstown NAACP cordially followed the protocol and procedure of its national organization. In fact, Corum's early administrative updates on NAACP activism in Pottstown impressed African American NAACP Department of Branches executive assistant Lucille Black in New York City so much that Black praised "the fine success" Corum and other Pottstown African Americans had with organizing early on.[192]

Second, even as the Pottstown NAACP's connection with the community slipped after Corum's departure, Corum's willingness to reengage NAACP work when the local chapter reorganized in 1951 meant that the new effort would enjoy a foundation and familiarity with working-class folk. Relatedly, the third significance of Corum's early tenure with the Pottstown NAACP would frame the later reengagement of the group as living connection to the past.[193]

Meanwhile, during World War II local NAACP activism can also be seen as clearly tied to working-class needs, such as access to the bustling war industries in Pottstown. In mid-January 1943, Pottstown NAACP secretary Frank W. Thomas Sr. revealed the branch's progress. "Industrial committee very active," Thomas wrote, noting precisely that it "succeeded in breaking down racial discrimination in one plant who never hired colored before" and that the workplace had "an average of dozen colored working in plant to date." Moreover, the Black NAACP secretary noted that the factory "promise[d] to hire more" African Americans.[194] "Often it was the initiative of black workers that was decisive," historian Beth T. Bates asserts, "turning the war effort into an opportunity for making inroads into war industries."[195]

In addition, Thomas's prior remarks could possibly relate to the connection between pragmatism and the hiring of local Blacks. Commenting on Pottstown companies during World War II, historian William H. McCabe contends that they severely lacked workers. Therefore, interpreting Thomas's remarks through this vein would suggest that Pottstown's labor deficiency was the ultimate rationale behind the local factory deseg-regating, thereby making the decision more pragmatically based rather than egalitarian or for the greater good of society.[196] At the same time, monetary challenges stemming from the working-class profile of its constituents likely contributed to the Pottstown NAACP's temporary disbanding by World War II's conclusion.[197] Moreover, borough residents experienced "post-war lay-offs in industry."[198] This, too, probably had something to do with the economic component of the Pottstown NAACP's brief disbanding in the late 1940s.[199]

In late March 1950, however, James Corum offered possibly one explanation on why the borough NAACP ceased existing soon after World War II. Yet when Corum made this argument, he was simultane-ously advocating for local African Americans who were about to lose their properties—a civil rights initiative that Heywood L. Butler additionally partook in as a representative of the FIA (see chap. 3). Moreover, Corum's assessment of the Pottstown NAACP and its ending spoke to the chal-lenges that laboring-class Blacks endured, particularly in relationship to the financial component of supporting civil rights activism. It was clearly not enough that the local Black population was extremely small. But since the populace was generally working-class as well, the economic struggle was even more perplexing than in other locales where African Americans had not only greater amounts of capital to disperse for NAACP activism but also greater representations from more affluent classes as well. None-theless, even with these economic handicaps, Corum still found fault among local African Americans. In fact, one frustration Corum exhibited regarded "the failure of the Negroes in Pottstown to form a chapter of the National Association for the Advancement of Colored People," announcing passionately that "the fault lies right here with us." Corum continued, "Too many of us were concerned only with the fact that we would have to pay $1 a year for membership. Now," he crowed, "we could have used such an organization." In short, by assessing Corum's transparent remarks, it is quite possible that the economic element was what directly contributed toward the Pottstown NAACP disbanding around the time that World War II ceased.[200]

Conversely, the tension between the pragmatism of equalization and other traditional Black internal improvement strategies and the moral correctness of refusing all but racial integration as a response to racial discrimination was additionally alleviated in the immediate postwar years with the emergence of a new liberalism in the national life that professed to embrace interracialism. "During the early years of the cold war," historian Doug Rossinow writes, "liberals at first accepted American capitalist democracy as a permanent framework for social improvement." These same individuals additionally started more concretely "to celebrate this society, while redefining liberalism as a movement for the inclusion of previously excluded groups in its bounties," with African Americans being one.[201] While the cold war raged, however, promoting acceptance among prior disregarded peoples had a grander agenda. And that, historian Mary L. Dudziak argues, concerned how the United States was perceived globally, ultimately to thwart communist expansion.[202]

Indeed, departures from traditional positions taken up by labor unions in the New Deal 1930s and by the federal government, particularly the presidency and the federal courts beginning in the 1940s, laid the groundwork for African Americans generally and organizations like the NAACP specifically to shift from strategies of equalization and other traditional Black internal improvement work. As such, civil rights groups like the NAACP adopted a willingness to incorporate the liberal interracialist strategy for Black advancement and civil rights change. Within this historical context, the Black freedom struggle commenced in Pottstown.[203]

Yet of all the local African American activists profiled in this chapter, James Corum would have by far the greatest, single-handed impact on local civil rights activism during World War II and in the years following.[204] As indicated previously, while both James and William were in the union (USW Local 2326, CIO), the older Corum sibling was the most active. To be sure, this aspect of his leadership profile—work with Local 2326—perhaps more so than any other, positioned him to play an influential role in advancement of the liberal interracialist philosophy in Pottstown, with its particular impact on the advent of civil rights work there.[205]

Historians Robert Korstad and Nelson Lichtenstein write, "The half million black workers who joined unions affiliated with the Congress of Industrial Organizations (CIO) were in the vanguard of efforts to transform race relations."[206] Without question, James Corum was no exception.

In fact, by the end of the 1940s, Local 2326 unionists had already named Corum president multiple times.[207] His fifteen-year period in office—which spanned three-decades (1940s–1960s)—is especially fascinating from a liberal interracialist tactic and "race relations" standpoint. As an African American leading an interracial union of hundreds of predominantly white workers, Corum was quite an aberration, especially when one understood his position of local power in the racist culture of the period, coupled with the minute size of the local Black population as compared to the white population. And the fact that the white unionists who dominated the rank and file of Local 2326 named Corum president time and again certainly demonstrates an anomaly of mid-twentieth-century "race relations" in America. As such, this chapter suggests that Corum was an outlier of the day.[208]

Because Corum headed a majority white labor union, making him an aberration of early postwar America, it should come as no surprise that upon retirement with Local 2326 in 1962, the *Baltimore Afro-American* praised the Black unionist. Specifically, the African American press proudly boasted how Corum presided over 1,300 whites as union chief (the Black newspaper noted that Corum was currently heading the Pottstown NAACP too).[209] This was a considerable increase from the 950 overall unionists reported by the *Pottstown Mercury* in late December 1948 that Corum headed.[210] In late July 1962, while commenting on Corum recently vacating his Local 2326 office, the *Pottstown Mercury* additionally categorized the African American factory worker as "one of the area's outstanding unionist." It also celebrated Corum's reign because he strongly advanced "labor-management relations."[211]

On the other hand, Corum had several leadership traits that reveal why he appealed to both Black and white members of Local 2326. First, Corum was fully dedicated. "His life is generally centered in the union," remarked the *Pottstown Mercury* in 1950. "He belongs to virtually no other organizations and has no other hobbies."[212] Second, the African American leader believed fervently in personal interaction for those he served. In 1955, Corum declared, "Unionism means more than just sitting around a table and negotiating with management." Rather, the Black factory worker continued, "You have to look after the well-being of your members, too."[213]

Third, and certainly most appealing toward local African American unionists, Corum did not divorce his labor activism at Stanley G. Flagg from his advocacy of empowerment within Black Pottstown. Nor did he condone or support any form of bigotry while on the job. For example, commenting in December 1948, Corum stressed his personal discontent toward any such practices. "There is no room for discrimination," the Black unionist sharply affirmed. Corum also pointed out that Local 2326 had an excellent record in supporting antidiscriminatory policies because of its CIO association.[214]

Consequently, the African American laborer demonstrated such commitment to the Black freedom struggle in Pottstown and beyond the small Pennsylvania locale. In late May 1946, Corum and roughly two hundred other Black CIO representatives traveled to Atlantic City, New Jersey, for a USW conference. Captured in the *Philadelphia Tribune*, these CIO African Americans announced that they supported the Fair Employment Practice Committee at the large-scale gathering. In solidarity, they also collectively endorsed "the anti-Poll Tax Bill" that was gaining momentum in Washington, DC, by congressional progressives.[215]

World War II–Era Activism as Foundational to Pottstown's Black Freedom Struggle

There are several points to take away from the Black-centered activism in Pottstown, which cemented the foundation for the local Black freedom struggle during World War II and beyond. Equalization and other traditional Black internal improvement strategies remained pragmatic necessities as the war began. Despite representing a continuation and expansion of racial discrimination, the financial and administrative assistance provided by white-led Edgewood Cemetery was, indeed, critical to Second Baptist Church's ability to acquire the Black graveyard in Douglass Township. Similarly, Black activists involved in the local YMCA's Negro Extension Work program used a patently racist policy—separating Blacks from whites and providing Blacks with inferior facilities and funding support—as an opportunity to build agency and autonomy without ceasing efforts to end discrimination in the organization. Finally, more so than in the South, where de jure segregation had the principal attention of activists, the Pottstown

NAACP branch's successes and failures demonstrate the centrality of economic, working-class concerns to the local Black freedom struggle against racial discrimination and other manifestations of white supremacist applications indigenous to the region's Jim Crow apparatus.

The ways in which southern-born African Americans relocated both before and during the Great Migration also facilitated the progress and development of the local Black freedom struggle. While Pennsylvania-born Blacks played important roles, southern African American transplants also held integral leadership positions that advanced civil rights activism efforts in the small northern borough. Additionally, while there is no evidence directly associating southern-born Blacks like Benjamin F. Corum with civil rights work during World War II, the very fact that they migrated to Pottstown before the war years led to their first-generation northern-born children having the opportunity to serve extensively in advancing civil rights initiatives that targeted the local African American community.

At the same time, the role of local African American women in promulgating and coordinating civil rights activism and essential programming germane to the betterment of the small Black collective is also important to emphasize. To be sure, Black activists Frances Young and Jennie Thornton's involvements are only a sample of the ways in which African American women took part in liberating and improving the local circumstance of the racial minority during 1940s America. Overall, how African American women like Young and Thornton struggled for racial justice in and around the borough would only continue well into the postwar years.

In total, the work launched in Pottstown during World War II was only the start of the local Black freedom struggle. YMCA Negro Extension Work activism, like the Second Baptist cemetery project and the Pottstown NAACP, revealed the genesis of civil rights activism to improve local Blacks' circumstances and conditions. Spearheaded by African Americans in the small northern borough, and assisted by local whites when applicable, their local Black freedom activism that emerged during the wartime only served as the impetus to multiple civil rights endeavors to come out of Pottstown in the years that followed. On the other hand, that same activist spirit unleashed during World War II held solidarity with the borough's white-led main newspaper, the *Pottstown Mercury*, which also came into its own as the global military conflict raged.

3

The *Pottstown Mercury* and the World War II Origins of Civil Rights Advocacy Work

In *Dear Sir*, Shandy Hill remarked on the ethos of racial progressivism that permeated the newspaper coestablished by him and white entrepreneur William M. Heister during the Great Depression. Launched in 1931, the *Pottstown Mercury*'s general philosophical current, which Hill himself largely cultivated, "was known mostly as a defender of the underdog, and a crusader for" the just.[1] Hill expressed at another time that "the newspaper exists only for public service." His *Philadelphia Inquirer* obituary also stressed how the white editor denounced "racial discrimination."[2] In the end, Hill and other white reporters employed by the *Pottstown Mercury* would apply similar racially progressive beliefs in their journalistic advocacy work that supported borough African Americans and the local Black freedom struggle. By doing so, the white journalists not only humanized African Americans in many of their news stories printed over the years but also collaborated directly with local Blacks on their earnest quest for racial equality, inclusion, and first-class citizenship during World War II and the postwar era.

Overall, Hill dedicated three chapters in *Dear Sir* to the *Pottstown Mercury*'s civil rights advocacy work, which helped improve conditions for local African Americans.[3] He also spoke about how the Pottstown newspaper was, in fact, before its time on several subjects relating to racial progress. For example, Hill underscored how his local newspaper "just didn't use the word 'Negro' to identify" an African American "who committed a crime." If the newspaper printed such information, then, he simply believed that the press did so because "it was necessary." "The 'sensitive' use of the word Negro," Hill likewise remembered, "gave The [Pottstown] Mercury no trouble." He also boasted proudly that his newspaper "never used the word 'colored'" when identifying an African American.

The *Pottstown Mercury* consistently spotlighted African American accomplishments as well. In fact, many times the press accompanied them with dignified images that both expressed and celebrated Black humanity to not only its readership but also its viewership. Another point Hill expressed in *Dear Sir* concerned the Pottstown newspaper having integrated "news columns." This practice, the white editor even argued, long preceded "the nationwide agitation" that exploded within the United States.[4]

In addition to the *Pottstown Mercury* consistently advocating for Blacks, it allowed the voices of local African Americans to make their way into the pages of the press. An early example of this was a *Pottstown Mercury* column written by local African American Sallie S. Sims. Born in 1889 close to Atlanta, Georgia (another illustration of the impact of southern Black migration on the northern borough), Sims wrote a column, "Happenings of the Colored Folks," for the newspaper that covered a variety of topics germane to the local Black community during the 1930s and early 1940s.[5] (While Hill stressed in *Dear Sir* that the Pottstown press did not utilize *colored* when identifying Black people, he was probably referencing local white newspaper staff, as indicated by the continual usage of it in the title of Sims's column.)[6] A *Pottstown Mercury* advertisement from early May 1938 described Sims's column with the phrase "Recognition of this large colony!"[7] Interestingly enough, this description supports an argument that Shandy Hill made in *Dear Sir*. In short, local Blacks isolated themselves consciously, Hill reflected, thereby choosing general separation from the white population because de facto segregation—the Jim Crow structure ubiquitous in the North—permeated the region.[8]

Outside her work with the *Pottstown Mercury*, Sims's own personal activist commitments to the Black freedom struggle in Pottstown is also worth mentioning. For example, she served with the borough's Young Women's Christian Association (YWCA) and the local Recreation Commission. However, Sims experienced discriminatory practices related to the localized structure of de facto segregation with both these Pottstown organizations.[9] Indeed, like the Pottstown YMCA during the northern Jim Crow era (see chap. 2), the YWCA practiced racial exclusion.

And although Sims labored with the local women's organization during its later integrated phase, she also worked there while it practiced de facto segregation, which lasted for almost thirty years, from its inception in 1913 until 1942 when, historian Paul Chancellor writes, the Pottstown YWCA finally started granting local Blacks "full membership" status.[10]

Similar to other strategies of traditional Black internal improvement and equalization activism during World War II, Sims additionally looked after African American youth as "Negro activities supervisor" for the Pottstown Recreation Commission—the same local entity the borough NAACP teamed up with as the global conflict raged.[11] As noted in chapter 2, the Pottstown NAACP fully backed the borough recreational commission's policy of northern Jim Crow—so much so that the branch NAACP, while not capitulating or even yielding to a relegated status, nonetheless, still willingly gave the commission one hundred dollars so that local Blacks could participate in de facto segregated programming during World War II.[12]

Yet even though Sims labored with both the local YWCA and the Pottstown Recreation Commission in capacities relevant to the local Black freedom struggle, it was her long-standing *Pottstown Mercury* column work that is, perhaps, her greatest and most impactful legacy, particularly because the writings do an excellent job in underscoring the vibrancies, inner workings and dynamics, and intricacies of the African American community in and around the borough both before and during World War II.[13] Moreover, partnerships like the one with Sims, as well as Pottstown African Americans more broadly, were further developed and cultivated during World War II and the postwar era. For these reasons, the *Pottstown Mercury*'s success in the realm of civil rights advocacy work from World War II throughout the 1960s rested largely on direct collaborations with local African Americans. While the newspaper indeed played its part in advocating for Pottstown Blacks—without direct African American participation, the local press would have not been able to have the editorial and reporting success that it did.

At the same time, because Pottstown African Americans, as this chapter (and others) reveals, involved themselves by serving as sources for the *Pottstown Mercury*'s civil rights reporting while also serving as willing partners and agitators in local Black freedom activism, they most certainly risked retaliation from the dominant white population on multiple levels, whether economic, social, or political. Altogether, this chapter demonstrates that even though the *Pottstown Mercury* played its paramount role in local civil rights advocacy work, it was only able to do so because of the determination and courage of African Americans. Clearly, Pottstown Blacks were at the forefront of their own liberation throughout the local civil rights struggle.

"The Shandy Hill School of Journalism"

Indeed, important surely were the roles played by local Blacks in combating the tyranny of northern Jim Crow in and around Pottstown. Yet one cannot overstate, or lessen, Shandy Hill's crucial part in supporting civil rights struggles endemic to the area. In fact, from World War II through the late 1960s, Hill almost single-handedly cultivated and created the overall journalistic atmosphere of the *Pottstown Mercury* and its guiding philosophies toward newspapering.[14]

Born in 1901 in Bethlehem, Pennsylvania, when Hill and Heister coestablished the *Pottstown Mercury*, the white editor was less than a decade removed from college. A journalism graduate of the prestigious Lehigh University in Bethlehem, in 1923, Hill—besides selling papers as a youngster—had around eight years of qualified, professional newspapering experience before the *Pottstown Mercury*. This included work for two nearby presses, the *Bethlehem Morning Sun* (Bethlehem, Pennsylvania) and the *Reading Times* (Reading, Pennsylvania). While employed with the *Reading Times*, however, Hill became acquainted with Heister, his future business partner.[15]

Although somewhat green to the newspaper industry, Hill was also the man who drastically shaped the general ethos of progressivism at the *Pottstown Mercury*. For example, while Heister largely financed the establishment of the newspaper, with capital stemming from a family inheritance from the fossil fuel industry, the white editor brought "the enthusiasm and knowhow" to the partnership.[16] Thus Hill, not Heister, became the central driving force behind the *Pottstown Mercury* and its philosophies toward journalism. Moreover, so influential was Hill at the *Pottstown Mercury* that the local press became not only acclaimed but also identified as "the Shandy Hill School of Journalism." Remarking further on his cherished press in *Dear Sir*, Hill fondly reflected on how "'the Shandy Hill School of Journalism' was a hard, demanding classroom." However, he continued, reporters "who survived" its difficult training would travel a long way "in the realm of metropolitan journalism."[17]

From the *Pottstown Mercury*'s inception, Hill also bragged in *Dear Sir* about his "crusading and campaigning" while leading the circular.[18] Additionally, he noted how "public service" constantly fueled his ambitions.[19] Here, Hill's perspectives go hand in glove with what communications scholar Aurora Wallace observes about "newspaper owners as citizens" and their general inclination toward orchestrating "a greater role in making change."[20] In the end, Hill's genuine concern "for the little guy," so to speak, coupled with his immense hatred of racism, explains why the *Pottstown Mercury* not only consistently advocated for African Americans but also, on numerous occasions, collaborated with them to improve developments within local civil rights conditions. The racially progressive philosophy he engendered during his thirty-six-year (1931–1967) tenure as editor at the borough newspaper also helps provide further clarity to the press's direct role in the local Black freedom struggle between World War II and the postwar era.[21]

An Outlier to Northern White Newspapers' Coverage of Civil Rights

Scholars have already documented the impact of both the Black and white press on American life during World War II and the postwar era. While World War II raged, they have even shown how African American newspapers were at the forefront of lambasting Jim Crow and white supremacy in the United States. For example, beginning with the *Pittsburgh Courier*'s "Double 'V' war cry," scholars have demonstrated the paramount function played by the Black press in exposing racial discrimination, both in the North and the South.[22] In the postwar years, Black newspapers only continued such fervent activism in the pages of their circulars, intimately capturing and examining the period African American civil rights activists Bayard Rustin identified as "the 'classical' phase of the struggle," 1954 to 1965.[23]

Yet only until recently have scholars begun to calculate the effect of white-oriented, or mainstream, print and broadcast journalism on the Black freedom struggle. Where consensus exists on this point, however, it holds that the advocacy of white-oriented news media in the postwar years greatly contributed to the emergence of the liberal interracialist agenda, shaping public opinion in support of civil rights protests and legislation. Moreover, most studies of white-oriented news media only concern themselves with civil rights events in the American South.[24]

Conversely, scholars have been very critical of northern white newspapers for their failure to capture civil rights activism above the Mason-Dixon Line.[25] Political scientist Jeanne Theoharis, for example, argues that "outside the Deep South . . . the media often stood in the way of the struggle for racial justice."[26] Also drawing her readership's attention to the fact that "the nation's leading print newspapers enabled the framing of civil rights and desegregation as Southern issues and helped to inoculate polite racism across the country," she additionally notes that "Northern segregation," on the other hand, "was treated as less systemic and more happenstance, and resistance to desegregation there as different and *not as segregationist* as Southern resistance." Regarding these last points, moreover, Theoharis points out that "much of the national media was located in the North."[27] Likewise, historian Matthew F. Delmont, who examines northern "busing," adds that "coverage of 'busing' for school desegregation reveals how mainstream media personnel based mostly in the North covered civil rights in the North differently than it did in the South." Although "news media helped underscore the urgency of the black civil rights movement in the South in the 1950s and 1960s," Delmont additionally writes, "by the mid-1960s and 1970s white 'antibusing' protestors received the vast bulk of media attention."[28]

The *Pottstown Mercury,* the small borough's main newspaper, however, was a northern white-owned and operated press that consistently advocated against de facto segregation and racial discrimination in its own backyard. For these reasons, the local civil rights advocacy work of the *Pottstown Mercury* during World War II and the postwar era demonstrates an outlier to standard historiographical interpretations of the northern white press and its relationship to the Black freedom struggle above the Mason-Dixon Line. By focusing on the Pottstown newspaper, this interpretation also shifts the geographical locus of civil rights advocacy work and investigation—particularly regarding the northern white press's central focus—from the American South to the North. Last, this fresh and insightful perspective on a small press above the Mason-Dixon Line simultaneously links together local northern civil rights activism of the World War II era and postwar years.

As World War II progressed, the *Pottstown Mercury* began unfolding its collaborative civil rights advocacy struggle with local African Americans in the Jim Crow North. Specifically, approximately three weeks following the Allied powers' D-day offensive in Normandy, the local newspaper started publishing "First of a Series," which centered on Black Pottstown. In effect, the article series examined a concern that had locals from both the Black and white communities anxious, "juvenile delinquency," a dilemma that even gripped Americans from across the United States during World War II.[29]

Black Pottstown and the Struggle for Community Policing

As shown in chapter 2, the Corum brothers James H. and William D. played vital roles in the local Black freedom struggle during World War II and the postwar era. However, so too was the case with another Corum sibling, Pottstown African American Thomas W. Corum. Like his brothers, Thomas Corum was one of the Black trailblazers from Pottstown who laid the groundwork for local civil rights activism. In the end, Corum inserted himself directly into the local civil rights struggle during World War II, which advocated for the improvement of community policing throughout Black Pottstown.[30]

In more recent years, historians such as Clarence Taylor and Leonard N. Moore have paid extensive attention to the ubiquitous practice of police brutality and its direct relationship to Black communities both above and below the Mason-Dixon Line.[31] Journalist Arthur Browne even captures the civil rights work of pioneering African American Samuel Battle, who became "Greater New York's first black cop" during the early 1910s. However, and like the general geographical vantage point of northern civil rights scholarship, Browne's important work mainly evaluates such activism across the large city sphere.[32] Thus, this chapter turns attention toward Thomas Corum, another Black pioneer residing within the Jim Crow North, and the ways in which the *Pottstown Mercury* assisted him in his groundbreaking activism, which integrated the Pottstown police force in the small northern borough during World War II.

Yet before Corum was the pioneering African American with the local policing department, he labored at Stanley G. Flagg in nearby Stowe (Pennsylvania), just like his siblings William and James. Born in Pottstown in 1906, while not as involved as his older brother James, Thomas, nevertheless, did partake in some union activism with his Stowe employer.[33] Similar to William and James, however, Thomas was heavily a part of Pottstown's African American community. Like William, he played with "Neville's All-Stars" and the "Pottstown Colored All-Stars."[34] A Black Boy Scout leader like James, Thomas also led African American youths associated with his and William's home congregation, Pottstown's Bethel AME.[35] While William sang for the all-Black group "the Keystone State quartet," Thomas managed it.[36] Similarly, Thomas was directly involved with Pottstown's "Colored Community Hospital auxiliary."[37] Finally, to demonstrate further Thomas's involvement in the local Black freedom struggle, in the fall of 1944, following his older brother James's initial reign as president of the Pottstown NAACP, Thomas became the chapter's second vice president. In sum, the evidence overwhelmingly displays Thomas Corum's long-standing, ongoing, and consistent commitment to local Blacks.[38]

Months prior to Corum beginning his tenure as vice president of the local NAACP, he teamed up voluntarily with white *Pottstown Mercury* journalist Larry Davis, the author of the three-part article series on Black juvenile delinquency in the borough. Yet while Davis served as the chief penman of the local juvenile delinquency series, for the articles to have the galvanizing effect needed, this required a direct voice, let alone personal connection, from Black Pottstown. In other words, someone from inside of Black Pottstown was desperately sought so the African American perspective could, in fact, be captured, expressed, and ultimately conveyed to *Pottstown Mercury* readership. In the end, because the *Pottstown Mercury* looked to illuminate the local Black perspective, Corum entered into the partnership. At the same time, this early interracial cooperation set the stage for later civil rights advocacy work in which the local newspaper would follow similar methods and practices when reporting on civil rights issues germane to local Blacks. Put differently, the Pottstown circular—especially during the postwar period—would consistently collaborate with local African Americans on their quest to obtain first-class citizenship and liberation from manifestations of anti-Black discrimination and other exclusionary practices connected to the pervasive structure of de facto segregation.

When the *Pottstown Mercury* published its series in late June/early July 1944, the issue of juvenile delinquency had the attention of many in Pottstown's Black and white communities.[39] Davis even mentioned that the concern began manifesting the same year (1941) America officially entered World War II.[40] More broadly, however, juvenile delinquency was a dilemma that had citizens across the United States feeling anxious, seeking ways to combat it. Historian Harvard Sitkoff, for example, even notes that across locations above the Mason-Dixon Line, "juvenile delinquency increasingly turned into racial gang fights." Sitkoff continues by also adding that nearby Pottstown, "Italo-American and Negro teenagers fought week-long battles in Newark and Philadelphia."[41] In addition to such biracial antagonisms, even in northern spaces like Detroit, which historian Karen R. Miller documents in the early 1940s, was the eruption of rioting throughout America as World War II raged. During this time, many young people were additionally involved. In sum, the wave of juvenile delinquency that permeated the home front had thus galvanized Americans. As such, they began fervently addressing the issue.[42]

Yet while juvenile delinquency was an issue both nationally and locally for whites, Corum, instead, focused on safeguarding local Black youths. Without question, the Black worker feared that juvenile delinquency had the strong possibility of causing racial tensions among African Americans and whites in the small northern borough. Responding to this potential interracial concern, however, Corum's solution to the juvenile delinquency dilemma was one based on pragmatism, as well as the strategy of equalization and other traditional Black internal improvement methods. In particular, Corum demanded the sanctioning of an African American "special police officer" by the Pottstown government. In his view, this was both the practical and precise way to address Black juvenile delinquency on the local front.

In that same spirit of equalization and other similar Black internal improvement work that percolated during World War II (see chap. 2), Corum's answer to curbing juvenile delinquency among African Americans in Pottstown was indicative of how Black resistance on the local front, at times, addressed discriminatory neglect. Specifically, such activism was framed without attacking cultures and practices fully germane to the borough's structure of de facto segregation vis-à-vis northern Jim Crow. At the same time, however, Corum firmly emphasized the imperativeness of the police officer being Black. Constructing arguments similar to what New York City's the *People's Voice* made during World War II, historian Clarence Taylor reveals, in Corum's mind, only an African American officer could "speak to his people in their own language." The Black factory worker added, only an African American special police person truly could reason with African American youths. Altogether, Corum stressed that he had the borough's Black youths' best interest in mind. He also rationalized that an African American special police person would help them move toward proper citizenship, especially since the individual was to serve as the "authority," which these Black youths desperately needed.

Continuing remarks reflective of New York City's the *People's Voice*, Corum was also adamant that white law officers were not equipped for such policing work within Black Pottstown. The way he saw it, they could not fully "meet the Negro on a common field." Nor could they have African Americans "common betterment" in mind. For these reasons, Corum emphasized that the Black special police officer was the one who could truly confront delinquency among African American juveniles and work fervently to check it. A man of action, Corum was so passionate about curbing juvenile delinquency in Black Pottstown that he offered his own service for the special police officer position. In fact, the Black worker even offered his own service, free of charge, over several months so that the issue was addressed not only firsthand but also by an African American like himself.[43]

Simultaneous to the *Pottstown Mercury* providing a space where Corum articulated his insightful perspectives on Black juvenile delinquency, Davis's own journalistic lens painted the African American laborer in a highly favorable, if not humanizing, light. Specifically, the white journalist did so by capturing the borough African American through "a politics of respectability" lens. As documented by Davis, Corum not only was cordial, married with children, gainfully employed with Stanley G. Flagg like his brothers in nearby Stowe (Pennsylvania), and self-reliant but also owned his own home.

Within the *Pottstown Mercury* series, Davis also expressed Corum's social ranking within Black Pottstown. Observing the Black worker's interactions among fellow African Americans, Davis noted that when strolling "through the Negro section of town," Corum recognized "everyone he passes." The white journalist continued, "Passers-by can usually determine where some of their acquaintances are or have gone," Davis noticed, "just by asking Tom Corum."[44] Moreover, Davis's series revealed that Corum was on a first name basis with "everyone in the [African American] community . . . and" that the Black homeowner understood clearly "how to speak, with authority, to his own people."[45]

In addition to Davis's juvenile delinquency series, the *Pottstown Mercury* published an editorial on June 30, 1944, entitled "The Negro Seeks to Solve a Problem," which sharply criticized the local government and how it handled Blacks who sought assistance with their juvenile delinquency dilemma. In short, the editorial argued that the Pottstown government had been failing African Americans because local policing efforts were lacking. Utilizing satire, it asserted that the local government was essentially telling the borough's African American population, "You're no part of us. We can't give you the same services whites are accorded. The problem's yours. Solve it yourself." The editorial continued, "At your own expense!" In fact, "Don't ask . . . for" any assistance from local government whatsoever.

The editorial also painted the African American juvenile delinquency and special police officer matter within the framework of the local Black freedom struggle, if not a broader spectrum of liberalism that both permeated and galvanized the hearts and minds of many Americans during World War II. Specifically, the *Pottstown Mercury* editorial emphasized that the Pottstown government was unequivocally discriminating against African Americans because their tax dollars afforded them such policing protection. Pottstown was not, therefore, holding up its governmental obligations, particularly toward African Americans and their community patrolling needs. On the other hand, the editorial urged the local government that if it employed an African American special police officer, the individual should receive identical benefits and respect as his white counterparts. By doing so, the newspaper argued, Pottstown would be demonstrating its forward thinking as a local governmental authority. In sum, such progressivism was certainly needed, the *Pottstown Mercury* added, particularly because the United States was currently fighting overseas against similar racist practices; indeed, the treatment of Pottstown Blacks as second-class citizens contradicted American values and ideological war objectives, aligning more with those of Nazi Germany and the Axis powers. Here, the *Pottstown Mercury*'s inconspicuous juxtaposition of the American government's central adversaries, ostensibly, and local manifestations of de facto segregation in the Jim Crow North, share striking similarity with the *Pittsburgh Courier* and its "Double 'V'" editorial advocacy during World War II.[46]

Aligning with the liberal interracialist strategy—the civil rights philosophy that began engendering large-scale support across mainstream, white America, especially during the postwar era—the *Pottstown Mercury*'s collaborative series with Corum, as well as its critical editorial, helped sway the local government (and local white public support) in favor of authorizing an African American special police officer. Clearly feeling the galvanizing pressure from the borough newspaper's civil rights advocacy work, on July 17, 1944, Pottstown officials approved Thomas Corum's special policing position.[47] "Mr. Corum, within the memory of present-day borough hall employees," the *Pottstown Mercury* declared, "is the first Negro to be appointed to the Pottstown force." Most importantly, however, "the biggest news is that his appointment broke down racial prejudice that prevailed in the department for years. For the courage in breaking tradition," the local newspaper concluded, "the Pottstown police committee is to be congratulated."[48]

A day after (July 18, 1944) Pottstown officials approved Corum's special policing position, the *Pottstown Mercury* printed remarks from African American Irving K. Merchant, who worked in New York with the Christian Commission for Camp and Defense Communities. Merchant additionally labored in Pottsville (Pennsylvania) during the 1930s, also conducting activism that was Black-centered. In sum, Merchant juxtaposed his Pottsville experience with the whole Black juvenile delinquency concern in Pottstown, even suggesting that greater factors contributed toward unruly behavior among African American young people in the borough. While Merchant thought Pottstown sanctioning an African American "uniformed policeman" made sense, precisely so that Black juvenile delinquency was combated firsthand, he argued how other measures were additionally demanded. According to Merchant, Black juvenile delinquency was "a problem that needs a thorough and far-reaching program underwritten both in finance and spirit by a group of public-spirited people in your city." He also added that local institutions would have to get on board as well if Pottstown wanted full-blown success when challenging Black juvenile delinquency.

Finally, Merchant gave an opinion on Corum himself, which was certainly positive. In fact, he celebrated Corum so much because the African American laborer—in the ethos of equalization and other traditional methods of Black internal improvement—took it on himself to address the local concern head-on. Pottstown's Black community, Merchant continued, should therefore value that Corum was a rare person. In his view, "one does not find such men everywhere." At the same time, however, Merchant confidently expressed that he was "sure Pottstown appreciates him."[49]

In Pottstown, Corum held this important Black policing position, which earned him sixty and a half cents hourly, in conjunction with his employment at Stanley G. Flagg.[50] By the following June (1945), however, borough governmental officials had named Corum a full-time "regular" officer, making him the pioneering African American with Pottstown law enforcement,[51] and historian Charles L. Blockson reveals that Pottstown was one of the initial locales in Montgomery County, Pennsylvania, to desegregate law enforcement.[52]

While Corum had a nineteen-year (1945–1964) career with the Pottstown Police, most notable about the tenure was the Black cop's interactions with local African Americans. "Mr. Corum pretty well knew how to handle obstreperous members of his own race," recalled the *Pottstown Mercury*. "That's where he served his department best." So effective was Corum, the local newspaper continued, that "he was able to keep the peace." On the other hand, the *Pottstown Mercury* reflected on the ways in which Corum benefited the entirety of the borough's African American population when it came to policing work. By doing so, the newspaper essentially made arguments that fell hand in glove with local traditions of equalization and Black internal improvement, specifically because Corum's "own race respected him for" being "able to keep the peace."[53]

Undergirded by the *Pottstown Mercury*'s publications of the juvenile delinquency series and editorial that lambasted local government, precisely because of its unequal racial treatment of Pottstown Blacks and their community policing needs, Corum's partnership with Davis served as the catalyst that ignited a long and fruitful interracial collaboration of local civil rights advocacy work. For the first time, Pottstown African Americans had both a consistent and a committed local white organizational ally, which publicly advocated the liberal interracialist cause. However, local Black activists and the *Pottstown Mercury*'s overall objectives within the cooperation need further clarity, let alone elaboration. Pottstown African Americans, for example, entered the partnership precisely because they demanded first-class citizenship and equal treatment throughout the economic, social, and political spectrums of the borough. In other words, what they ultimately wanted and desperately sought was a level playing field and accesses precisely when it came to the same privileges and opportunities afforded to the dominant white population. In a more subconscious fashion, perhaps, local Blacks chiefly inserted themselves into the collaborative civil rights advocacy work with the sincere intention that the *Pottstown Mercury* and its majority white readership, after reading and digesting the series, would, in turn, publicly acknowledge both the humanity and dignity of local African Americans.

Yet as far as the *Pottstown Mercury* went, while it too supported equality among Blacks and whites—as demonstrated in its joint journalistic advocacy work that partnered with local African Americans from World War II through the late 1960s—the newspaper also had professional, if not philosophical, incentives behind its cooperative work. For example, the progressive ethos of the *Pottstown Mercury*, which Shandy Hill almost single-handedly cultivated, meant precisely that the newspaper was, indeed, morally obligated to speak out and publicly lambaste local injustices and discrimination indicative of de facto segregation. Moreover, because the *Pottstown Mercury* was so passionately committed to supporting "the underdog," as it were, the press, in turn, also simultaneously created an atmosphere in which it zealously pursued justice work across multiple facets of the local front. Whether such justice work centered on race relations or governmental effectiveness, to name a few, the local newspaper fervently took up the just and morally progressive causes of the time.[54]

During the early 2010s, white Montgomery County (Pennsylvania) district attorney Risa Vetri Ferman lionized Corum's policing legacy.[55] However, Corum was not present. In fact, his lengthy tenure with Pottstown law enforcement ended tragically.[56] During the evening of January 20, 1964, while working, Corum was in the process of subduing local African American Charles Davis. The Black policeman, however, had a heart attack.[57] Rushed from the scene, moments later the local African American "was pronounced dead in Pottstown hospital at 10:23 p.m."[58] In addition to heart failure, Corum's death certificate identified that "diabetes mellitus" was a contributing factor.[59] Four days following Corum's untimely death, Pottstown's Bethel AME held his homegoing service. Over two hundred individuals—an interracial crowd—flocked into the local African American church, paying their final regards to Corum, who was "a member of an old and respected Pottstown family," the *Pottstown Mercury* reflected. Moreover, the event brought together law enforcement officials from throughout the area as well as the mayor of Pottstown, among others.[60]

The Creation of Pine Forge Institute and Northern White Pushback

The *Pottstown Mercury*'s juvenile delinquency series was not the last thread of civil rights advocacy work that collaborated the borough newspaper and local African Americans in waging combat against racial exclusion and other manifestations of racial oppression indigenous to Jim Crow in the North. Roughly four months after the United States dropped the atomic bombs on the Japanese cities of Hiroshima and Nagasaki, directly pressuring imperial Japan's capitulation in early September 1945, thereby ending the Pacific Theater of World War II, Black Seventh-day Adventist (SDA) transplants nearby Pottstown in Pine Forge (Pennsylvania) started materializing a long-awaited educational project. Sharing a strikingly similar tone with the juvenile delinquency series, the *Pottstown Mercury*'s next collaborative civil rights advocacy work with local Blacks was the first of three episodes between 1945 and 1950, which involved specific instances of activism that sharply lambasted de facto segregation ubiquitous to the local racial landscape of postwar America.

In December 1945, the all-Black Allegheny Conference of the SDA Church began the acquisition stages of the massive Rutter Estate—"575 acres of beautiful, rolling farmland"—in Pine Forge from white medical doctor Thomas B. Snyder.[61] Situated in Douglass Township (Berks County, Pennsylvania) and largely rural, Pine Forge was during this period a predominantly white community. In fact, when the Allegheny Conference initially entered the Berks County region, Shandy Hill estimated it had roughly four thousand white inhabitants; however, he was most likely including other local areas in this estimate as well, specifically since, according to US census records, Douglass Township had only 1,410 residents in 1940 and 1,843 in 1950.[62]

During the century prior, the historical record documents at least one Pine Forge white whose honorable actions indicated that he firmly embraced liberal racial viewpoints toward African Americans. In fact, historian William J. Switala writes, white Underground Railroad activist John P. Rutter not only occupied Pine Forge but also aided and abetted enslaved Africans on their path to freedom.[63] Nearby Pottstown additionally played a direct role with Underground Railroad activism.[64] However, historian W. Edmunds Claussen argues that Pottstown was never solidly "an abolitionist community."[65]

Yet by the time the Allegheny Conference started obtaining the Rutter Estate, liberal white sentiments like John P. Rutter's regarding African Americans largely escaped the area. In fact, once "word of the sale leaked out," Snyder "was the target of criticism from nearby farm owners," respected "officials and run-of-the-mill citizens" precisely since he sold his property to the all-Black group. Indeed, the white medical doctor was the individual responsible, many local whites believed, in drastically altering the racial landscape of Pine Forge.

Upon news emerging about the Rutter Estate's sale, accounts also circulated about racially restrictive "secret agreements" between local whites. The stories stated, Shandy Hill asserted, "that no home owner ever would sell to a Negro, no real estate dealer would rent or sell living space to a black man." While the white editor was not able to fully certify such gossip, he supported its validity, specifically because of the absence of African Americans in Pine Forge when the Black Adventist group arrived.[66]

In December 1945, the all-Black Allegheny Conference was less than a year old when it began acquiring the Rutter Estate. Officially organized on January 1, 1945, Black Adventists throughout Pennsylvania, Delaware, New Jersey, Virginia, West Virginia, Maryland, and Washington, DC, made up the conference's membership. Moreover, the conference was a faction within the Columbia Union Conference, one of several organizational groups of the overall SDA Church. With its central office located in Washington, DC, Black SDA minister John H. Wagner first headed the African American conference.[67]

Similar to Pottstown Blacks like Willis Strawther, Thomas B. Carter, Isaiah E. Glenn, and Heywood L. Butler (see chap. 2), Wagner was a southern African American transplant involved in local civil rights struggle. A North Carolinian by birth (1902), he was formerly the Columbia Union's "Colored Secretary." And upon the university-trained Black minister taking the helm of the Allegheny Conference, its African American membership numbered around four thousand. In addition to his responsibilities as the conference's president, Wagner was largely behind the Rutter Estate transaction as well.[68]

Prior to Wagner's work in Pine Forge, he also lived in multiple locations both North and South, where he pastored Black SDA congregations. In fact, the African American minister oversaw SDA houses of worship in Memphis; Baltimore; Pittsburgh; Washington, DC; Paducah (Kentucky); Newark; and Nashville. An African American son of the South, Wagner even completed his college degree with the historically Black SDA institution of higher education, Oakwood College (now Oakwood University), in Huntsville, Alabama.[69]

Because Wagner was a Black southerner by birth like previous local African Americans noted (see chap. 2), he must have had a clear understanding of equalization and other traditional Black internal improvement strategies.[70] Likewise, this would have probably related to the clerical organization Wagner was a part of. The historian Samuel G. London Jr., for instance, documents that the broader white-led and controlled SDA Church practiced structural and systemic racism toward its African American congregations. Black Adventists, however, did not just lie down and capitulate to the white-led SDA Church and its racist protocol. Instead, they fought back on several occasions. For example, at a gathering of top-brass of the SDA Church during April 1944, African American congregants—among them Black Morgan State College (Baltimore, Maryland) alumnus Addison V. Pinkney—disseminated the report "Shall the Four Freedoms Function Among Seventh-day Adventists?" Supported by another Black-centered Adventist group, their document argued "for the complete and immediate integration of the church." White Adventist leadership in attendance, however, generally did not want desegregation within their pews. Thus, the leadership created the Allegheny Conference—along with the other African American "regional conferences."[71]

While Wagner geographically relocated multiple times during his life both above and below the Mason-Dixon Line, his direct connection to the Great Migration, coupled with his SDA work, was what eventually led him to the small southeastern Pennsylvania locale of Pine Forge.[72] According to Black SDA minister Jacob Justiss, African American Walter Caution was the first to hear that the Rutter Estate was for sale. At the time, Caution worshipped some forty miles away from Pine Forge at Philadelphia's Ebenezer SDA Church, which Black minister Frank L. Brand pastored. Caution notified Brand about the real estate opportunity. Thus, Brand contacted Wagner. Once Wagner received such pertinent information, he and several Allegheny Conference Blacks traveled to Pine Forge so they could closely examine the Rutter Estate.[73] Yet before their travels, "the [Columbia] Union and the General Conferences had voted to allow the Allegheny Conference to purchase a piece of property for a permanent camp ground, junior camp site, and boarding school."[74]

Following a vote of Wagner and five other Allegheny Blacks, the group ultimately went forth with the Rutter Estate endeavor, "which, as will be seen later, was a pricey venture, more than $42,000." Moreover, it is worth noting that a Black Adventist woman and Philadelphia doctor named Grace Kimbrough advanced and gifted the Allegheny Conference some desired capital. Ostensibly, the very fact that the Black SDA Conference utilized her monies suggests, perhaps, that the group was not that financially secure. If so, then the Black SDA group shared the economic insecurity exhibited by the equalization work and other traditional internal improvement initiatives transpiring among Pottstown African Americans that had launched during World War II (see chap. 2 especially). Whatever the case, the Allegheny Conference happily received the Black doctor's capital, and it served as the down payment for the massive Rutter Estate.[75]

Although the Allegheny Conference started purchasing the Rutter Estate in December 1945, Black Adventists had long desired some educational space in the North that they could identify as their own. Indeed, so passionate about this long-standing ambition was he that Wagner even constructed poetic verse. "Of a northern school we dreamed," the Black minister wrote in late August 1946, "For a century it seems."[76] Another source notes that Wagner himself "had a burning desire to establish a boarding school somewhere in the northern states for the Black young people of the church."[77] Moreover, when reflecting on the Rutter Estate full transaction in April 1946, Wagner declared, "We [the Allegheny Conference] are now anxious to lay plans to start school for our young people in order to meet a demand that has been evident for some time."[78] Yet while Wagner stressed this extended goal embraced by Black Adventists, it was only articulated via print in the month prior to the beginning acquisition stages of the Rutter Estate. Published in the November 8, 1945, edition of the *Columbia Union Visitor*—the conference's official publication—the periodical revealed that during a Newark, New Jersey, Allegheny Conference workers' gathering, "the subject that had priority was that of the prospective Allegheny Academy site."[79]

The Allegheny Conference's acquisition of the Rutter Estate initiated on December 14, 1945. In short, this venture put the all-Black group on its eventual path of complete ownership. However, the Adventist faction still had to raise a good amount of capital.[80] In late December 1945, although the *Columbia Union Visitor* mentioned that "officers of the Conference signed for the purchase of this site at the price of $42,500," it additionally emphasized how much cash was still desperately needed.[81]

Around the same time, the *Baltimore Afro-American* reported "the purchase agreement" being signed among the Adventists and Snyder.[82] Moreover, the *Pottstown Mercury*, in early January 1946, noted how the Black SDA group was not going to fully "take possession of the property" until months later.[83]

For the interim period, therefore, the Allegheny Conference needed to raise substantial capital to obtain full and complete ownership of the Pine Forge property.[84] Moreover, to address this massive task, Wagner utilized the *Columbia Union Visitor* as the place to not only report the Allegheny Conference's progression in the complete acquisition of the Rutter Estate, but he (and fellow colleagues) also solicited monetary donations from its Black congregants for the property.[85] "Please," Wagner pleaded, "if you have not already done so, do your best to finish your quota so that we can take possession" of the Pine Forge holding.[86]

In addition, the Black SDA minister encouraged and inspired Allegheny Conference congregants in the large-scale endeavor through the press. "Newspapers the country over are filled with news about our acquisition of this historic property and our intention of using it for a boarding school. WE CANNOT RETREAT," Wagner announced in a militant tone, "WE MUST GO FORWARD! Everyone," he passionately continued, "arise and do your bit!"[87] Ostensibly, Wagner's tactics seemed to work. "After engaging in a campaign of about three and a half months' duration," reflected the Black minister in April 1946, "the Allegheny Conference, by the help of God, was able to pay for this property and take the deed." On March 22, 1946, the Allegheny Conference finally secured the massive Rutter Estate.[88]

While the Allegheny Conference tackled this large financial battle so that the group could completely obtain ownership of the Rutter Estate, it had to concurrently participate in another conflict gaining momentum in Pine Forge. Over a month after the Allegheny Conference began its acquisition, there were already audible rumblings from whites locally, which concerned the Black SDA group. Adventist scholars such as Jacob Justiss stress that the Allegheny Conference wanted an educational institution in the North, precisely so its Black youth would have the possibility to study in an area away from the deep embedded racism of the American South. In effect, such arguments fall in line with the generalized dichotomy of the racist and bigoted South, on the one hand, juxtaposed to the liberating and progressive-minded North, on the other hand.[89] Although this historiographical dichotomy is largely prevalent in scholarship on civil rights history, it is not totally factual when assessing the Allegheny Conference and its experience in the Rutter Estate venture. In fact, Wagner and other Blacks of the conference soon learned that racism strongly permeated the beliefs of multiple whites in Pine Forge as well.[90]

To be sure, the northern white pushback or hostility that began percolating toward the Allegheny Conference in Pine Forge during the age of de facto segregation extensively predated the "massive resistance" developments in the American South. As historian John A. Kirk points out, "massive resistance" began arising soon after *Brown v. Board of Education* (1954). This southern white opposition, therefore, was about eight years later than the white pushback that started crystalizing in Pine Forge.[91]

Thus, the Valley Improvement Association (VIA) during the early postwar in the Jim Crow North was the greatest organized resistance from local white Pennsylvanians, who specifically targeted the Black SDA group and its Rutter Estate venture. First conceived on the frigid night of January 22, 1946, local white I. Grant Irey was the central organizer and president of the VIA. Irey resided near Pine Forge in Douglasville, Pennsylvania.[92] On that January night two hundred whites, including Irey, gathered at Pine Forge in "the Amity township high school auditorium and voiced concerted opposition to the sale of the" property. Individual testimonies began the assembly. In solidarity, they declared that the Allegheny Conference and its place in Pine Forge was indeed horrible for area whites.

On the one hand, local whites believed the ultimate transaction "would deprive the townships of [Amity and Douglass] much needed tax money," while, on the other hand, be "detrimental to property owners" within the region. Eventually, Irey took over the gathering. He not only proposed the VIA's establishment so that "the reported sale" of the Rutter Estate was thoroughly examined, but Irey wanted preventive steps in place that stopped the acquisition, providing, of course, such an initiative was viable or not. Moreover, that same night, the massive crowd had chosen Irey as VIA president. Alongside Irey, there were five other white VIA officials nominated. The officials resided in either Amity or Douglass Townships. In fact, northern white pushback toward the Allegheny Conference had centralized within these two predominately white Berks County Townships.[93]

Earlier the same month, the *Pottstown Mercury* published an article, which highlighted the salient points regarding the Allegheny Conference and its beginning Rutter Estate transaction. In turn, this essay galvanized local whites into direct dissent.[94] In fact, the newspaper report was the catalyst of the large-scale gathering on January 22. At the same time, during the massive assembly, one of the white VIA's vice presidents (the group had two) emphasized how the issue was "not a matter of race discrimination." He continued, "Certain things are damaging to a community and this sale is one of them."[95]Although the individual stressed his argument was in no way racially driven, someone else present had another viewpoint, which was indeed diametrical. White Douglass Township resident Harper Diener, who headed Pottstown's Congress of Industrial Organizations (CIO)–affiliated union, Local 644, could "not see how any property owner can be prevented from selling," providing that the individual wanted to. When commenting directly on the notion that the white-led VIA was prejudiced, Diener identified the vice president's argument as unequivocally racist.[96]

Weeks later, the *Pottstown Mercury* captured similar racist remarks from the same white VIA leader. In fact, the vice president made them when the group met leadership of the historically Black Allegheny Conference, including Wagner, for the first time in person during another evening assembly. Again, this gathering brought together many. On February 14, 1946, the white VIA leader centralized his argument around "the [proposed] school" impacting nearby proprietors. However, regarding the role played by white racism in the Rutter Estate equation during this era of pervasive yet clandestine segregation in the Jim Crow North, the VIA chief maintained that "real estate men" informed "him [that] the presence of Negro schools depreciated real estate values."[97] Interestingly enough, it is worth noting how the VIA leader's argument coincided with the Grand Rapids Real Estate Board during the postwar as well. The organization, historian Todd E. Robinson points out, followed racially discriminatory policy that the National Association of Real Estate Board disseminated about "property values" being harmed.[98]

It should come as no surprise that on February 14, Wagner rejected the VIA leader's racially charged argument. Yet while Wagner rebutted the thesis centering on Black educational institutions lowering property worth, the interracial gathering, overall, left the African American SDA minister with a general sense of disenchantment. In some concluding remarks on the entire affair, Wagner announced cynically how he, and his Allegheny Conference colleagues, "came here for an understanding." However, the Black minister felt that the VIA—and other local whites' presence during the massive gathering who were also combative toward the Allegheny Conference setting up shop in the region—did not give them one.

Surely, evidence from the February 14, 1946, gathering indicated that the white-led, VIA resistance was not going to budge an inch on its hostility toward the Allegheny Conference.[99] By the end of March 1946, however, the VIA's pushback had capitulated. On March 26, the white northern group (and others) gathered in front of another massive crowd, where it reversed its stance on the Allegheny Conference. In fact, the group now collectively endorsed—as did many others present—the Allegheny Conference's prospective educational site. The endorsement, however, was a direct by-product of both sides compromising.

On the white-led VIA side, supporters decided that Amity and Douglass citizens had to cooperate fully when it came to the Allegheny Conference's Pine Forge undertaking. On the Black-centered Allegheny Conference side, Wagner and team agreed to three crucial points. While the *Pottstown Mercury* article from March 27 does not explain why the group had more points to compromise upon juxtaposed to the white-led VIA, nonetheless, the Black SDA faction yielded.[100]

Foremost, the Allegheny Conference recognized it "would pay the equivalent of taxes" currently taken "from the farm property." Amity and Douglass authorities would also sit directly "on the board of governors of the [prospective] school," thus making them involved with and partially "responsible for the orderly conduct of the enterprise." The last point that the Black SDA faction settled on was essentially a contingency plan. Providing that the Allegheny Conference decided not to build an educational facility, it had to give local authority the earliest opportunity to acquire the vast landholding.

Even though the *Pottstown Mercury* praised the white-led, VIA's about-face on the Allegheny Conference's Pine Forge initiative—stressing how sound judgment luckily triumphed over "blind opposition"—it still concurrently provided an appraisal, which sharply criticized the faction. "In this day and age," the *Pottstown Mercury* article, published March 28, 1946, declared, "when we are preaching the necessity for getting along with all peoples of the world, it was a sad commentary on the present-day trend to see a local group opposing such a laudable venture as the founding of a preparatory school." The newspaper continued by demonstrating how egregious the VIA's racist policy was when contextualized within the recently ended World War II. As noted by the *Pottstown Mercury* article, "Tolerance, equal rights and all the liberties millions of Americans fought, bled and died for, were forgotten for a moment in a narrow, community, prejudicial fight." Yet although critical, the fact was this: the *Pottstown Mercury* still celebrated the VIA's ultimate capitulation, arguing that good prevailed over evil. In the end, though, the borough newspaper reflected its approval of the triumph of the local Black freedom struggle nearby Pottstown in Pine Forge by entitling the March 28 article "Victory for Democracy."[101]

In *Dear Sir*, Shandy Hill captured how Black Adventists praised him and the *Pottstown Mercury* for their civil rights agitation on behalf of the Allegheny Conference in Pine Forge. As noted by Hill, one Black Adventist leader reflected how "The [Pottstown] Mercury"—under the white editor's direct supervision—advocated for the conference's "entrance into" Pine Forge. "We needed a friend in a desperate way and you came forward to help us." Moreover, because Hill guided the *Pottstown Mercury* toward addressing the situation in the early postwar years—encouraging its "reading public to know that they should not judge a group before giving them a chance to prove themselves"—the Black faction, wrote the African American Adventist, remained grateful. Another esteemed Black Adventist argued that Hill and his advocacy newspaper had simply been "our champion," specifically because it fervently combated the mounting dissent of the white-led VIA and friends.[102]

At the same time, the *Pottstown Mercury*'s civil rights advocacy work on behalf of the Allegheny Conference even caught the attention of nationally renowned Black activist and central leader of the National Council of Negro Women, Mary McLeod Bethune, who publicly celebrated it.[103] By the early postwar, Bethune most certainly had an extensive history that advocated "interracial cooperation and first class citizenship for African Americans nationwide," historian Maxine D. Jones writes.[104] As such, on August 2, 1949, Bethune likewise responded to a recap published by the *Pottstown Mercury* weeks earlier (July 9). The recap, in short, highlighted the white-led, VIA resistance against the Allegheny Conference in Pine Forge.[105]

Not surprisingly, the early July 1949 article from the *Pottstown Mercury* zealously lambasted the white faction, stressing to its audience through the liberal interracialist lens, "so long as any minority among us is not free, all of us are" endangered.[106] In response, Bethune wrote Shandy Hill in late July directly.[107] A few days later, on August 2, the *Pottstown Mercury* published her remarks in the newspaper's "Readers Say"/ letter-to-the-editor section. Aligning with the liberal interracialist ethos, Bethune, who labeled the account "a beautiful story," declared, "It just shows us that we can live together in peace if we are willing to let the other fellow have his right to live and work in order that he might obtain for himself some of the good things of this life."[108] The following day (August 3) Hill then sent Bethune a celebratory letter for her thoughtful remarks on the *Pottstown Mercury*'s intentional assault. Yet this struggle that lambasted white attempts at supporting and maintaining Black exclusion and other policies linked to the ubiquitous yet clandestine practices of northern Jim Crow in Pine Forge during the early postwar only went hand in glove with the grander spectrum of civil rights advocacy work and the liberal interracialist ethos engendered by Hill and his racially progressive newspaper.[109]

While the white-led, VIA resistance was gaining momentum in Berks County, Pennsylvania, the Allegheny Conference, under the leadership of Wagner, had simultaneously been organizing and coordinating initiatives on behalf of its Pine Forge landholding. The Allegheny Conference especially wanted its projected education center, Pine Forge Institute, up and operating that September 1946. In the interim, Wagner spearheaded a militant drive in the pages of the *Columbia Union Visitor*, so that the Allegheny Conference utilized its Pine Forge property sooner rather than later. Ultimately, the prospective school became the central focus of Wagner's radical campaign. "Our slogan in Allegheny is," the Black SDA minister zealously declared, "HEED THE CALL, A SCHOOL BY FALL!"[110]

Albeit Wagner (and others) militantly organized and inspired his African American congregants in the *Columbia Union Visitor*; the *Pottstown Mercury*, concurrently, kept its readership abreast with updates of the Allegheny Conference's ongoing developments close by the borough. In effect, the local newspaper's advocacy culminated with Pine Forge Institute officially starting on September 9, 1946, with a coeducational roster that exceeded one hundred. Early the following June (1947), Pine Forge Institute graduated its pioneering six pupils.[111] In time the Pine Forge property even became the Allegheny Conference's center of operations and activism. The massive landholding also served as the place of the Allegheny Conference's annual camp meetings, which brought together Adventists from across not only the United States but also the world.[112]

Unequivocally, the creation of Pine Forge Institute (now called Pine Forge Academy) is one of the greatest long-lasting achievements of the local Black freedom struggle, which the *Pottstown Mercury* helped attain. "In many newspaper campaigns there is no recognition when a battle is [achieved]," Hill observed. However, he continued, it was "not so in this case," for multiple Black Adventist congregants celebrated the civil rights advocacy work of the *Pottstown Mercury*.[113]

The Pottstown Bowling Association and Black Recreational Exclusion

While the conflict in Pine Forge ended soon after its genesis, the fight was not the last civil rights advocacy work that the *Pottstown Mercury* conducted during the early postwar years. In 1949, a little over two months after the *Pottstown Mercury* printed Black activist Mary McLeod Bethune's celebratory remarks on Pine Forge, the newspaper examined a local recreational access issue inextricably related to the ubiquitous yet covert structure of de facto segregation. In sum, the issue was a part of a grander civil rights affair being directly challenged at the national level.[114]

Yet as activists struggled for integrated bowling on the national level, the mainstream white sporting world had already started desegregating.

Shortly following World War II, the most famous example concerned Black athlete and Georgia native Jackie Robinson. Robinson smashed through "the color barrier" soon after (1947) as the pioneering African American baseball player with the Brooklyn Dodgers of Major League Baseball.[115] At mid-twentieth century, Earl F. Lloyd was the pioneer as well for his athletic profession when the Black Virginian by birth desegregated the National Basketball Association as a member of the Washington Capitols.[116]

Although the rise of the liberal interracialist ethos helps explain why integration in the professional athletic world began unfolding following World War II, it does not necessarily mean that all mainstream, white sporting organizations willingly capitulated to such progressivism in the contemporary racial landscape. In fact, communications scholar Patricia L. Dooley demonstrates that the white-led American Bowling Congress (ABC) represented the latter, and "by 1940 . . . was the most powerful bowling association in the country."[117] In the end, while the ABC formally integrated in 1950, the white organization did not do so without a fight, seeking desperately to cling on to its long-standing history of Black exclusion in early postwar America.[118]

As indicated earlier, Pottstown activists were a part of this larger desegregation bowling struggle unfolding at the national level. Moreover, in the fall of 1949, the *Pottstown Mercury* and local white representatives from the Congress of Industrial Organizations (CIO) took on the Pottstown Bowling Association (PBA). Specifically, the two activist groups did so because of the PBA's racist provision that prevented African Americans from joining. In other words, the PBA, which was the local associate of the ABC, followed the national organization's exclusionary provision. And since 1916, the ABC's governing charter possessed "a 'white male sex' clause," which guaranteed that the organization's authorized competitions remained fully segregated.[119]

Yet while the ABC removed its racist provision in May 1950, the white-led entity only did so because several activist groups on the national level applied pressure. For instance, the CIO not only combated the ABC's discriminatory provision nationally during World War II but also continued similar nationwide work in the years following the global conflict. Likewise, the Catholic Youth Organization was another group that went against the ABC's long-standing racist policy both during and after World War II, especially across the national sphere.[120]

To be sure, during the early to mid-twentieth century, Americans as a whole had a passion for bowling. Not surprisingly, Pottstown residents share that same enthusiasm.[121] Yet to satisfy such interest across the area, historian Paul Chancellor notes, "league competition" relating to the nonprofessional sport mainly converged "in . . . church, industrial, and veterans' leagues."[122] By the late 1940s, Pottstown additionally had multiple lanes for bowlers, located in places such as the local YMCA and Arrow Recreation Bowling Alleys, which was, by far, the borough's biggest.[123] Moreover, several fraternal organizations had alleys at their establishments.[124]

As far as the ABC went, however, Pottstown's inauguration with the group occurred in 1934, when local bowlers traveled to Peoria, Illinois, to participate in an ABC-sponsored competition.[125] From thereafter, Pottstown bowlers remained active with the national organization, especially through its local associate, the PBA.[126] In fact, by the time that the *Pottstown Mercury* and local white CIO leadership challenged ABC policy, most bowling establishments in Pottstown held authorization from the powerhouse organization.[127] At the same time, Pottstown's ABC associate, the PBA, noted that it represented "220 teams in 23 leagues" on the local scene.[128]

Albeit, the *Pottstown Mercury* would not address the ABC's racial provision in the small northern borough until the fall of 1949, it began covering the organization's policy on the national level and its oppositional groups earlier that year. In Atlantic City, New Jersey, the ABC held another competition under its policy of racial segregation. Taking place in March, while the newspaper documented several Pottstown bowling teams currently participating in the contest, it also illuminated how ABC leadership in Atlantic City once again kept in place the discriminatory provision. Even following protest from multiple activist groups such as the Anti-Defamation league, the Japanese-American Citizens League, the NAACP, and the CIO United Autoworkers, the ABC leaders still maintained the decades-old clause.[129] Moreover, days later in Atlantic City "delegates to the ABC convention," like the previous two years, once again did not support "by voice vote an amendment," which demanded erasing "the words 'individuals of the white male sex'" within the organization's constitutional document.[130]

On the other hand, the *Pottstown Mercury*'s initial coverage of the ABC on the national level did inspire an African American who resided near Pottstown to write an interesting letter to the editor of the local press. In the correspondence, he placed the phenomenon of the ABC's discriminatory article in a broader, contemporary context.[131] This was not, however, the only time that the *Pottstown Mercury* would print a "Readers Say" correspondence from local African American James H. Downing. In fact, from 1948 to 1950, the *Pottstown Mercury* published a total of four "Readers Say"/letters to the editor pieces from the local Black civil rights activist.

Downing's writings, which heavily utilized Christian themes, focused on the plight of contemporary African Americans.[132] To be sure, his correspondence published by the newspaper on March 30, 1949, about the ABC was by no means any different. In the letter, Downing stressed that the ABC's policy should not be taken as abnormal. But the ABC's bigoted provision reflected multiple well-respected "civic, political, educational, fraternal, social, charitable, and religious organizations" across the United States. Thus, Downing continued, singling out the ABC was simply foolish. Rather, the real issue at hand related to "American hypocrisy and insincerity." In his mind, specifying the ABC only failed to illuminate the larger societal practice and acceptance of excluding African Americans.[133] Downing made similar claims about insincerity when it came to addressing racism in the United States the year before (1948) in his correspondence to the *Pottstown Mercury* editor, where he wrote that "racial prejudice is a disease of the mind" and that "America has a prolific endemic."[134] In his 1950 letter, Downing further lambasted the United States. Centering his argument within the context of the current Cold War, Downing asserted, "It is high time that some of the millions being spent to combat Communistic aggression be used to fight our national policy of racial segregation and discrimination."[135]

When the *Pottstown Mercury* and local white CIO leaders took on the ABC's racial provision in Pottstown, the national activist strategy of the bowling organization revolved largely around the premise of fighting the group in the court system. In fact, historians John C. Walter and

Malina Iida reveal that "a legal approach" was what ultimately ended the ABC's racist practice.[136] Locally, however, activists addressed the ABC mainly through the *Pottstown Mercury* on the one hand, coupled with sit-down discussions between local CIO and PBA and ABC associates on the other hand.[137]

Not surprisingly, the *Pottstown Mercury* advocated the antiracist, liberal interracialist position, publishing an article in early October 1949 that illuminated the ramifications of ABC protocol and how it directly affected African Americans in the small northern borough. Like Downing's letters, the article, entitled "Discrimination Here," contextualized ABC racism within late 1940s America. It did so, however, by noting the backwardness of the ABC's provision, especially when juxtaposing it and other sports—professional and amateur—and how they had been integrating rather than excluding African Americans. "In this day of tolerance," the *Pottstown Mercury* remarked, "when even the major leagues don't draw the line, when northern college football teams now go into the deepest South and use Negroes, it is hard to imagine Pottstown discriminating against any bowler." The newspaper article also emphasized particularly that "industrial leagues"—another point that further demonstrated the small northern borough's ubiquitous working-class composition—were the ones mainly affected, precisely because African Americans were in their rank and file. The *Pottstown Mercury* radically suggested, then, that they "should rebel when this discrimination is mentioned at a local ABC" gathering.

Additionally, the *Pottstown Mercury* reported on some positive news in Pottstown about the ABC's national provision, which, in fact, came from one of the local bowling establishments themselves. The Pottstown YMCA, which recently desegregated its entire facility additionally in 1949 in the borough (see chap. 2), revealed publicly that African Americans would certainly be granted bowling privileges there.[138] Although the YMCA's bowling lanes were ABC sponsored in Pottstown, the local branch noted that it did not plan on enforcing and following the organization's racist charter. Furthermore, like the *Pottstown Mercury*'s coverage of the Allegheny Conference and the white-led VIA, the newspaper painted the bowling struggle on the local front in terms of the postwar, liberal interracialist ethos. "It will take courage to fight the ruling."

However, the paper concluded, "it will be a battle for tolerance and brotherhood" in the end.[139]

In *Dear Sir*, Shandy Hill, while not naming the business directly, revealed how "a Pottstown labor leader" informed him about an establishment, which refused Black bowlers access there. This local organization, Hill continued, was "Pottstown's only public alley." Although the white editor left out the business's name, he was most likely referencing Arrow Bowling Alleys, which was, as indicated, the small northern borough's biggest bowling venue. At the same time, the unionist, Hill said, inquired if the white editor "would help 'desegregate' the bowling alley," thus further demonstrating how inconspicuous yet pervasive the structure of northern Jim Crow was. Moreover, Hill juxtaposed this instance of the local Black freedom struggle that centered on integration during the late 1940s, which was a nonviolent affair, with southern African American activism roughly twenty years later, which ended both violently and tragically with law enforcement killing "three Negro youths" who were seeking "to 'liberate' a bowling alley." Finally, Hill expressed how after "a few" meetings between both sides, where some disputing even took place, the local editor eventually assisted in radically changing the white owner's perspective on Black exclusion at his business.[140]

Whatever the case, days following the *Pottstown Mercury*'s "Discrimination Here" article, Pottstown CIO representatives from United Auto Workers Local 644 entered the civil rights struggle. Specifically, they did so by holding a verbal sparring match with ABC workers and the PBA during the association's yearly gathering at the West End Fire Company in nearby Stowe.[141] Following in similar footsteps of the CIO's national take on the ABC, the two white unionists wanted the PBA to depart immediately from the bowling organization. The PBA should return, they demanded, solely when the ABC removed its bigoted provision. One of the leaders even stressed, "You are not only discriminating against Negroes and other racial groups but against all other bowlers in non-sanctioned leagues." In the context of "the past three national [ABC] conventions," the second CIO activist emphasized how "we must think of the American principles in the world of sports." Although he acknowledged "that the rule must be left to the convention," the CIO activist additionally asked, "Where are we?" He continued, "It is time we stood to be counted." The same CIO unionist also noted that since most athletic organizations in the United States had stopped excluding African Americans, ABC policy was, therefore, essentially archaic. Finally, the white unionist demonstrated how hypocritical the provision was when juxtaposed with the fact that African Americans served in the US military, yet the ABC excluded them from its rank and file. "If a man goes to fight for his country," the white unionist declared, then "he should have equal rights in sports" too.

Both the PBA and ABC officials provided direct rebuttal arguments to the white CIO unionists. Regarding the PBA needing to leave the ABC, the PBA chief argued that the position was fundamentally flawed, specifically because "all affiliated leagues in the local association" signed up fully knowing about the ABC's exclusionary article. Certainly, since the provision was not some covert pact hidden from Pottstown ABC associates, then there should thus be no debate surrounding its blatant exclusionism, countered the PBA head.

Likewise, when the ABC leaders responded, they defended the organization's decades-old provision, emphasizing choice. First, the leaders noted that during "the past three national conventions," ABC delegates upheld the exclusionary article "by overwhelming majorities." It is also interesting to mention that one of the ABC officials even juxtaposed the bowling congress with "any fraternal or other" group who excluded within their rank-and-file membership. In the end, therefore, because ABC representatives had consistently backed the organization's bigoted article, it was essentially their choice as Americans.

Another ABC officer posed the second rebuttal point. He did so, however, by directly questioning one of the unionists themselves, inquiring whether the individual "would resign from a fraternal organization" since the association excluded African Americans. Paradoxically, the labor leader responded no. His justification was even more contradictory. Essentially, the white unionist argued that that was the group's prerogative. His voice and authority in their exclusionary decision was thus immaterial.

Nevertheless, even though the CIO leader's remarks were indeed inconsistent, the white unionist remained committed to the fight to allow Pottstown African Americans to bowl alongside whites.[142] Well over a month following the PBA's yearly gathering, the labor official continued demanding that the Pottstown group protest the ABC's exclusionary provision. Simultaneously, however, the *Pottstown Mercury* reported on how local bowling athletes were largely positioning "themselves" together "behind repeal of the Negro discrimination clause." A PBA representative from Pottstown, the newspaper additionally noted, was "very likely" going to Columbus, Ohio, the following May to attend the ABC gathering. The PBA's president also stressed two reasons why the representative was going. First, the rep was to travel there because Pottstown bowling athletes were planning on competing. Second, and most important concerning the local Black freedom struggle, the PBA leader stressed how "the delegate will be advised to vote for repeal of the discrimination clause if it is put to a vote."[143]

While the *Pottstown Mercury* captured local bowlers' competitive endeavors during the ABC affair in Columbus the next year, it failed to mention anything about how the Pottstown representative ultimately lined up with the national decision on the ABC's discriminatory provision. However, the *New York Times* announced that out of "the 518 delegates" present, those supporting the ABC's long-standing policy were not the majority. In fact, it divulged, "only a few delegates shouted nays."[144] While there is no evidence of the PBA rep's direct vote, taking the aforementioned evidence altogether, it seems safe to assume that the Pottstown rep not only followed the will of the PBA majority but also was in direct concert with the majority of ABC comrades during the historic Columbus gathering that May 1950.

Finally, even though the ABC reps disbanded racial exclusion that May 1950, John B. Sbarbaro, an Illinois justice, legally ruled against the historically white organization the previous month. Specifically, Sbarbaro applied "a $2,500 fine on ABC leaders," even declaring intimidatingly "to revoke the association's state charter" in late April 1950. Yet while shortly after that May, the ABC officially desegregated, Dooley adds, one must also acknowledge how paramount "bowling activists'" impactful agitations were as World War II raged.[145]

Hemlock and Cottage Rows and the Fight for African American Housing in Stowe

As civil rights activists were able to put direct pressure nationally on the ABC to annul its long-standing racist policy of exclusions in 1950, that same year another local civil rights struggle in Pottstown was already in full swing. It, too, shared a direct correlation to the national plight of African Americans. This connection, however, focused specifically on African American experiences with enduring local housing inequality during the age of northern Jim Crow. In the end, such residential activism ultimately engendered cooperation between local Blacks and whites both conscious and interested in promoting African American equality and fairness in and around the small northern borough during early 1950s America.

Like the *Pottstown Mercury* juvenile delinquency series from 1944, the borough newspaper again launched another "series" that examined civil rights developments within the local Black freedom struggle during the early postwar. In short, this series was a collaboration between white *Pottstown Mercury* journalist Frank J. Dostal and local African Americans from a predominately Black neighborhood nearby Pottstown in Stowe: Hemlock and Cottage Rows. Unlike the juvenile delinquency articles, however, the *Pottstown Mercury* series from the spring of 1950 did not center primarily on one local African American voice. Instead, for this series, the paper teamed up Dostal with several Stowe Blacks, who both publicly and intimately revealed the housing challenges they endured particularly relating to the de facto segregation of early postwar America.[146]

Following World War II, many Americans faced the challenge of obtaining adequate living quarters, so much so that the US government responded directly. "The housing shortage continues to be acute," Democratic President Harry S. Truman declared in early January 1949. "As an immediate step," Truman added, "the Congress should enact the provisions for low-rent public housing, slum clearance, farm housing, and housing research which I have repeatedly recommended."[147] That July, the president authorized and approved the Housing Act of 1949. In effect, the main purpose behind the act, Truman contended, was that all United States residents had sufficient housing.[148]

"Segregated housing," historian Jason Sokol writes, "was the scourge of the North." The practice "was alternately subtle and overt," he adds.[149] Indeed, while Pottstown's housing situation mirrored the national landscape of postwar America, it was especially troubling for local Blacks.

Moreover, although the conditions were clearly horrendous during World War II, as demonstrated in chapter 2, the postwar era did not fare much better.[150] "The only blot is the slum area in which many" local African Americans reside, declared a Pottstown white in early August 1949. However, she continued, "that isn't their fault."[151] Later the same month, while present during a gathering of Pottstown officials on the construction of prospective government living quarters, local Black NAACP activist Joseph Young, Frances's dad (see chap. 2), stressed how Pottstown African Americans had issues that pertained directly to obtaining "decent homes."[152] The following March 1950, moreover, Second Baptist's Heywood L. Butler shed further light on local housing insecurity among African Americans. "It has been" approximated, Butler argued, that "there are 1500 Negroes in Pottstown," with "less than one-tenth of that number" possessing "their own homes." Ostensibly, Butler's rough calculation is high, considering the 1950 US census marks the borough's Black population at 844. Nevertheless, the approximation principally conveys the housing dilemma local African Americans were in by the mid-twentieth century.[153]

In a somewhat similar vein, locals outside Hemlock and Cottage Rows—the predominately Black neighborhood in Stowe that served as the locus of the housing civil rights struggle thoroughly documented by the *Pottstown Mercury* in 1950—even utilized negative connotations such as "slums" or "sub-standard" when identifying the properties there.[154] "A lot of effort is being spent in getting rid of the slums in Cottage and Hemlock rows so that new homes can be built," wrote a Pottstown resident in early February 1950. "Sure, this will help clean up Pottstown."[155] The *Pottstown Mercury* was also guilty when describing the residencies as such in its reporting.[156]

These labels, of course, bothered the Black residents in Stowe. While the brandings were warranted to an extent, it was the Pottstown government, nevertheless, that enabled some of these low-quality conditions in the first place during the age of northern Jim Crow. For example, the local government failed at building an adequate drainage system for Hemlock and Cottage Row buildings. Left with no indoor plumbing, Black residents utilized outdoor lavatories. Additionally, the Pottstown government did not pave the roadways of Hemlock and Cottage Rows.

In fact, that was precisely why the African Americans poured concrete pathways to surround their properties.[157]

The unmodern roadway also had ramifications on waste collection. "Since it is not an ordained street, [waste] collectors" simply sailed past the properties. Yet to neutralize trash accumulation among their properties, Hemlock and Cottage Row Blacks worked as a collective unit during the summertime to remove the waste. In effect, Hemlock and Cottage Rows' lack of modern trash disposal—a direct consequence of the unpaved roadway—only contributed to the low-quality identifications bestowed on them. Moreover, because the local authority neglected these buildings, Hemlock and Cottage Row African Americans responded by doing all in their own power to modernize the residencies. In the end, the local Blacks made these refurbishments, so the buildings were both habitable and respectable living places.[158]

Like their white counterparts throughout the United States, African Americans have historically believed that owning one's residency was both sacred and noteworthy, something worth obtaining. Historian Patrick D. Jones even argues poignantly that among American Blacks' collective consciousness, "homeownership and open access to housing bore a special historical resonance." In particular, Jones continues, since the African American enslavement period in the United States, followed by decades under the oppressive and legally codified southern Jim Crow system, as well as northern Jim Crow, whites have both forcefully and clandestinely stripped away Blacks' constitutional privileges as US citizens, thus stymieing African Americans real possibility as homeowners.[159]

For all these reasons alluded to by Jones, one can thus understand clearly that while Pottstown-area locals outside Hemlock and Cottage Rows constructed negative opinions of the Stowe residences, the African Americans living within them held contrasting sentiments. Indeed, pride was the strongest of these. For example, African American Robert Parsons, who worked for Stanley G. Flagg and resided at 27 Cottage Row, illuminated such prideful feelings by stressing how much time and effort he spent modernizing his place and space. "[Growing] up on Cottage row," Parsons recognized plainly "the task of turning a house into a modern home would not be an easy one when he started buying four years ago." However, Parsons "bowed to his job and began the long years of work which lay ahead."[160]

Similarly, Black homemaker and Georgia native Corrine Nixon lived at 40 Hemlock Row with her spouse, African American Walter Nixon, a North Carolinian by birth and local steel mill worker. Like Parsons, Corrine shed light on the extreme sacrifices she and Walter had made for their humble abode. Moreover, the Nixons' situation represented Hemlock and Cottage Row Blacks' housing plight overall. "They purchased half of the double house in which they live for $850 and then began buying the other half by paying $30 each month. In six months," Dostal continued, "both halves of the house will be theirs." Moreover, even though "the purchase of their home used up their savings and has continued to be a constant fight," the white journalist added, "they have tried to improve their property over the years."[161]

To be sure, the economics of buying and renting Hemlock and Cottage Row properties were also not the sole financial hardships that these local working-class African Americans experienced; fixing-up and modernizing the residencies were the others. As indicated, multiple Blacks manufactured concrete walking paths, which bordered their properties so "mud and dirt" were not tracked within them.[162] Other exterior enhancements they completed included shingling sides and roofing restoration alongside window and patio replacements. Interiorly speaking, some added sleeping and living quarters, lavatories, and cooking rooms, among other refurbishments.

These expenditures were not cheap. In fact, African American industrial worker and South Carolina native Columbus Massey, the breadwinner of 23 Cottage Row, talked about how pricey such renovations had been.[163] An employee of Pottstown's Doehler-Jarvis plant, Massey's restorations left him nearly dead broke. The Black breadwinner approximated that his enhancements priced out at over $4,000. Nonetheless, that did not stop him or African American domestic worker and North Carolina native Elizabeth Massey, Columbus's spouse, from zealously restoring 23 Cottage Row. In fact, around the time the *Pottstown Mercury* reported the Black housing plight, all the Masseys had left was some minor stuccoing.[164]

Interestingly enough, Parsons revealed that he spent $450 on shingling. Certainly Parsons's amount was a hefty price, especially considering "the seasonal nature of his work" with Stanley G. Flagg and Co. meant it was not steady capital. Nevertheless, the African American worker scraped together the little monies he had so that the restoration got done.[165] In short, Black residents like the Nixons, Masseys, and Parsons made these efforts precisely because they took pride in modernizing and revamping their properties.[166]

Yet as Hemlock and Cottage Row Blacks navigated their everyday lives, events outside their control began materializing. In early March 1950, news spread from Norristown (Pottstown's county seat) that the Montgomery County Housing Authority (MCHA) had started drafting the preparation stages for the building of an additional two hundred public housing units adjacent to Pottstown's Penn Village, a federally funded residential complex.[167] The two hundred "low cost public housing units" had initially received sanction by the Public Housing Administration, a department associated with the Federal Housing and Home Finance Agency, roughly six months ago.[168] Thus, the MCHA approved several steps that launched the initial phase of the massive building task. Moreover, one step in this undertaking was "the demolition of sub-standard homes on Cottage and Hemlock rows" nearby Pottstown in Stowe.[169]

In particular, these structures included eighteen houses as well as Mount Herman Baptist Church's building (another Black congregation). Finally, in Pottstown local government organizations openly cooperated with the MCHA's clearance endeavors.[170] However, Hemlock and Cottage Row African Americans fervently resisted them.

Yet even though Hemlock and Cottage Row African Americans faced such housing expulsion in early 1950, they had already walked this path. Shortly after World War II, they endured possible residency loss when their proprietor wanted to sell the buildings away. During this time, Hemlock and Cottage Row Blacks did not own these properties. However, Corrine Nixon revealed that the proprietor gave them two choices: namely, they could purchase their residences "or get out." Because "there was no place for us to go," Nixon stressed that they acquired the dwellings. Granted "first choice" before additional prospective buyers, these Blacks also had two courses in which they could obtain property ownership. Option 1 was that the African Americans paid the full price for their properties, thereby having complete ownership. Option 2, on the other hand, equated to them putting one-tenth of the money down, and then over time completely purchasing the buildings with rental monies. Generally speaking, these African Americans—as illuminated by the Nixons' example—selected option 2, although it was certainly still financially taxing on these working-class African Americans.[171]

In addition to Hemlock and Cottage Row Blacks' holding civil rights solidarity, they felt a keen sense of cohesiveness. An institution that helped cultivate such African American unity was Mount Herman Baptist Church, located at 41 Hemlock Row. Mount Herman congregants constructed their place of worship in the early 1940s. Black minister Daniel Charles, another Virginia native and industrial worker, pastored Mount Herman.[172] Moreover, while Mount Herman worshippers resided in both Stowe and Pottstown, Hemlock and Cottage Row African Americans' economic activism was the main reason that the physical house of God existed. Specifically, these Black working-class locals made their capital work in tandem so that Mount Herman was ultimately finished.[173]

At the same time, Hemlock and Cottage Row African Americans highlighted their respectability as local citizenry, which gave further credence to the nobility and honor of their housing cause. For example, these local Blacks emphasized how they broke no laws but were, rather, good, upright people. Employed as "a truck dispatcher" with the local Doehler-Jarvis factory, John H. Harper of 38 Hemlock Row illuminated such an argument. Born in the Deep South in Alabama, Harper also argued for the decency of Hemlock and Cottage Row African Americans. Specifically, he stressed two influential factors. Not surprisingly, the first was Mount Herman. The congregation's presence, he noted, continually affected the Black families there for the greater good.[174] Additionally, Corrine Nixon celebrated Mount Herman in a similar vein. In her view, she stressed that the house of worship created a real sense of safety and security—something nonexistent prior to its Hemlock Row occupancy, especially when individuals traveled the area during the evening time.[175]

In addition to Mount Herman being a place of neighborhood importance, Harper spotlighted the property enhancements of Hemlock and Cottage Row African Americans as the second impactful component for the small Black community. In fact, the way Harper shingled 38 Hemlock Row's exterior served "as a model for other residents." Yet Harper's standing among Hemlock and Cottage Row African Americans went even farther than an outdoor refurbishment. Indeed, neighborhood Blacks categorized Harper as a leader and a generally highly regarded individual. Moreover, Harper's reputation transcended Hemlock and Cottage Rows. Not only was Harper Doehler-Jarvis's pioneering African American in Pottstown—initially employed in 1943—but over his outstanding tenure the company sought his advice. In particular, Harper supplied Doehler-Jarvis with names from local African Americans seeking employment. By Harper acting as such, he also further revealed how Black networks played out on the local front.[176]

Finally, it is worth stressing that Hemlock and Cottage Row African Americans utilized militant discourse when protesting the potential loss of their properties. Specifically, they did so in response to the frustration they felt over investing so much energy and capital into their residencies only to have to vacate them because of the projected two hundred federally funded homes. Indeed, Columbus Massey's frustration related directly to the fact that his place was nearly finished—notwithstanding some brief stuccoing—and now government forces threatened to snatch it right out of his hands. He stated cynically, therefore, "Why the devil should I put any more money into it?" In addition, Massey blatantly criticized the Pottstown government's failure in providing Hemlock and Cottage Rows an adequate roadway. The Black worker also called out local officials who solely cared about the neighborhood African Americans during ballot season. Thereafter, Massey continued, these same officers totally neglected the needs of Hemlock and Cottage Row Blacks.

However, Massey's most militant assertion came when he stressed how Black residents would not tolerate their local government's second-rate treatment anymore. He did so by using metaphor. "If they insist on treating us like dogs," Massey proclaimed, "they should remember that a dog will take only so many lickings before he bites back."[177] African American domestic and Virginia native Neva L. Goffigon of 46 Hemlock Row utilized another radical metaphor, enslavement, when demonstrating the plight of Hemlock and Cottage Row African Americans. An angered Goffigon announced, "You could almost call these two row slavery."[178]

On the other hand, a last fascinating point Corrine Nixon illuminated went directly against an argument conveyed by a MCHA representative.

Specifically, the MCHA rep suggested how qualified Hemlock and Cottage Row Blacks, like whites, had an identical chance at residing within "the 200 new homes . . . around Penn Village."[179] Consequently, Nixon's remarks further demonstrated the tangible challenges local African Americans endured in the realm of civil rights and sufficient housing during the postwar years. The way Nixon saw things, "she doubted strongly that the families from the home on both Hemlock and Cottage rows would be given room in the new [Penn Village] units anyway," particularly since "all are Negroes." Nixon continued, "I know people who have applied for rooms there and they are still waiting."[180] A *Pottstown Mercury* editorial published on April 26, 1950, entitled "Penn Village Charges," substantiated Nixon's position as well. In fact, it added that multiple local Blacks affirmed how Penn Village practiced bigoted sentiments toward African Americans seeking residency there, further demonstrating the pervasive yet clandestine structure of de facto segregation and how it permeated the local front during the early postwar period.[181]

Such racial discrimination in Penn Village, however, did not end there. Indeed, Hemlock and Cottage Row Blacks noted quite a few racially charged episodes involving the complex. First, even though neighborhood kids attended "school with the children in Penn Village," the youths "were prohibited from crossing the project's property to get the school bus." Moreover, Penn Village had "a Summer playground" and the complex asked Hemlock and Cottage Row residents that they "keep their children" away from it. Hemlock and Cottage Row adults faced similar discriminatory constraints as the younger people when using Penn Village as a short cut. In fact, Penn Village also barred them from traveling on its land—another demonstration of the inconspicuous and covert local structure of northern Jim Crow.

While white *Pottstown Mercury* journalist Frank Dostal provided a forum where Hemlock and Cottage Row African Americans intimately and passionately revealed their housing grievances, he additionally advocated several points for the local Black residents. First, Dostal painted Hemlock and Cottage Row African Americans in a specific way that its readership could sympathize with. Defenseless "before the onward sweep of government progress, a little group of Pottstown families are watching their chance to be independent homeowners and a credit to their community rapidly disappear."[182] In another passage, the white journalist declared that "the tragic loss of the homes for which they have strived so long is not the only price the residents of Hemlock and Cottage rows must pay for government progress."[183]

Second, and similar to his colleague Larry Davis, Dostal utilized "a politics of respectability" lens. "The Negro 'Y'" across the United States conspicuously represented "a politics of respectability," especially before World War II, as historian Thomas J. Sugrue astutely observes, and woven throughout Dostal's coverage on Hemlock and Cottage Row Blacks during the early 1950s was the fact that these working-class African Americans were not only gainfully employed, hardworking, church-going, and family-oriented but "law-abiding" as well.[184] Third, Dostal stressed the failure of the Pottstown government to provide Hemlock and Cottage Row Blacks an adequate roadway. In particular, he asserted how the Pottstown government unequivocally neglected the neighborhood's African Americans since it "never . . . constructed a sewer to the" residences. Corrine Nixon even noted how the neighborhood African Americans had no quarrel with "pay[ing] his share if a sewer was put through here for us."[185] Moreover, Dostal revealed that local government never finished constructing the street. "The past year," he additionally noted, "tarvia was spread over the 'street' which wanders over the householders' properties." Notwithstanding, Hemlock and Cottage Row African Americans were not satisfied with such second-class refurbishment.[186]

Meanwhile, the *Pottstown Mercury*'s Shandy Hill inserted himself directly into the local Black freedom struggle. Around this time, however, his newspaper informed its readership about the MCHA revamping its original position for Cottage Rows. Now, the MCHA announced, Cottage Rows were remaining intact. Thus, Hill turned his energies toward the plight of Hemlock Rows. Specifically, Hill did so by personally corresponding with the MCHA, informing it about "several alternative sites" where "the proposed 200-unit expansion of Penn Village" could potentially be placed. Hill included "a map" with these various locations as well. The MCHA, moreover, forwarded such pertinent information to Philadelphia's Public Housing Administration branch.[187] In addition to Hill's correspondence, the *Pottstown Mercury* published passionate editorials like "Save Hemlock Row" and "Hemlock Row—Pottstown's Sin."[188]

Hill also sent out a correspondence to the NAACP's central location in New York. Dated April 29, 1950, three days following the "Penn Village Charges" article, which Hill also referenced in the document, he informed the NAACP that "we are continuing our fight here against discrimination." At the same time, the white newspapermen let the national civil rights organization know that his local press was not against receiving its direct assistance. "Anything youcan [*sic*] do to help us will be appreciated," he declared. With the Pottstown NAACP not revitalizing until 1951, Hill's last point particularly makes sense.[189]

The *Pottstown Mercury* was not, however, the only group working on behalf of Hemlock Row African Americans. In fact, local Blacks outside the neighborhood inserted themselves directly into the conflict too. Second Baptist's Heywood L. Butler was the earliest. To be sure, the African American minister cared deeply about Hemlock Row Blacks, so much so that Butler even advised some African Americans, who ultimately purchased houses in the neighborhood. As an activist with Pottstown's Frankford Improvement Association (FIA), the group that actively worked within the confines of the strategies of equalization and traditional Black internal improvement (see chap. 2), Butler was also fervently supportive of African American homeownership. As such, the Black minister's activism further demonstrates his rightful connection and place within the local Black freedom struggle.[190]

Pottstown African American leaders James H. and William D. Corum also backed Hemlock Row Blacks. President James H. Corum's biracial Local 2326 put forward "the first offer of financial as well as moral help for the residents of Hemlock row who are threatened with the loss of their homes." Corum even added how some Blacks residing there not only worked at Stanley G. Flagg but that the African American laborers were card-carrying Local 2326 unionists too. Moreover, Corum, "the aggressive labor leader," basically endorsed Corrine Nixon's claim about Penn Village being discriminatory toward local African Americans seeking occupancy there.[191] His younger brother, William D. Corum, celebrated how local African Americans, especially churchgoers with different religious beliefs, came together in solidarity. By putting "Christianity first, and church affiliation second," something that Corum argued even played a direct role in previously causing factionalism among local Blacks, "then we'll" begin progressing ahead.[192]

In addition to Local 2326, Hemlock Row Blacks had backing from Local 138 of the Amalgamated Clothing Workers—another Pottstown CIO union.[193] Moreover, the American Legion Milton E. Simms Post 955 backed the Stowe African Americans housing plight. Pottstown's Black-led Masons organization, alongside local African American congregations, had additionally united on behalf of Hemlock Row Blacks and their housing quandary inextricably linked to de facto segregation in the age of northern Jim Crow.[194]

Furthermore, Hemlock Row Blacks received interracial backing from outside the local collective. African American lawyer, civil rights activist, and Pennsylvania native Herbert C. Nelson entered the local Black freedom struggle as an FIA associate.[195] An alumnus of historically Black Howard University School of Law, decades later historian Charles L. Blockson even argues that Nelson represented Montgomery County's "first prominent black lawyer."[196]

To be sure, Nelson demonstrated such lawyering skills during the Hemlock Row affair. He also provided counsel at no cost to the working-class African Americans. In sum, Nelson involved himself precisely because he was so passionate over the local Black freedom activism. "This is not just a fight for a home," the Black counselor announced, "it is a fight for a principle. If you need the services of a lawyer, forget about money," he militantly proclaimed, "I'm offering my services here and now." In effect, Nelson viewed the Black housing dilemma as "a righteous" struggle.[197]

Another Hemlock Row backer (among others, Black and white) was Pennsylvania white Republican senator Lloyd H. Wood, who was currently making pertinent "plans for his election campaign." Wood announced that he was "very anxious to be of service in this matter." In fact, the white senator continued, "I want to do every and anything I can to be helpful to" these Stowe African Americans.[198] Less than a year later, the senator became Pennsylvania Republican governor John S. Fine's lieutenant governor.[199]

Altogether, the civil rights advocacy work that paired up local African Americans and the *Pottstown Mercury* paid Hemlock Row Blacks real dividends during the age of Jim Crow in the North. Most importantly, the cooperative civil rights work pressured the MCHA into leaving Hemlock Row properties completely intact, so much so, that the MCHA relocated the projected Penn Village additions, finalizing the decision on April 6, 1950.[200] About three weeks after the April 6 judgment, Penn Village additionally welcomed its pioneering Black residents. The Whites, who were the "first members of their race to crack the barriers at the Federal housing project," moved into Penn Village.[201]

Outside the *Pottstown Mercury*'s initial reporting, only *Dear Sir* mentions the Hemlock and Cottage Rows housing struggle. The passage, which Dostal mostly penned, brings up two fascinating points.[202] First, Dostal emphasizes how the local Black freedom struggle over housing in Stowe was "long before civil rights became such a burning issue." Whether intentionally or inconspicuously, Dostal's remarks demonstrate how civil rights history in Pottstown and nearby areas from World War II throughout the late 1960s goes against traditional historiographical interpretations that center especially on the Black freedom struggle.

At the same time, when Hill found out about "the powerful Federal Government" and its desire to take away the local Blacks residencies, Dostal recalls the white newspaperman identify the situation as blatantly discriminatory. The white editor, therefore, informed Dostal to "fight them," which further expresses the ethos of civil rights advocacy work and racial progressivism engendered from Hill and his zealous press. Dostal gloats, "A solid thirty-day campaign mobilized the support of churches, unions, businessmen, industry and some powerful behind-the-scenes allies." In turn, the white journalist continued, such advocacy directly pressured "the U.S. Housing Authority" into capitulation. Thus, the local Blacks held on to their residences.

Furthermore, Dostal sheds light on how these same African Americans housing victory was, nevertheless, "another award—for public service." This victory, Dostal argues, transpired well before the US Supreme Court's *Brown v. Board of Education* decision from 1954. Ostensibly, the white journalist's remarks propose, perhaps, how the civil rights housing struggle from 1950 centering on Hemlock and Cottage Rows not only benefited the local Blacks involved but also had greater possibilities in the realm of equality and inclusion, which would, indeed, benefit the greater good of society at large.

In the end, Dostal's insightful reflections captured in *Dear Sir* suggest how the Hemlock and Cottage Rows dilemma pushes back against overall traditional conceptualizations and generalized theoretical frameworks of the twentieth-century Black freedom struggle. His commentary likewise supports how the local civil rights struggle from 1950 inextricably complicates the southern-primacy narrative, coupled with the consensus, beginning, time frame argument, which centers precisely on the US Supreme Court's monumental *Brown* ruling.[203]

The Pottstown Civic League and Traditional Black Internal Improvement

What also materialized from the Black freedom struggle that focused on the plight of Cottage and Hemlock Row African Americans across the northern Jim Crow structure on the local front was the Pottstown Civic League (PCL), which was established on April 3, 1950.[204] In short, the PCL stressed equalization and identical traditional Black internal improvement strategies that centered on ameliorating "the educational, economic, social and moral advancement of" local African Americans.[205] Fervently supporting the Stowe African Americans endeavors in acquiring Pottstown governmental provisions and amenities, which would benefit them, the Black-centered PCL was "a formal non-profit corporation with receipt of its charter from the State."[206] Finally, it is worth noting that the PCL's initial establishment even caught the Pennsylvania government's attention. Thus, the state's Department of Internal Affairs published an article on the PCL in September 1950.[207]

Heywood Butler, James and William Corum, and eleven-other local African Americans helped establish the PCL. James Corum was even the group's initial secretary. Yet the most notable PCL official was Black physician Daniel Lee, the body's first president. Born in Georgia (1918) but raised in Philadelphia, another example of how the Great Migration directly benefited the local Black freedom struggle, Lee attended the historically Black Lincoln University in Chester County, Pennsylvania, graduating in 1940 with a biology degree. About two years after Lee completed his undergraduate work, he enrolled in another historically Black institution, Howard University School of Medicine (Washington, DC). Lee finished there in 1945. Before settling in Pottstown, however, Lee additionally spent time interning with New York City's Harlem Hospital (1946), followed by a stint working at his alma mater Lincoln (1946 to 1948).[208]

Eventually, Lee migrated to Pottstown in June 1948. In addition, later that same month, Pottstown Hospital hired him, making Lee its pioneering Black physician. Moreover, upon arriving in Pottstown, Lee did not waste time getting involved in the local Black community. In addition to working at Pine Forge Institute as its doctor, Lee gave his time to YMCA Negro Extension Work programs, the local NAACP, and Pottstown's Second Baptist Church. Later in life, he also worked with the Pottstown Committee on Human Relations (PCHR). In the end, one can argue persuasively that Lee would make his most significant local civil rights contributions through service to the PCL as well as the PCHR.[209]

Overall, the PCL emphasized academics. It not only directed local educational competitions but provided Black pupils academic funding. The PCL, in the same traditions of equalization and Black internal improvement work on the local front utilized during World War II, also purchased a facility—the Scout House—so that local Black Boy Scouts had a space to work. Lee's PCL funded the Boy Scout group, too. Furthermore, the PCL sponsored public discussions from regional leaders, including African Americans.[210]

Yet in the immediate postwar years, the local Black freedom struggle became demonstrably interracial, as indicated by the *Pottstown Mercury*'s journalistic advocacy work. This same activism illuminated greater participation and visibility from local whites than witnessed previously. Collaborating with multiple local African Americans, the local newspaper helped attain civil rights achievements that were directly germane to area Blacks.

At the same time, the *Pottstown Mercury*'s civil rights advocacy work assisted in presenting humanizing and dignified portrayals of local Blacks to the white majority of the area. To be sure, the northern newspaper not only illuminated the humanity of these local African Americans but also provided them the opportunity to voice their grievances and arguments, which sharply lambasted indigenous manifestations of racial inequality that permeated the local sphere of de facto segregation. In sum, the *Pottstown Mercury*'s journalistic advocacy work that began mushrooming during World War II served as foundational work for the local Black freedom struggle more broadly. In due time, the civil rights advocacy work of the *Pottstown Mercury* would also demonstrate that the local newspaper organization remained the most steadfast and committed white ally to African Americans in the area, and their Black freedom work for first-class citizenship and inclusion.

Of course, the liberal interracialist strategy that began crystalizing and forming in Pottstown during World War II and the early postwar years was not pertinent only to the small northern industrial borough of southeastern Pennsylvania. But throughout the United States, African American and white activists began both firmly and passionately embracing this racially egalitarian idea, as historians such as Nina Mjagkij and Stanley Keith Arnold indicate.[211]

In 1954, following the United States Supreme Court declaring public school segregation illegal in *Brown v. Board of Education*, once again the *Pottstown Mercury* demonstrated its ongoing commitment to civil rights struggle across the area. Collaborating with local African Americans, the newspaper would focus its reporting on discrimination and civil rights homegrown to the local front. Clearly, so impactful was the liberal interracialist work in Pottstown that it eventually galvanized national civil rights responses, consciousness, and awareness.

Yet before such work made its way to the national sphere, it began percolating locally. In particular, area residents wrote into the *Pottstown Mercury*'s "Readers Say"/letter-to-the-editor section in *Brown*'s subsequent aftermath, discussing the ways in which race relations played out in the local Jim Crow landscape. While *Brown* took center stage in the national civil rights drama, the high court judgment would locally both morph and inspire residents in and around Pottstown to begin discussing whether or not racial discrimination and other manifestations of anti-Black exclusion permeated the borough. Moreover, the *Pottstown Mercury* demonstrated journalistic objectivity by capturing both sides of the racial discrimination debate. In due time, however, the local newspaper ultimately aligned with the chorus of perspectives suggesting that racial prejudice undergirded by the northern Jim Crow structure was indeed not only entrenched but also covert throughout the small locale of southeastern Pennsylvania.[212]

4

Emerging Civil Rights Discourses and Pottstown Shortly after *Brown v. Board of Education*

The events following the United States Supreme Court's May 17, 1954, ruling in *Brown v. Board of Education*—which nullified legally (de jure) segregating Blacks and whites in public schooling—reflected the ways in which the national sphere impacted Pottstown's Black freedom struggle.[1] Like others in the nation, shortly after *Brown*, local residents pondered the federal judgment and its significance in challenging the long-standing structure of legal discrimination in America and its public educational sphere, especially in the South. Yet while locals celebrated the decision and provided commentary on it, they soon turned their attention away from the larger ramifications of the US Supreme Court announcement. Instead, they began assessing the state of race relations in the area. Becoming pressingly interested in the status of local African Americans, these writers started sharing their views on the borough's racial landscape in the *Pottstown Mercury*.

Between May 22 and June 18, 1954, the *Pottstown Mercury* printed articles and "Readers Say" letters to the editor relatively frequently. In sum, the writings not only related to local African Americans but also connected to whether Pottstown had its own problems with a more inconspicuous brand of racial exclusion. This type of racial oppression—de facto separation—contrasted from the de jure structure of the South. Specifically, the de facto brand did not legally codify segregation among African Americans and whites. In the end, the discourses that emerged in the *Pottstown Mercury* shortly after *Brown* paved the way for an apex in the borough's history of the local Black freedom struggle and beyond.[2]

In his examination of African American school reform in Milwaukee, historian Jack Dougherty argues that locals in the northern city tailored the meaning/purpose of *Brown* specifically for their own struggles in seeking first-class citizenship. Moreover, Dougherty shows that local African Americans in Milwaukee used the larger premise of the *Brown* ruling as an avenue to ultimately advocate for more Black public school teachers employed in the city. Eventually, the strategy worked.

This chapter and the one that follows lean heavily on Dougherty's theoretical framework, especially as it pertains to the ways in which activists in Milwaukee custom-fitted the ramifications of the *Brown* decision for their fight for first-class citizenship. However, chapters 4 and 5 also demonstrate a more nuanced yet wide-reaching assessment of Dougherty's interpretation. In particular, because the impact of *Brown* transcended multiple areas locally in and around Pottstown, the chapters reveal how activists fervently committed to equality called out the practice of northern Jim Crow in both public and private local employment sectors. Put differently, the impact of the *Brown* decision in Pottstown and beyond transcended desegregation efforts, even going outside public schooling.[3]

Of course, Pottstown did not have public school segregation legally mandated at the time of *Brown*, for Pennsylvania had lawfully barred the discriminatory practice within its government-funded school system in the late nineteenth century. Nevertheless, Black exclusion and white racism did, in fact, make their way more inconspicuously into the local, public, educational structure. However, where the influence of *Brown* was in the area concerned this: it encouraged locals to begin examining rigorously the racial landscape of their own community and the plight of African Americans. In sum, Pottstown's Black freedom struggle, which aligned with the liberal interracialist ethos that permeated the national sphere during the postwar era, agitated beyond public schooling into other employment spaces in the private and public sectors. The local Black freedom activism also advocated for more integrated spaces outside employment, including leisure organizations and activities.[4]

Interestingly enough, most "Readers Say" authors did not identify themselves with their full names shortly after *Brown*. In fact, many of them used either an initial, a first name, a word, or a phrase as identifications. Ostensibly, the writers signed their letters as such because they did not want their real identities divulged, suggesting that they had real concerns about the political, economic, or social repercussions for their remarks from individuals who had both access to and control of local power.

Nevertheless, while the correspondence writers did not outright state who they were, the fact remains that their opinions provide great insight into the conditions of the local racial landscape in and around Pottstown, especially following *Brown*. The "Readers Say" authors also illuminated their role in laying the groundwork for ensuing civil rights activism in the local Black freedom struggle, which will also eventually receive attention by individuals and organizations across the United States (see chap. 5). In sum, this same civil rights work that combated de facto segregation in and around Pottstown only weeks preceding *Brown* might, in fact, be one of the earliest direct responses to the US Supreme Court ruling in the North, if not the country.[5]

Black and White Leadership Discuss *Brown* in Pottstown

The *Brown* ruling most certainly captivated many Americans in its subsequent aftermath. Whether in support or disagreement, American citizens had their opinions on the monumental case.[6] Days following *Brown*, one survey even marked 55 percent of Americans favoring the judgment, whereas 40 percent were not for it. In June 1954, another study revealed that those who supported the decision slightly dropped to 53 percent; then about six months later (December 1954), it moderately reduced by one percentage point to 52 percent. From 1955 to 1961, approximately 60 percent of Americans polled had also endorsed the ruling. In the end, while there was both a majority and increased endorsement of *Brown*, the evidence does not demonstrate collective solidarity among the American people and the ways in which they saw the ruling.[7]

Editorials throughout the United States also reflected that Americans held contrasting views soon after on the US Supreme Court's May 17, 1954, ruling. The June/July 1954 edition of the NAACP's official publication, the *Crisis*, for example, spotlighted remarks from newspapers across the United States. Writing in the affirmative, New Jersey's *Trenton Times* proudly announced, "What is especially encouraging about the Supreme Court decision is its frank and unqualified insistence that this country has no room for second-rate citizenship of the type implicit in a system of segregation." Similarly, the *Newark-Star Ledger*, also located in the Garden State, wrote, "The historic decision yesterday by the Supreme Court—declaring unconstitutional race segregation in the public schools—is one of the most important developments in the touchy problem of race relations since the emancipation of the slaves during the Civil War."[8]

While the parts of the South that sat on the outermost edge of what previously made up the Confederate States of America usually embraced *Brown*, even promising to implement it, historian Brian J. Daugherity writes that such sentiment was not the case for "the Deep South."[9] For example, Alabama's *Tuscaloosa News* declared, "Action by the United States Supreme Court in ruling that segregation in public schools is unconstitutional is a terrific blow to Southern custom and sentiment." The *New Orleans State* (Louisiana) echoed the prior exclusionary remarks, stating, "To say that its decision in this matter was not entirely popular with many Southern elected officials is to state the obvious."[10] At the same time, however, one must also note that viewpoints existed toward *Brown* even within the Deep South that contrasted the antidesegregation feelings illuminated by the Alabama and Louisiana presses.[11]

Yet as far as residents in and around Pottstown went, their views reflected the affirmative position on *Brown*, thereby aligning with the majority public sentiment found across the North on the US Supreme Court's revolutionary announcement. On May 19, 1954, two days following the declaration, the *Pottstown Mercury* interviewed prominent individuals from in and around the locale, inquiring about their feelings on the historic case. Published the next day (May 20), like the viewpoints of other progressive-minded Americans across the nation who supported racial integration and the liberal interracialist strategy, the interviewees expressed positive yet practical remarks on the breakthrough decision. Indeed, Black physician Daniel Lee, local activist who was on a hiatus as president of the Pottstown Civic League (PCL), declared that *Brown* was "the greatest thing since the Emancipation Proclamation." Lee also saw the judgment as a watershed moment in allowing Black America to have "greater respect" and trust toward the United States, which was finally following through with its long-overdue promises; African Americans could now truly experience equality. The Black professional was not, however, naive about how long it could possibly take for the whole South to implement the case. In fact, he acknowledged, *Brown* "may take a few years to make this change" in the region.

Likewise, African American activist and current head of the PCL, James H. Downing, the same local Black who wrote multiple *Pottstown Mercury* letters to the editor as mentioned in chapter 3, interpreted *Brown* as a game changer that transcended beyond public school doors. Downing argued, "We've been waiting for this a long time." The PCL activist additionally declared that "it will have tremendous influence—not only in the schools but everywhere." Black reverend and affiliate from the Pottstown branch of the NAACP, Ozzie Garlington, argued that *Brown* "would 'work out fine.'" Yet Garlington also lambasted "educators" who continued practicing the "outworn traditions" of separate but equal education. Nevertheless, Garlington was overall hopeful, particularly about the youth of the day and their separation from those discriminatory practices. In his mind, they were more progressive-thinking than those who preceded them. "I don't think the younger people are so eager to follow these traditions as their elders were" because "people today are more enlightened than ever before," Garlington observed. In fact, he continued, "Even in the South . . . eyes are being opened to the policy of equal rights for all."[12]

The same *Pottstown Mercury* article also documented leading Pottstown African Americans' comments on *Brown*'s global implications and importance. For example, Black educator E. I. Watson, who served as Pine Forge Institute's headmaster, contextualized his remarks in terms of the current Cold War between the United States and the Soviet Union. "It's about time our country came out like this and gave Communism a good blow in the teeth." Watson's remarks, while pro-American, nonetheless, conveyed a sharp critique of the United States' longtime practices of discrimination and injustice toward its Black population. Ostensibly, although he puts forth a common anticommunism Cold War argument, Watson also inconspicuously centers his declaration on promoting African American equality.[13]

Around the same time, the historically Black *Pittsburgh Courier* made identical anticommunism assertions as the African American SDA administrator following *Brown*.[14] Yet even closer to home, the *Pottstown Mercury*'s initial coverage of *Brown* spotlighted national NAACP heads constructing their rationalizations in fashions identical to Watson's as well as that of the African American newspaper. In one of their assessments of *Brown*, for instance, the NAACP heads declared how "the ruling 'gives the lie to the Communist propaganda that American democracy is decadent' and will have 'a great effect on American relations and prestige throughout the world.'"[15]

Likewise, local African American leadership further articulated international comparisons, as did Blacks throughout the United States responding directly to *Brown*. "If we can't live together in justice here," Garlington lamented, "we have no right to preach to other countries about 'one world.'" Black cleric Enoch N. Martin, who pastored Pottstown's Bethel African Methodist Episcopal (AME) congregation, made statements similar to Garlington's. In particular, Martin viewed America as the country, which others worldwide tried passionately to replicate—both philosophically and legally. Physician Lee, moreover, saw *Brown*'s global significance for his own nation. In the Black doctor's mind, the historic case had the real possibility in encouraging international "brotherhood," something he saw as "key to the world's" issues.[16]

In addition to *Brown*'s global influence and ramifications, the *Pottstown Mercury* noted remarks from prominent locals on whether the historical case would contribute to white pushback or hostility throughout the American South. In contrast to views held by southern white segregationists like Mississippi Democratic politician James Eastland, area leaders forecasted "that the States would abide by the court's decision." As far as violent backlash went, Watson even had faith in white southerners obeying and respecting the legal judgment. Indeed, Garlington and Martin echoed his optimistic position.

Yet a local white boarding school principal representing the Hill School in Pottstown had the most pragmatic yet sobering interpretation of *Brown* as it pertained to the manifestation of southern white pushback. Ostensibly, his analysis even had foreshadowing overtones. *Brown*, Edward T. Hall announced, rested on how each southern state implemented the legal case. Hall warned, "The significance of this decision may depend very largely upon the reaction of the governments in the individual states most concerned." In sum, Hall's remarks would prove especially true throughout the American South in the years following *Brown*.[17]And while not all southern whites responded to *Brown* with extreme pushback and consternation, as historian Clive Webb points out, there were those who did.[18]

Notwithstanding, the *Pottstown Mercury* article from late May 1954 shows that leadership from local African American and white communities still viewed *Brown* as a significant advancement in postwar America's overall Black freedom struggle. Clearly, local African Americans praised the legal decision and spoke about it in terms centering on the Cold War and American exceptionalism. At the same time, they conceptualized international-based arguments in order to help ameliorate Black America's overall agendas of equality, freedom, and interracial inclusion to their audience. Moreover, their remarks inconspicuously lambasted the hypocrisy of the American government preaching democracy to the world; however, their same comments additionally specified the indisputable fact that oppression and bigotry were largely African Americans' realities at home.

Most of the leadership spotlighted in the *Pottstown Mercury* article also had no anticipation of *Brown* causing any sort of interracial ruckus in the American South. Instead, for the most part, they saw the American South transitioning relatively smoothly as *Brown* unfolded. Yet the words of the Hill School's Hall represented insightful commentary and the only voice of ostensible descent in the rank and file of those leading Pottstown residents—African American and white. In hindsight, however, southern whites substantiated Hall's foreshadowing analysis with their steadfast, even militant, "massive resistance" to the liberal interracialist efforts that would catapult because of *Brown*.[19] In effect, the public statements captured on May 20, 1954, from the *Pottstown Mercury* provide a glimpse into how local leadership was, in fact, processing and viewing the high court announcement. They also show that *Brown* was undoubtedly captivating leading African Americans and whites in and around Pottstown.

Yet such discourses pertinent to *Brown* would not end there. Shortly after the US Supreme Court's historic civil rights judgment, the *Pottstown Mercury* began printing other local perspectives in its letter-to-the-editor section that shared contemporary relevance to *Brown*. Rather than evaluate

Brown from a national or even international perspective, however, the letters penned from locals essentially analyzed the liberal interracialist philosophy behind the landmark decision of postwar America. Specifically, the writers remarked on whether the desegregationist ethos of *Brown* had any significance or relevance to the plight of local African Americans. In the end, these "Readers Say" commentators illuminated in the *Pottstown Mercury* reveal early examples that shed light on how locals utilized the aftermath of *Brown* to ponder and reflect on the treatment of Blacks in the area. As a result, their remarks would serve as the groundwork to a subsequent era in developments across Pottstown's local Black freedom struggle.[20]

"Is Pottstown Segregated?"

Throughout the American South, white bigots began resisting *Brown* shortly after the ruling. Indeed, their "massive resistance" developments eventually mushroomed to include other discriminatory efforts, which targeted African Americans and grander attempts at integration.[21] In July 1954, for example, the White Citizens' Council appeared. Indianola (Mississippi) was the location of the inaugural council, and many more soon followed in the South. Moreover, enrollment within the White Citizens' Council reached about a quarter million individuals who opposed desegregation.[22]

At the same time, white southern politicians like Virginia congressperson Harry Byrd and Governor Thomas B. Stanley of the same state below the Mason-Dixon Line sharply lambasted *Brown* soon following its declaration. The white politicians even officially announced that they would fiercely protest public school desegregation efforts in their southern state.[23] Likewise, the *Register* out of Danville in the Old Dominion State sharply echoed the sentiments exhibited by Byrd and Stanley succeeding *Brown*. "Our own opinion is that a turn-coat court has misinterpreted a Force Amendment to strike a foul blow at public education in the South and at a way of life in the South which no court ruling can end by dictum," the *Register* lamented.[24]

Contrastingly, southern African Americans celebrated *Brown*.[25] Their Black counterparts across the industrialized North did so as well, historian

Jason Sokol adds, precisely since the ruling gave them some sense of optimism, let alone hope. Northern African Americans even saw the possibility of the verdict transcending the de jure power structure of education in the South, and thereby addressing racial inequality and injustices that permeated the similar, more inconspicuous structure on the northern side of the Mason-Dixon Line. However, many whites in the North rejected all points trying to relate their region's educational institutions' exclusionary practices toward African Americans with *Brown*. Of course, northern Blacks believed otherwise, demonstrating their opposing beliefs by concrete protest actions.[26]

While examining the North, historians outside Jack Dougherty have generally not captured much when it comes to the early aftermath of *Brown* and how the period relates directly to civil rights developments catapulting within the Black freedom struggle. Yet this was not the case in Pottstown. In short, *Brown* would inspire local citizens to write the *Pottstown Mercury* on topics connected to race in and around the small northern borough. Captured in its letter-to-the-editor section, these opinions transcended the judgment of the US Supreme Court. Moreover, while *Brown* declared the unlawfulness of segregation within public schooling, the correspondences published by the press addressed whether Pottstown was also guilty of similar exclusionary practices germane to the borough's own Jim Crow structure that targeted local African Americans. In sum, local Blacks and whites let their voices heard on the status of race relations in Pottstown and nearby and if racial discrimination was a local problem. The same locals' correspondences also forcefully articulated whether change needed to occur on the local front.[27]

Five days following *Brown* on May 22, 1954, the *Pottstown Mercury* published the first of the "Readers Say" letters. Centering on Pottstown churches practicing de facto segregation, the writer—who signed the correspondence as "One of the Majority," thereby suggesting that he or she was white—spotlighted a recent decision by Pennsylvania's Lutheran Ministerium to terminate "racial segregation in its churches." Writing within the context of the recent *Brown* announcement, the author continued, "I would suggest that all the churches take this position and actually put it into practice." Citing personal experience, the writer additionally centered his or her analysis on the local front, announcing, "I have lived in the Pottstown area for nearly 10 years and I have yet to see any Negroes admitted to white congregations."

In effect, the rationality behind the "Readers Say" writer's scathing correspondence was "not intended to stir up any racial animosity." Instead, the author desired "to point out that the soul of a man is the same in the sight of God regardless of the color of his skin." Next, the same writer noted the paradox of how Pottstown residents, Black and white, labored together "side by side" at their jobs—how their children went to school together—while congregations remained racially closed off and lamented, with even more animation and poignancy, "The color line has been established at the church door. No where [*sic*] else in our fine community does it exist." Following these sorrowful remarks—that indeed have a hint of African American intellectual and freedom fighter W. E. B. Du Bois to them—the author ends the thought-provoking essay by offering a solution to combating Pottstown church segregation. Specifically, the white contributor summoned "liberal-minded church leaders to assert themselves and put Pottstown" at the vanguard behind the American democratic, as well as the liberal interracialist, concept that unbiasedly demanded "liberty and equality for all."[28]

To be sure, the "Readers Say" writer's comments centering on segregation within the pews of Pottstown churches were not aberrations of mid-twentieth-century America. Historian Peter C. Murray and religious scholar Stephen R. Haynes have even demonstrated how such exclusionary practices permeated congregations located above and below the Mason-Dixon Line.[29] In February 1958, Dr. Martin Luther King Jr. likewise made points similar to the Pottstown letter-to-the-editor writer when responding to a white Oklahoman's correspondence in *Ebony* magazine. In short, the Oklahoman explained in the letter her disconnect with the contemporary white church and its racial exclusion of Blacks. She even felt combative against "*the word Christianity*" since whites exhibited such ungodly feelings "*toward the colored peoples of the world.*" She felt so strongly that she could not bring herself to congregate at a Christian assembly as long as racial prejudice permeated the institution. Moreover, the writer added that Oklahoma did not have congregations in which both Blacks and whites gathered, which made her rather disregard public assembly in the segregated space.

In response, King sharply concurred with her analysis of segregated congregations. The Black civil rights activist even noted how shockingly correct the following statement was, "that eleven o'clock on Sunday morning, when we stand to sing 'In Christ There Is No East or West,' is the most segregated hour in Christian America." Altogether, though, King finished his remarks about the white church on a positive note. However, his initial critique still blatantly rebuked the ways in which predominantly white congregations allowed racial bigotry within their Christian assemblies.[30]

While the *Pottstown Mercury*'s "Readers Say" author from May 22, 1954, specified de facto segregation within local congregations, the letter would also play an organic role in sparking a local debate on whether racial prejudice transcended houses of worship in the small northern borough. Thus, the writer made all who read the letter have to start sincerely reexamining how racially integrated and harmonious Pottstown was during the age of northern Jim Crow. At the same time, the "Readers Say" author essentially informed his or her readership, especially white readership, to examine themselves. In doing so, they can then look at how they treated their Black counterparts.

The general clarion call put out by "One of the Majority" for white Pottstown to truthfully examine itself on the ways in which it treated local African Americans was initially met with outright rebuke to the extent that one group responded shortly after, denying that the practice of de facto segregation transpired in local churches. On May 25, 1954, white pastors who led seven Pottstown congregations of the Lutheran denomination jointly authored a response piece in the "Readers Say" section that straightway rebutted the prior remarks. Specifically, the white clerics fervently declared that they had remorse when it came to the correspondence's conclusion from May 22. Referencing the Lutheran meeting, the white clerics even publicly announced how they attended the gathering and unequivocally agreed with the Christian organization's racially progressive decision.

Moreover, the white ministers directly challenged a central argument made by "One of the Majority." In the clerics' view, their congregations and other church-related functions welcomed everyone "without regard for racial origin." Rather, they asserted, all that was required by the white ministers' was that individuals accepted their congregations' Lutheran doctrines.[31]

Four days later (May 29), an individual identifying as "Methodist" echoed the white pastors' sentiments. In short, the writer questioned whether the May 22 author attended church services because, according to "Methodist," a few local congregations actually had African Americans and whites worshipping together. At the same time, the author "Methodist" lambasted the prior letter writer's statements about if local clergymen excluded Blacks from their assemblies. "I have lived in Pottstown longer than One of the Majority," the May 29 contributor declared, "long enough to know that the ministers of our churches will admit anyone who follows the Christian faith." In closing, the writer finished the combative essay by praising the white Christian pastors' public rebuke to the May 22 correspondence.[32]

On May 28, another "Readers Say" author from Pottstown, who identified only by the masculine first name "Jimmy," composed an analysis that supported both the Lutheran clerics' and the Methodist writer's assessments. However, while the writer concurred that Pottstown churches were racially integrated, he simultaneously believed that de facto segregation existed "in some privately-operated places of amusement and recreation" within the small northern locale. Moreover, the contributor finished his analysis about African American discrimination within Pottstown by pointing out that Pennsylvania law prohibited "racial segregation at any public place." Ostensibly, however, his tone suggests that he thought the situation was unfortunate. "Wouldn't it be wonderful if these conditions could be eliminated without court action," the contributor Jimmy lamented.[33] Interestingly enough, Shandy Hill made similar reflective observations about the local northern Jim Crow structure in *Dear Sir*. "The Supreme Court decision made it clear that the 14th Amendment was deemed to preclude segregation in the public schools," Hill remarked. "Pottstown wasn't concerned with this," he added. "Its schools were desegregated." However, Hill asked, "Would the decision have any bearing on segregation of other kinds?" In sum, one type that Hill noted regarded racial discrimination that was not legally mandated. Put differently, the white editor specified the more inconspicuous yet pervasive brand of anti-Black oppression, especially prevalent outside the South, which was de facto exclusion.[34]

In a somewhat similar vein, another May 28, 1954, "Readers Say" correspondence remarked on private enterprises in Pottstown. In particular, these May 28 writers, who identified themselves as "Two June Graduates," illuminated how such enterprises practiced the northern brand of Jim Crow, which was more camouflaged and unobtrusive, yet still solidified throughout the local front. Set to graduate the following month from Pottstown High School, their foremost premise in writing into the borough newspaper was to bring awareness to the employment plight of their African American classmates. In addressing the topic that had so galvanized recent "Readers Say" responses—"Is Pottstown segregated?"—the authors began by providing a generalized assessment about what, in their view, most in Pottstown's opinions were on the segregation question. "Many of us are led to believe that Pottstown is not segregated. Is this really a true statement?" The writers then pointed out that "in many aspects, this is not a true statement." Yet as far as employment went, they contended, racial exclusion in Pottstown was particularly accurate.

Like the "Readers Say" writer Jimmy, the essayists Two June Graduates then contrasted their previous statements with Pottstown's own racism, which was, in their minds, largely prevalent. In fact, they passionately declared that "when it comes to jobs," the locale exceptionally practiced de facto segregation. "Take, for instance," the writers charged, "the job situation confronting Negro high school graduates—especially the commercial students." They continued, "Is it because they do not want a Negro boy or girl to sit behind a desk and perform secretarial or stenographic duties[?]" The authors then posed an analysis that challenged Pottstown whites' prejudice while simultaneously bringing into question if they also held socioeconomic biases toward the borough's African Americans. The writers asked their audience, "Are we much more content to have them scrub our floors or clean our houses[?]"

Following their sincere remarks, the "Readers Say" writers then turned their attention to an example of an established business owner. During the early 1950s, they noted, the individual demonstrated both his uprightness and his commitment to the liberal interracialist ethos. In particular, the business owner smashed through "this so-called 'ice'" by hiring an African American female "as a stenographer." In an optimistic tone, the writers also added that few other African Americans received local employment offers within the same field.

To be sure, a deeper examination into the language of the Two June Graduates' May 28 "Readers Say" letter suggests that the writers were liberal-thinking whites sympathetic to the occupational discrimination that their Black classmates encountered firsthand in Pottstown. For example, when talking about their peers, "Negro high school graduates," and the hopeless Pottstown employment market that awaited them, the writers utilized the pronoun "they." In doing so, the writers distinguished themselves from the individuals on whom the argument centered: their Black classmates, as well as Black Pottstown more broadly. At the same time, the essayists' observations corroborated larger themes African Americans experienced of discrimination, inequality, and suffering. Moreover, when asking whether local white employers did "not want a Negro boy or girl to" work for them in skilled positions, the writers used the pronoun *we*. Again, the contributors aligned themselves with the white employers who were only satisfied with Blacks working as unskilled laborers and domestics. From both demographic and racial standpoints, by using *we*, the "Readers Say" writers additionally identified as members of Pottstown's white population. Finally, the authors subtly labeled themselves as whites when they employed the pronoun *our* in the clause "our floors or clean our houses."[35]

"Is There Discrimination?"

In addition to the previous letter to the editors, articles published by the *Pottstown Mercury* in early June 1954 further highlighted the unequal treatment that local African Americans endured. In short, the writings suggest that the borough newspaper was most certainly paying direct attention to what was on the hearts and minds of its local readership. Therefore, one way to interpret the rationale behind the newspaper's articles, this chapter suggests, was to galvanize readership into expressing their personal views toward whether racial discrimination was a problem in the small northern borough via the *Pottstown Mercury*.[36]

As the US Supreme Court ruling in *Brown* spotlighted the pervasiveness of inequality across the sphere of public education during the early postwar, the *Pottstown Mercury* simultaneously put the local front on notice by lambasting the entrenched presence of racial equality within the borough. To draw attention to the current state of local race relations in the Jim Crow North, however, the borough newspaper documented the academic milestones of African American scholar Jessie L. Matthews. A distinguished June 1954 Pottstown High School graduate, Matthews had an impressive résumé while at the local educational institution.[37] According to the school's yearbook, *Troiad 1954*, Matthews was in the "*Honor Club*" as well as "*Troiad Editorial Staff, Troiad Business Staff*," and the "*Library Council*."[38] Her participation in the library council turned into a lifelong interest, for she followed a similar path in her college focus by majoring in library science.[39]

Interestingly enough, Matthews and her family did not grow up in the area, once again demonstrating how Black migration affected the small northern borough. In fact, before Pottstown, they lived in Charleston, West Virginia. Moreover, when comparing her Pottstown educational experience with the one as a West Virginia student, Matthews noted how "Pottstown schools" were more exceptional. Matthews additionally recalled how "West Virginia [then] . . . had the separate schools" for white and Black students. However, the Black scholar gladly continued, the recent *Brown* decision nullified such discriminatory policies.[40]

Echoing statements like the "Readers Say" letter writers who supported the argument that de facto segregation permeated structures within the locale, the *Pottstown Mercury* reflected on Matthews's recent accomplishments to speak about the larger discriminatory conditions faced by local African Americans. In an editorial entitled "The Same Opportunity?," the newspaper pointed out the sad realities that Pottstown Blacks endured. In particular, it noted that Matthews would soon matriculate into Kutztown State Teachers College (Kutztown University of Pennsylvania) to study library science. However, the newspaper asked its readership several poignant questions. First, would Matthews obtain employment solely "at a 'colored' school?" The second question then drove the analysis back home, inquiring directly about how racially progressive Pottstown was. "Would Pottstown, for instance" give Matthews's employment "in the public schools?"

From there, the same *Pottstown Mercury* editorial finished the clear-headed questioning by inquiring whether the ethos behind the small northern borough's progressivism related to not only local hiring practices but also the forward thinking of its white citizenry. "Would Pottstown school authorities employ a 'colored' teacher?" the newspaper asked, and "Would Pottstown parents have any scruples against Negroes teaching their children?" The second question must have most certainly struck a nerve with local white readership since it directly questioned their own personal sensibilities, emotions, and perspectives toward their Black counterparts.

On the other hand, the same *Pottstown Mercury* editorial understood clearly that readers could plausibly view the June 11 column as "a touchy subject," particularly for local African Americans. Nonetheless, the newspaper pointed back to the *Brown* decision and how the announcement fostered "much discussion on discrimination." Yet juxtaposing Pottstown with the American South, which shared extreme consternation when it came to integrated schooling among Black and white pupils, the *Pottstown Mercury* revealed that such worriment was not an issue within the small northern borough. Specifically, the press asserted, because racial "segregation" was not legally enforced like the de jure structure. At the same time—and to further demonstrate that the *Pottstown Mercury* paid specific attention to its "Readers Say" section and the recent discourses surrounding the racial landscape of the small northern locale—the newspaper mentioned the letters from May 22 and 25, respectively. "When a correspondent to Readers Say recently hinted that Pottstown's churches would not accept 'colored' parishioners," it conveyed, "a large segment of the clergy rose in wrath." Moreover, the newspaper wrote, the white clerics contended outright that their worship centers allowed everyone—whatever racial and ethnic background—into their local assemblies.

While the *Pottstown Mercury* editorial agreed that Christian congregations in Pottstown did not totally exclude local African Americans, it also continued by making a fascinating differentiation. In sum, it wrote in an emphatic tone, "There's no segregation in Pottstown!" However, "What of discrimination?" The newspaper continued by spotlighting examples of employment sectors in Pottstown and the lack of African American workers within them. Specifically, do local companies employ Blacks at all, the

Pottstown Mercury inquired, as well as offer "them the jobs whites perform and pay them the same wages?" Ostensibly, the *Pottstown Mercury* editorial reflected on how a few businesses impartially employed local African Americans. In fact, the newspaper noted, Pottstown even had an influential and sole Black labor unionist who "led for many years."(James H. Corum was probably the African American referenced.) However, the newspaper editorial expressed, this was not the standard when it came to companies that operated in and around the small northern borough.

Finally, the *Pottstown Mercury* editorial went on by questioning whether Pottstown businesses even gave local African Americans opportunities when it concerned "white collar" employment. Citing the Hemlock Row Black freedom struggle in nearby Stowe (see chap. 3) from early 1950, it declared that the answer was emphatically no. In fact, these local Blacks only held "domestic jobs" and employment at "dry cleaning plants," while clerical and other professional-related work excluded them in Pottstown. Therefore, the same newspaper editorial wondered what the real purpose was, then, behind local African Americans like Matthews even attending university. In the end, the provocative *Pottstown Mercury* editorial finished by further stirring the sensitive topic on the state of local race relations. Specifically, it did so by leaving those who read the article with the following inquiry: "Is there discrimination?"[41]

To be sure, the *Pottstown Mercury* articles, corroborated by the "Readers Say" letters on the small northern borough, reflected the larger exclusionary experience of Black Americans around the mid-twentieth century. For example, the statements examining practices of racial exclusion in "white collar" work coincided. In 1950, Blacks comprised 2.6 percent of the entire "clerical" occupation field in the United States and only represented 3.9 percent of the same field ten years later (1960). The same also related, for instance, to domestic work that the "Readers Say" authors essentially noted. Here, African Americans tallied 28.5 percent of "service workers" in both "private" homes and outside such living quarters in 1950. In 1960, Blacks occupied 27.1 percent of the same "service workers" categories nationwide.[42] Furthermore, as far as exclusion went outside employment, remarks that the "Readers Say" authors made in 1954 also corroborate the larger discriminatory conditions endured by African Americans during the postwar era.[43]

"Not Even Considered"

The almost monthlong debate analyzing the racial landscape of Pottstown and the area in the pages of the *Pottstown Mercury* continued into mid-June (and beyond, see chap. 5). Four days after the June 11, 1954, editorial, the *Pottstown Mercury* published a "Readers Say" letter that pushed back against the column's assessments of racial bigotry germane to the local Jim Crow structure. Appearing on June 15, the writer, who penned the letter as "T.M.W.," found the earlier piece problematic. "Since the question of 'segregation' or 'discrimination' has been raised again," the writer said, "I would like to say something that was passed along to me by a friend of another race."

Writing from nearby Pennsburg, Pennsylvania, the author did agree that local Blacks only desired the same chance as whites pertaining to acquiring employment. However, the writer also argued that it was not all right for African Americans to obtain work predicated solely on their racial makeup. From there, the writer continued by pointing criticism back toward Pottstown African Americans, especially those who exclaimed "discrimination" upon finding out that they did not get hired. In the correspondent's view, this untrue claim created "a persecution complex," which, in turn, strongly influenced other Blacks' psyche. In sum, the writer wanted his or her audience to know that such accusations surrounding racial prejudice were not necessarily always legitimate.[44]

Before going any further, it is worth noting that the previous writer makes arguments identical to former Black communist Manning Johnson in his 1958 book, *Color, Communism, and Common Sense*.[45] Once an active communist, Johnson eventually became disenchanted and thus departed "the party."[46] Ultimately, he even helped the American government in its ideological crusade against communism during the Cold War as "an FBI [Federal Bureau of Investigation] undercover agent."[47] In short, Johnson commented in *Color, Communism, and Common Sense* on how erroneous "red trickery" was because the far-left doctrine put "the blame for all the Negroes' ills at the door of the white leaders in America." By doing so, communism absolved any "responsibility" Blacks had in improving their own conditions. "The result is a persecution complex," Johnson continued, "a warped belief that the white man's prejudices, the white man's system, the white man's government is responsible for everything."[48] Some five years later, several passages from *Color, Communism, and Common Sense* were even noted to the US Senate's Committee on Commerce during discussions of S.1732, *A Bill to Eliminate Discrimination in Public Accommodations Affecting Interstate Commerce* (1963).[49]

Evidence does not explicitly reveal whether there is an ideological link between the "Readers Say" writer from Pennsburg's letter and Johnson's *Color, Communism, and Common Sense*. However, the interpretations of the two aforementioned documents at least speak to the fact that "a persecution complex" argument was not solely confined to discourse, rationale, and intellectual space in southeastern Pennsylvania. Rather, it transcended the Jim Crow region in early postwar America. On the other hand, the ethos behind "a persecution complex" perspective ostensibly aligns with whites in the North, who emphasized that the practice of "color blindness" permeated their communities. However, they utilized "color blindness" within an intellectual framework laced in contradictions and paradoxes. As historian Jason Sokol writes, "the ideology of color blindness helped explain how one could vote for a black politician . . . and how one could at the same time countenance segregation in school. In two different realms—electoral politics and school integration," he continues, "whites' commitment to color blindness produced two very different results."[50] Political scientist Jeanne Theoharis and historian Brian Purnell likewise observe, "Color-blindness blamed social inequality and lack of access on the motivations, choices, and culture of the individual, not on systems, institutions, or power structures" entrenched throughout the American North.[51] In the end, and similar to "a persecution complex" argument, regional whites' interpretation when it came to "color blindness" deflected unequal conditions in society back on their marginalized Black counterparts and not the ubiquitous yet clandestine practices of de facto segregation that they endured during the postwar era.[52]

Now with the continual back-and-forth discussion taking place in the "Readers Say" section of the *Pottstown Mercury* subsequent to *Brown*, it should come as no surprise that a Black writer from the borough responded to the June 15, 1954, correspondence with blatant criticism. The African American graduated from Pottstown High School the same month as Jessie Matthews. In a correspondence published on June 18, the contributor viewed the premise behind the June 15 piece as simply inaccurate. Moreover, the writer acknowledged that locally, "the subject of 'segregation' has been of such great interest during the past month." In an antagonistic tone, the Black writer additionally called out the Pennsburg correspondent. "He needs someone to straighten him out," the Pottstown African American zealously declared, "and I take this upon myself."

From there, however, the writer's response piece at times reads more like an analytical appraisal than an opinion letter, soberly dissecting claims made in the June 15 correspondence. For example, the Black author concurred that employment must be grounded on skill set rather than racial background. In the Pottstown author's view, however, local African Americans were not being granted employment interviews. Thus, the June 15 argument centering on so-called rejection had no merit whatsoever. In other words, since Pottstown African Americans were not receiving employment offers, how, then, could they exhibit the sentiment of feeling turndown, the writer asked. In further clarification, the Black essayist declared that local African Americans only desired a level playing field and that opportunities be based on the individual's qualifications juxtaposed to race. However, as the author saw it, upon finding out an applicant was Black, the individual was "automatically refused"—that is, the writer clarified, excluding "Civil Service employment," because it was directly under the government's authority.

Furthermore, the Black "Readers Say" author lambasted the subjectivity of the June 15 contributor, suggesting that the individual conveyed judgments based on "facts" rather than "opinions." In closing, the African American writer turned attention back to Jessie Matthews and her academic accomplishments. While Matthews had such scholarly qualifications, would the soon-to-be Kutztown student have the same employment opportunities within Pottstown, the Black author inquired. Instead, the contributor finished the question, would Matthews have to seek employment outside Pottstown, that is, he directly posed, "or must she go South?" [53]

As the *Pottstown Mercury* printed the "Readers Say" correspondences and articles, local newspaper staff, including Shandy Hill, meanwhile, had been hard at work behind the scenes on an important project. In short, this "series" would eventually serve as the munition that helped ignite the high point of the local Black freedom struggle in Pottstown and beyond. Nevertheless, the *Pottstown Mercury* letter-to-the-editor correspondences previously mentioned indeed demonstrate how Blacks and whites in the area already had direct interest as far as the plight and circumstances of the local African American collective went.[54]

"We Shall Continue to Do So"

According to legal historian Michael J. Klarman, the US Supreme Court justices' unified decision in *Brown* was not necessarily an obvious conclusion. In fact, by assessing previous opinions from the nine before the May 1954 ruling, one sees that the members genuinely disagreed and vacillated over the correct announcement to make. Nevertheless, in due time they eventually ruled their undivided position in *Brown*.[55]

Yet as the justices exhibited ambivalence toward the constitutionality of *Brown* in its lead-up, the *Afro Magazine*—an edition published by the *Baltimore Afro-American*—about five months before printed correspondences from outside editors, centering on how their presses would interpret an announcement about desegregation within public education from the high court. The *Afro Magazine* additionally printed the letters on December 12, 1953, only days following the *Afro-American* publishing "the historic reargument of the five school segregation cases before the Supreme Court was" commenced, which the NAACP spearheaded.[56] "If the Supreme Court outlaws segregation in public schools," the *Afro Magazine* inquired, "what position will your publication take editorially on this decision[?]"[57] In short, Shandy Hill wrote one of the letters, and his correspondence shared printed space with letters from editors of six other newspapers. They included the *Chicago Tribune* (Chicago, Illinois), *Hertfort County Herald* (Ahoskie, North Carolina), *Trenton Times Newspapers* (Trenton, New Jersey), *Richmond News Leader* (Richmond, Virginia), *News-Journal Company* (Wilmington, Delaware), and the *News* (New Castle, Pennsylvania).

Interestingly enough, all of the editors' responses to the *Afro Magazine* query at least stated that their newspapers would back the high court's judgment. Some of the editors, including Hill, even expressed that provided the US Supreme Court outlawed the discriminatory practice within public education, they would, in turn, praise the announcement outright. By doing so, therefore, they demonstrated both their subjectivity and their racial progressivism on the matter. Hill, the *News*, and the *Trenton Times Newspapers'* editors also stressed that government did not legally sanction racial separation in their regions above the Mason-Dixon Line. At the same time, Hill and the *News* editor made similar points that spoke to the ways in which their locales had more harmonious race relations.[58]

Now when thinking about the *Pottstown Mercury's* journalistic record of accomplishments, it should come as no surprise that Hill gave the *Afro Magazine* feedback that fully backed the liberal interracialist strategy. Writing in that same racially progressive ethos that permeated the consciousness of many in postwar America, Hill boldly declared, "We have been plugging anti-discrimination and bigotry for the twenty years I have occupied the editorial desk." He continued, then, by unwaveringly affirming, "We shall continue to do so." At the same time, Hill conveyed how the *Pottstown Mercury* "made progress" locally toward beating racial prejudice. In particular, he stressed that his Pottstown press even had "the friendship of the little fellow who" was, in fact, enduring such anti-Black sentiments across the local northern Jim Crow structure. Overall, Hill's arguments expressed in the *Afro Magazine* most certainly had validity, especially when one stresses the professional partnership between the *Pottstown Mercury* and the local African American community that began crystallizing during World War II.[59]

In the end, it was under Hill's leadership and in the aftermath of *Brown* that the *Pottstown Mercury's* same commitment Hill corresponded the *Afro Magazine* in early December 1953 that continued to foster and percolate. Indeed, the *Pottstown Mercury's* letter-to-the-editor pieces and articles in 1954 eventually launched civil rights discourses in and around the borough that, in turn, catapulted tangible Black freedom activism. Altogether, the local newspaper would not again match the same intensity, impact, or reach of journalistic advocacy work that it had shortly following *Brown*.[60]

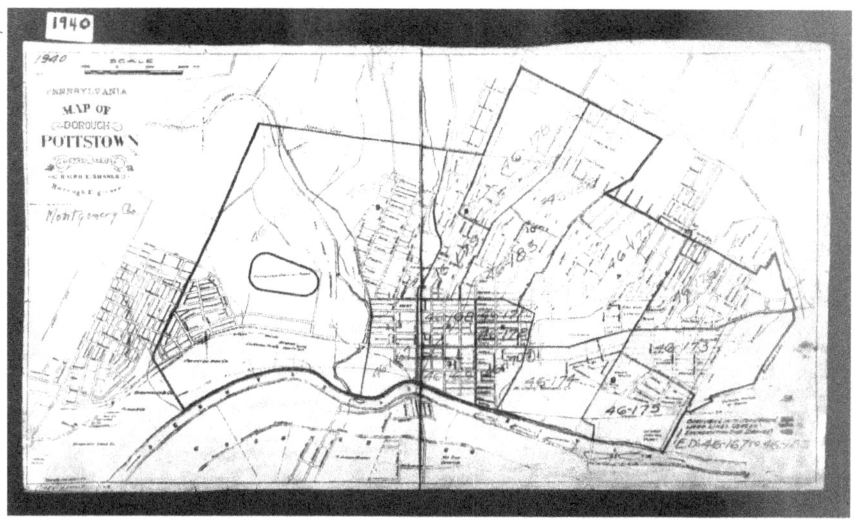

Census map of Pottstown from 1940. Courtesy of the US National Archives and Records Administration, https://catalog.archives.gov/id/5838037.

Another Virginia native, Reverend Heywood L. Butler was actively a part of the local Black freedom struggle during both World War II and the postwar period. March 1950. Courtesy of the *Pottstown Mercury*.

Like his brothers, William D. Corum was largely involved with local civil rights work through World War II and the postwar period. October 1949. Courtesy of the *Pottstown Mercury*.

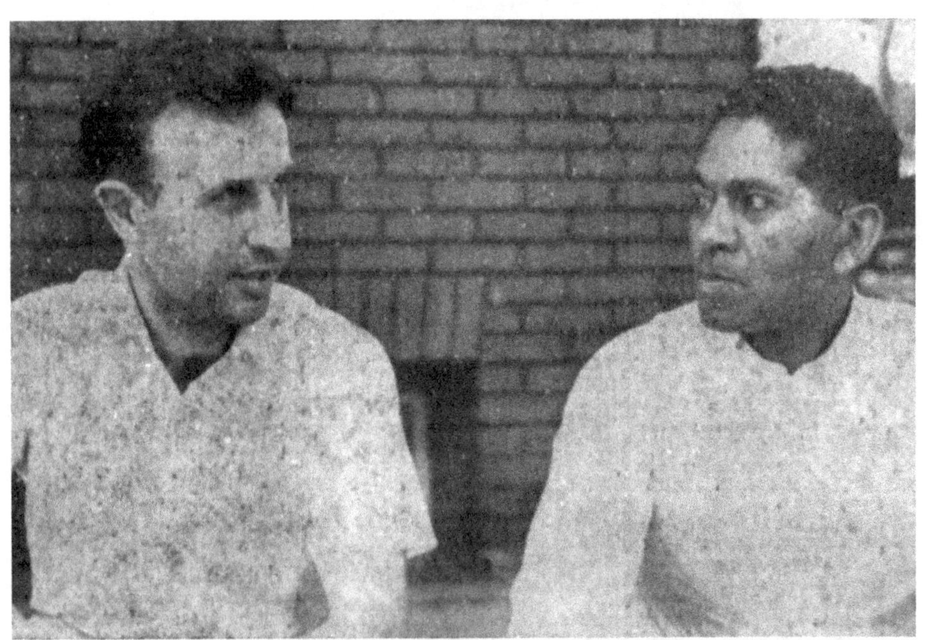

Picture of James H. Corum, accompanied by another labor activist, as Local 2326 president. June 1946. Courtesy of the *Pottstown Mercury*.

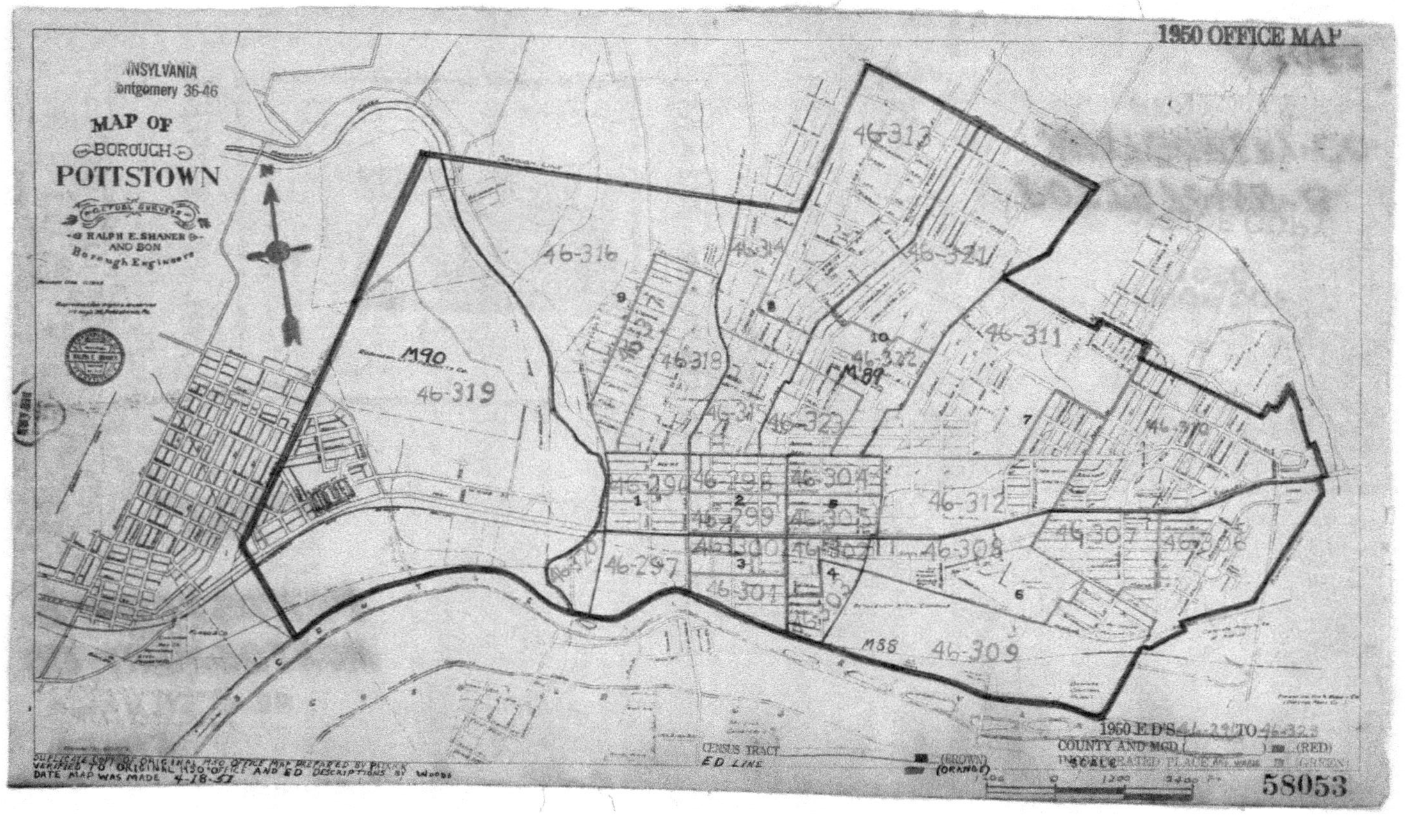

Census map of Pottstown from 1950. Courtesy of the US National Archives and Records Administration, https://catalog.archives.gov /id/36433303.

Shandy Hill almost single-handedly cultivated the ethos of racial progressivism, let alone progressivism more broadly, that both pervaded and infused the *Pottstown Mercury* during his lengthy tenure, especially from World War II through the late 1960s. August 1969. Courtesy of the *Pottstown Mercury*.

Thomas W. Corum was actively involved in the local Black freedom struggle, as well as civil rights activism, which led particularly to him becoming Pottstown's pioneering Black police officer. The illustration commemorated his lengthy policing tenure only a few years after he died in service to the local community. May 1969. Courtesy of the *Pottstown Mercury*.

Picture of a structure being renovated before the official opening of Pine Forge Institute. August 1946. Courtesy of the *Pottstown Mercury*.

Plans for Their Modern Home Are Shattered

An industrial laborer with Stanley G. Flagg, Robert Parsons was one of several local Blacks from Stowe, Pennsylvania, that white *Pottstown Mercury* journalist Frank J. Dostal interviewed regarding the civil rights housing struggle, which examined Hemlock and Cottage Rows. March 1950. Courtesy of the *Pottstown Mercury*.

Homes from Cottage Row as they looked in early 1950 during the civil rights housing struggle in nearby Stowe, Pennsylvania, that partnered the *Pottstown Mercury* and local African Americans. March 1950. Courtesy of the *Pottstown Mercury*.

Business and Professional Week Inaugurated in Pottstown

Both Reverend Heywood L. Butler and physician Daniel Lee played active roles in the local Black freedom struggle. June 1949. Courtesy of the *Pottstown Mercury*.

Civil rights discourses centering on the academic milestones of Jessie Matthews assisted directly in igniting the height of Pottstown's Black freedom struggle. August 1954. Courtesy of the *Pottstown Mercury*.

Pottstown Mercury journalist Normand Poirier wrote "the series," which demonstrated emphatically that Jim Crow permeated the local front. June 1954. Courtesy of the *Pottstown Mercury*.

Does Jim Crow Live in Pottstown!

To get the answer to this question, The Mercury assigned Staff Writer Normand Poirier to conduct an exhaustive survey concerning all phases of Pottstown life. His intensive investigation took him into Pottstown schools, stores, hotels, plants—in fact, anywhere discrimination against Negroes might exist. The results of this month-long survey will be told in a series of news stories in The Mercury next week. Watch Monday for the first of the series: "Does Mister James P. Crow, Esquire, Live in Pottstown?"

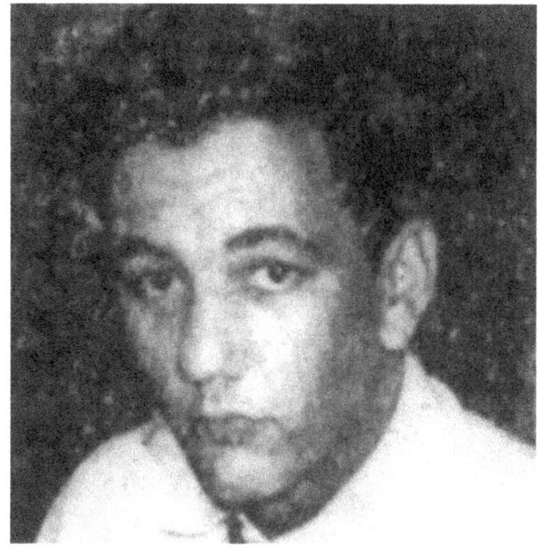

Normand Poirier's summer 1954 "series" examining local manifestations of Jim Crow in the subsequent aftermath of *Brown v. Board* helped launch both local and regional developments across the Black freedom struggle, even sparking national interest. April 1955. Courtesy of the *Lincoln Clarion*, https://digital.shsmo.org /digital/collection/LUClarion/id/2419.

The last article from Normand Poirier's "Jim Crow, Yankee Style" series, which notes that physician Daniel Lee was the main contact regarding individuals interested in combating the covert yet pervasive anti-Black policies on the local front. August 1954. Courtesy of the AFRO American Newspaper Archives, Baltimore, Maryland.

ENDORSEMENTS

"Any plan to create a spirit of friendliness and brotherhood which tends to elevate the social standing of humanity deserves the wholehearted support of freedom loving people." CAPT. C. ROBERT FLINN, Salvation Army.

* * *

"The POTTSTOWN PLAN is certainly within the realm of the democratic way of life and goes beyond the political patterns of our society and embraces the religious conviction of the "Fatherhood of God and the Brotherhood of Man." I heartily endorse this plan." REV. MAURICE E. HOOVER, Searles Memorial Methodist Church.

* * *

"I am happy to endorse the Pottstown Plan. We shall only be victorius when we believe these things in our hearts and as individuals live them day by day. As the Plan makes clear, the issue depends on the individual." H. BERT SHAW, President of The Pottstown School Board.

* * *

"Equal opportunity for all is a part of our American heritage. The efforts of the Human Relations committee of Pottstown should be supported by every citizen of our community." ROBERT C. CONNER, International Representative, UAW-CIO.

* * *

"I am happy to endorse any movement which will relieve tension between racial and religious groups in these United States of America." CHARLES R. WYLIE, President, Board of Directors, Memorial Hospital.

* * *

"I think this is a wonderful plan which should teach us to live together just as harmoniously as we, in sports, have learned to play together." RICHARD "DICK" RICKETTS, JR.

* * *

"With one purpose in mind — the betterment of humanity — let us all stand united under one God for the equal rights and privileges of all mankind. With this statement I sincerely endorse the Pottstown Plan." I. WAYNE KNAUSE, President, Borough Council.

* * *

"The Pottstown Plan is a definite step forward, a step that merits the support of all of us." JOSEPH PRINCE, Attorney.

* * *

"The Catholic Church, throughout its history, has recognized the dignity of the human beginning as a child of God. Since the Pottstown Plan is based on that premise I heartily endorse it." REV. WILLIAM BEGLEY, Rector, St. Aloysius Church.

Patron
Rural Route 2
Local

THE POTTSTOWN PLAN

¶ Pottstown is a good town. We like it very much. Otherwise, we wouldn't be here. But recently, we've come to see that it could be an even better town for each of us if it were equally good for all of us. This is what we mean: last Summer, the Pottstown Mercury uncovered some disturbing facts. That newspaper made it clear that some of our citizens have NOT found our city a friendly place to live.

¶ These are Americans, as we are. But racial and religious discrimination keep them from sharing fully in community life. Discrimination makes it very hard for them to find a good home, obtain a good job, and raise their families right.

¶ Like you, we believe in fair play. We don't like these facts. We believe something can and must be done to change the picture. And this is the time. All over the country cities — big and small — are facing up to the business of assuring "liberty and justice for all." Perhaps our POTTSTOWN PLAN can help others in other towns — for it is a simple patriotic plan that requires no expense and no new organization.

¶ Big jobs get done when there is a will to do them and the muscles to carry out the will. The muscles of Pottstown are its schools, churches, hospitals, business groups, labor unions, service clubs, veterans' organizations, news media. The will to do it is our love for justice, a love natural to Americans.

¶ The POTTSTOWN PLAN is simply to have the community flex its muscles and take THE FIRST STEP — that is, that every group in town, from the Chamber of Commerce to the smallest Cub Scout den, is asked to consider the problem, talk about it, and come up with ONE PROJECT, no matter how small, which will help build a fairer, friendlier Pottstown.

¶ Each group will be asked to name its project and to report to the committee on how it is progressing. The Mercury will be asked to publish the reports.

¶ When each group — each muscle — moves, Pottstown will be taking a FIRST STEP which may be felt around the world!

WHAT OTHERS ARE DOING

1.—One nearby school system has set up short in-service courses in human relations for its teachers with credit given for the course.

2.—Some PTAs are raising money to send teachers to Summer workshops in human relations. And they're educating parents on the subject through lectures and discussions.

3.—Churches, both Catholic and Protestant, and synagogs are giving time and thought to the problem. One churchmen's group began a now famous Forum which unites one hundred men out of every racial, religious and nationality group in town for regular supper meetings to work for understanding in their community.

4.—A Junior Chamber of Commerce gives an award each year to the person who has done the most for racial and religious justice.

5.—A hospital, recognizing the great need for nurses, is making a special effort to recruit colored girls for training.

6.—Some service clubs are putting special program emphasis on human relations. One is backing a "Music of the Faiths" evening when choirs sing for democracy.

WHAT WILL YOU AND YOUR GROUP DO? YOU CAN MAKE A DIFFERENCE!

COMMITTEE MEMBERS:

Arnold Markowitz	Carl M. Herbine
William Barber	Marjorie Penney
Samuel Frost	Frank McCord
Rev. Arthur Simpson	Henry Dozier
J. Wayne Knause	Rev. A. V. Pinkney
Willard Hetzel	Mrs. Evelyn Gaut
James Corum	Rev. Brent T. Watson
Frank Bundy	Joseph Prince
Norman Poirier	Mrs. Carl Pickar
Francis Banks	Dr. Daniel Lee
Dr. Herbert Haslam	Morris Miller

For further information write THE POTTSTOWN PLAN, PO BOX 186

ENDORSEMENTS

"Any plan to create a spirit of friendliness and brotherhood which tends to elevate the social standing of humanity deserves the wholehearted support of freedom loving people."

CAPT. C. ROBERT FLYNN, Salvation Army.

* * *

"Equal opportunity for all is a part of our American heritage. The efforts of the Human Relations committee of Pottstown should be supported by every citizen of our community."

ROBERT C. CONNER,
International Representative, UAW-CIO.

* * *

"I am happy to endorse any movement which will relieve tension between racial and religious groups in these United States of America."

CHARLES R. WYLIE,
President, Board of Directors, Memorial Hospital.

* * *

"I think this is a wonderful plan which should teach us to live together just as harmoniously as we, in sports, have learned to play together."

RICHARD "DICK" RICKETTS, JR.

* * *

"With one purpose in mind — the betterment of humanity — let us all stand united under one God for the equal rights and privileges of all mankind. With this statement I sincerely endorse the Pottstown Plan."

J. WAYNE KNAUER,
Borough Council.

* * *

"The Pottstown Plan is a definite step forward, a step that merits the support of all of us."

JOSEPH PRINCE,
Attorney.

* * *

"The Catholic Church, throughout its history, has recognized the dignity of the human beginning as a child of God. Since the Pottstown Plan is based on that premise I heartily endorse it."

REV. WILLIAM BEGLEY,
Rector, St. Aloysius Church.

ENDORSEMENTS

"I am pleased for this opportunity to congratulate your group for the splendid work you have done in our community in the past, and hope that you will continue on with the same success in the future."

JOHN B. HARTENSTINE, JR.,
Burgess of Pottstown.

* * *

"Good human relations among all of its people is essential to the health and progress of any community. I believe the Pottstown Council on Human Relations should receive the cooperation of every one in its work against prejudice and bigotry."

ROBERT H. McKINNEY, JR.
Borough Manager.

* * *

"That all men should enjoy equal opportunity in every field whether politics, industry, religion, the law is a basic tenet of the American way of life. Fortunately for Pottstown, the Human Relations Council is actively helping us to unite into a common brotherhood. I heartily endorse the Pottstown committee for striving to make that equality a reality in our community. I pledge my help to this momentous task."

RAYMOND F. NESTER,
President Borough Council

* * *

"Those people who have been responsible for the progress made under the Pottstown Plan are to be congratulated. The cause for which they have labored deserves the support of every public spirited citizen of this borough."

HAVARD E. FOSNOCHT,
Superintendent of Schools.

* * *

"Two years ago in the beginning of the Pottstown Plan I was happy to add my endorsement. Since then great strides have been taken and many achievements accomplished. I can again be grateful for the opportunity of adding my endorsement and do believe in the years that lie ahead "Greater Things Then These" shall be accomplished."

H. BERT SHAW,
President School Board.

* * *

"God has made of one blood all nations of men. In Christ we are all the sons of God and therefore brethren. In Him there is neither Jew nor Greek, male nor female, black nor white! I most heartily give my personal endorsement to the Pottstown Plan. I conscientiously cannot do otherwise as a Christian minister."

LUTHER A. KROUSE,
Pastor Emmanuel Lutheran Church.

THE POTTSTOWN PLAN

What has happened in two years

A TOWN CAN DO SOMETHING ABOUT BIGOTRY AND PREJUDICE

SHORTLY AFTER THE NATIONALLY FAMOUS SERIES OF ARTICLES IN THE POTTSTOWN MERCURY EXPOSED "JIM CROWISM" IN OUR TOWN, A SMALL GROUP OF CITIZENS SAT AROUND A TABLE AND ASKED THEMSELVES THAT QUESTION. WHAT COULD BE DONE? THAT GROUP BECAME THE CORE OF THE POTTSTOWN COUNCIL ON HUMAN RELATIONS, AND IN THE TWO YEARS SINCE, POTTSTOWN HAS SEEN MANY CHANGES.

---

1 Pottstown now has its first Negro teacher.

2 The School of Nursing has accepted its first Negro students.

3 All major industries in town now hire without prejudice or discrimination.

4 A number of Negro girls working in offices.

5 Speakers from the Council's Doll Library and Speakers Bureau have appeared before more than a score of civic and church organizations stressing the need for equal opportunity for all citizens.

6 The Jr. Chamber of Commerce is making an Annual Award to the person doing the most in bettering community relations.

7 The YMCA is sponsoring an Incident Control Course thru their Adult Education Committee.

8 A Negro has been appointed for the first time in Pottstown's history to a municipal authority.

9 A Committee of the Human Relations Council receives and acts on complaints and rumors of discrimination.

10 A town wide meeting in November 1955 with Judge Hastie of the Federal Court as principal speaker, attracted more than 500 people. A music-drama, "Count Me In" based on the Pottstown Plan, was presented. This meeting drew mention in several National magazines.

A NEW SPIRIT IN POTTSTOWN!

THE POTTSTOWN COUNCIL ON HUMAN RELATIONS DOES NOT TAKE CREDIT FOR THESE ACCOMPLISHMENTS. THE CREDIT BELONGS TO THE COMMUNITY. THERE ARE AS MANY MORE INTANGIBLE RESULTS AS THE STATED TANGIBLE ONES FOR WHICH POTTSTOWN CAN WELL FEEL PROUD.

WHERE DO WE GO FROM HERE?

OUR JOB IS FAR FROM FINISHED, MUCH MORE REMAINS TO BE DONE. THE HUMAN RELATIONS COUNCIL FOR THE COMING YEARS PLANS THE FOLLOWING.

★ DRAWING UP A DIVERSE SERIES OF PROGRAMS WHICH WILL BRING TO THE VARIOUS GROUPS AND ORGANIZATIONS IN OUR TOWN.

★ MAKING A DETERMINED EFFORT TO BRING OPEN HOUSING TO POTTSTOWN.

★ CONTINUING THE VISITS OF THE SUB-COMMITTEE WHEREVER COMPLAINTS OR NEW OPPORTUNITIES ARE BROUGHT TO ITS ATTENTION.

★ SENDING A COMMITTEE TO NEARBY SCHOOL COMMUNITIES TO SUGGEST AND HELP IN HIRING OF MINORITY GROUP TEACHERS.

★ COOPERATION WITH OTHER HUMAN RELATION COMMITTEES IN THE TRI-COUNTY AREA.

WHAT CAN YOU . . . A CITIZEN OF POTTSTOWN DO?

••• JOIN THE COUNCIL.

••• ASK FOR A SPEAKER FOR YOUR ORGANIZATION.

••• MAKE A PERSONAL EFFORT TO SEE THAT MINORITY GROUPS ARE REPRESENTED IN THE ORGANIZATIONS TO WHICH YOU BELONG, WHETHER IT BE PTA, VETERANS GROUP OR SERVICE CLUB.

••• SEE THAT YOUR ORGANIZATION BEGINS ONE PROJECT IN THE FIELD OF HUMAN RELATIONS.

••• STUDY YOUR OWN PREJUDICES. GET RID OF OUTWORN RACIAL AND RELIGIOUS PREJUDICES. MAKE YOUR OWN FIRST STEP TO BETTER NEIGHBORLY RELATIONS.

FOR FURTHER INFORMATION . . .

WRITE COUNCIL OF HUMAN RELATIONS, BOX 186
OR
WRITE OR PHONE MRS. MARTIN ULAN
661 BLUE SPRUCE COURT, POTTSTOWN, 2856

THE COUNCIL

CO-CHAIRMEN
REV. RUSSELL BARBOUR
CARL HERBINE

TREASURER
HENRY DOZIER

SECRETARY
MRS. MARTIN ULAN

MEMBERS
WILLIAM D. BARBER
REV. ARTHUR SIMPSON
WILLARD HETZEL, ESQUIRE
JAMES CORUM
NORMAND POIRIER
MRS. DORA OHRENSTEIN
REV. A. PINKNEY
REV. ERCEL WATSON
JOSEPH L. PRINCE, ESQUIRE
MAURICE MILLER
ROBERT GARBER
MARTIN ULAN
HARRY POLLOCK
MRS. JOSEPH HUNSICKER
DAVID COOPER
MRS. JOHN DeVINCENTIS
ALEXANDER DOWNIE
JAMES GAUT
EDWARD HALE
MRS. RICHARD RICKETTS
MISS CHARLOTTE ROPETER
REV. WILLIAM CORUM
RABBI EMIL SCHORSCH

In the aftermath of *Brown v. Board of Education*, the Pottstown Committee on Human Relations printed the following pamphlets; note that the Pottstown Human Relations Council is another appellation of the PCHR. Courtesy of the Special Collections Research Center, Temple University Libraries, Philadelphia, Pennsylvania.

Locals in and around Pottstown fully embraced the Pottstown Plan, which the Pottstown Committee on Human Relations launched. The large poster in front of Penn Village, a local federally funded residential complex, is one illustration of how locals embraced the Pottstown Plan. Moreover, by holding hands, the two young children in the photograph symbolize what the Pottstown Plan stood for: complete racial equality. March 1955. Courtesy of the *Pottstown Mercury*.

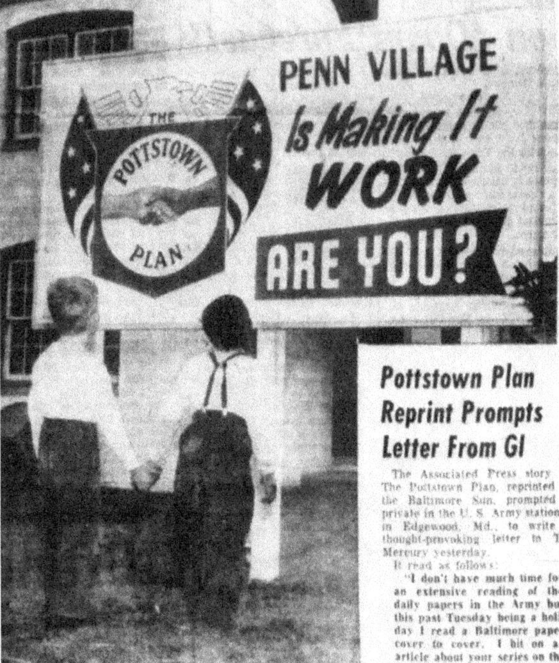

Local law enforcement detained Barney Strickland, charging that he was "terrorizing" Stowe residents. Accompanied Strickland was West Pottsgrove officer James V. Guadagno. August 1951. Courtesy of the *Pottstown Mercury*.

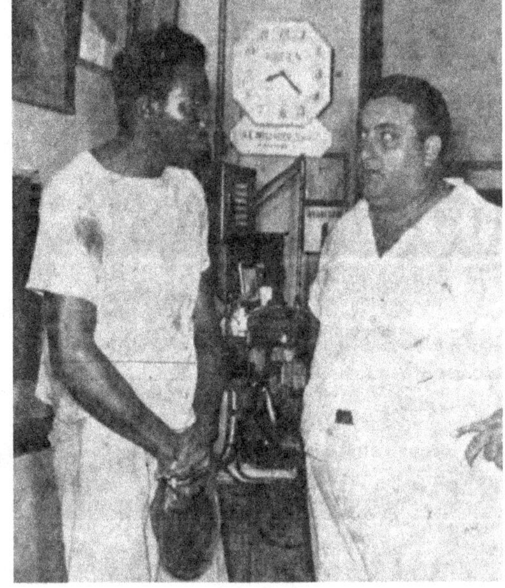

During the postwar era, the Pottstown NAACP was most active under the presidency of local civil rights activist Newstell Marable. March 1967. Courtesy of the *Pottstown Mercury.*

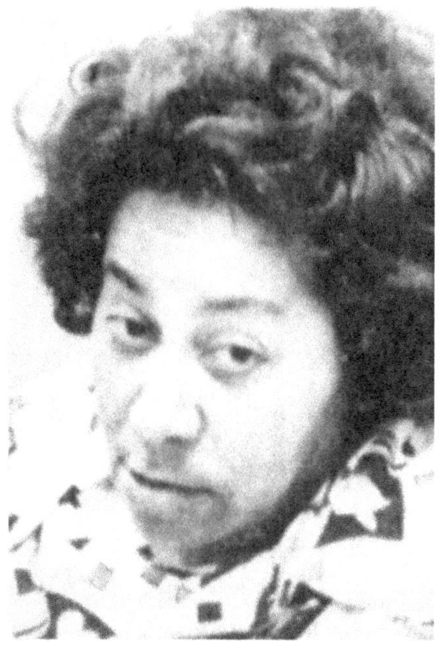

Millicent Marable, local civil rights activist, and wife of Pottstown NAACP president Newstell Marable. June 1977. Courtesy of the *Mercury.*

Pottstown-Phoenixville NAACP activist Newstell Marable, alongside branch affiliate Nathan Moffatt, being accompanied by law enforcement officers following the massive sit-in they orchestrated in late March 1969 close by Pottstown in Phoenixville Area Senior High School. April 1969. Courtesy of the *Pottstown Mercury*.

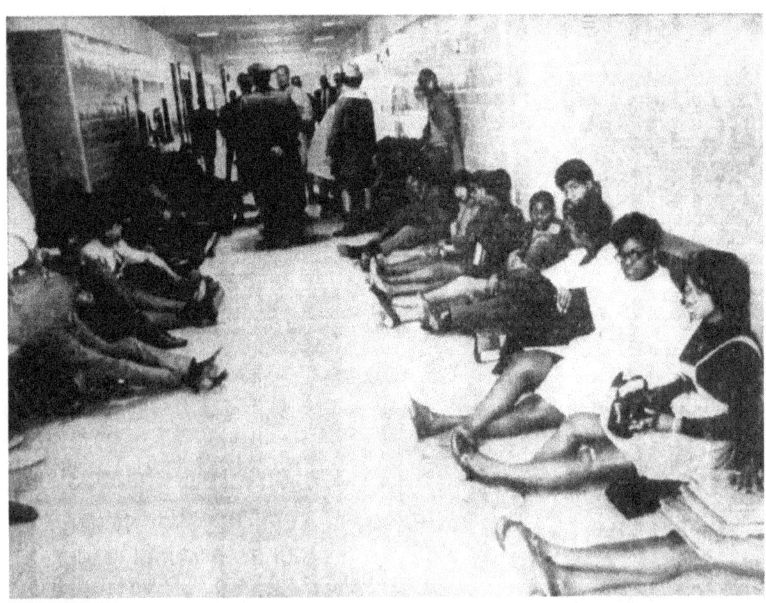

Totaling fifty, Phoenixville pupils represented the majority of those that local law enforcement detained in the massive sit-in in late March 1969, which the Pottstown-Phoenixville NAACP spearheaded. April 1969. Courtesy of the *Pottstown Mercury*.

5

The Pinnacle of Civil Rights Struggle in Pottstown and Beyond following *Brown v. Board*

Although the litigants of the United States Supreme Court's decision in *Brown v. Board of Education* would not completely feel its direct effect until years, even decades later, the African American civil rights experience in Pottstown proved substantially different.[1] In addition to the *Pottstown Mercury* publishing the letter-to-the-editor correspondences and newspaper articles shortly following *Brown* (see chap. 4), it printed another "series" on local discrimination approximately five weeks later. Subsequently, what emerged from this fascinating series being disseminated was the height of civil rights activism in Pottstown. The series played a direct role in catapulting not only local advancements in the Black freedom struggle but also national developments.[2]

From a legal perspective, *Brown* had no bearing on public education in Pottstown. As shown in chapter 4, Pennsylvania had legally barred racial segregation within its public school system in the late nineteenth century. Nevertheless, while the public school system in the state was technically desegregated, de facto segregation still manifested within it. To be sure, school segregation was firmly entrenched throughout the American North by the time the US Supreme Court announced *Brown*. While northern activists waged battles toward such institutional racism before the historic case—especially within tinier populaces similar to Pottstown, for instance—following the decision, agitators from large urban centers additionally came into the fold, radically protesting this Jim Crow practice above the Mason-Dixon Line.[3] It should come as no surprise, then, that the topic of school segregation has remained on the radar of historians focusing on northern civil rights, such as Thomas J. Sugrue and Davidson Douglas. Moreover, these same historians demonstrate how pervasive racism was throughout the American North.[4]

Yet the influence and impact of *Brown* in Pottstown, as noted previously (see chap. 4), transcended discriminatory practices in education. While the *Pottstown Mercury* illuminated injustices within the borough's public educational system, the newspaper additionally provided a more expansive and elaborate analysis of white racism endemic to the area and how it manifested across the local Jim Crow structure. In addition to the letter-to-the-editor correspondences and newspaper articles disseminated by the *Pottstown Mercury*, *Brown* served as the impetus for the local newspaper to conduct its civil rights investigation throughout the small borough. In fact, because *Brown* ruled against white supremacy, the local newspaper, in turn, demanded to know whether Pottstown African Americans themselves encountered similar evidences of bigotry. Like the letter-to-the-editor writers and local newspaper pieces published in the subsequent aftermath of *Brown* (again, see chap. 4), the *Pottstown Mercury* series from summer 1954 proved that local Black people endured the oppressive structure of de facto segregation along multiple fronts, as did African Americans in other northern locales. Such racial oppression, however, was more inconspicuous than overt.

For this local civil rights investigation, the *Pottstown Mercury* approximated Pottstown's Black populace at 1,200 in the early summer of 1954. The following March (1955), the *Baltimore Afro-American* wrote that Pottstown had 100 more (1,300) African Americans than had been given in the *Pottstown Mercury*'s prior assessment. Indeed, when compared with the number specified by the Black newspaper for Pottstown's overall 1955 populace (25,000), local African Americans comprised 5 percent with respect to the borough's total population. In any case, both estimations seem plausible, particularly because the numbers are between the 1950 and the 1960 US census tallies. In 1950, Pottstown had 844 African Americans, which equated to almost 4 percent of the overall populace (22,598). By 1960, the US census recorded 1,633 African Americans, or a little over 6 percent of the entire Pottstown population (26,144).[5]

"An Average Northern Community"

The civil rights advocacy work and activism that begun in Pottstown following the US Supreme Court's ruling in *Brown* continued reflecting the emerging liberal interracialist ethos and strategy of the postwar era. Symbolic of this, the white-oriented local newspaper, the *Pottstown Mercury*, documented the legitimacy of Pottstown Blacks' grievances and advocated for their cause. From late June to early July 1954, the local newspaper published its "series of news stories" that shed direct light on the local Black circumstance. As throughout the postwar years, the *Pottstown Mercury* incorporated journalistic techniques that humanized African Americans and the tangible issues they faced in the realm of civil rights. Moreover, the newspaper additionally provided them a public space where they could articulate said experiences. In the end, such activism eventually mushroomed into other local civil rights developments.[6]

Yet in comparison to the previous civil rights advocacy work conducted by the *Pottstown Mercury*, which began crystalizing during World War II (see chaps. 2 and 3), its late June/early July 1954 series departed from the earlier approaches along several lines. To begin, the African Americans whose perspectives the borough newspaper utilized in the reports remained nameless. Ostensibly, the *Pottstown Mercury* did this so that the local African Americans who voiced their complaints did not face any social, economic, or political repercussions from the dominant white populace. Moreover, the borough newspaper did the same for the whites it spotlighted within its reporting. These whites, however, were not necessarily supporting local civil rights. Rather, they were simply remarking on such homegrown prejudice for Pottstown in the age of Jim Crow North, so much so that a local white person, when asked directly whether borough whites practiced prejudice toward African Americans, remarked, "I believe in letting sleeping dogs lie." Indeed, for many, Pottstown was simply "an average Northern community."[7] Finally, the most obvious difference between the series in the summer of 1954 and the previous two *Pottstown Mercury* civil rights series was that it was indeed more ambitious. The reporting was not only of greater depth in both scope and research, but such advocacy once again saw direct collaboration between the *Pottstown Mercury* and local African Americans interested in combating anti-Black racism evidenced throughout the de facto segregation structure indigenous to the area.

Unlike the previous two series on local civil rights (see chap. 3), white *Pottstown Mercury* journalist Normand Poirier's summer 1954 series would go on and have greater impact on the Black freedom struggle in the borough and beyond, even reaching the national sphere. Born in 1928 in Worcester, Massachusetts, Poirier obtained a journalism degree from Cornell University in Ithaca, New York. A US naval veteran of World War II, by the time Poirier landed his newspapering gig in Pottstown, he had already labored with the *Worcester Telegram & Gazette*, located in his hometown, as well as the *Lafayette Daily Advertiser* in Lafayette, Louisiana.[8] After the *Pottstown Mercury*, Poirier had employment with *Life*, *Newsday*, and the *New York Post*. It was at *Esquire*, however, where he conducted his most celebrated journalism. Yet before *Esquire* printed Poirier's "An American Atrocity"—"one of the first" accounts highlighting Vietnam War cruelties (August 1969)—the white journalist composed another galvanizing investigation targeting Black inequality on the southeastern Pennsylvania home front. Moreover, instead of letting a large northern city like nearby Philadelphia taking center stage, Poirier set his reporting sniper scope, so to speak, directly on a small borough of the North, Pottstown, to demonstrate how Jim Crow practices unambiguously pervaded there.[9]

Not surprisingly, *Brown* helped inspire the summer of 1954 *Pottstown Mercury* articles on local civil rights. Just as the ruling galvanized locals to write into the press's letter-to-the-editor section, and led to the publication of subsequent newspaper pieces (see chap. 4), so too did it influence the Pottstown newspaper to create the upcoming series. For example, during this time, white journalist Charles D. Treleven was the local newspaper's managing editor. Moreover, decades later Treleven penned reflections in the Arizona-based *Prescott Courier* that highlighted the connection between *Brown* and the *Pottstown Mercury*'s subsequent civil rights investigation. According to Treleven, who identified Poirier as "a man of razor-sharp intellect and acute powers of observation," the two had been discussing *Brown* shortly after its ruling. Inspired, Poirier then put several inquiries directly to his managing editor. "We have only a few small black areas in town," Poirier said, "but do they really have equality of opportunity in employment, in leadership, in housing?" The white journalist continued, "Aren't we discriminating?"

Next, Treleven recalled how he and Poirier gathered alongside their "managing editor," brainstorming "a series of articles," which shed extensive light on de facto segregation practices "long embedded in the fabric of the community."[10] Here, Treleven must have meant "General Manager" Shandy Hill and not the *Pottstown Mercury's* managing editor, which was his (Trevelen's) position.[11] In 1955, moreover, Poirier identified his "editor" as the one who initially conceptualized "an idea" regarding Pottstown African Americans and their local status/treatment.[12]

Finally, Treleven argued, "the newspaper had no reporter other [than] Normand Poirier qualified for such a sensitive assignment." In fact, it was Poirier's audaciousness, Treleven remembered, which made him perfect "to withstand the wrath of the 90-percent white population that the articles seemed certain to arouse"—thereby further suggesting how racially discriminatory sentiments permeated the local white majority—even if his findings proved valid. Ultimately, the animosity Treleven and Poirier forecasted eventually manifested from local whites. In fact, following the *Pottstown Mercury's* initial dissemination of the civil rights reports, whites frequently sent hostile correspondences directly to the two journalists.[13] In late April 1955, Poirier noted how seven hundred communications streamed "into the [*Pottstown Mercury's*] office," albeit such correspondence had mixed responses.[14] Most protestors, Treleven reflected, even targeted Poirier specifically. Nevertheless, he continued, Poirier handled their racist remarks rather skillfully.[15]

Throughout Poirier's examination into white exclusionary initiatives in Pottstown, he utilized the American South as his comparison point or barometer. In fact, Poirier named the series' inaugural report "Jim Crow, Yankee Style, Stalks Streets of Pottstown." Within the series, Poirier also labeled Pottstown racism "under the name of Mister James P. Crow, Esquire,"[16] as did newspapers across the United States. Roughly eight months following the publication of the *Pottstown Mercury* series, the newspapers encapsulated Pottstown's own racism "as a Northern style Jim Crow system and an informal—but airtight—form of segregation." Ultimately, such juxtaposition illuminated direct continuity between the South's formal de jure structure and the North's "informal" de facto construction, an argument that Poirier articulated at the time too.[17]

At the same time, Poirier formulated his journalistic work centering on Pottstown so that it highlighted a broader point about African Americans and the North. In short, the white journalist suggested that the small locale "might be called an average Northern community." Surely, therefore, his investigatory journalism had implications and connections that transcended Pottstown. To be more precise, Poirier's series demonstrated how the exclusionary conditions that Pottstown Blacks endured throughout the locale were indeed indicative of the plight and discriminatory conditions analogous of African Americans across the northern United States.[18]

The questions that drove Poirier's reporting concerned how segregated Pottstown was on the one hand, coupled with how far or whether local Blacks had integrated within the small borough's social, economic, and political life on the other hand. Moreover, on the front page of the *Pottstown Mercury*'s June 26, 1954, edition, the press asked its approximately twenty-two thousand subscribers an important inquiry, which centered on whether borough whites excluded local African Americans: "Does Jim Crow live in Pottstown?"[19] Two days later, the *Pottstown Mercury* began publishing the summer of 1954 civil rights reports. On June 28, following his extensive examination into local civil rights, Poirier revealed multiple startling illuminations that focused solely on African Americans being excluded.

Overall, Poirier's central thesis showed that white racism permeated numerous spaces across Pottstown. He did so, however, by first demonstrating the fact that locally, African Americans were not "a member of a service club in Pottstown." They included Rotary, Lions, ABC, Optimists, and Kiwanis. Nor did Blacks have memberships with "a fraternal or social organization" locally, such as Moose, Doehler Die-Caster Club, Orioles, Odd Fellows, Elks, Eagles, Knights of Columbus, Owls, and Maria Assunta. Moreover, not one African American was "a member of a 'white' veteran's organization." These local groups included AMVETS, Veterans of Foreign Wars, and the American Legion. Brookside Country Club likewise shut out Blacks by withholding membership. This too was the case with Pottstown's "fire companies."

Work opportunities throughout the borough were also discriminatory toward Pottstown African Americans. For instance, Poirier noted that although Pottstown's "three public utilities," which were Bell Telephone, Philadelphia Electric, and Pottstown Rapid Transit, employed Blacks, at the time that employment was only within "a janitorial capacity." This was also the case when it came to Blacks laboring "for the Pottstown school system." The same local school system as well never employed Black teachers. Similarly, African Americans never held jobs "as a salesgirl or salesman" locally. Nor did Pottstown under any circumstance have "a [Black] mailman" employed. Poirier additionally lambasted the fact that solely "one Negro girl has an office job in all of Pottstown" at the time and how just "one Negro girl has ever worked as a nurse in either Pottstown or Memorial hospital."

For African American pupils themselves, Poirier noted further local discrimination. "Only one Negro Senior High school graduate," he found, was "ever . . . sent out on a job interview from the school's job placement office." He also spotlighted specific institutions, announcing that "no Negro girl has ever been admitted to the Pottstown hospital School of Nursing."[20] Ultimately, Poirier argued that Pottstown's exclusionary practices had manifested along "subtle methods" rather than the southern de jure structure, which was, indeed, publicly exposed and conspicuous.[21] In other words, Pottstown's "color line" existed inextricably throughout the locale—that is, Poirier added, aside from "school and work."

Nevertheless, even though the local job market and educational situation illuminated spaces where Blacks experienced integration, Poirier revealed that these same institutions still discriminated against African Americans in more inconspicuous fashions. Regarding livelihood, for example, a local African American approximated a little under two hundred Blacks had industry jobs in the area. He additionally identified Stanley G. Flagg and Co. as most likely having the highest number of Black employees, followed by Concrete Products of America. However, even local factories like these that hired African Americans still covertly excluded them too. Moreover, nailing down such exclusionary policies was indeed challenging, he continued, because staff supervisors running these places denied that they discriminated. Of course, local African Americans argued otherwise. The same Blacks even contended that "one of the largest plants in town" solely employed African Americans "for janitorial and maintenance work."

In addition to these so-called integrated spaces, Poirier illuminated several local occupations that nearly fully excluded African Americans.

Essentially, these were white-collar professions. According to Poirier, merchant-related jobs principally excluded African Americans. He also singled out public education in Pottstown—namely, its teaching profession (as indicated prior)—which African Americans had at no time labored within. Like the local factory that employed African Americans solely to conduct custodial-related tasks, just "one Negro has ever worked for the Pottstown school system. He was a janitor." Finally, like merchant-related occupations, Poirier revealed how local Blacks—particularly African American women who at the time mostly conducted domestic-based jobs—especially had issues obtaining clerical-related occupations.

Now even though local Blacks did not work as educators within the Pottstown educational system, Poirier did stress that the borough's public institution granted African American youths access within it. In fact, he added, Black students received similar guidance as their white counterparts. However, unlike their white classmates, younger African Americans had to deal with blatant racism. Poirier even emphasized how emotionally damaging such racism was on the youths' subconscious. "There have been cases," Poirier revealed, "[of] the official use in lower grades of picture books based on the adventures of 'Little Black Sambo'" that incorporated racially discriminatory depictions of African Americans. (Poirier did note, however, that once local African Americans informed the proper educational authority about them, it revised such practices.) Another example Poirier spotlighted happened somewhat recently. As noted by the white journalist, "three young Negroes . . . couldn't take part in their class picnic in Pottstown because the [white] man who owned the site" would not permit African Americans entrance there, even so intolerantly arguing how "business reasons" had swayed him.[22]

Poirier also shed light on Pottstown African Americans and certain housing challenges they endured. Here, it is worth noting that Poirier's illustration aligned with the *Pottstown Mercury*'s examination of Hemlock and Cottage Row African Americans from 1950, as captured in chapter 3, especially those who were trying to get into the federally funded Penn Village residential project. As noted by Poirier, an African American "applied for admission to a housing development in Pottstown." However, the development's supervisor eventually informed the African American during their "final meeting" that he could complete "an application if you like and I will accept it." Yet the same white supervisor told the local African American that he did not recommend it. In his view, "I don't believe your application would be approved." Thus, the potential Black house-hunter accepted "the man's advice." Inquisitive, Poirier additionally found out that the manager's judgment rested largely on race, particularly because multiple whites residing there wanted no part in having Black neighbors whatsoever. Regarding this racist residential dilemma, Poirier even stressed continuities between Pottstown and his days reporting way below the Mason-Dixon Line in Lafayette, Louisiana.[23]

Yet while Poirier illuminated elements of racism which local African Americans encountered, Pottstown Blacks, he determined, needed to do more on their end to help with the integration process. Specifically, Poirier argued that local Blacks "fear of rejection" handicapped them "from striving to become an integral part of the community." In several instances, in fact, he stressed how African Americans in the area never sought opportunities—even employment—within Pottstown because they had consternation about the organizations declining them. This mentality, Poirier affirmed, therefore explained aspects of why the post office, as well as the Pottstown Hospital School of Nursing, to name a few, generally lacked African American occupants. Poirier's harsh appraisal, however, also criticized whites. In particular, it lambasted their long-standing oppression of African Americans. In fact, Poirier—just like the "Readers Say" Pennsburg writer mentioned in chapter 4—suggested that such injustice was what gave Pottstown Blacks "an inferiority complex." Moreover, providing African Americans fully escaped their mental bondage, he continued, whites could still be hostile toward integration.

Whatever the case, Poirier stressed that local African Americans—as well as their counterparts throughout the nation—needed to make the effort. If Blacks failed to do so, it implied that they were only reciprocating similar bias toward whites in general—even those who demanded full-blown African American integration and civil rights.[24] On local whites, however, Poirier made two central observations. First, he argued that Pottstown whites denied that the small borough practiced any forms of bigotry toward local African Americans. Commenting directly on *Brown*, Poirier even noted that most identified it as solely a southern concern because the borough, and the rest of the American North, were indeed integrated spaces.

Second, Poirier found whites to believe that Pottstown African Americans were—on all occasions—content with their local existence. In a sense, Poirier supported this latter assertion since, in his view, local Blacks had reservations about fully integrating within Pottstown. However, he understood the motive behind them exhibiting such sentiment. Bluntly stated, Pottstown African Americans wanted no part in so-called integration, Poirier observed, because whites in the locale had no desire in fully accepting them in terms of being equal.[25]

Yet even though local whites argued that their African American neighbors had the same opportunities afforded them in Pottstown, Poirier countered such an argument by throwing light from another Black viewpoint. African Americans, an unnamed Black leader remarked, had no connection to Pottstown, outside being taxpayers. The same African American also highlighted Pottstown's Black collective and what its local existence centered on. According to the African American, Pottstown Blacks navigated only a few places—"his church, his job, his house." Such isolation even supported Poirier's comments that Pottstown African Americans preferred to remain by themselves. However, it additionally spoke to their perceived status in Pottstown, which a second leading African American commented directly on. "It's not a bad town at all," the African American declared. "But we are treated as Negroes." Interpreting these remarks, Poirier emphasized that while the white populace "tolerated" Pottstown African Americans "on some levels," it saw them as far from being their equal counterparts. Rather, he continued, these local Blacks were second-class citizens to the majority white group.[26]

Finally, although Poirier's journalism shed light on white racism and the ubiquity of northern Jim Crow in and around Pottstown, that was not its sole objective. Its other purpose was to galvanize residents into combating prejudice in the small northern locale. Continuing the *Pottstown Mercury*'s liberal interracialist strategy and civil rights advocacy activism tradition that began solidifying during World War II (see chaps. 2 and 3), Poirier's seventh article in the summer of 1954 series, subtitled "A Plan of Action for Pottstown," stressed just that. Summoning locals, he informed his readership that all they needed to launch such "a movement" was several committed individuals. Poirier additionally let them know that Pottstown activist and Black PCL president Daniel Lee was the main contact. At the time, in fact, Lee had an idea about establishing "a committee on human relations" similar to those forming in the wake of *Brown* in many southern states, as historian John A. Kirk reveals, so that prejudice evidenced within the local Jim Crow structure was combated firsthand.[27]

The *Pottstown Mercury*'s 1954 investigation on civil rights continued a local liberal interracialist response. Once again, dialogue emerged within the newspaper's "Readers Say"/letter-to-the-editor section that appraised the borough's civil rights issues. In addition to the subsequent letters published shortly following *Brown* (chap. 4), the *Pottstown Mercury* printed more "Readers Say" responses both during and following Poirier's local civil rights investigations. Moreover, one should note that the majority of "Readers Say" letters backed Poirier's findings.

At the same time, many "Readers Say" authors at this specific juncture following *Brown* did not sign their full names. In a vein similar to the white and Black participants that Poirier utilized within his civil rights reports, most likely individuals left out their full identities so that they did not receive any form of local reprisals—whether economic, social, or political. Yet there were some locals—mostly identifying as African Americans—who certainly risked retaliation by penning their full names. In sum, these responses provide excellent insight into Pottstown African Americans and the homegrown racism they endured across the local Jim Crow structure.[28]

Out of the multiple "Readers Say" responses, African Americans Frances Young Williams and Mary V. Reid's correspondences paint the best picture of local Blacks and the racial hardships they endured. Both women not only grew up in Pottstown but also were a product of the borough's educational system. Moreover, they agreed how Pottstown African Americans began battling racism from early on.[29] Williams, maiden name Young—the former local YMCA Negro Extension Work activists captured in chapter 2—even correlated her own experience with southern African Americans. However, she found her plight in Pottstown worse because the northern locale—unlike those communities below the Mason-Dixon Line—masked its own racism, whereas the southern brand was not covert. "As a child," Williams remembered, "I was reared and received my schooling in Pottstown." She continued, "Let me say that there were times during my childhood that led me to believe that conditions for Negroes in Pottstown were not half as good as they were for Negroes in the South." Specifically, Williams believed that "at least in the South a Negro knew where he stood and he did not have to face embarrassment by attempting to seek social life, entertainment or jobs above a certain level or field." Ostensibly, therefore, what really bothered Williams was the belief centering on local African Americans having identical "opportunity as the other races for betterment of his conditions." In her view, however, she found the small northern locale only wanted African Americans within the capacities of "labor, factory or domestic type" work. In other words, Williams declared, Blacks were wanted solely in unskilled employment and not white-collar employment.[30]

Reid, who in this same correspondence lambasted the ways in which de facto segregation vis-à-vis the local Jim Crow structure was ubiquitous to Black burial (chap. 2), articulated similar points as Williams. Reid even added that such discriminatory practices permeated all facets of Black life throughout Pottstown "from birth until death in our little borough." Regarding her youth, Reid recalled, "I lived next door to white children and we went to the Jefferson playground together." She continued, however, by writing, "The colored children were called into a group and told that they were being given a colored supervisor and special times to use certain facilities at the playground." Of course, Reid's last argument went hand in glove with the traditions of equalization and similar Black internal improvement activism in Pottstown that percolated especially during World War II (see chaps. 2 and 3).

Reid also lambasted Pottstown's educational system, arguing fervently that local African Americans time was largely filled with "humiliating experiences, bitter disappointments and a nauseous fear of being rejected." Interestingly enough, Reid sharply criticized Pottstown public school teachers too, which, therefore, challenged Poirier's assessment in the series. Finally, like Williams, Reid illuminated her own challenge in obtaining white-collar employment in Pottstown. Eventually, Pottstown left her feeling disenchanted. Thus, Reid moved to Philadelphia, where she found, in her view, better racial treatment.[31]

While Pottstown resident Raymond C. De Wald did not fully back Poirier's findings, he affirmed that providing the investigations proved true, then such prejudices demanded fixing. At the same time, De Wald lambasted whites who were directly against African Americans obtaining civil rights advancements. In his view, "Intelligent, fair-minded people certainly must realize that 'separate citizenship is second-class citizenship' and should want to see that their Negro neighbors are guaranteed the same rights and privileges as they have." He continued, "If these conditions do exist, those who object to their correction must be either blindly prejudiced or else completely indifferent to the principal of equal rights," which considers "all citizens." Ultimately, even though De Wald never fully celebrated Poirier's civil rights assessment, he did at least concur with its fundamental premise, which demanded that whites and Blacks both had equality.[32]

Early National Responses to the *Pottstown Mercury* Series

In addition to catalyzing an early local liberal interracialist response, soon after the *Pottstown Mercury* disseminated Poirier's final report, the historically Black *Baltimore Afro-American* started publishing the same civil rights investigation. While it is not clearly known how the Black newspaper found out about Poirier's series, the *Pottstown Mercury* did have earlier professional contact with the Baltimore press, as shown in the *Afro Magazine*'s early December 1953 publication (see chap. 4). In recap, the *Afro Magazine* printed Hill's letter that responded directly to the inquiry: "If the Supreme Court outlaws segregation in public schools, what position will your publication take editorially on this decision." The white editor wrote back in an affirmative position to the *Afro Magazine's* inquiry. And, of course, the US Supreme Court eventually answered and shed greater light on the Black newspaper's speculative questioning roughly six months later in the *Brown* decision.

Moreover, because Hill openly endorsed the anticipated, perhaps forecasted, historic decision from the highest court in the land, he came out publicly once again, this time in the esteemed Black newspaper, as a white civil rights advocate, if not ally, for African American equality and inclusion. At the same time, by Hill sending in his racially progressive statements to the *Afro Magazine*, he was, in fact, further demonstrating his commitment to the larger Black freedom struggle, which was in full development and blooming throughout various spaces, North and South, at the time. Finally, under local Black activist and physician Daniel Lee's leadership, the PCL had a professional connection to the historically Black Baltimore news outlet, even before Poirier's summer series. In sum, these two professional contacts possibly shed light on how the *Afro-American* got wind of the *Pottstown Mercury*'s series—the journalistic advocacy which, indeed, ultimately ignites further developments across the local Black freedom struggle in Pottstown and beyond.[33]

On the other hand, the historical record does reveal the motives behind the *Afro-American* publishing the *Pottstown Mercury*'s 1954 civil rights series. Foremost, the Black newspaper circulated Poirier's work so "its readers" plainly understood how *Brown* was nationally relevant and not just confined primarily within the American South. The *Afro-American* additionally printed the powerful essays that examined anti-Black discrimination across the northern Jim Crow structure within Pottstown, believing that they might inspire everyone who perused them to doing something about combating said racial injustice in early 1950s America.[34]

Because the *Afro-American* circulated the *Pottstown Mercury* 1954 series, it inspired an early national dialogue that centered on the small northern locale and the normalization of Jim Crow oppression that permeated the borough. On July 17, 1954, the Black newspaper published these responses in its section entitled "WHAT AFRO READERS SAY—." Most likely, these opinion writers were all African Americans, specifically because of the ways in which the writers responded to Poirier's work on white prejudice and the structure of de facto segregation indigenous to Pottstown. Moreover, not only did the "Afro Readers Say" contributors reside above and below the Mason-Dixon Line, but most of them also wholeheartedly celebrated Poirier's eye-opening series.[35]

One of the southern "Afro Readers Say" writers, Portia Madison, who resided in Atlanta, Georgia, called out the contradictions individuals above the Mason-Dixon Line made in seeing white racism as only a southern phenomenon. The way Madison viewed the subject, "Northerners who are always breaking their fingers pointing at the South need to examine the situation in their own backyards." Southern "Afro Readers Say" author Edward Evans from Richmond, Virginia, argued that there was continuity between the two regions' discriminatory practices too. "The proscriptions of the color bar had been just as harsh and just as cruel in Richmond, Ind.," Evans announced, "as they often are in Richmond, Va." Writing out of Savannah, Georgia, Mrs. Phoebe Dudley made perhaps the most powerfully accurate assessment of racial discrimination among the two geographical regions in the "Afro Readers Say" space. According to Dudley, what differentiated "Jim Crow–Dixie style and Jim Crow–Yankee style is the difference between honesty and hypocrisy." She continued by viewing the regions' racism as a dichotomy. "Jim Crow is brazenly out in the open down here and no attempt is made to hide it." She continued, "In the North Jim Crow works undercover while those who practice it stubbornly deny its existence." Altogether, Dudley saw each Jim Crow practice uniformly exasperated.[36]

In addition, the *Afro-American* captured "Afro Readers Say" contributors from the northeastern United States who found similarities with Poirier's reports and their own particular cities. Like Poirier, two of the responders resided in Pennsylvania. Mal Jordan from Philadelphia highlighted the national importance of Poirier's informative assessments relating to Pottstown's discriminatory practices. In Jordan's view, Poirier's reports "can be repeated in just about every town" across America, "North and South." Moreover, the white journalist's findings, Jordan believed, firmly provided graphic evidence of how *Brown* was not entirely a southern issue. Jim Halperin from Harrisburg viewed Poirier and his investigatory journalism comparing nicely with white prejudice in the state's capitol. Notwithstanding "very few changes," Halperin asserted, the *Pottstown Mercury* series essentially described Harrisburg and how "Mr. James Crow's activities" manifested there.[37]

Not every northern "Afro Readers Say" writer, however, praised "Poirier's penetrating analysis of the racial situation in Pottstown" outright.[38] For example, Georgine Clark from Detroit, Michigan, was not shocked at all by what Poirier demonstrated. When juxtaposed with the Motor City, the small Pennsylvania locale, Clark argued, was "the Promised Land . . . to racial conditions" there. Similarly, Ray Powell from Chicago, Illinois, took issue with the journalist's report on certain private associations that denied Blacks membership in Pottstown. They included the Lions, Rotary, Kiwanis, and Optimist societies. As noted by Powell, this was "not startling news." In fact, he continued, "I have never heard of these . . . organizations" having Black affiliates anywhere throughout America. In short, Powell finished his response by suggesting how the Lions, Rotary, Kiwanis and Optimist societies associations uniformly excluded Blacks from their rank and file. In fact, "I have heard that their by-laws restrict membership to 'white males only,'" he added. Of course, Powell's last argument goes hand in glove with the local and national civil rights struggles involving the Pottstown Bowling Association and the American Bowling Congress (see chap. 3).[39]

Although critical, Joseph Daniels from Cleveland, Ohio, provided a more nuanced view of Poirier's findings than that of both Clark and Powell in the "Afro Readers Say" national space. Moreover, Daniels revealed he had firsthand expertise with northern and southern discrimination from having resided in each region. Like previous writers, Daniels saw how white racism manifested in the regions as a dichotomy. On the one hand, he noted how the southern brand was overtly antagonistic toward Blacks. On the other hand, he asserted that the northern method presented African Americans "with utter indifference." Finishing his well-articulated remarks, Daniels concluded his assessment on a more cynical note, declaring, "I haven't made up my mind which of the two is the worst."[40] Poirier expressed a similar sentiment. "Segregation," the white journalist noted, "whether brought about with Jim Crow signs in buses and restaurants" like the de jure structure "or . . . the more polite, subtle methods" relating to de facto separation locally across Pottstown, as well as the North more broadly, "is exactly the same thing."[41]

In addition to the *Afro-American*, another nationally respected historically Black newspaper, the *Pittsburgh Courier*, soon after started printing Poirier's examination into African American inequality in Pottstown and how the northern Jim Crow structure manifested there.[42] Yet the two Black presses were not the only newspapers that recirculated the *Pottstown Mercury* series. South Carolina's *Rock Hill Herald*, and the *News-Argus* out of Goldsboro, North Carolina, did so as well. These newspapers, however, were white presses. In fact, white South Carolinian Talbot Patrick not only owned and edited the *Rock Hill Herald* but also provided introductory remarks to Poirier's initial essay. In sum, Patrick reflected comments that the *Afro-American* publicized. Specifically, he expressed how both the North and the South equally oppressed African Americans. Patrick also spotlighted how Poirier's series depicted Pottstown as "a typical Northern small city."[43]

Like the *Afro-American* and *Rock Hill Herald*, under Henry Belk's editorship, the *News-Argus* constructed commentary that emphasized that white racism was an issue that permeated above and below the Mason-Dixon Line. "It is a problem for all of us to work at quietly, sanely, soberly in every community where races are thrown together in juxtaposition," the *News-Argus* added.[44] In a vein similar to Shandy Hill's influence on *Pottstown Mercury* writers, historian George W. Troxler argues correspondingly that underneath Belk's supervision as well as leadership, a good amount of younger journalists employed with the *News-Argus* went on and obtained important occupations across the newspaper profession.[45]

Interestingly enough, the *News and Courier* out of Charleston, South Carolina, suggested how "in an average Northern community such as Pottstown," African Americans might actually have it worse than Charleston. In particular, the *News and Courier* argued, Charleston Blacks had substantial employment opportunities across white-collar work; indeed, much greater than locales in the Jim Crow North like Pottstown. Thus, the *News and Courier* suggested, ostensibly, how Charleston African Americans fared better from an equality and a socioeconomic standpoint than Pottstown Blacks.[46]

So galvanized by Poirier's initial civil rights essay, which he perused in the *Pittsburgh Courier*, conservative white journalist William Loeb decided to write to the *Pottstown Mercury* itself. Loeb not only edited New Hampshire's *Manchester Union Leader* but also presided over Associated Newspapers incorporated, which, at the time, printed five New England news publications. Published in the *Pottstown Mercury*'s "Readers Say"/letter-to-the-editor section in late July 1954, although Loeb's remarks aligned with the consensus—that is, white racism transcended the American South—they also demonstrated his political conservatism. "It especially pleased me because there is a very repugnant type of self-righteousness among our Northern 'liberals,'" Loeb crowed, "who delight in pointing their finger at those 'dreadful Southerners.'" However, he continued, they do practically nothing when it came to searching "for the mote in their own eyes."[47] Years later, Shandy Hill reflected in *Dear Sir* on general remarks he gave "at an Associated Press [AP] managing editors' conference." Like Loeb's comment, Hill utilized an illustration from the Bible, calling out "Many editors" who roared arrogantly "in behalf of downtrodden minorities." However, he continued, they declined "to examine the beam in their own eyes while calling attention to the moat elsewhere."[48]

As the *Pottstown Mercury* printed the final articles from Poirier's local civil rights series, Black SDA worker and civil rights activist Addison V. Pinkney—the same individual briefly mentioned in chapter 3—wrote African American newspaperman Claude Barnett on July 1, 1954.[49] Born in Sanford, Florida, in 1889, Barnett eventually moved to Chicago and launched the Associated Negro Press the year after World War I finished. The establishment of his Black newspaper also coincided with "Red Summer," a series of race riots that ignited across the United States, especially within Barnett's transplanted home of Chicago, which resulted in thirty-eight deaths, with African Americans comprising twenty-three of the slain and whites fifteen.[50]

Within the July 1 correspondence, Pinkney informed Barnett about Poirier's "series of articles featuring Jim Crow as it exist[ed] in Pottstown." The Black SDA also requested that Barnett contact Shandy Hill.[51] Barnett answered Pinkney's request and the following day, July 2, penned the *Pottstown Mercury* editor, letting Hill know that he acquired "four issues of the Pottstown Mercury, carrying your series on discrimination" and that his press was "very much interested." Moreover, Barnett remarked how he "had come from a small mid-western town not even as liberal as Pottstown." The Black newspaperman additionally commended the *Pottstown Mercury* for "the objective manner in which" it examined the topic and noted bluntly how the locale was "typical" with respect to tiny urban locations above the Mason-Dixon Line.[52]

Hill responded to Barnett six days later (July 8). Within the correspondence, he acknowledged Barnett's celebration of Poirier's series. Yet Hill informed the Black newspaperman that the *Pottstown Mercury's* simple purpose behind such local civil rights advocacy was the press struggling "to lift our small voice against discrimination, bigotry and intolerance." Moreover, Hill emphasized the fact that whether "it is heard, and if it is heeded by only one person," then, he asserted in an upstanding yet racially progressive liberal interracialist tone, "we think we will have achieved a good." The white editor also asked Barnett whether it would be OK if he "reprint[ed]" Barnet's correspondence "in our 'Readers Say' column," excluding "personal [subject] matter."[53] The Black journalist responded two days later (July 10) and informed Hill that that was certainly all right. However, evidence does not suggest that the *Pottstown Mercury* actually republished Barnett's correspondence in its letter-to-the-editor section.[54]

The Pottstown Committee on Human Relations and the Liberal Interracialist Strategy

Shortly following the *Pottstown Mercury* publishing Poirier's final civil rights piece, PCL president Daniel Lee got the local "human relations" organization he so passionately desired.[55] While Lee played an instrumental role in the establishment of the Pottstown Committee on Human Relations (PCHR)—a volunteer-based, private local civil rights organization fiercely committed to true racial equality in the northern borough and beyond—the Black-advocacy reports disseminated by the *Pottstown Mercury* served as its impetus.[56] In March 1956, the PCHR additionally stressed that "following the publishing of a series of articles in the Pottstown Mercury describing the local human relations situation," it was founded.[57] Furthermore, like the summer of 1954 *Pottstown Mercury* series, scholars have fully ignored the PCHR's proper place in the history of northern civil rights during the early postwar.

In mid-July 1954, local activists created the PCHR. Although Lee was the early head and principal developer, during roughly the next two years many Black and white advocates joined the PCHR too.[58] Almost a year later (June 1955), an individual narrated the PCHR as thus: "The organization is totally a lay man group. They do not even represent organizations." The author continued, "They do represent the people who are concerned and who want to do something to make the town a better place for all."[59] Some notables among the PCHR included African American brothers James H. and William D. Corum; Black SDA ministers Pinkney and Ercell I. Watson from the nearby Pine Forge Institute; and *Pottstown Mercury* journalist Poirier.

Moreover, white civil rights activists Marjorie Penney and A. Herbert Haslam joined the PCHR early on as representatives from Fellowship Farm in Fagleysville, Pennsylvania. In fact, these two-seasoned activists, through Fellowship Farm and their main location, Fellowship House in Philadelphia, would play a fundamental role in helping the PCHR have an impact locally (as well as regionally and nationally).[60]

Activists officially established Fellowship House in Philadelphia during the early 1940s, and it had direct origins with Philadelphia's Young Peoples' Interracial Fellowship (YPIF), which came about early the decade prior.[61] Yet by the time the PCHR launched, Fellowship House's "Farm" was only about three years old. Started in late June 1951, the farm was a pivotal organizational space. In fact, historian Stanley Keith Arnold argues that the location was an essential "training ground" where "a generation of civil rights activists" received instruction in promoting equality.[62] A November 1955 report from Fellowship House additionally noted that it was "a summer training, workcamp, and conference center." Inextricably interracial, from an organizational standpoint, the farm was directly tied to Fellowship House. Moreover, in the year following the PCHR's launch, Fellowship House and Farm had eleven other affiliated organizations situated in Pennsylvania; New York; Maryland; Ohio; Washington, DC; Tennessee; and Missouri.[63]

Surely the PCHR's greatest contribution to the local Black freedom struggle concerned "the Pottstown Plan."[64] Yet the only mentioning of the Pottstown Plan outside contemporary sources is found in regional scholars Jean Barth Toll and Mildred S. Gilliam's massive anthology, *Invisible Philadelphia: Community Through Voluntary Organizations* (1995). This account, however, is extremely brief. Moreover, it does not document the origins of the Pottstown Plan in relationship to the *Pottstown Mercury* civil rights series or its connection to the PCHR itself. Rather, the version solely emphasizes Fellowship House and Farm's part in implementing the Pottstown Plan.[65]

Even though the PCHR was completely "a lay man group" that did "not even represent organizations," the fact remained that it still needed organizational backing, especially in promoting the Pottstown Plan. In late February 1955, the PCHR, in collaboration with both the *Pottstown Mercury* and the Fellowship House and Farm, distributed over ten thousand pamphlets that conveyed the Pottstown Plan's central aims.[66] Entitled "The Pottstown Plan: A First Step," the pamphlet's front cover illustrates the PCHR's goal for civil rights activism in the locale. While the backdrop itself has scattered clippings of the summer of 1954 *Pottstown Mercury* series, in the center of the cover are two young children. One is Black and the other white, and they are holding hands. This simple gesture symbolizes the PCHR and Pottstown Plan's grand objectives: full-blown African American integration coupled with unapologetic civil rights promotion and egalitarianism.[67] Interestingly enough, Penney articulated a similar viewpoint months earlier. In a correspondence dated September 8, 1954, Penney wrote Black justice and civil rights activist William Hastie, who also sat on Fellowship House's board, about the pamphlet's prospective civil rights imagery. Specifically, she notes how the document had "an attractive front-page picture of a Negro and a white baby taking first steps toward each other," thereby visually promulgating the liberal interracialist ethos on the local front.[68]

On the inside jacket, the pamphlet mentions how the Pottstown Plan ultimately catapulted, emphasizing Poirier's civil rights reporting. Moreover, because certain prejudices barred Pottstown African Americans "from sharing fully in community life," the pamphlet summons local organizations. Specifically, it asserts, "The POTTSTOWN PLAN is simply to have the community flex its muscles and take THE FIRST STEP— that is, that every group in town, from the Chamber of Commerce to the smallest Cub Scout den, is asked to consider the problem," speak "about it, and come up with ONE PROJECT, no matter how small, which will help build a fairer, friendlier Pottstown."[69]

Before going any further, a note on the language of the Pottstown Plan pamphlet is worth emphasizing. In essence, the document utilizes broader inclusive statements rather than explicitly identifying that Pottstown's African American population was the group receiving the brunt end of racism indigenous to the northern locale. Likewise, Arnold sheds light on Fellowship House and Farm's utilization of inclusive discourse in promoting civil rights. Fellowship House and Farm, Arnold even suggests, put in place an able foundation "for a philosophy" eventually recognized "as multiculturalism," thus further demonstrating the organization's unprejudiced objectives.[70]

Since the PCHR collaborated with Fellowship House and Farm and had activists from the Philadelphia group as well—it should not be surprising the way the Pottstown Plan document was configured. However, even though the Pottstown Plan booklet is arranged in such a way, the fact remains that the *Pottstown Mercury*'s summer 1954 civil rights series demonstrates what local people were most certainly experiencing the bulk of inequality evidenced by the northern Jim Crow structure in and around Pottstown. Unequivocally, they were Pottstown African Americans.

The Pottstown Plan document also suggests how the borough initiative could not only possibly assist individuals "in other towns" but that the local civil rights endeavor, providing how local organizations directly involved themselves, might even have international reach. Here, the international argument also goes hand in glove with Fellowship House and Farm's inclusive message.[71]

While the PCHR disseminated the Pottstown Plan booklet in early 1955, the organization really started working on the initiative shortly after its establishment. In fact, the PCHR initially announced the Pottstown Plan roughly four months earlier.[72] Outside of the PCHR itself, as indicated, the two main organizations that promoted the Pottstown Plan were Fellowship House and Farm and the *Pottstown Mercury*. While Fellowship House and Farm workers Penney, Haslam, and another white colleague named Mitzi R. Jacoby, labored in promoting the Pottstown Plan, Poirier and the *Pottstown Mercury* did the same.[73]

Last—but certainly not least—the evening before the PCHR and collaborators released the Pottstown Plan booklets in late February 1955, Lee publicly endorsed it. In fact, he made egalitarian arguments like the ones found in the document itself. Unequivocally, the African American physician declared "that the big majority of the people in Pottstown feel just as we do about discrimination. Most people realize how ignorant and unjust it is." Lee then juxtaposed his assessment of Pottstown with that of the United States overall. Remarking within the vein of the liberal interracialist ethos, Lee argued that "most people . . . in Pottstown," as well as "every town—would like to do something about" combating prejudice. On the other hand, because Pottstown had such a plurality who held egalitarian views, it appeared, therefore, seemingly logical that these local residents should receive the PCHR's proposal cheerfully. "We think this plan will give us all the chance that we've been" wanting desperately, Lee affirmed.

Lee also demonstrated the PCHR's fervent commitment to inclusion by highlighting the fact that people from various ethnicities and backgrounds have experienced bigotry firsthand, while simultaneously they have also dished it out. Thus, he saw the real issues which plagued the day relating to "human" concerns rather than solely "racial." Indeed, by Lee further painting the PCHR along these inclusive lines, he was only helping the group in having a larger appeal to the borough's entire population.[74]

Among the Fellowship House and Farm workers, Haslam was the most involved in conceptualizing the Pottstown Plan. Born in 1897 in Norristown, Pennsylvania, he attended Bucknell University (Lewisburg, Pennsylvania) and Columbia University (New York City), as well as Andover Newton Seminary (Newton Centre, Massachusetts). A cleric by vocation and fervent advocate of African American civil rights, doctor Haslam started working with Fellowship House in the late 1940s. However, before his Fellowship House tenure, Haslam pastored in Pennsylvania and Ohio too. Moreover, he had a history laboring within civil rights–minded organizations like the American Civil Liberties Union (ACLU), the National Association for the Advancement of Colored People (NAACP), and the Philadelphia Fellowship Commission, among others.[75] Yet "THE POTTSTOWN PLAN for integrating small communities was Dr. Haslam's last project."[76] In fact, when the PCHR and collaborators initially disseminated the plan's booklet on February 21, 1955, Haslam had already been dead about a week.[77]

Following Haslam's death, Penney and Jacoby were Fellowship House and Farm's main promoters of the Pottstown Plan. Born in 1908 in Philadelphia, Pennsylvania, Penney was one of the main leaders and organizers of both the YPIF and the Fellowship House and Farm. Like Haslam, Penney had an extensive history as a civil rights activist. In fact, she received the Philadelphia Award—a distinguished honor that celebrated initiatives that directly ameliorated conditions in the City of Brotherly Love—in 1947. More precisely, Penney obtained the honor because of her activism that assisted in launching the Fellowship Commission over World War II.[78]

Like Haslam and Penney, much of Jacoby's professional life centered on civil rights and communal-based activism, especially while working with Fellowship House and Farm (and beyond). A Philadelphia native like Penney, and born in 1931, Jacoby was the youngest of the three white activists. College educated, Jacoby completed her degree at Temple University in the city as well.[79]

When the *Pottstown Mercury* publicly announced on February 21, 1955, that the Pottstown Plan was being disseminated that day, the newspaper simultaneously informed its readers that it demanded to know what they thought. In fact, the *Pottstown Mercury* continued, they should utilize the newspaper's "Readers Say"/letter-to-the-editor section to articulate their "pro and con" remarks about the PCHR as well as the Pottstown Plan.[80] Here, two responses are worth mentioning since they demonstrate the debate from both sides.

First, Pottstown African American Bessie M. James definitively praised the PCHR's proposal. "In a civilized world there is born into the life of all mankind a hope—a hope of a better life, a hope of a better world in which to live." Therefore, James continued, "The Pottstown Plan is a step forward in making that hope become a reality in our community," specifically because it promoted egalitarianism throughout the small northern locale. More broadly, the Black woman's comments were indeed analogous to the liberal interracialist ethos, which both galvanized and impacted many progressive Americans during this early postwar period. James's thought-provoking remarks also specifically summoned all locals to take part fully in the Pottstown civil rights project.[81]

Second, Pottstown resident Bert Dobry represented a voice of dissent about the PCHR's egalitarian initiative. Interestingly enough, Dobry rationalized his argument by centering attention on the current Cold War. "Segregation and integration is only to promote Socialism." Moreover, he continued his analysis by criticizing African Americans directly, asserting that Blacks—as well as Jews—were hypocrites in terms of racial exclusion. "Truthfully," Dobry complained, "how many Negroes do we see going to the synagogs [*sic*] and how many Jews do we see going to the Negro church?" Finishing his short response, Dobry announced, "First, let them practice what they preach and stop blaming others for the very same thing they are doing—segregating." While Dobry did not name the PCHR or its proposal directly, he did indirectly criticize the egalitarian principles it promulgated.[82] In a similar vein, shortly after the *Pottstown Mercury* started printing the summer 1954 civil rights series, another "Readers Say" author sharply lambasted the reports too, declaring that such rabble-rousing would only create animosities between local whites and African Americans.[83]

For the most part, however, the PCHR and its progressive civil rights endeavor was unequivocally embraced throughout Pottstown. Concerning the Pottstown Plan in particular, the colorful pamphlet's back page illuminates some of the organizations, as well as their leadership, which were in direct solidarity with the innovative scheme. In addition to borough clerics (Protestant and Catholic) and the government, the local public approved of the Pottstown Plan, notably stemming from leadership of Pottstown Memorial Hospital, the United Auto Workers of the Congress of Industrial Organizations, the Salvation Army, and the Pottstown School Board. The *Pottstown Mercury* also revealed that leadership from the Young Women's Christian Association, the Kiwanis Club, and the Pottstown Council of Girl Scouts (among others) thoroughly championed the Pottstown Plan.[84]

"'The Pottstown Plan' . . . an anti-bigotry movement," additionally had local bipartisan support. "Our party has always been in the forefront in the struggle for equal rights," local white Republican William J. Boden announced. "We welcome and will do all we can to help the Pottstown Plan," Boden concluded. Moreover, leading white Democrat Maurice Miller echoed Boden's sentiments. Asserting how his political party consistently labored "in human relations" too, Miller emphasized the Pottstown Plan's importance, providing "everybody does his part." By doing so, the white Democrat continued, the local civil rights initiative would, consequently, create "a 'Community of True Opportunity' for all," no matter their individual background.[85]

In addition to Fellowship House and Farm directly collaborating with the PCHR in organizing and implementing the Pottstown Plan, the organization reached out to other civil rights activists about the plan at both the national and the regional levels. In fact, Penney and Jacoby's correspondences relating to the Pottstown Plan demonstrate how far of a reach Fellowship House and Farm had within its expansive civil rights web. Alongside Justice Hastie, for example, Penney corresponded with national African American NAACP head Roy Wilkins. "Fellowship House has been greatly concerned as to what a small community, not big enough to maintain a Fellowship House or other human relations agency with staff, might do in the integration picture." Penney continued, "We think that this ['the Pottstown Plan'] may be a partial answer which will at least build atmosphere in which real changes can take place."

Penney sent Wilkins the previous correspondence on February 23, 1955.[86] In response, Wilkins—whom Penney also included with the late February communication the Pottstown Plan pamphlet itself—demonstrated how impressed he was by the local civil rights initiative. "I can say only that this is the kind of work that needs to be done, and the way you are going about it should be a lesson to hundreds of communities." The NAACP activist continued, "You are too experienced in the field of human relations for me to more than mention that if profound and permanent changes are to take place in community thinking and living they" should both include let alone further engender careful activism "on the community level as a follow-up to the spectacular 'break-throughs' by national organizations in the field." Wilkins, then, cheerfully finished his correspondence. "I shall be glad to have you advise me from time to time on the developments in Pottstown," he positively remarked.[87]

Dedicated to the liberal interracialist cause, Penney also utilized Fellowship House and Farm's expansive web of connections to inform other white organizational leaders about the Pottstown Plan. Three notable civil rights activists among them were William H. Gremley, who directed Kansas City's (Missouri) Mayor's Commission on Human Relations; Marshall Bragdon, who led Cincinnati's (Ohio) Mayor's Friendly Relations Committee (MFRC); and George Schermer, who held a similar leadership position as the prior two with Philadelphia's Human Relations Commission.[88]

Interestingly enough, both Bragdon and Schermer made identical points in their response letters to Penney. Bragdon was the first, however, who penned back. "Thanks so much for the Pottstown material," said his early March 1955 correspondence, "which is mighty interesting in itself and also strikes me as a partial answer to the important question, What can the small community do in this direction?" From there Bragdon expressed why he had such expertise with respect to civil rights within smaller locales like Pottstown. Essentially, the white activist contributed such knowledge with his MFRC activism, alongside his involvement with the National Association of Intergroup Relations Officials (NAIRO). With NAIRO, Bragdon continued by adding that its members had even talked through "this problem on the Board, in the Local Public Services department," ultimately seeking "to be helpful to the Local Private Services department."[89]

Roughly a month later, Schermer wrote to Penney a similar letter that celebrated the Pottstown Plan. Specifically, he loved how it called with respect to all individuals, whatever age or socioeconomic background, in taking part within the local civil rights activism. Like Bragdon, Schermer also demonstrated his professional familiarity within tinier populaces such as Pottstown. "The venture interests me very much because I have had some experience with efforts in smaller cities and have been impressed with what a small group of concerned people can do." Having labored previously "with a handful of people in Grand Rapids, Michigan—a town that is famous for its conservatism"—an astute observation historian Todd E. Robinson additionally makes when identifying the major political ethos that permeated the Michigan locale—Schermer remembered, "There were times when, as a 'big city' man, I tended to reject some of their ideas as being too much for a small voluntary organization." However, he continued, "In time I had to take back what I had said because that little group put out two of the most expert community studies that I have seen anywhere." Finally, it is worth mentioning that within the same correspondence, Schermer additionally let Penney know how Haslam had already briefed him on the Pottstown civil rights endeavor, particularly during its early phase.[90]

In addition to the NAACP and the three civil rights–centered organizations spotlighted previously, Penney contacted, for example, national leadership within the American Friends Service Committee (AFSC), the Anti-Defamation League of B'nai B'rith (ADL), and the National Council of the Churches of Christ in the United States of America (NCCCUSA) about the Pottstown Plan. By doing so, Penney further demonstrated Fellowship House and Farm's vast civil rights web.[91] "A good many groups across the country . . . are watching to see what can happen,"

Penney wrote Gremley in late June 1955, respecting the Pottstown Plan.[92] In two separate letters, Penney made similar points on the local civil rights initiative. For example, Penney's early November 1955 communication noted how it got "so much interest from other states," while the following July (1956) she corresponded that her organization mailed out scores of the Pottstown Plan document throughout America.[93]

Ultimately, Penney identified why the Pottstown Plan had such potential, specifically because this "human relations" initiative "for small communities" had so many prospects nationwide. "There are literally hundreds of towns all over the United States faced with the business of changing the moral climate. We think the Pottstown Plan is a door opener, nothing more," Penney wrote to white Philadelphia governmental worker William Rafsky in late March 1955.[94] Similarly, in a Fellowship House report from November 1955, while it identified where the civil rights program originated—Pottstown—the survey also emphasized how its creators arranged the initiative with "small communities" as their utmost priority. Moreover, the report stressed that the Pottstown Plan wanted residents participating "in promoting better human relations" within the borough. Examples the survey utilized included overseeing "an interracial event, or opening up" spaces "or employment opportunities" that formerly discriminated. Alternatively, the last illustration spotlighted carrying out "some other tangible" collaboration that communicated equality, while also firmly embracing fairness among locals, African American and white.[95]

Regionally, another individual with whom Penney corresponded about the Pottstown Plan is worth emphasizing. In late February 1955, she wrote white sociologists Milton M. Gordon from prestigious Haverford College (Haverford, Pennsylvania), who responded weeks later in early March. Throughout his life, Gordon published extensively on assimilationism and its relationship to American minorities. In fact, one of his notable works is *Assimilation in American Life: The Role of Race, Religion and National Origins* (1964). Like the previous white activists, Gordon celebrated the PCHR's scheme. "This kind of action is greatly needed, and I am happy to add my hearty endorsement of the plan." However, Gordon additionally articulated his utmost desire "that minority group organizations in Pottstown will also be invited to initiate action." More specifically, he believed "it is important to stress the cooperative effort for a common goal and" thereby circumvent "the idea that this is entirely a one-way affair with one group 'doing something' of a charitable nature for another less privileged group." Within the same correspondence, Gordon also found the PCHR's civil rights program an excellent commemoration of Haslam. Gordon even lamented that Haslam's departure "was a great loss to the cause of justice and brotherhood for all people," whatever background.[96]

While Penney communicated the Pottstown Plan with outside organizations, Jacoby was mainly the one marketing it to the affiliated Fellowship House and Farm works such as Kansas City, Brooklyn, Columbus, and Washington, DC. Moreover, she publicized the Pottstown Plan in regional Fellowship House and Farm affiliations, which included Media, West Chester, and Reading—all in Pennsylvania.[97] Regarding the Media Fellowship House affiliate, Jacoby emphasized via correspondence to an individual there in early May 1955 how "Pottstown . . . has begun this year a human relations program unique in the country."[98]

Similarly, white Pottstown Burgess John B. Hartenstine, Jr., authorized October 27, 1955, officially as "'THE POTTSTOWN PLAN' DAY." Hartenstine even boasted via newsprint how Pottstown was "the first small community" throughout America that constructed such an initiative that emphasized amelioration "of its citizens"—whether Black or white. "The future of the success of the Pottstown Plan," Hartenstine announced, "is, in its very nature, in the hands of each resident of our Town."[99] Correspondingly, Poirier revealed how "committees and organizations against discrimination, for brotherhood," were indeed ordinary across the majority of large urban centers such as San Francisco, Chicago, Los Angeles, New York, and close by Philadelphia. However, the white journalist continued, Pottstown was clearly an aberration because "no similar experience has been reported from a community anywhere near" its smaller population configuration.[100]

Like Fellowship House and Farm, the *Pottstown Mercury* demonstrated as well that the PCHR's proposal was surely acquiring recognition both nationally and regionally. In fact, the borough media-outlet noted on March 1, 1955, how "newspapers from coast-to-coast have printed the story of the plan—and what it hopes to accomplish." These presses did so, the *Pottstown Mercury* continued, because AP initially circulated a description that highlighted the Pottstown-based civil rights initiative across "its national wires."[101] For instance, newspapers located in Wisconsin, Maryland, Michigan, Georgia, Texas, California, Kansas, Minnesota, Missouri, Florida, West Virginia, South Dakota, and New Jersey, all grabbed the AP account.[102] In Pennsylvania, publications such as the *Gazette and Daily* (York), the *Scranton Times* (Scranton), the *Indiana Evening Gazette* (Indiana), and the *Plain Speaker* (Hazleton) also publicized the Pottstown civil rights endeavor.[103]

Likewise, Fellowship House and Farm revealed how organizations throughout America passionately inquired about obtaining numerous printings of the Pottstown Plan document itself. For example, a representative from the Northern California Regional Office of the AFSC wrote Penney in June 1956, requesting one hundred additional duplicates from the initial texts it had.[104] The previous June (1955), Black executive director J. Oscar Lee of the NCCCUSA's Division of Christian Life and Work Department of Racial and Cultural Relations, located in New York City, sought roughly one hundred Pottstown Plan booklets from Penney as well. Lee even let Penney know via letter how Interracial News Service, an organizational publication, already printed data on "the Pottstown project."[105] Ultimately, however, Penney wrote both organizational representatives back that Fellowship House and Farm was not able to fulfill such large-scale requests at those specific junctures in time, citing document shortages. That said, within her same correspondence to Lee (June 15, 1955), Penney did include ten Pottstown Plan booklets.[106]

Similar to Fellowship House and Farm, shortly after the PCHR disseminated its booklet in late February 1955, the *Pottstown Mercury* informed its readership that it was already getting attention throughout the United States. In fact, four inquiries—stemming out of Milwaukee, Wisconsin, Ann Arbor, Michigan, Columbus, Georgia, and nearby Baltimore, Maryland—contacted the *Pottstown Mercury*, seeking the local civil rights booklet itself. For example, the Maryland Congress of Parents and Teachers (MCPT) first heard about the PCHR's scheme through the *Baltimore Evening Sun*. Moreover, the MCPT requested fifty Pottstown Plan duplicates. The organization wanted the documents, the MCPT declared, because its members were indeed concerned "in the studying samples of programs or projects which tend to" reduce discrimination.[107]

At the same time, when the *Baltimore Sun* publicized the AP's Pottstown Plan account, white army soldier David Chaplin wrote to the *Pottstown Mercury* directly. Interestingly enough, Chaplin correlated Pottstown's racial struggles as captured by Poirier and the PCHR in general with his alma mater, Amherst College (Amherst, Massachusetts), where he penned an essay that illuminated identical discriminatory issues that Blacks endured there. By Chaplin making these juxtapositions, he demonstrated further how ubiquitous white racism across Pottstown reflected other diminutive northern locales. At the same time, Chaplin's remarks aligned with arguments articulated previously and corroborated how apparent Jim Crow racism was above and below the Mason-Dixon Line. Summarizing his bachelor's degree experience, Chaplin recalled that "race relations" there were similar to all northern small communities. Within these locations, Chaplin continued, they were "governed by a subtle Jim Crow line, as fixed as the obvious one down South." For instance, he added how Amherst African Americans "could not get a haircut, go into a 'nice' restaurant or hotel, or find homes in any 'desirable' areas." Blacks there "could find work only as menials," he added, and not within white-collar work, leading to them residing "in the run down fringes of town," Chaplin observed. In summary, though, how Black exclusion played out in Pottstown had surely both captivated and enthralled Chaplin, thereby explaining why he directly wrote to the *Pottstown Mercury* itself.[108]

Two national presses—the *Christian Science Monitor* (Boston, Massachusetts) and the *Pittsburgh Courier*—additionally made specific inquiries to the *Pottstown Mercury* with respect to the Pottstown Plan. On the one hand, the *Christian Science Monitor* asked the *Pottstown Mercury* for "a special 800-word" piece on the PCHR's initiative. The *Pittsburgh Courier*, on the other hand, wanted the illustration the PCHR utilized on its Pottstown Plan booklet.[109] Eventually, the Black newspaper disseminated the cover page within its April 30, 1955, *Magazine Section*. Moreover, on the same page, it is worth mentioning that the *Pittsburgh Courier Magazine Section* identified the PCHR's civil rights project as "the crusade."[110]

In a vein identical to the imagery found on the front page of the Pottstown Plan booklet, the *Pottstown Mercury* captured other symbolic gestures. On the front page of its March 1, 1955, edition, the small northern newspaper printed an illustration that truly symbolized the main justifications behind the launching of the PCHR as well as its Pottstown Plan. Indeed, the illustration has several salient points to take away from it. First, a billboard is in the picture. Within the advertisement is a circle. Engraved inside the object is the phrase "POTTSTOWN PLAN" (right above and outside the circle is the word "THE"). Pottstown is at the top of the circle, while the word plan is at the bottom. Most moving, however, is what is inside the circle's middle: a hand shake between white and Black hands. In short, the gesture further symbolizes the Pottstown Plan's unequivocal objective, which was full-blown racial integration. On the other hand, it is worth stressing that directly outside the circle are two American flags on each side as well as an eagle right above the circle. Here, such images both conceptualize and visualize how the Pottstown Plan was in direct concert with American ideals and values. Furthermore, to the right of the aforementioned images are the words "Penn Village Is Making It Work," and directly underneath, the question "Are You?"

A last powerful graphic found on the *Pottstown Mercury*'s front-page article goes hand in glove with the cover page of the Pottstown Plan document itself. Captured in the image are two young people (a little older than the ones illustrated on the Pottstown Plan booklet itself). One is Black while the other is white. Dressed in the fashions of the day, they are holding hands and directly gazing on the billboard constructed at Penn Village. Again, by holding hands, they are further symbolically showcasing what the PCHR and the Pottstown Plan demanded locally when it came to African American advancement and civil rights. Moreover, by looking on the enormous poster, the gesture demands that everyone else in the small northern locale follow suit as well. Finally, when providing direct commentary on the aforementioned picture, the *Pottstown Mercury* emphatically declares: "The eyes of the Nation have turned to Pottstown to see how the plan works out."[111]

"Count Me In"

Countrywide responses to the *Pottstown Mercury*'s summer of 1954 reports on local civil rights resulted in prominent distinctions. Indeed, during the

same month (February 1955) that activists began circulating the Pottstown Plan pamphlet, the National Conference of Christians and Jews
(NCCJ) granted the *Pottstown Mercury*, alongside thirty-four additional
"media" representatives, accolades. Specifically, the NCCJ acknowledged
their marvelous "contributions [in] promoting the cause of good-will and
understanding among the people of our nation." Additionally, the NCCJ
placed the *Pottstown Mercury*'s journalistic advocacy work within its "top
ten" distinctions. As noted by the *New York Times*, the NCCJ praised the
southeastern Pennsylvania newspaper because it "painstakingly and fairly"
analyzed Pottstown Blacks' status; consequently, such local activism thereby
springboarded the PCHR. Moreover, accompanying the *Pottstown Mercury* on this reputable list were many other esteemed organizations such as
the United Nations, the *Christian Science Monitor*, and Columbia Broad-
casting System, to name a few. That same year, Poirier's civil rights investigation even shared glorious space with white antiapartheid activist and
South African author Alan Paton.[112] In addition to the NCCJ, weeks following the publication of the *Pottstown Mercury* series, the NCCCUSA
commended the civil rights reporting.[113] Similarly, the Pennsylvania Society
of Newspaper Editors celebrated the *Pottstown Mercury* by bestowing "an
editorial excellence award" on the local press, particularly for Poirier's captivating Black freedom struggle work.[114]

In April 1955, Lincoln University in Jefferson City, Missouri, personally acknowledged Poirier's journalistic work on African American civil
rights in Pottstown. Specifically, the historically Black institution invited
him to speak about it during the university's "7th Headliner Banquet." In
fact, Lincoln University made Poirier the main speaker of the special program, where he addressed more than two hundred individuals.[115] Moreover, Lincoln University's School of Journalism gave the *Pottstown Mercury*
its "Award for Significant Contributions to Better Human Relations."[116]
Here, the educational center acknowledged how the southeastern Pennsylvania press was "a model, vigorous, and resourceful newspaper whose
enlightening exposure of subtle race discriminatory practices stems from a
publishing enterprise of high motive."[117] Lincoln University's honor continued, Shandy Hill recalled, noting that the *Pottstown Mercury* was in fact
aiding and assisting the small northern locale toward racial egalitarianism,
thereby promoting "a model of neighborly love and justice."[118]

The civil rights advocacy work spearheaded by the *Pottstown Mercury*'s summer of 1954 reports also greatly assisted in another victory on the home front in its fight toward eradicating racism inextricably caused by the local Jim Crow structure. In 1956, Elaine Hill became Pottstown's pioneering Black instructor, where she taught geography in local public education. As noted by the *Philadelphia Tribune*, Hill visited an event the PCL sponsored. While there, the group acquainted her with multiple influential locals.[119] Originally from Darby, Pennsylvania, Hill obtained her bachelor's degree from West Chester State Teachers College (now West Chester University of Pennsylvania) in 1956.[120] While working as an educator in Pottstown, it is also worth mentioning that Hill served with the Pottstown Human Relations Council, another appellation of the PCHR.[121]

In *Dear Sir*, Shandy Hill reflected on this prior civil rights achievement and the *Pottstown Mercury*'s direct relationship to the local Black freedom struggle. While addressing Seventh-day Adventists about Elaine Hill's hiring and its egalitarian significance over summer 1956, the white editor emphasized—whether consciously or subconsciously—how the Black educator's teaching position demonstrated broadly how Pottstown was chipping away at previously entrenched biases there. "A few years ago," Shandy Hill remembered, "the superintendent of public schools recoiled in horror when" the editor and his newspaper staff revealed that their campaign "for anti-discrimination would be" assisted significantly providing "the school board were to hire" an African American educator. While it took some time, Hill observed, the *Pottstown Mercury*'s labor was not in vain because Elaine Hill got appointed. Moreover, speaking of the *Pottstown Mercury* staff overall, the white editor asserted that it did not conceptualize Elaine Hill's hiring "as [a] personal" victory. Rather, Shandy Hill continued in an optimistic retelling, it foreshadowed ultimate racial equality throughout employment.[122]

In addition to the Pottstown Plan booklet, the PCHR printed another pamphlet-style document later that highlights the group's civil rights achievements in and around the small northern locale. The document's entitled "Pottstown Human Relations Council . . . For Equality: The Pottstown Plan; What Has Happened in Two Years?" In essence, it provides excellent insight into the PCHR's history as well as its successes as a local activist organization. Like the Pottstown Plan booklet, this document stresses how the *Pottstown Mercury* series was the impetus that led concerned residents to launch the PCHR.[123]

Regarding the PCHR's accomplishments, the second PCHR document mentions that Pottstown had already employed an African American educator, although without mentioning Elaine Hill's name explicitly. The text also captures how the small northern government employed an African American. Like Hill, he was another Black pioneer. However, he initially held the position within the local "municipal authority." Like Hill, his name is not revealed in the PCHR pamphlet itself. But the Pottstown African American and Pennsylvania State University (State College) alumnus was William D. Barber.[124] While Barber eventually obtained governmental employment in York, Pennsylvania, it must also be noted that he helped establish the PCHR, thereby demonstrating his proper place in local, as well as northern, civil rights history.[125] Similarly, Penney wrote glowing reference letters for Barber in late August and November 1955 which additionally praised his role as an activist within Pottstown.[126] Barber, Penney declared in late August, "is the kind of leadership I seldom see."[127]

Yet Hill and Barber's pioneering work was not the only local accomplishments emphasized by the second PCHR pamphlet. It also boasts that Pottstown's School of Nursing at last welcomed an African American pupil. "All major industries" within the northern borough at the time, reported the second PCHR document, "hire[d] without prejudice or discrimination." Demonstrating the degree to which the post-*Brown* Black freedom struggle had tapped into white Pottstown's liberal interracialist sensibilities, the PCHR even had a designated committee that kept a watchful eye over local grievances as well as "rumors of discrimination," expecting such matters received direct attention. The same document noted that within the PCHR, activists already addressed "a score of civil and church organizations." Here, PCHR representatives emphasized while also simultaneously demanded "equal opportunity for all citizens." Local groups like the YMCA and Junior Chamber of Commerce, the second pamphlet additionally reported, were also incorporating civil rights–centered programming that went hand in glove with PCHR advocacy work.[128]

At the same time, both PCHR booklets illuminate how the local civil rights organization directly influenced multiple entities, including other associations, throughout Pottstown. For instance, they reveal that "service clubs," congregations, Parent Teacher Associations, and so forth started conducting initiatives because the PCHR launched its innovative and inclusive, civil rights–centered work.[129] "One churchmen's group began a now famous Forum which unites one hundred men out of every racial, religious and nationality group in town for regular supper meetings to work for understanding in their community," notes the initial PCHR pamphlet.[130]

Along with the two small booklets, another PCHR document, dated March 14, 1956, provides further light into the group's civil rights activism. While this evidence supports the pamphlet's assertions, it also suggests that the PCHR had an influence and reach that went beyond Pottstown. At this time, the report states that the PCHR was already creating connections among different "Human Relations Committees in Montgomery County," Pennsylvania—the county where Pottstown is situated. Moreover, locations outside the small northern locale were not only "following the lead of Pottstown," but "exchange relationships" were also transpiring. Indeed, the paper both corroborates the two booklets also in revealing that such activism transcended Pottstown and even Pennsylvania—including not only Baltimore, Maryland, but also Wilmington, Delaware.[131]

Moreover, the same document from March 1956, sheds light about the PCHR being "an informal information center." Historians such as Thomas J. Sugrue and Matthew J. Countryman have already demonstrated the role of various networks in organizing, implementing, and ultimately promoting civil rights activism throughout the twentieth century. Thus, this examination of the PCHR falls in line with their interpretive assessments.[132] In fact, within the PCHR's civil rights network/web, activists remained diligent swapping data about local issues. These activists stayed vigilant, the report continues, because they wanted better insight let alone conflict-free answers that addressed "problem areas" within Pottstown.[133]

Finally, the PCHR had other civil rights achievements that were directly linked to a late October 1955 gathering where well over five hundred spectators convened. News of the PCHR gathering even caught the attention of the NAACP. Fascinated by the entire affair, the national civil rights organization documented it in its December 1955 edition of *Crisis*. "The 'town meeting'" the PCHR promoted, indeed, only demonstrated another overall achievement that the small northern organization conducted, so much so, the December 1955 *Crisis* edition continued, that the PCHR began "the nationally-known 'Pottstown Plan.'" The NAACP publication also noted that thus far, representatives in "38 states" had already contacted the PCHR about its civil rights program.[134] Correspondingly, the PCHR's second pamphlet documented how the same late October 1955 gathering received acknowledgment "in several National magazines."[135]

Held in Pottstown Junior High School (PJHS), Justice Hastie served as the principal orator. Overall, the Black justice centered his evening talk on dismantling "religious and racial" hurdles. In his view, such obstacles were the main culprits behind keeping individuals from living together in harmony. Although Hastie delivered an insightful oration, the PCHR had another initiative on full display in PJHS. "For all of Hastie's eloquence and charm," the December 1955 *Crisis* edition noted, "the spotlight was stolen by the premiere production of an original musical-play based on the formation of the Pottstown Committee and the Pottstown Plan."[136] While not identified in the aforementioned NAACP *Crisis* publication, the pioneering artistic endeavor alluded to was "COUNT ME IN." The previous June (1955), Fellowship House Farm printed an organizational document that illuminates further information about *Count Me In.* Named "Cast Down Your Buckets Where You Are," the packet writes that *Count Me In* was "an original musical drama" which reveals "the story of the Pottstown Plan, a program that citizens of Pottstown worked out to make their city a friendlier place in which to live."[137] Moreover, it is worth noting that the December 1955 *Crisis* publication revealed that *Count Me In* lasted sixty minutes in duration.[138]

Scholars have already shed light on Fellowship House's integrated "Singing City" chorale, which was established during the late 1940s. The intention behind the choral, historian Stanley Keith Arnold writes, pertained specifically "to be a musical expression of racial tolerance." However, Arnold and others fully ignore the events and people surrounding *Count Me In,* and its proper place in northern civil rights history.[139] Although *Count Me In* was a PCHR creation, the fact was that Fellowship House and Farm activists were intimately involved in both organizing and implementing the artistic endeavor.

To begin, white Fellowship House associate Nettie Mae Hare (maiden name Merritt) composed *Count Me In*'s musical and lyrical content. Born in Springfield, Massachusetts, in 1923, Hare was also a part of Singing City, where she labored directly under its nationally esteemed leader, conductor, and establisher, white civil rights activists Elaine Brown (not to be confused with the African American activist of the same name associated with the national leadership of the Black Panther Party for Self-Defense). By the time Hare constructed *Count Me In*, she had already obtained several college degrees.[140]

Like the PCHR booklets, *Count Me In* makes egalitarian points. In particular, it stresses how Pottstown African Americans, as well as other local minority groups, experienced discrimination firsthand. Thus, individuals should not tolerate such bigotry. "Prejudice overflows like a river and hurts ev'ry single person in this town."[141] Unlike the two PCHR brochures, however, *Count Me In* directly illuminates examples of the local de facto segregation structure and particularly the pervasive racism endured by Pottstown African Americans. Indeed, the following sample taken from *Count Me In* demonstrates the latter points most cogently:

Newsboy (sung)	Extra, extra, read all about it! (yelled) Jim*Crow, Yankee-style, stalks the streets of our town! (sung) Northern town with a Southern exposure. (yelled) Nurses needed desperately!
Girl's voice, reading slowly	Our hospital is not training negro nurses.
Newsboy (sung)	Secretaries needed in vital industries.
2 people reading together	Our businessmen refuse to hire Negro secretaries.
Newsboy (sung)	Student counsellors advise Negro students, "take a general high school course."
3 people reading	White counsellors refuse to to [*sic*] recommend Negro students for white collar jobs after high school.
Newsboy (sung)	Only menial jobs open to Negros. (pause) Housing and churches segregated.
5 people	Average Negro in our town is fearful of his white neighbors because of treatment he has received.

Newsboy (sung)	Fearful.
7 people	Fearful
Newsboy (sung)	Jim Crow
9 people	Jim Crow!
Newsboy (sung)	In our town.
All (spoken)	IN OUR TOWN![142]

Activists associated with High School Fellowship, an educational civil rights endeavor that Fellowship House initially launched during the early 1940s, were the ones responsible for publicly executing *Count Me In*. Jacoby even supervised High School Fellowship while *Count Me In* was being staged.[143] Moreover, on September 1, 1956, Penney informed Lee of the NCCCUSA's Department of Racial and Cultural Relations that greater "than six thousand teen-agers and adults, in public and private schools, churches and synagogues, town meetings, and department stores" had witnessed *Count Me In* being performed. Indeed, African American singer Harry Belafonte, an esteemed individual active within the broader Black freedom struggle himself, was arguably the most notable among the thousands. At the same time, *Count Me In* captivated Belafonte. Thus, Penney revealed, the Black entertainer strongly wished "to make a recording of the song" included in *Count Me In* entitled "There are People."[144]

Like their promotional work for the Pottstown Plan, Jacoby and Penney utilized Fellowship House and Farm's civil rights web so that *Count Me In* was extensively marketed. In fact, they not only informed individuals about when and where *Count Me In* was being performed but also struggled diligently so that the civil rights musical might obtain sponsorship for printing as well. Within the same September 1, 1956, letter, Penney informed Lee of the NCCCUSA's Department of Racial and Cultural Relations that her organization was "receiving requests from groups and individuals across the country—for copies of the [*Count Me In*] script." Because Penney's Philadelphia-based organization had no economic means to sponsor *Count Me In*, she asked Lee whether the NCCCUSA "or any [other] group you know" could. Indeed, Penney explained why *Count Me In* was worth such economic investment. "There is a sad scarcity of simple, pointed plays on human relations," she wrote to Lee, "and this is eminently useable with both adult and youth groups." Concluding her letter to Lee, she bluntly stated, "Do help us—if you can."[145]

On the same day, Penney wrote Jewish Rabbinical scholar and ADL activist Arthur Gilbert an identical letter.[146] That December (1956) she wrote to white NCCCUSA worker Robert A. Elfers too, letting him know that "we have not the funds to reproduce the score."[147] Although the two additionally penned Penney, even showing interest, nothing materialized.[148] Eventually, Hare copyrighted *Count Me In* herself.[149]

Yet even though Penney expressed the real economic challenge that Fellowship House faced in sponsoring *Count Me In*, the civil rights organization did assemble an aspiring "preface page" for the artistic work. Like the PCHR's two previous booklets, the preface stresses both the intention and the genesis behind *Count Me In*. "This is a musical that got written <u>not</u> because the composer sat down to write a musical," the document reads, "but only because there was a true and wonderful story to be told, andthere [*sic*] just had to be songs to go with it! The story is really more important than the music" since "it's the story of Americans, folks like you and me, who got together to solve the very real human relations problems of their town." While "the names of people in the musical are fictitious," the preface continues, "the musical itself tells what really happened in 1954 in Pottstown, Pennsylvania." The paper then highlights what directly stimulated *Count Me In*'s dawning. "It all began when a crusading newspaper revealed 'Jim Crow-ism,'" the ubiquitous de facto segregation structure, "in the town." Inspired, driven individuals responded by plunging "into action." Thus, the preface writes, "a small group of citizens consulting with Fellowship House (a nearby human relations agency) worked out its own plan for building a friendlier, more democratic town."

At the same time, Fellowship House saw *Count Me In*'s content as having tangible potential in personally inspiring its viewership toward conducting further activism, essentially resembled the Black freedom work in Pottstown. "We hope you'll enjoy this musical," the preface asserts, "but more than that, we hope you'll <u>use</u> it in your own community to help more Americans get together and discover how exciting and rewarding the practice of democracy really is." Moreover, like the two previous PCHR booklets, *Count Me In*'s preface makes arguments centered on egalitarianism, once again demonstrating Fellowship House and Farm's direct influence on the PCHR's own civil rights activism.[150]

The Local Black Freedom Struggle Presses Forth

The PCHR remained a local civil rights organization over the 1950s and 1960s in Pottstown.[151] However, the group never again matched the same impact as its civil rights activism in the two years or so following *Brown*.[152] On the other hand, it is worth noting that leadership within the PCHR went on and had success in other civil rights ventures. For example, by the end of the 1950s, Lee was working in Coatesville, Pennsylvania (Chester County), under African American physician, civil rights activist and fellow Howard University Medical School graduate Whittier Atkinson. During the late 1930s, Atkinson launched a pioneering medical facility in Coatesville that accommodated local African Americans within a city that blatantly discriminated. Soon after, Lee branched out from Atkinson, providing medical services for many Coatesville Blacks. In addition to his professional life, Lee labored with the NAACP following his Pottstown Civic League and PCHR activism in Pottstown. In the end, Lee was one of several activists from the PCHR who went on and continued similar civil rights work in and outside Pottstown. Another individual was Pottstown African American William D. Barber and his later activism in York, Pennsylvania.[153]

While the *Pottstown Mercury* series and subsequent work spearheaded by the PCHR led to both regional and national buzz surrounding the liberal interracial work, the fact remained that such civil rights activism had its most significant and lasting impact on the local front. Indeed, during this age of northern Jim Crow, local employment sectors in both private and public industry capitulated to the demands of the salient Black freedom work in the aftermath of the *Brown* ruling. These arguments also demonstrate links between "the local with the national," historian Steven Lawson observes, especially when it comes to analyzing and assessing the history of the Black freedom struggle.[154]

Although the *Pottstown Mercury* stepped out and illuminated local civil rights issues in the aftermath of *Brown*, it was not alone in such activism. To be clear, without the direct participation of Pottstown African

Americans—taking part in the process by directly sharing their lived experiences and know-how—the work would have never materialized and gone on to having the large-scale impact that it ultimately did. The civil rights reporting disseminated by the *Pottstown Mercury* engendered reactions from across the United States as well. When it came to the realm of civil rights, however, this was the *Pottstown Mercury*'s first time having such large-scale attention and impact. In some sense, though, the closet resemblance to the small northern newspaper's activism captured above was when it focused on Hemlock and Cottage Rows African Americans in early 1950, as chapter 3 shows. Yet while that activism influenced governmental authorities to leave the Stowe properties alone, it was nowhere near as far-reaching as the *Pottstown Mercury*'s work following *Brown*.

Like the PCL, the PCHR was another homegrown civil rights organization. Yet what made the PCHR different from the PCL was that it had fervent and consistent organizational backing, particularly from the *Pottstown Mercury* and Fellowship House and Farm. Such support allowed the PCHR to have the local, regional, and national impact that it ultimately had. Moreover, Fellowship House and Farm contributed to the PCHR's success through the use of its vast civil rights web. It utilized this network to promote the PCHR's local civil rights work, namely, the Pottstown Plan. In a similar sense, because the *Pottstown Mercury* allowed other newspapers to pick up its summer of 1954 series on civil rights, and because it eventually promoted the Pottstown Plan as well, the local press contributed to the rapid success and impact of the PCHR.

While the PCHR commanded national attention, it was still, nevertheless, able to transform conditions for African Americans on the local front. Indeed, the PCHR continued the work started by previous activists' groups in Pottstown like the local NAACP, the Black-centered YMCA activism, and the PCL. Therefore, even though the PCHR began during the traditional time frame of civil rights, a period already well-documented within the scholarship, it was, to borrow language from historian Jacquelyn Dowd Hall, essentially continuing that "long"—albeit noncontinuous nor monolithic—fight of the local Black freedom struggle that began taking shape in Pottstown during World War II.[155]

As the PCHR played such an essential component in Pottstown's Black freedom struggle in the aftermath of *Brown*, it was not the most consistent local civil rights group during the postwar area. Unequivocally, the Pottstown NAACP was. And in the early 1950s, it revitalized following an approximately six-year disbandment.

Yet while the local NAACP was not necessarily a direct and major participant in the impactful work that began materializing after *Brown*, it was, arguably, the most active local civil rights entity of the 1950s and 1960s. Moreover, one of the PCHR activists would go on and play a fundamental leadership and activist role within the borough NAACP, spearheading multiple civil rights initiatives on the local front. Like Daniel Lee, Newstell Marable was another native son of the South.[156]

6

The Pottstown NAACP and the Postwar Industrial North

Published on July 31, 1951, the *Pottstown Mercury* circulated information on an African American reportedly "terrorizing" locals since about mid-month. In response to the suspect's activity, two West Pottsgrove law enforcement officers, accompanied by twenty-five other white males holding firearms, patrolled the township seeking the alleged Black perpetrator. Understanding the possible risk of utilizing local citizens in such a radical capacity, one of the white police officers, James V. Guadagno, cautioned them "to shoot only to cripple the man if they have to use their weapons."[1]

While the *Pottstown Mercury* captured the dramatic events unfolding in West Pottsgrove, Pennsylvania, that did not mean it agreed with arming citizens to help township police do its job. As a continual supporter of the liberal interracialist ethos and civil rights advocacy work, the newspaper published an article the following day, August 1, entitled "Don't Take Law into Own Hands!" In short, the newspaper argued that equipping "vigilantes" was seriously dangerous. On the one hand, the press brought up how bad the practice was from a legal standpoint. Because "the armed men have [not] been deputized as police officers, their patrolling is contrary to law." Therefore, the individuals could not, under any circumstances, "take the law into their own hands." On the other hand, the newspaper pointed out that township law enforcement had wiser, more legal options than its current methodology. County and state police forces, for example, were far better choices. Moreover, the *Pottstown Mercury* took direct issue with Guadagno's advice, which stressed shooting "to cripple" the alleged Black perpetrator, cautioning that bloody mayhem could result. "Let there be a 'trigger-happy' man in that patrol," the newspaper continued, "and there's likely to be a mass killing!"

In addition to laying out practical reasoning that lambasted radical vigilantism's promotion, the *Pottstown Mercury* brought up the very tangent threat the white militant gang had on local African Americans. Rational minds, the newspaper argued, should obviously acknowledge "the danger of angered mobs looking for a Negro of vague description." The press continued additionally, admonishing "that any Negro . . . might be harmed if mob psychology rules a horde of angered townsmen."[2] Here, the local African American community's connection to migration both before and during the Great Migration is worth stressing. Not-too-distant memories of lynchings perpetrated by southern white terrorists had to have been in the hearts and minds of local Blacks as this episode of potential violence took center stage in Stowe.[3] At the same time, Pennsylvania had its own history with similar racial violence. Earlier in the twentieth century, whites lynched and then dismembered African American Zachariah Walker in Coatesville, a region close by Pottstown that had a similar working-class composition.[4]

In addition to the trepidation likely on the conscious of local Blacks, the *Pottstown Mercury* pointed out that the white band also prospectively threatened everyone's safety as well as security in Stowe. Consequently, the borough newspaper vehemently encouraged West Pottsgrove law enforcement to not only demobilize the radical gang immediately but also apprehend all individuals not licensed to bear arms in the area. The *Pottstown Mercury* also demanded that the district attorney of Montgomery County get involved and suspend "the movement" posthaste.[5]

Outside southeastern Pennsylvania, NAACP headquarters in New York City also found out about West Pottsgrove's racial dilemma. Black NAACP activist and civil rights pioneer Thurgood Marshall even provided direct commentary. In short, Marshall noted publicly how his organization dispatched with urgency newly hired African American NAACP laborer John W. Flamer to the scene. When addressing the West Pottsgrove affair directly, however, Marshall identified it as being "loaded with dynamite."[6]

In the end, the central NAACP sending Flamer helped ease tensions in West Pottsgrove. An organizational document dated soon after (August 2) reported that Flamer conducted "a conference with law enforcement officers and other officials of the town and with community leaders in an effort to" avoid violent encounters. Therefore, "it was agreed to restrict the carrying of fire-arms on the open highway and to disband the groups of men roaming the area," the NAACP document concluded.[7]

It is also worth noting that West Pottsgrove police detained the alleged perpetrator, Stowe African American Barney Strickland, on August 1.[8] Montgomery County Prison then incarcerated Strickland for thirty-seven days; however, the jailing facility ended up letting Strickland go on September 6 because the evidence against him collapsed.[9]

The Postwar Pottstown NAACP

While the local Pottstown NAACP branch relaunched in the early 1950s, overall, the civil rights organization also endured its own makeover. About midway through the 1950s, it underwent "generational change as early leaders" such as African Americans Walter White alongside W. E. B. Du Bois died "or retired from active work in the Association." For instance, White's demise in 1955 placed Black NAACP leadership into the capable hands of the progressive organization's assistant secretary and "Pottstown Plan" commentator Roy Wilkins.

As such, the launching of the Wilkins era (1955–1977) of NAACP leadership coincided with more extensive historical developments across the African American civil rights struggle for first-class citizenship and equal rights of the early postwar.[10] Historians Kevern Verney and Lee Sartain also point out conflicts between representatives from the NAACP's central location in New York City as well as smaller auxiliary chapters, even from the 1950s to 1960s.[11] Nevertheless, like many other NAACP chapters both above and below the Mason-Dixon Line, the reestablished Pottstown NAACP waged continual assaults on white supremacy and other manifestations of anti-Black racism ubiquitous to the local and regional Jim Crow landscape of southeastern Pennsylvania during the postwar period.[12]

While the Pottstown NAACP ceased existence around World War II's conclusion, it would officially revamp in early October 1951.[13] From after World War II to the autumn of 1951, however, efforts locally and by NAACP representatives from outside the small northern borough had also transpired.[14] "I am very much interested in the progress of our people and I am trying very hard to put this program over," wrote Stowe African American Charles Prince in late October 1949 to the NAACP's central location in New York City. "This is the reason I am riting [*sic*] your office," continued Prince, a blue-collar worker with the local Bethlehem Steel Corporation who would head the Pottstown NAACP during most of the 1950s. In the same correspondence, Prince also acknowledged that an NAACP branch was previously active on the local front.[15]

Outside Pottstown, NAACP representatives like Flamer also sought to relaunch the local branch. He started with the NAACP in April 1951.[16] However, regarding Pennsylvania locations that needed direct attention, a document addressed to Flamer and dated July 31, 1951, targeted Pottstown as one of nine places the NAACP wanted specifically focused "on . . . the next two months."[17] At this time, the NAACP also identified the Pottstown branch as nonfunctioning, albeit it did acknowledge how the local civil rights organization was surely operative until 1945.[18] Thus, Flamer planned to visit Pottstown in late September of the same year.

Yet although Flamer initially targeted visiting Pottstown in late September 1951, talks about the local NAACP reformulating had already begun crystallizing weeks before. In late August—not too long after the white vigilantism dilemma in nearby Stowe—Black activists had started strategizing developments locally "for organizing a branch," so much so that during a Pottstown Civic League (PCL) gathering that Black physician Daniel Lee administered, NAACP representatives from outside the borough, African Americans Joshua Thompson and Dr. Harry J. Green, assisted Lee in planning initiatives. Moreover, the NAACP reps appointed "a temporary committee to enlist workers for an organizing drive." Indeed, James H. Corum and Prince (as well as another individual) were on the short-term committee, even before both headed the reemerged Pottstown NAACP during the 1950s and early 1960s, as this chapter shows.[19]

By 1963, however, African American Newstell Marable started leading the Pottstown NAACP. Born in Birmingham, Alabama, and a product of the Great Migration, Marable was especially capable of spearheading local Black freedom work, as chapter 1 reveals. In reflection on Marable's death, the *Mercury* additionally described him as "a passionate advocate for equal opportunity and employment for all races and genders."[20] Recalling her late spouse of almost six decades in January 2015, Millicent Marable likewise emphasized his compassion toward people, whatever their background. Furthermore, Black minister Vernon Ross, who headed Pottstown's Bethel AME, Marable's former church, even argued that the Alabama native honestly subscribed to "the message of Dr. Martin Luther King's dream for equality."[21]

Finally, one must also note that during Marable's extensive time in the area, he served in leadership capacities with the borough "Jaycees," local Boy Scouts, the Montgomery County Opportunity Board, and Pottstown's "Federation of Men's Bible" courses.[22] As far as employment went, however, Marable labored, for instance, at places such as Pottstown Planting Company. The Black activist worked close to Pottstown with Rahns, Pennsylvania's Techalloy Company as well. Although Marable was university trained, the brief sample here of the companies he worked for demonstrates the fact that he must have had an intimate familiarity, as well as conceptualization and understanding, of both the needs and the concerns of local working-class African Americans in the decades after World War II.[23]

"Mr. James P. Crow, Esquire. . . . A Sequel"

During the postwar, the reestablished Pottstown NAACP utilized local Black spaces to conduct its racial justice work. Such spaces included congregations like Mount Herman Baptist, Bethel AME, Friendship Baptist, and the House of God.[24] The role of white-led interracialist entities was critically important as well.[25]

Yet while local civil rights activism had support from whites in the area, that did not mean all from the majority population honestly welcomed, let alone embraced, more significant steps toward racial equality and access to resources. In fact, many local whites—most, perhaps—did not entirely cling to the changes in the realm of Black equality that reverberated the American home front of the early postwar period. Rather, many from the dominant populace withstood this perceived African American assault on white privilege in housing, education, employment, and similar arenas. Moreover, these same whites wished desperately to keep local Blacks in their historically inferior circumstances—a condition in which the local northern Jim Crow structure had both promulgated and undergirded. As a result, local white pushback or opposition to integration efforts began surfacing during the early 1960s. Here such pushback, which predated the national civil rights legislation of 1964 and 1965—the time frame that traditional historiographical interpretations argue is the high-water mark—frustrated desegregation attempts conducted by the Pottstown NAACP during the decade. Indeed, the borough branch at this time was the principal civil rights organization that directly attacked the pervasive yet clandestine local structure of de facto segregation during the 1960s.[26]

From June 11 to 21, 1963, the *Pottstown Mercury* printed reports on local civil rights activism from white journalist Paul F. Levy entitled "Mr. James P. Crow, Esquire. . . . A Sequel." Continuing in the same vein of civil rights advocacy work and the liberal interracialist ethos of World War II and the early postwar years—not surprisingly—the newspaper's 1954 "series" inspired Levy's own work. Moreover, Pottstown NAACP activists Marable and Corum served as major voices from Black Pottstown in the white journalist's ten-report series.[27]

Clearly the *Pottstown Mercury* 1963 series covered similar topics as the 1954 reports of the plight of local Blacks and how they endured oppressive conditions germane to de facto segregation. One topic, for example, concerned the role that local white real estate workers played in African American housing exclusion. Levy argued that they had an inconspicuous "unwritten" yet "unbroken code" that residentially segregated Pottstown African Americans. To support this argument, Levy also noted the all-white examples of the Brookside Gardens, Belmont, and Colonial residential complexes and how they principally excluded local Blacks.

To be sure, like many other Blacks across the Jim Crow North during the early postwar, Pottstown African Americans had already begun experiencing aspects of residential segregation or "ghettoization."[28] One space in particular where ghettoization already started crystallizing was "Chicken Hill." Historians Norman B. Cohen and Lawrence E. Cohen trace local manifestations of ghettoization within the Pottstown region even back before World War II. Largely southern-born and newly arrived, thereby illuminating further instances of African American migration in Pottstown, these Blacks resided throughout "Chicken Hill." Yet these local Blacks' socioeconomic status, Cohen and Cohen add, was overwhelmingly depressed.[29] During the mid-1960s, historian Gordon P.

Griffiths additionally corroborates that the Pottstown African American community existed "clustered around . . . 'Chicken Hill'" by the early 1920s. Locals negatively gave the region the name, Griffiths continues, since "residents frequently raised chickens" there.[30]

Yet even as decades past not much had changed on the local front when it came to the predominantly African American area within Pottstown. In late August 1954, the *Pittsburgh Courier* verified the relationship between ghettoization and "Chicken Hill" too. The Black newspaper additionally made the point to contextualize the small northern borough with the remainder of the nation, declaring emphatically that "Pottstown, like other cities in the South and North," refused African Americans "the right to live in certain areas."[31] Like the *Pittsburgh Courier*, Shandy Hill, as indicated earlier, emphasized how Pottstown African Americans residing within "Chicken Hill" also essentially endured ghettoization.[32]

Furthermore, two more pieces of data that support the Pottstown residential ghettoization thesis are worth mentioning. In July 1988, white Pottstown native Daryl Hall—a teenager during the 1950s and 1960s who went on to have fame with the musical group Hall & Oates—bragged in *Spin* about how "the suggestive R&B [rhythm & blues] oozing out of Chicken Hill," Pottstown's African American "ghetto," inspired him artistically.[33] Yet perhaps Levy, in his 1963 *Pottstown Mercury* series, was the most emphatic about the ways in which residential segregation within the structure of de facto separation permeated the small northern locale during the early postwar era. Writing in a concise yet blunt manner, the white journalist declared, outrightly, that "the Pottstown Negro lives in a ghetto."[34]

Indeed, since at least shortly following the Pottstown NAACP's revitalization in 1951, local issues with Black housing and residential amenities received consistent attention from the small borough chapter, so much so that the Pottstown branch even branded its activism in this way, informing local African Americans that the group was there so they could receive assistance in ameliorating "living conditions."[35] Moreover, the Pottstown NAACP addressed tangible everyday living needs with respect to local working-class African Americans, which even included "road, sewer and water facilities."[36]

In its quest for racial justice and fairness during the early postwar era of northern Jim Crow, the Pottstown NAACP also vigorously worked for African Americans' access to quality schooling. For example, in early 1961, the Pottstown School Board put together an initiative that tried separating Pottstown's junior high schools (there were two). By doing so—whether purposely or not—many Black "children and those of low income families" would mostly compose Central Junior High's population. Consequently, the Pottstown NAACP protested the Pottstown School Board's ruling, identifying it as discriminatory. At the same time, one white school administrator in early 1961, while he acknowledged how surely "the colored race in Pottstown is congregated in certain areas," he also noted, "so are the people of certain income groups." In response, Pottstown NAACP president James H. Corum called out specific points stated by the school administrator, correcting what, he viewed, mispresented the situation. While Corum agreed that Pottstown African Americans "congregated in one area," this local reality was by no means "a matter of choice." Rather, the Black NAACP activist continued, "We don't confine ourselves to certain ghettos because we're clannish." African American minister Foster H. Worten Sr. from Bethel AME made somewhat similar points as Corum. A Pottstown NAACP activist himself, Worten viewed local Blacks' residential difficulties inextricably linked, or at least intersected, with their "income brackets, race and locality."[37]

Interestingly enough, another episode of discriminatory education policy nearby Pottstown, in Pine Forge, also brought the borough NAACP into protest actions.[38] In this civil rights struggle, local NAACP activism revolved around five orphaned Black youths in the parental custody of two white families. Overall, the event received extensive media reporting throughout Pennsylvania by news presses like the *Morning Call* (Allentown), *Gettysburg Times*, and *Indiana Evening Gazette*.[39] However, the two main African American newspapers in the state, the *Philadelphia Tribune* and the *Pittsburgh Courier*, and the historically Black *Baltimore Afro-American* also covered the struggle in Pine Forge.[40]

In late September 1960, news spread about the majority white Pine Forge Elementary School. Located close to Pottstown in Douglass Township, the elementary school prohibited African American pupils Charry Jones, Richard Jenkins, Clementine Jones, Maria Cash, and Claudine Jones from attending the public institution. In essence, leadership from

Pine Forge Elementary, which began its ruling on the Black youths on September 6, argued that the five were being excluded since the institution had "overcrowded conditions." Moreover, the African Americans' "'non-resident' status in the township," coupled with "substantial and completely unwarranted" financial costs, white Pine Forge School Board solicitor Philip Salkin argued, was precisely why Pine Forge Elementary disallowed them.[41] Salkin also underscored how the schooling affair was "not a 'colored-white'" dilemma.[42]

English scholars Laurie Grobman and Gary Kunkelman's edited compilation *Woven with Words: A Collection of African American History in Berks County, Pennsylvania* (2006) is the only secondary source that mentions anything about the Pottstown NAACP and its direct involvement in Pine Forge during late 1960, and even this mention, in the essay entitled "Segregation and Racism in Berks County," is extremely brief. Thus, this chapter elaborates further on the Pottstown NAACP's role in the local Black freedom struggle, which centered specifically on African American access to educational space in the Jim Crow North. What also adds to this lengthier account of the race-based educational exclusion in Pine Forge is that it shares cohesion with the plight of many other northern Black students who had to deal with both navigating and wading through the inconspicuous yet pervasively entrenched structure of de facto racism above the Mason-Dixon Line.[43]

Not surprisingly, the Pottstown NAACP had a familiar white ally who also took part in the local Black freedom struggle in close by Berks County. Indeed, alongside the Pottstown chapter, the *Pottstown Mercury* spearheaded the local activism that challenged the Pine Forge Elementary ruling, so much so that Prince informed the public about the Pottstown NAACP's unequivocal backing of the orphaned youths. In the *Baltimore Afro-American* in early October 1960, he declared, "We have turned the case over to our legal redress committee for study and recommendations." Moreover, Prince continued by demonstrating how the borough NAACP had "no intentions of dropping this case before the children are admitted to the school."[44] While providing in-depth coverage of the entire affair, the *Pottstown Mercury* additionally printed a passionate editorial on September 23. Entitled "No Room for Them," it sharply lambasted the move orchestrated from Pine Forge Elementary leadership.

Ostensibly, the *Pottstown Mercury* even suggested that the ruling possibly had exclusionary "overtones" instead of "the 'over-crowded'" argument.[45]

In the end, it was precisely in this context of postwar America that the revitalized Pottstown NAACP labored across the small northern borough and beyond. While the work spearheaded by the Pottstown Committee on Human Relations soon after *Brown* was the height of the local Black freedom struggle's regional and national impact, the Pottstown NAACP was the most active civil rights organization in the small locale throughout the 1950s and 1960s. Continuing in the vein of the liberal interracialist strategy, Pottstown NAACP activists directly addressed discriminatory conditions indigenous to the local Jim Crow landscape. Moreover, while the borough NAACP had four Black presidents from 1951 to 1969, who included Prince, Corum, and local African American Randolph Henry, who also briefly served during the early 1960s, the tenure of Newstell Marable was the most active time of the group in conducting local civil rights struggle.[46]

"An Ingenious Evasion of the Law on Public Accommodations"

During the 1960s, the Pottstown NAACP also protested three establishments in Pottstown that excluded African Americans on the local Jim Crow front. They included two private clubs, Die-Casters and Sunnybrook Swim, as well as North End Fire Company. To challenge these organizations, the Pottstown NAACP did so by not only marching on the organizations' premises but lambasting their racist policies in public discourse too.[47]

Initially, white journalist Normand Poirier underscored the practice of racial exclusion by the Die-Caster Club in the inaugural report of the *Pottstown Mercury*'s 1954 civil rights series, "Jim Crow, Yankee Style, Stalks Streets of Pottstown."[48] Interestingly enough, the *Pottstown Mercury* reported in 1965 on how the local Die-Casters allowed African Americans the ability to hold gatherings inside the establishment (providing they paid, of course). Black performers worked there as well. However, Pottstown's Die-Casters never admitted an African American as a member. In fact, white Die-Casters associates blocked several Black potential constituents from enrolling. During this time, fifty-two associates took part in the decision; only one supported Black acceptance into Pottstown's Die-Casters.[49]

Clearly the way the leadership of Die-Casters, Sunnybrook, and North End rationalized such exclusionism policies was that they grasped onto their organizations being "private" entities. This, in turn, meant that their members decided whom they included. In late June 1963, the *Afro-American* even captured remarks illuminating such an assessment. At the time, local white Richard Moser headed the small northern borough's firehouses. Moser conceded how the firehouses—North End, Empire Hook and Ladder, Good Will, along with Phillies—had no desire at all in admitting African Americans.[50]

Weeks earlier Levy captured Moser's opinion on the same matter in the *Pottstown Mercury* series from 1963. Moser argued that because the firehouses were "private institutions charted by the State," their membership had privileges as American citizens. More specifically, he continued, membership had the final say on whom it included. To the same point, Moser made remarks which, the white Pottstown leader felt, further justified exclusion—even boastfully citing the United States Constitution. The document, Moser argued, fully endorsed individual members of private organizations and their ability to include—as well as exclude—outsiders seeking potential association. Whatever Moser's own personal beliefs were on African Americans, he contended, the fact remained that his position on private organizations and choice, supported racial ostracism. As long as whites desired organizational separation from African Americans, Moser believed, then they were only exercising their rights as US citizens—not bigots.[51]

Conversely, the *Afro-American* explained that the Pottstown NAACP's main vantage point rested on the fact that these "private" firehouses received "public" funds. By late June 1963, for example, Pottstown firehouses took in almost $80,000 in tax-financed support from the government. Thus, local NAACP leader Marable criticized the organizations for grasping on to any claim of being private. In his view, since the firehouses unbiasedly took government dollars that African Americans and whites both gave, then the organizations forfeited the privilege of identifying as "private institutions."[52]

Similarly, the Pottstown NAACP countered Sunnybrook and North End's private enterprise arguments during the 1960s by emphasizing their relationship to the "public" sphere. Interestingly enough, Levy initially criticized Sunnybrook and its exclusionary practice in the *Pottstown Mercury* series from June 1963.[53] Additionally, argued Marable in late May 1966, because Sunnybrook was "a 'public place,'" it landed below Pennsylvania "law which requires that such facilities provide equal service to all."[54] In early July 1966 during a local government meeting, white Pottstown NAACP activist James Gaut also publicly lambasted Sunnybrook, arguing how banning African Americans from utilizing "the pool . . . was done by 'an ingenious evasion of the law on public accommodations.'"[55]

The historian Stanley Keith Arnold writes that Fellowship House worker Mitzi Jacoby Barnes, the same activist captured in chapter 5, played an active role supervising integrationist initiatives orchestrated from the racially liberal Philadelphia-based organization. One space specifically, Arnold adds, where Barnes spearheaded such desegregation work concerned "swimming pools."[56] Likewise, Fellowship House and Farm evidence sheds even greater light on the Pottstown NAACP and its integrationist efforts with Sunnybrook Swim Club. In fact, it reveals that the Pottstown NAACP initially tried desegregating the club under Corum's presidency (Marable was currently the group's treasurer). During both Corum's and Marable's reigns as Pottstown NAACP president, however, it is important to note that Gaut was intimately involved in the desegregation endeavors.[57] Born on October 19, 1921, in Pennsylvania, Gaut was a United States Navy veteran of World War II.[58] Like James H. Corum, Gaut was largely involved in Pottstown unionism. Employed by Doehler-Jarvis, he worked directly in a leadership capacity with the company's union, Local 1056 of the United Automobile Workers of the American Federation of Labor and Congress of Industrial Organizations, including on civil rights issues.[59] In further relationship to local civil rights, it is worth revealing that Gaut was a part of the Pottstown Human Relations Council (PHRC) as well.[60]

A Fellowship House and Farm document approximates that between 1961 and 1968, local African Americans tried utilizing the Sunnybrook location on several occasions.[61] Gaut even wrote to the chairman of the

Pennsylvania Human Relations Commission (HRC), Harry Boyer, in early September 1961, about the borough NAACP's own investigation of "public accommodations" and whether the organization was in compliance. "The recent test was arranged so that a white person first gained admission to show the routine used," Gaut noted. "Then a Negro group tried to swim and different treatment resulted. Two whites next tried, but did not get in." He continued, "Perhaps the management was wary of a test by that time." Moreover, Gaut provided Boyer with further detailed accounts of the August 27, 1961, incident, even penning one of them himself.[62]

Entitled "Report of the Test of the Sunnybrook Swimming Club August 27, 1961 Pottstown, Pennsylvania," Gaut captured his own direct participation in trying to desegregate the Jim Crow space. The white NAACP activist, accompanied by his stepchild Eddie Augustine (who was also white), did not hold memberships with Sunnybrook Swim Club. However, the organization let them purchase visitor passes, which gave them access inside. Shortly after two Pottstown African Americans tried entering Sunnybrook. These two Blacks included Randolph Henry, the vice president of the Pottstown NAACP at the time, along with his child Aubrey. During the early 1960s, as indicated earlier, the elder Henry briefly headed the local NAACP branch too.[63]

Personal testimony from Randolph Henry documents how Sunnybrook Swimming Club denied their request. "We can only admit members," an associate there informed the Henrys. In response, Randolph inquired about Sunnybrook's "requirements to become a member," which the helper answered, "You will have to get an active member to recommend you."[64] Following the Henrys being barred, "two [white] girls, Barbara Richards and Judy Becker," were also denied entrance. Now, white Sunnybrook associate Ray Hartenstine Jr., who was the space's supervisor, took notice.[65]

Hartenstine's father, Raymond Sr., established the Sunnybrook organization, which included other amenities such as its nationally renowned ballroom, where esteemed musical performers like Bob Crosby, Benny Goodman, and Bunny Berigan, to name a few, entertained everyday people.[66] Eventually, the younger Hartenstine met with Gaut, giving him back the payment that Sunnybrook collected earlier. However, the supervisor also kicked Gaut (as well as Eddie) out. Before Gaut left, moreover, Hartenstine informed him about the process "to make application for membership" with the Sunnybrook Club.[67] In the end, the Pottstown NAACP lambasted Sunnybrook because the organization had "a double standard of admission" for whites and African Americans.[68] Its activism even ended up getting Black NAACP tristate field director Phillip H. Savage involved, as well as the Pennsylvania HRC (as mentioned previously).[69]

Decades later Newstell's spouse, Millicent E. (maiden name Corum) Marable, also recalled local civil rights activism directed toward Sunnybrook. Born in Pennsylvania and the daughter of Pottstown civil rights and labor union activist James H. Corum Sr., Millicent graduated from Pottstown Senior High School in 1949, where she was a part of the "Glee Club" as well as the "Safety Patrol."[70] According to the 1950 US census, Millicent worked as a "Baby Sitter" for a "Private Family."[71] In corroboration years later, Millicent even noted how "I used to baby-sit for" Newstell's mom, "and she would tell me about her life and her children," adding further biographical information with respect to the background leading to the married couple's initial encounter.[72] At the same time, however, in late May 1960, the *Pottstown Mercury* noted that Millicent was currently working for Stanley G. Flagg—clearly in footsteps similar to her father and uncles, as chapters 2 and 3 show.[73] On the Pottstown social front, Millicent not only was actively involved with Bethel AME like her husband Newstell but also was a part of activism programming relating to the local Girl Scouts.[74]

In reflection on Sunnybrook in February 2015, Millicent briefed white *Mercury* journalist Evan Brandt with respect to one incident in which "a fire hose [was] turned on" activists (including Millicent) who were demanding that Sunnybrook capitulate and fully embrace African American inclusion.[75] In another *Mercury* article published in late January 2015 and written by Brandt, the white journalist described Millicent revealing that Newstell "was among the black men who climbed the fence at the pool at Sunnybrook Ballroom," an organization that excluded African American "members" during the age of northern Jim Crow.[76] Furthermore, Brandt conducted a video interview with Millicent that the *Mercury* published in mid-February 2015 that provides more insight into the local civil rights affair.

In the interview, Millicent notes that the civil rights activism was a collaborative effort that partnered Fellowship Farm, as well as borough NAACP activists. Here, her argument illuminating the involvement of Fellowship Farm in Sunnybrook makes particular sense, especially since the civil rights organization was not only participants in previous activism within the local Black freedom struggle, as chapter 5 has noted, but the fact that Pottstown NAACP records are also archived in the Fellowship House and Farm collection at Temple University in Philadelphia supports this same assertion. Continuing her remembrance of Sunnybrook in the same video interview, Millicent likewise recalls that the local rabble-rousers also conducted such Black freedom work on the weekends, particularly since the activists during the week had their employment commitments and obligations.[77] She additionally remarks that these local civil rights demonstrations took place in the summertime thus, she recalls the heat.[78] In sum, the previous recollections articulated from Millicent's vantage point shed even greater light on the ways in which the Pottstown NAACP struggled both passionately and fervently for local African Americans and their honorable quest of racial inclusion and equality during the postwar period.[79]

Interestingly enough, Sunnybrook Swimming Club was similar to Die-Casters in the sense that it allowed African American musical performers there. Nationally famous Blacks such as Cab Calloway, Duke Ellington, Count Basie, and Louis Armstrong, among many others, entertained fans.[80] Similarly, an undated document entitled "Open Letter to People at Sunnybrook," notes that "The Sunnybrook facilities—such as the Ballroom, Restaurant, and cocktail lounge" were totally desegregated, even during the 1960s.[81]

Like the Die-Casters Club, Poirier initially revealed in 1954 that North End—as well as Pottstown's other firehouses—excluded African Americans from membership. Paul F. Levy followed similar course with the *Pottstown Mercury* series from 1963. While Levy noted how the small northern NAACP publicly lambasted Pottstown's fire stations' racist practices in June 1963, the local civil rights group became intimately involved in civil rights work about three years later, demanding that North End integrate. In 1966, the *Pottstown Mercury* documented the borough NAACP's integrationist efforts, which combated Jim Crow on the local front.

Pottstown native Sage E. Glenn, an African American employed by the local Firestone Tire and Rubber Company who was also an ex-serviceman with firefighting experience, tried becoming affiliated with North End. However, the firehouse denied him. Marable responded during a local government meeting in June that "if the fire company discriminated against Glenn because of his race," then the local government had an obligation "to withhold taxpayers' money being appropriated" there.[82] The following month during an identical assembly, the local NAACP president again discussed North End. Moreover, Marable noted how a local interracial consensus had emerged. Like the Pottstown NAACP, it believed firmly that the firehouse refused Glenn on the fact that he was an African American.[83]

Meanwhile, if one compares the four Pottstown NAACP presidents' times in office, the revitalized chapter conducted its best civil rights work in demanding employment opportunities for African Americans under Marable. Indeed, like the 1954 *Pottstown Mercury* series, Levy's 1963 reports provide excellent insight into the employment plight of Pottstown Blacks. Within the series, moreover, Levy captured commentary from Marable that lambasted how local governmental jobs marginalized African Americans, especially among "white collar" positions.

Regarding the private sector, Marable articulated similar points. In his view, "there is almost complete discrimination in white collar jobs in local industries and only 'token employment' in production jobs." Marable contended that such posts were essentially dead ends, specifically because they did not have any growth possibility.[84] In 1965, Marable once again chastised Pottstown businesses that continued exercising "token" desegregation. As Marable viewed the situation, because these companies capitulated in employing African Americans symbolically rather than an earnest, sincere effort, their actions were essentially perfunctory, if not superficial. Furthermore, the Pottstown NAACP president even publicly called out Pottstown companies such as Dana Corporation, Firestone Tire and Rubber, along with Mrs. Smith's Pie, among others. Specifically, Marable condemned the small number of African Americans they had on their payrolls.

Conversely, the local NAACP leader praised Pottstown companies like March Brownback, Stanley G. Flagg, and Bethlehem Steel, to name a few. According to Marable, these companies practiced true democracy, generally because they executed colorblind policies in the hiring of African Americans.[85] On the other hand, Marable, especially in comparison with NAACP presidents Prince and Corum, unquestionably spearheaded more civil rights work that incorporated direct confrontational methods on the local scene. In fact, one of the earliest civil rights initiatives that Marable directed concerned the Collegeville Fire Company, located near Pottstown in Collegeville, Pennsylvania (Montgomery County). In late January 1963, the Pottstown NAACP notified the firehouse about modifying "its annual minstrel show." The chapter argued that such presentations not only demeaned African Americans but also perpetuated interracial animosity. Therefore, providing the firehouse did not comply, then the Pottstown NAACP, in cooperation with the Norristown chapter, would "picket the show."[86]

"An 'Orderly Demonstration to Secure Our Just Demands'"

Because Marable's tenure occurred during the explosive 1960s, the Pottstown NAACP had to address the real probability that the small northern borough could erupt into large-scale racial pandemonium rapidly and without warning. The historian Peter B. Levy notes that from 1963 to 1972, the United States had more than "750 urban revolts." These many uproars throughout the nine-year period, what Levy identifies as "a 'Great Uprising,'" certainly had to have influenced Marable and other Pottstown NAACP activists during the 1960s.[87] Likewise, the *Pottstown Mercury* reported on July 27, 1967, that Marable and the local NAACP were creating an initiative to avert potential interracial conflict.

Indeed, Marable's decision to establish Teenagers Organization for a Productive Summer—TOPS—followed consultation with higher NAACP leadership. In short, he wished that TOPS would alleviate interracial conflicts on the local scene.[88] Earlier in July 1967, the *Afro-American* captured remarks from NAACP tristate field director Savage—who oversaw group work in Pennsylvania, among two other states—which proposed TOPS. Aligning with Marable's comments from later in the month, Savage believed TOPS could serve as an important subdivision of local

NAACPs, specifically in curbing interracial conflicts, as well as violent flare-ups.[89]

Finally, the *Pottstown Mercury* article from late July 1967, questioned Marable if Pottstown might potentially erupt in "racial violence." In his view, he did not believe that "a militant spirit" strongly existed throughout the small northern locale. However, Marable continued, never say never, especially because all locals needed was an unfavorable event to ignite interracial chaos.[90] Months earlier during a local governmental gathering, Marable made an identical point. In response to the Pottstown government constructing "two stop signs" where African Americans largely resided, Marable suggested that "something as serious as a race riot could result from auto injuries" occurring there. He continued later by elaborating on "how a traffic incident can set things off, and I wouldn't like to see it happen down in this neighborhood because some child is struck or killed."[91] A few days later, the *Pottstown Mercury* identified Marable's assertion as essentially hyperbole, which possibly suggests a disconnect between the advocacy newspaper and Pottstown Blacks. At the same time, Marable's remarks surely illuminate the challenging relationship among African Americans and whites, even within a smaller northern geographical region, in the United States during the chaotic 1960s.[92]

Before going any further, it is interesting to note that in 1968, the *Philadelphia Inquirer* captured remarks that went hand in glove with Marable's own trepidations about biracial antagonisms. On March 17, the *Philadelphia Inquirer* printed an article entitled "'Clean Up Penn Village': A Teen Evaluates Pottstown." In short, the article illuminated some of the challenging circumstances that younger African Americans, particularly those living in Penn Village, endured at the time. In addition to the housing development's economic and social issues, the essay highlighted commentary from an African American sixteen-year-old Penn Village local named Gary Walton. Interestingly enough, Walton took his opinion much further than Marable's concern, contending that Pottstown would unequivocally have an uprising. In his view, however, "outsiders" would probably start it. Walton even envisioned African American militant "Rap Brown"—who took part in racial unrest the previous year only a few hours away from Pottstown in an even smaller southern locale,

Cambridge, Maryland—"and his boys," leading many other Black radicals in this uproar.[93]

Walton's remarks became partially true.[94] In early April 1968, days following Dr. Martin Luther King Jr.'s murder, the *Pottstown Mercury* spoke about African American juveniles behaving briefly one night "like a bunch of rioters." However, it emphasized that such unrest was in no way "a race riot." Rather, the situation was only young Blacks letting out some energy. In other words, they demonstrated no malice in the public display at all.[95] Of course, when comparing the aforementioned event in Pottstown with the remainder of the United States following Dr. King's slaying, it pales in the bucket, so to speak, to the rioting that engulfed the nation. For example, Levy notes how "looting, arson, or sniper fire occurred in 196 cities in thirty-six states plus the District of Columbia." Among other disturbances, "forty-three men and women were killed, approximately 3,500 were injured, and 27,000 were arrested," Levy additionally writes.[96]

Yet while radicalism was not a central component to the ways in which the Pottstown NAACP operated, the local branch did eventually take part in civil rights work that exhibited elements of Black militancy. In late March 1969, the small borough chapter, now identified as "the Pottstown-Phoenixville NAACP" (during the late 1960s, the *Pottstown Mercury* started identifying the local NAACP as such) waged an all-out assault toward combating African American inequality near Pottstown in Chester County. Interestingly enough, Marable identified the large-scale sit-in that transpired on Monday, March 31, in Phoenixville Area Senior High School as "an 'orderly demonstration to secure our just demands.'"[97] In sum, the event received coverage throughout Pennsylvania from various media outlets such as the *Pottstown Mercury*, *Philadelphia Inquirer*, *Hazelton Standard-Speaker*, and *Indiana Evening Gazette*.[98] It was also documented by the Lemberg Center for the Study of Violence at Brandeis University (Waltham, Massachusetts) in its publication entitled *U.S. Race-Related Civil Disorders, January–June, 1969* as well as the NAACP's *Annual Report* (1969).[99]

It is worth mentioning that Phoenixville pupils had conducted an identical sit-in on the previous Friday, March 28. Such activism, however, ceased following "a brief counter-demonstration by white students."

Phoenixville's school board then got involved. On April 1, the *Philadelphia Daily News* noted how between Friday and Monday, it embraced an uncompromising "hard-line" position "that . . . would not tolerate disruptions of school operations and would prosecute" wrongdoers.[100] More broadly, Phoenixville's school board's inflexible position, as well as other responses to disciplinary actions captured in this chapter, coincided with the ethos behind the "law and order" argument both popularized and embraced by whites in the late 1960s, even in smaller places like nearby York, Levy reveals.[101]

Nevertheless, the March 31, 1969, sit-in represented the culmination of recent African American student activism, which sought that the Phoenixville School Board fully endorse fourteen "demands." Captured in the *Pottstown Mercury* on April 1, the activists' first and foremost militantly requested "that black students expelled from school last Fall be asked to return immediately"—albeit the article does not elaborate on why the pupils got kicked out. Outside this initial urging, however, their dictates broke down into consciousness efforts, greater employment possibilities, and everyday African American student initiatives.

Regarding consciousness efforts, the activists wanted Phoenixville High School to have "a course in Swahili," coupled with African American "history on all grade levels." Moreover, they desired for Phoenixville public schools to have an "assembly program dealing with black culture so that both white and black pupils can 'be made aware of black contributions to our society.'" Their next request stemmed directly from what happened in April 1968. Because of Dr. Martin Luther King Jr's murder, the African American students wanted his "birthday . . . as a school holiday."

Next, the greater employment appeals rested in both white- and blue-collar work. Regarding white-collar employment, the student activists demanded that Phoenixville employ an African American guidance "counselor 'so that black students can be assured of a counselling service that adequately meets their needs.'" They wanted additional African American educators, "a black athletic director," along with "a black administrator and a black principal." As far as blue-collar labor went, the student activists believed firmly that Phoenixville needed greater amounts of African American kitchen workers.

Finally, the third grouping of their fourteen requests directly linked to everyday life of the African American student body. Outside coursework, students sought African Americans on "the varsity and junior varsity cheerleading squads" alongside "black leadership representation in all school clubs and activities." They also pleaded for equal treatment of African American and white students, specifically regarding punishment administered by schooling officials. However, the activists additionally petitioned for "representation in all discussions involving pupil suspensions and expulsions" from both groups. The students' last of the fourteen requests concerned their sit-in activism itself. Put bluntly, they wanted schooling officials to not penalize them. In their view, they did nothing wrong but were only engaging "in an orderly 'expression of our rights.'"[102]

In response to the sit-in, Phoenixville law enforcement detained fifty-three African American activists on March 31. It gave them all "disorderly conduct" violations as well. Marable and two other Phoenixville Blacks named Nathan Moffat and Ginnie (Virginia) Ramsey, who had spearheaded the sit-in,[103] received a "trespassing" infraction too. Marable, Moffat, Ramsey, and Phoenixville African Americans Bruce L. Jackson and Orlando P. Jackson (who, although over eighteen, still went to Phoenixville High) were the only adult activists apprehended. Forty-eight minor students comprised the rest seized by law enforcement. Like Marable, additional evidence links Moffat and Ramsey to the Pottstown-Phoenixville NAACP.[104]

The Phoenixville High School sit-in of March 31, 1969, was so vast that almost the entire Phoenixville police force was on the scene to handle the situation. Detained, Marable's, Moffat's, and Ramsey's bonds were one hundred dollars. Since they were eighteen-year-old students, Jackson and Jackson's bonds were twenty dollars. The remaining underage African Americans' bonds were only five dollars. Interestingly enough, the African American civil rights activists comprised "the bulk of the 67 black students in the [Phoenixville] school district's junior and senior high schools" that altogether had 2,200 registered youngsters.[105] The Phoenixville sit-ins of March 28 and 31, particularly the role African American students played, also coincided with the emergence of the Black studies movement of the late 1960s. Throughout the United States, historian Peniel E. Joseph reveals, African American students in both secondary and higher education vigorously sought that educational institutions begin providing curriculum which specified and centered on the Black experience. They also wanted more representations from Blacks like themselves in multiple positions throughout education. Understanding these points, therefore, is indeed crucial to contextualizing the late March 1969 Phoenixville sit-ins within the larger historical narrative of Black student activism.[106] At the same time, the importance with respect to this activism in Phoenixville is that it coincides with similar work conducted during the 1960s by "secondary students" in Grand Rapids (Michigan), historian Todd E. Robinson writes, a demographic largely excluded within the historiography. Instead, Robinson adds, historians have usually targeted pupils' activism across higher education spaces.[107]

Yet while Black militancy played a direct role in the Phoenixville School sit-ins of late March, there were no manifestations of violence. However, the same was not true for what transpired in Phoenixville a little over a month later, causing the Pottstown-Phoenixville NAACP to become directly involved. On May 8, 1969, soon after Phoenixville High School dismissed students for the day, violence erupted among white and African American students. A rock launched by one individual served as the catalyst that ignited the brawl. Later in the night, forty young whites continued the mayhem when they entered Phoenixville's African American portion of town. There, further interracial violence ensued. Soon after, however, Phoenixville law enforcement intervened. While the local cops handled the first skirmish quite easily, others would eventually erupt throughout Phoenixville. Law enforcement, therefore, remained occupied that night disbanding "gangs" throughout Phoenixville, as well as averting additional situations. Ultimately, it took eighty law enforcement officers, many from outside Phoenixville in neighboring communities located in Chester and Delaware Counties (Pennsylvania), alongside even "state police from [nearby] Exton [Pennsylvania]," to assist in controlling the uprising. Before the pandemonium ended, however, it hospitalized several young people involved—a byproduct of the interracial violence. The uprising also damaged some vehicles.[108]

On May 9, 1969, the *Philadelphia Daily News* suggested that the impetus that caused the uprising was Phoenixville's yearly "Dogwood Parade." African American pupils contacted borough authorities, demanding that they consent to them holding "their own parade" prior to "the traditional" exhibition. However, the local administrators denied them, the *Philadelphia Daily News* revealed. In sum, when examining the uprising that transpired in Phoenixville, local Black participation aligns directly with many other African Americans across the United States who displayed similar militancy and radicalism during the late 1960s.[109]

Yet while law enforcement played an important component in settling down the May 8 ruckus, so too did the Pottstown-Phoenixville NAACP. Because Pottstown-Phoenixville NAACP activist Ramsey resided in Phoenixville, she was directly present. On location, Ramsey assembled alongside local authorities such as Phoenixville's white mayor, Joseph E. Dougherty, among others. The time was now 12:00 a.m., May 9, 1969.

In the end, the early-morning conference proved fruitful. Satisfied, Ramsey went back "to a mass meeting" where the NAACP activist addressed three hundred African Americans. Her words helped ease tensions, so much so that around one o'clock in the morning Phoenixville had peace. Against manifestations of interracial violence, Ramsey, like local NAACP president Marable, took it on herself to make sure local African Americans remained calm. Generally speaking, Phoenixville stayed peaceful during the early morning—notwithstanding some brief incidents.[110] On Sunday evening, Pottstown-Phoenixville NAACP activists Marable, Moffat, and Ramsey gathered again with Dougherty and associates. During this gathering, they game planned potential ways that Phoenixville could maintain interracial peace in light of the recent uprising. By doing so, the local NAACP once again demonstrated its rejection of violence and its radical commitment to the liberal interracialist strategy, thereby aligning with many other racial progressives of postwar America. At the same time, the local NAACP's rejection of militancy and more radical political solutions contrasts sharply from many other activists' strategies in places like Cambridge, Maryland, and nearby York, as Levy shows.[111]

Successes, Shortcomings, and Rising Northern White Pushback

By far, the revitalized Pottstown NAACP was most active under Marable. However, that did not mean the group had its greatest success during his presidency. For example, while Charles Prince and James Corum conducted fewer civil rights projects in and around Pottstown, they had higher tangible achievement rates than Marable. In 1955, NAACP activism under Prince's leadership saw the Pottstown government finally construct Hemlock Row's sewer lines.[112] In 1960, Prince's NAACP successfully helped press the Pennsylvania government to intervene in the Pine Forge Elementary school affair. Thus, the Pennsylvania government overruled the local choice initiative designed to discriminate against the Black pupils.[113] Likewise, under Corum, the local NAACP successfully lambasted the Pottstown School Board in early 1961, in its attempt to separate "the borough's pupil population between two Junior High school buildings on grounds that the boundary embodied 'unintentional racial and social segregation.'"[114]

At the same time, even though Marable conducted more civil rights work than other Pottstown NAACP presidents, especially Prince and Corum, his tenure during the 1960s realized fewer immediate achievements. For instance, the failed actions with Die-Casters, Sunnybrook Swim, and North End Firehouse are examples of his frustrations.[115] Here, it surely appears that white appetites for the liberal interracialist ethos—or, at least, the lengths some seemed willing to go to test and thereby get rid of race discrimination on the local front—seemed to wane. For example, the Pennsylvania HRC in 1966 ruled (following a complaint filed on behalf of an African American teen by the Pottstown NAACP) "that the Sunnybrook Swim club" was "a bona fide private club and hence outside the jurisdiction of the commission under the State public accommodations act."[116] Moreover, it is even worth noting that Savage wrote to the Pennsylvania HRC in early February 1967. Unfiltered, he expressed that the NAACP hated the Pennsylvania HRC's resolution.[117]

Likewise, where *Pottstown Mercury* exposés and opinion pieces during the 1950s and early 1960s had worked as calls to liberal interracialist actions and sensibilities, by the late 1960s, they seemed only frustrating reminders of the durability of the local de facto segregation structure vis-à-vis Jim Crow in the North. In early August 1967, for example, *Pottstown Mercury* journalist James E. Shapiro revealed several damnable practices continually transpiring. "Many clubs, social organizations and fire companies still" excluded Blacks, Shapiro reported.[118] Such local discriminatory practices, as the *Pottstown Mercury* summarized in an article published in early August 1967, must have surely started already having an adverse impact on Black optimism, that is, that things locally would change so that racial inclusion was an actual, complete reality. "Much progress has been made" locally "the past ten years." However, the *Pottstown Mercury* article continued, "much progress is not enough progress."[119] In early August, an African American woman echoed cynical remarks seemingly akin as the previous points. "I think Pottstown is a pretty town. Yes, I do." Yet Pottstown "ain't going to change [local] housing, and you're kidding yourself if you think" contrarily, the Black woman bluntly stated.[120]

Nevertheless, Marable's tenure as Pottstown NAACP president did have some tangible accomplishments. In collaboration with the Norristown branch, under Marable the Pottstown NAACP's condemnation of the Collegeville firehouse utilizing "blackface" during its yearly "minstrel show" succeeded. In fact, shortly after the Pottstown NAACP first publicly lambasted the firehouse, it ceased using the racist greasepaint.[121] The *Philadelphia Inquirer* even reported the following January 1964 that the Collegeville Fire Station planned on not incorporating "blackface" for its upcoming yearly presentation.[122] Furthermore, the calming of the Phoenixville uprising in early May 1969 can, in fact, be attributed to the Pottstown-Phoenixville NAACP while Marable was its president.[123]

At the same time, the multiple civil rights projects that Marable spearheaded as president of the Pottstown NAACP, whatever his success rate, did not go unnoticed. On November 2, 1965, the *Philadelphia Tribune* revealed that Marable and five others received awards "for civil rights achievements" during a gathering of the Pennsylvania NAACP in nearby Norristown. In a related vein, while Marable was Pottstown NAACP president, the Montgomery County Opportunity Board appointed the Black activist to a position in early March 1967. In short, these two awards demonstrate that Marable's ongoing activism in the realm of civil rights during the 1960s certainly caught the attention of others.[124]

As noted, although the Pottstown NAACP had some success under Marable, it faced hurdles such as the integration of Die-Casters and Sunnybrook Swim clubs as well as the North End Fire Company. One way to interpret the failure of these integrationist efforts, therefore, relates specifically to local whites pushing back against the liberal interracialist philosophy of postwar America and rather grasping at the customary policies of northern Jim Crow. Indeed, because this white antagonism especially coincided with Marable's NAACP presidency, one can further understand why civil rights efforts did not always fully meet white capitulation to racial equality on the local front.[125]

Yet while the pinnacle of interracial civil rights work conducted out of Pottstown began almost a decade before the civil rights legislation of 1964 and 1965—the time period that the traditional historiographical interpretation suggests being the high-water mark—northern white pushback or opposition to local civil rights started formulating before those laws had passed. Most noticeably, public enthusiasm and response to Paul Levy's 1963 civil rights essays did not come anywhere close to what transpired out of Pottstown in the two years or so following the *Pottstown Mercury*'s publication of Normand Poirier's 1954 series. In a comparison between these two periods, Pottstown's racial climate and activism mobilization for civil rights change were by far more apparent following Poirier's reports than they were in the aftermath of Levy's "Mr. James P. Crow, Esquire. . . . A Sequel."[126] In *Dear Sir*, for example, Shandy Hill captures the following passage from Paul Levy, which illuminates northern white pushback to the white journalist's 1963 essays. "As each article was written and printed, the town seethed a little more," Levy asserts, "and by the time the fifth or sixth one arrived on the doorsteps, the communications had become a two-way street." Moreover, Levy reveals how many correspondences where sent "to Hill, to the Letters to the Editor column, and" himself. "Mine started off almost identically," Levy recalls, "as if they had been punched out on a mindless xerox machine" with the racist introduction "Dear Nigger Lover."[127]

The *Pottstown Mercury*'s "Readers Say" section documents further evidence of local white pushback or resistance to Black freedom work in and around the borough, mostly during Marable's NAACP presidency as the tumultuous 1960s raged. Although the "Readers Say" writers did not identify themselves outright as white, the tone and language of their letters strongly suggests they were. Interestingly enough, the *Pottstown Mercury* published a correspondence in early September 1961 that criticized the NAACP itself. "I think it's about time the National Association for the Advancement of Colored People slow down and quiet down," argued a Pottstown resident who signed the letter with the initials "M. C. F." While the writer believed in equality among African Americans and whites, he or she felt strongly in "a limit as to how to go about the advancement." Finishing off the essay, the author antagonistically declared, "The NAACP is trying to force the colored people into everything too rapidly."[128]

In early May 1963, the *Pottstown Mercury* printed another letter in its "Readers Say" section that chastised the NAACP. Here, a Pottstown resident who went by the name "Tom Stie" lambasted the NAACP because, in his view, the group failed ordinary African Americans' daily existence. "With all the money behind its powerful organization," Stie argued, "instead of promoting grandstand plays for desegregation and paying its lawyers to fight such trivial things as minstrel shows and books like Huckleberry Finn, the NAACP take some of its seemingly unlimited supply of money and spend some of it in a constructive way" like assisting "to pay for their people's share of hospital expenses."[129] Essentially, Stie's point aligns with Pottstown's working-class composition, specifically since they emphasize tangible class-based concerns—namely, eradicating medical debts among ordinary African Americans—rather than initiatives that he felt had no pragmatic impact on their everyday life. The *Pottstown Mercury* published similar comments in late January 1963 from the Ivorys, a white King of Prussia (Pennsylvania) married couple; the Ivorys saw the Pottstown and Norristown NAACPs demonstration against the Collegeville Firehouse's "minstrel show" as also focusing on something inconsequential—if not frivolous.[130]

In late August 1965, a "Readers Say" writer captures a further example of local white pushback or resistance to civil rights change. This letter, however, lambasted the recent Watts uprising. The Pottstown author, who signed the letter with only the initials "LMM," wrote in frustration about an African American Los Angeles official seeking "the government to send $100 million to the riot area." The writer then demonstrated his or her distaste for "my tax money going to this kind of people," suggesting that civil rights groups like CORE (the Congress of Racial Equality) or even the NAACP spend their own capital so that Watts was put back together.[131] In summary, the aforementioned evidence compiled suggests local whites were most certainly dissatisfied with aspects of civil rights. While the Pottstown NAACP had white allies locally, the fact remained that not all whites were on board with the group's civil rights projects, thereby potentially explaining some of the integrationist failures under Marable's presidency across the stormy and tempestuous decade otherwise known as the 1960s.

Beyond its important local work, the revitalized Pottstown NAACP demonstrated its solidarity with civil rights activists in the American South. Only months after its revitalization in 1951, the Pottstown NAACP demonstrated such unity when it joined national sentiment across America that sent the US attorney general formal protests about the murders of Harry T. and Harriette Moore, Florida African American NAACP activists who were slayed in cold blood.[132] Following the June 1963 assassination of Mississippi African American NAACP activist Medgar Evers, slightly over thirty locals, including borough NAACP chief Newstell Marable, donning "a black armband of mourning," quietly paced Pottstown streets.[133]

Likewise, a few months later in late August 1963, Pottstown NAACP membership joined over 200,000 activists in the March on Washington for Jobs and Freedom in the nation's capital. "The harmony among the demonstrators was enough to convince you that we'll overcome the segregationists," Millicent Marable declared.[134] Recalling her time there decades later, Marable additionally remembers the tranquil and harmonious atmosphere. Moreover, when traveling back home with other activists, she remembers vividly discussing how impactful and profound Dr. Martin Luther King Jr.'s "'I have a Dream' speech" was.[135]

While not explicitly linked to public activism that the Pottstown NAACP initially launched, toward the end of Charles Prince's presidency, a borough resident took part in one of the iconic Greensboro, North Carolina, direct confrontational sit-ins to combat racism below the Mason-Dixon Line. Pottstown white Margaret Jean Neff's southern activism did, however, ultimately inspire some local civil rights work conducted by the Pottstown NAACP. In collaboration with Fellowship House and Farm, the activism transpired during Prince's latter NAACP presidency.[136] Finally, outside historian Deidre B. Flowers, whose short study lists the Pottstown activist, scholars have really not written anything about Neff and her Greensboro connection.[137]

On April 21, 1960, Greensboro law enforcement apprehended Neff, a twenty-year-old student from historically Black and all-female Bennett College (Greensboro, North Carolina), alongside forty-four other civil rights "sit-down movement" activists in S. H. Kress & Company. The activists attended either Bennett or historically Black North Carolina Agricultural and Technical (A&T) College (Greensboro, North Carolina). Moreover, local authorities seized them because the activists' disobeyed orders and would not remove themselves from S. H. Kress & Company. Besides twenty-one-year-old Mary Ellen Bender, a fellow northerner who also attended Bennett College, Neff was the only other white activist detained that day. Processed and freed that same day, Black North Carolina A&T students Joseph A. McNeil and Ezell Alexander Blair Jr., two of the initial four sit-in activists, were also among the forty-five detained by local law enforcement.[138]

Multiple newspapers located in the eastern and northern United States captured the story behind Neff and her fellow arrestees.[139] On April 23, 1960, the *Philadelphia Inquirer* even printed a photograph centering on the Pennsylvanian's activism.[140] Locally, moreover, the *Pottstown Mercury* celebrated Neff, thereby further demonstrating its continued and ongoing commitment to civil rights advocacy work and the liberal interracialist ethos of postwar America. "A Pottstown girl trying to crack racial bias was arrested . . . during a lunch counter fracas in Greensboro, N.C.," the newspaper announced on its front page shortly after Neff's detainment. Drawing from information released by Greensboro law enforcement, the *Pottstown Mercury* also noted that Neff—as well as Bender—took part "in other pro-Negro demonstrations in recent days." Furthermore, the same article provided commentary from a relative of Neff, who stressed that she was long concerned with supporting "the rights of down-trodden" African Americans for sometime now.[141]

In addition to the favorable reporting, the *Pottstown Mercury* published a correspondence saluting Neff in its "Readers Say"/letter to the editor section. Printed on April 26, 1960, the author viewed "Neff . . . and the heroic young people of the South" as individuals fervently struggling "to make democracy work." The Pottstown writer also blatantly called out the hypocrisy behind America's current racial landscape, especially if contextualized from a historical standpoint, arguing "that more than lipservice is paid to the great ideals of democracy." The zealous essayist continued, "How can we presume to be leaders of the free world when we permit the vestiges of slavery to exist in our midst?" In fact, the writer emphatically concluded, "There can be no democracy without full equality and dignity for" all.[142]

Additionally, Neff's personal involvement in the April 21 Greensboro sit-in mobilized the Pottstown NAACP. On August 28, 1960, the local NAACP held "a fund raising" gathering close to Pottstown on the property of Fellowship House Farm in Fagleysville, where 125 assembled. The reformulated Pottstown NAACP planned on utilizing the capital acquired to aid and assist southern sit-in activists. Moreover, Neff attended and spoke at the late August assembly.[143]

Similarly, the Pottstown NAACP orchestrated multiple initiatives, which sent money, supplies, and statements supporting southern civil rights activism.[144] Yet perhaps the ultimate show of solidarity with the larger Black freedom struggle came in the aftermath of the murder of Dr. Martin Luther King Jr., in Memphis. On April 8, 1968, four days following King's murder, 1,200, including local NAACP head Newstell Marable, assembled at Pottstown Senior High School, paying their respects. Addressing the vast crowd, Marable informed the audience that because King was not physically alive "to carry on the fight for justice and freedom for all, it is our responsibility to see that his dream is" accomplished.[145] Surely in the aftermath of Marable's own death almost fifty years later, the Black freedom fighter's commitment that centered on "King's dream for equality" still reverberated on the local front.[146]

Lessons Learned from Pottstown's Black Freedom Struggle

Although a small northern borough, Pottstown was able to serve as an important hub of civil rights struggle from World War II through the postwar era. Working through various borough organizations, local Black and white activists took it on themselves to fight against racial inequality and other manifestations of second-class citizenship that specifically targeted local African Americans. While some of their civil rights initiatives did not have tangible successes, many activists in and around Pottstown were able to still break down local walls of bigotry, prejudice, and exclusion that permeated the locale. In sum, such activism spearheaded by locals was in direct response to the long-standing practices of de facto segregation characteristic of Jim Crow above the Mason-Dixon Line.

Of course, civil rights activism originated and came about by local activists in Pottstown during World War II, a time when African American resistance in particular still pursued traditional strategies of equalization and other Black internal improvement work. Surely it was the honorable efforts of local African Americans connected to entities like Second Baptist Church, the Pottstown NAACP, and the Pottstown YMCA's "Negro Extension Work" that demonstrate the historical starting point and manifestation of the local Black freedom struggle.[1] Moreover, as local African American activists utilized equalization strategy and other traditional Black internal improvement methods—practices that shared similarities to activism in the South—the laborers concurrently worked for racial reform within discriminatory environments laced in anti-Black racism. In time, however, local activists did eventually shift toward a more aggressive and racially equitable tactic, precisely when opportunities to do so became both palatable and practical in the postwar years. Additionally, most of the Black activists who got their start during World War II would later play integral roles in local civil rights developments and programming. In review, it should also be noted that many Pottstown African Americans involved in such racial justice work from the early 1940s to the late 1960s not only were natives of Pennsylvania but also had direct connections to southern Black migration both before and during the Great Migration.[2]

At the same time, however, these local Blacks did not only pursue equalization and other traditions of internal improvement work as tactics to advance the African American condition in and around the borough. Instead, and especially within the context of the rise of a Cold War domestic agenda after World War II, they employed and encouraged the liberal interracialist method. Unequivocally, this latter modus operandi greatly influenced civil rights activism catapulted from Pottstown and beyond. Beginning in the 1940s and concluding during the late 1960s, the trajectory of the liberal interracialist philosophy defined much of the objectives of local civil rights struggle. The ethos of the liberal interracial vantage point also engendered how local Black and white activists approached racial justice work and equality more broadly.

Yet even though local whites got on board and started both adopting and embracing the liberal interracialist perspective, that does not in any way diminish the crucial roles played by African American freedom fighters in their own liberation from traditions and customs of racial injustices ubiquitous to the local Jim Crow structure. Throughout Pottstown's civil rights struggle, local Blacks from both the North and the South were the orchestrators of impactful and sustaining civil rights activism. At the same time, it is important to stress that from the beginning local African Americans had always desired true equality, liberties, and privileges afforded to their white counterparts. Put differently, from inception, local Black activists demanded the same opportunities as the majority white population. For these reasons, Pottstown African Americans never let the small size of their population handicap them from consistently pressing for first-class citizenship. In addition to supplying grassroots activists, the Black community provided local civil rights work with its many leaders. In fact, when examining Pottstown and civil rights work in its entirety, Black activists composed a consistent element that made the liberal interracial work possible, continual, and sustainable during World War II and the postwar era.

When comparing Pottstown's Black and white organizations, especially their involvement in local civil rights work, there are several points to consider. The first point concerns organizational consistency. Although African American activists remained a constant in civil rights activism over three decades (1940s–1960s), they did so across multiple groups in the small northern borough. In other words, during this time period, there was not one main local organization through which African Americans worked directly to impact civil rights change. With that said, civil rights activism with the Pottstown NAACP was by far the most consistent. While the Pottstown NAACP incorporated aspects of the equalization strategy and other traditional Black internal improvement activism during World War II, when it revitalized in 1951, the branch advanced, if not solely promulgated, the liberal interracialist strategy across the local front.

The fact that the Pottstown NAACP was initially established during World War II before its revitalization in 1951 is also worth noting. In short, because the small borough NAACP had a history dating back to 1942, when the time came to revitalize some nine years later, the group already had a relationship, specifically an administrative one, with the organization's headquarters in New York City. Thus, the Pottstown NAACP was not starting from scratch, so to speak.

Moreover, when juxtaposing the World War II–era Pottstown NAACP and the revitalized group in the postwar, the extent of activism was by far greater during the latter period. As in the World War II era, the Pottstown NAACP of the postwar influenced the local Black community for the better in the realm of civil rights advancements and progress. Especially under the presidencies of local African Americans Charles Prince, James H. Corum, and Newstell Marable, the revitalized Pottstown NAACP fought against inequalities germane to the northern Jim Crow structure in local housing, employment, and education, as well as public and private spaces. The organization also challenged negative portrayals of African Americans. In sum, when conceptualizing Pottstown and civil rights activism, particularly the role played by African Americans in local organizations, without any question, the small borough NAACP was the most consistent.

What this study has also demonstrated about local African Americans is the function played by multiple Black institutions in sustaining civil rights activism. Indeed, African Americans incorporated multiple local Black institutions such as Second Baptist, Bethel African Methodist Episcopal, and Mount Herman Baptist Church to advance and implement civil rights work. Local African Americans used their own residences for similar purposes as well. Additionally, this book has highlighted how local Blacks utilized spaces from the majority community like the Pottstown YMCA and Bethany Recreation Center, among others, to implement Black-centered activism throughout the local scene.

While local African Americans integrated various institutions from Black and white Pottstown to advance civil rights work, undoubtedly, the *Pottstown Mercury* was at the forefront of activism among the small borough majority population. Thus, the borough newspaper was able to promote further its civil rights advocacy work that, in turn, went hand in glove with the national liberal interracialist philosophy of World War II and postwar America. At the same time, when reflecting on Pottstown's white population and its actual commitment to furthering first-class citizenship among African Americans, the borough newspaper certainly had a leading position in civil rights activism launched from the small northern locale. Indeed, even though *The Jim Crow North: The Struggle for Civil Rights in Pottstown, Pennsylvania* has captured several white journalists from the newspaper and their specific work in advocating local civil rights, the overall role played by Shandy Hill was what largely empowered them. Moreover, because Hill was the central architect behind the *Pottstown Mercury* being an advocacy-centered newspaper, the work compiled by white journalists such as Larry Davis, Frank J. Dostal, Normand Poirier, and Paul F. Levy (in addition to the many articles utilized throughout this study on Pottstown and civil rights) followed suit. In other words, since Hill had already set the philosophical standard of the *Pottstown Mercury* early on, when the time came for the white journalists to construct their advocacy work, they knew what type of reporting he demanded. In the end, Hill would not accept anything less from his journalists than full exposure of the racial injustice that plagued the everyday experience and lives of local African Americans during World War II and the postwar period.

Surely a crucial component as tantamount to the successes of the *Pottstown Mercury*'s impactful Black freedom activism was its collaboration with local African American freedom fighters in advancing civil rights advocacy work through the liberal interracialist philosophy. As demonstrated, the borough newspaper continuously cooperated with African Americans. By doing so, it shed light on many of the discriminatory conditions they experienced. Since the *Pottstown Mercury* provided a public forum where African Americans in and around the borough could freely express the racial hardships they endured, the newspaper's journalistic work also made it quite an outlier of the time. As noted, the *Pottstown Mercury*'s local civil rights work with African Americans contrasted sharply from "the national media" that also resided above the Mason-Dixon Line.[3] Although these presses recognized "Southern Black people and the movements they built . . . as noble and necessary," political scientist Jeanne Theoharis argues that the news outlets simultaneously painted "Northern Black people and the movements they built" as "marginal, unreasonable, and disruptive."[4]

Conversely, between World War II and the late 1960s, *The Jim Crow North* has argued that the *Pottstown Mercury* was a civil rights advocacy press that fought with the objective of local African Americans fully receiving the rights and privileges guaranteed them as United States citizens. Moreover, as the *Pottstown Mercury* conducted civil rights advocacy work through the prism of the liberal interracialist strategy, it continually humanized local Blacks. As such, the newspaper was able to provide African Americans in and around the locale a platform where they could articulate their humanity and dignity to its readership. At the same time, the civil rights work of the Pottstown Committee on Human Relations (PCHR) is the best example of the local liberal interracialist method and ethos reaching across the United States. The PCHR not only mobilized local activists but also inspired civil rights workers from outside the small northern borough to get involved. Nationally speaking, the evidence has also shown that many activist-minded individuals directly contacted PCHR affiliates, inquiring about receiving further information and materials from the Pottstown-based civil rights organization.

In addition to arguing that the small size of Pottstown's Black community related to the absence of the locale experiencing large-scale violence, racial unrest, or police brutality, *The Jim Crow North* has suggested that the long-standing commitment of local Black and white activists to the liberal interracialist cause possibly explains why the northern borough did not experience such antagonisms. At the same time, the lack of militancy among local activists played a direct role in the absence of wide-reaching interracial friction in the small locale. Consequently, this study departs from much of the current scholarly literature, which emphasizes the relationship between such radicalism and racial unrest. Nonetheless, even though Pottstown lacked serious interracial strife, especially in comparison to other urban locales across the industrialized North, this does not mean that activists from both the white and the Black communities never had any anxieties about such chaos unleashing with fury on the local front.

The Relevance of Pottstown's Black Freedom Struggle in Twenty-First-Century America

Local African Americans and whites from World War II through the late 1960s played definitive roles in combating de facto segregation ubiquitous to the area. Thus, the story has pragmatic utility that individuals today can both incorporate and review. Surely by examining the past and concrete illustrations, including Pottstown, they can gain better insight toward understanding, contextualizing, and addressing twenty-first-century America and more recent racially centered wrongdoings like the horrific events surrounding George Floyd and Ahmaud Arbery, two African Americans tragically and appallingly slayed.[5]

Yet how locals struggled to implement racial justice and democratic change in and around Pottstown can also have current-day relevance that centers on similar smaller-size communities both above and below the Mason-Dixon Line. In an analysis of recent civil rights work such as the Black Lives Matter movement, *Institute for Policy Studies* journalist Karen Dolan writes that outside large urban centers within the United States, civil rights activism is also transpiring. Published in June 2020, from there, Dolan continues her analysis by noting how inside "small towns around the country"—locales not usually thought of seeing such activism—individuals "are having protests with signs" that declare "Black Lives Matter" as well as "I Can't Breathe." Specifically, locations like Dolan's "tiny town in . . . Maryland," as well as another smaller "conservative coastal enclave" above the Mason-Dixon Line where her acquaintance resides (Massachusetts) have additionally launched contemporaneous initiatives supporting racial equality and inclusion.[6]

Providing demographic evidence that supports Dolan's previous arguments, *New York Times* journalist Maggie Astor reveals that as of 2020, 8 percent of American citizens inhabited locations that United States "census officials call 'micropolitan' areas," urban spaces "or other population centers" that are under fifty thousand yet over ten thousand individuals. Astor also notes how 6 percent of citizens resided across "rural parts of the country." In the end, even though most US residents as of 2020 were a part of "metropolitan" locales, totaling 86 percent, the fact is that a substantial minority populace still claims smaller regions as residencies.[7] Consequently, activist-minded individuals like Dolan and those across the smaller places alluded to by Astor would surely benefit from both closely evaluating and assessing how interracial collaborations fostered sustaining and impactful civil rights work in Pottstown and adjacent areas from the early 1940s to the late 1960s.[8]

Interestingly enough, the twenty-first-century Pottstown NAACP is continuing similar civil rights work that the local branch initially launched during World War II and sustained across the 1950s and 1960s. Moreover, the modern-day Pottstown NAACP advocates collective solidarity in protest work—activism that even has direct connections to the national sphere.[9] In early June 2020, for example, following George Floyd's brutal murder, *Mercury* journalist Evan Brandt writes, "Pottstown hosted yet another peaceful rally for racial justice Sunday, [June 7, 2020,] expanding exponentially on the number of people who showed up to call for equal treatment under the law for all Americans." Moreover, one local civil rights organization directly involved, Brandt adds, was the Pottstown NAACP.[10] Yet the Pottstown NAACP is not alone in promoting civil rights change on the local front. The Pottstown Area Health & Wellness Foundation, for example, is another local twenty-first-century organization also taking part in impactful civil rights work that seeks to improve area conditions.[11] Furthermore, one must also understand clearly how the twenty-first-century *Mercury* continues excellent journalistic reporting, which, indeed, only stems from the extensive traditions of civil rights advocacy work and the liberal interracialist ethos that Shandy Hill for decades had almost single-handedly cultivated, honed, and refined, as this book has shown.[12]

Pottstown's civil rights struggle from World War II through the late 1960s can also serve as "a usable past." Within this context, "a usable past" conceptualization illuminates how locals during the time pragmatically combated de facto segregation firsthand. Thus, even though recent scholars have heavily scrutinized the concept of de facto segregation, the analytical construct is still beneficial in order to try to understand manifestations of racial discrimination and anti-Black racism, which, woefully, have manifested more recently in the United States. In the end, a close reading of the history of Pottstown's Black freedom struggle is an excellent place for activists today to examine and compare and contrast to today's efforts in order to find pragmatic solutions to address contemporary civil rights challenges. Arguably, twenty-first-century America faces challenges that resemble de facto racism, as identified throughout this study of Pottstown, rather than the South's de jure exclusionary scheme.[13]

Last, the potential impact of *The Jim Crow North* on local and national historiography is worth stressing. For the first time, the African American experience in Pottstown has been captured at length. Earlier scholarly treatments, generally speaking, have given only cursory accounts of local Blacks and their relationship to the area. Therefore, one hope of this book is that it serves as an impetus to study local African Americans further. To be sure, African Americans have been present in the Pennsylvania area for several hundred years, and regional scholars have sorely neglected their influential part in local history throughout the entire period.[14]

In addition to the utility of *The Jim Crow North* to civil rights–minded activists of the early twenty-first century—as well as its impact on historiographical interpretations of local history in and around Pottstown—this book has the potential to inspire others to look away from large urban cities of the North and thus begin focusing more on smaller regions above the Mason-Dixon Line. While recent scholarship has started underscoring such locales, more work is still desperately needed. Did equalization and other traditional Black internal improvement strategies manifest within these other communities? Was the liberal interracialist tactic a staple there? What role did militancy play in these spaces? Did these communities have a local newspaper that continually promulgated and promoted the liberal interracialist agenda? Or did their newspapers pay no attention to local civil rights work? In sum, until areas like Pottstown and those even smaller are fully incorporated into the scholarly literature of northern civil rights will a better picture begin to emerge of the twentieth-century African American struggle for equal opportunities, inclusion, and first-class citizenship in the North.[15] Only then will historians and other scholars gain a greater understanding of what, in the words of *Pottstown Mercury* journalist Normand Poirier, "Jim Crow, Yankee Style" really was. And perhaps still is.[16]

Acknowledgments

First, I give all honor and praise to God Almighty Jesus Christ for His continual love, guidance, and strength during this process.

While I grew up in the Pottstown area and recognize the region's influence on me writing *The Jim Crow North: The Struggle for Civil Rights in Pottstown, Pennsylvania*, the work has only benefited and evolved over time because of the expertise and encouragement of a community of scholars. Therefore, thanks to David Taft Terry, Will Guzmán, Charles L. Chavis Jr., Jeremiah I. Dibua, Peter B. Levy, Lawrence Peskin, and Robert W. Morrow for their keen insights and helpful suggestions. Thanks also to my colleagues at Prairie View A&M University, especially Ronald E. Goodwin and William T. Hoston.

Many archivists at the Library of Congress in Washington, DC; the Special Collections Research Center at Temple University in Philadelphia, Pennsylvania; and others have tremendously benefited this book. Sincere thanks to them. Thanks as well to the *Mercury* for allowing me to utilize its vast newspaper collection. I am also truly appreciative and grateful to staff at the University Press of Kentucky for their combined efforts and scholarly contributions to *The Jim Crow North*. Moreover, I am grateful for the awarded financial support given that helped in the progress of this book from Prairie View A&M University's Mellon Center for Faculty Excellence. Likewise, sincere thanks to the Faculty Enhancement Program of the Brailsford College of Arts and Sciences at Prairie View A&M University for awarding financial support that assisted significantly in the completion of *The Jim Crow North*.

I want to also take this time to express gratitude to my family. Heartfelt thanks to my precious wife, Hannah Kristine, for her continual love and support. Wholehearted appreciation and thankfulness to the newest addition to our family, our beautiful daughter Madelyn Grace. Furthermore, thanks to my parents, in-laws, siblings, the extended Washington family, and friends.

Material and content examined throughout this manuscript has appeared both previously and similarly in a short chapter entitled "Examining Interracial Civil Rights Activism in 1950s Pottstown, Pennsylvania" in *Contemporary Debates in Social Justice: An Interdisciplinary Approach to Exploring the Lives of Black and Brown Americans*, edited by Farrah G. Cambrice, William T. Hoston, and Marco Robinson (Dubuque, IA: Kendall Hunt Publishing Company, 2021), 131–41.

Finally, I accept full responsibility for any errors in this book.

Notes

1. Pottstown, Pennsylvania, a Center of Civil Rights Significance

1. "Community Icon Newstell Marable, Longtime Pottstown NAACP President, Dies at 84," *Mercury*, January 26, 2015, 8:33 p.m. EST (updated September 24, 2021, 3:31 a.m. EST), https://www.pottsmerc.com/2015/01/26/community-icon -newstell-marable-longtime-pottstown-naacp-president-dies-at-84/; "Pottstown Bridge Named in Honor of Newstell Marable Sr.," *Mercury*, May 18, 2019, 4:19 p.m. (updated September 23, 2021, 8:37 a.m.), https://www.pottsmerc.com/2019/05 /18/pottstown-bridge-named-in-honor-of-newstell-marable-sr/. For Alabama A&M University, see "About," Alabama A&M University, accessed September 5, 2023, https://www.aamu.edu/about/index.html. For Great Migration, see J. Trent Alexander et al., "Second-Generation Outcomes of the Great Migration," *Demography* 54, no. 6 (December 2017): 2250–71, http://www.jstor.org/stable/45047340.

2. "Negroes Here Plan Cemetery," *Pottstown Mercury*, November 4, 1942; Robert Dunphy, "They Make Unions Tick: 'Jim' Corum Is Loyal Employe [*sic*] of Flagg's, 100% Labor Man," *Pottstown Mercury*, December 24, 1948; "Negroes Organize Group in Pottstown," *Pottstown Mercury*, November 23, 1942; "Negro Leaders Form Pottstown Civic Group for Self-Improvement," *Pottstown Mercury*, April 4, 1950; *The Pottstown Plan: A First Step*, Other Orgs: Pottstown Human Relations Council, 1955, Box 82/folder 84, Fellowship House (Philadelphia, Pennsylvania) Records, SCRC 281, Special Collections Research Center, Temple University Libraries, Philadelphia, Pennsylvania (hereinafter, FHPA-Temple). On Millicent's familial connection to James H. Corum, see Millicent E. Corum, Line 24, Sheet 8, Enumeration District 46-312, Pottstown Township, Montgomery County, Pennsylvania, Seventeenth Census of the United States, 1950, Record Group 29, Records of the Bureau of the Census, National Archives and Records Administration, Washington, DC, accessed January 10, 2023, https://1950census.archives.gov/.

3. Sallie Sims, "Happenings of the Colored Folks," *Pottstown Mercury*, August 18, 1937; Sims, "Happenings of the Colored Folks," *Pottstown Mercury*, January 5, 1938; "Scout Forum: Troop 17—Bethel A.M.E.," *Pottstown Mercury*, March 5, 1935; Sims, "Happenings of the Colored Folks," *Pottstown Mercury*, February 10, 1938.

4. "Zion's Young People to Hear Talk," *Pottstown Mercury*, February 24, 1934; "Needle-Eye Social Club Holds First Dinner: Keystone State Quartet Sings; Paul Green Gets Fan," *Pottstown Mercury*, May 6, 1935; Sallie Sims, "Happenings of the Colored Folks," *Pottstown Mercury*, September 29, 1936; Sims, "Happenings of

the Colored Folks," *Pottstown Mercury*, October 25, 1938. On another initiative relating to Pottstown's "Colored Community Hospital," see "Children Give 2250 Items to Hospital: Auxiliary Expresses Thanks for Foodstuffs," *Pottstown Mercury*, November 3, 1936.

5. "Final Plans Made for Negro Center," *Pottstown Mercury*, January 26, 1945; "Rev. William Corum Accepts Charge at Bethlehem Church," *Pottstown Mercury*, October 24, 1949; "Negro Leaders Form Pottstown Civic Group for Self-Improvement"; *Pottstown Plan*, 1955, FHPA-Temple. On Black YMCA history more generally, see Nina Mjagkij, *Light in the Darkness: African Americans and the YMCA, 1852–1946* (Lexington: University Press of Kentucky, 1994).

6. Larry Davis, "Beech St. Brews Trouble, Negro Worker States," *Pottstown Mercury*, June 29, 1944; "Corum Gets Council OK as Officer: Negro Special Policeman Begins Duties at Once," *Pottstown Mercury*, July 18, 1944. For family connection of Corum's, see "Bad Heart Cause of Corum Death: Autopsy Shows Policeman Succumbs of Natural Causes, Patrolmen Dies While Arresting Man," *Pottstown Mercury*, January 22, 1964.

7. "Community Icon Newstell Marable, Longtime Pottstown NAACP President, Dies at 84"; "Pottstown Bridge Named in Honor of Newstell Marable Sr."; "Human Relations Council Conducts Election of Officers," *Pottstown Mercury*, May 5, 1958; *Pottstown Human Relations Council . . . For Equality: The Pottstown Plan; What Has Happened in Two Years?*, Other Orgs: Pottstown Human Relations Council, 1955, Box 82/folder 84, FHPA-Temple; *Pottstown Plan*, 1955, FHPA-Temple; James E. Gaut to Harry Boyer, September 5, 1961, "Jim Gaut" Activities Programs, [Test Cases] Sunnybrook Swim Club, 1961–73, Box 28/folder 491, FHPA-Temple; "Marable Named Head of NAACP," *Pottstown Mercury*, December 10, 1962; "Area Swim Club Is Picketed by NAACP Group," *Pottstown Mercury*, May 31, 1966.

8. "Pottstown Bridge Named in Honor of Newstell Marable Sr."

9. Paul Chancellor, *A History of Pottstown Pennsylvania, 1752–1952* (Pottstown: Historical Society of Pottstown, 1953); *Encyclopedia Britannica Online*, s.v. "Pottstown," May 11, 2018, https://www.britannica.com/place/Pottstown. This book expands much further on my doctoral work. See Matthew G. Washington, "'Jim Crow, Yankee Style': Civil Rights and Working-Class Pottstown, Pennsylvania, 1941–1969" (PhD diss., Morgan State University, 2019), https://mdsoar.org/handle/11603/17921.

10. "The History of Pottstown's Second Baptist Church," *Mercury*, February 4, 2012, 10:14 p.m. EST (updated September 24, 2021, 10:16 a.m. EST), https://www.pottsmerc.com/2012/02/04/the-history-of-pottstowns-second-baptist-church/; "Negroes Here Plan Cemetery"; "Negroes Organize Group in Pottstown."

11. "Final Plans Made for Negro Center." Regarding equalization, see John A. Kirk, "The NAACP Campaign for Teachers' Salary Equalization: African American Women Educators and the Early Civil Rights Struggle," *Journal of African American History* 94, no. 4, Special Issue: "Documenting the NAACP's First Century" (Fall 2009): 530, https://www.jstor.org/stable/25653977.

12. The phrase *liberal interracialist* and similar conceptualizations are already utilized within the scholarly literature. See David Taft Terry, *The Struggle and the Urban*

South: Confronting Jim Crow in Baltimore before the Movement, Politics and Culture in the Twentieth-Century South (Athens: University of Georgia Press, 2019), 157, 161, 164. For liberal interracialist conceptualization in World War II and after, also see Harvard Sitkoff, "Racial Militancy and Interracial Violence in the Second World War," *Journal of American History* 58, no. 3 (December 1971): 662, https://www.jstor .org/stable/1893729; Kevin Daniel Ryan, "Catholic Liberal Interracialism in the Archdiocese of Chicago in the 1960s and 1970s" (PhD diss., State University of New York at Buffalo, 2016).

13. "Negroes Here Plan Cemetery"; "Negroes Organize Group in Pottstown"; "Final Plans Made for Negro Center"; "Negro Leaders Form Pottstown Civic Group for Self-Improvement"; *Pottstown Plan*, 1955, FHPA-Temple.

14. For local coverage of *Brown v. Board*, see "Supreme Court Rules Public School Segregation Must End: Further Hearings Set for Fall," *Pottstown Mercury*, May 18, 1954; "NAACP Hails Move as 'Vindication' of 45-Year Battle," *Pottstown Mercury*, May 18, 1954. For PCHR launching, see "Human Relations Group Will Meet Tonight," *Pottstown Mercury*, July 28, 1954; "Human Relations Group Will Meet," *Pottstown Mercury*, July 14, 1954. On *Brown*'s greater impact, see Charles J. Russo, J. John Harris III, and Rosetta F. Sandidge, "*Brown v. Board of Education* at 40: A Legal History of Equal Educational Opportunities in American Public Education," *Journal of Negro Education* 63, no. 3 (Summer 1994): 297–309, https://www.jstor.org /stable/2967182. Regarding *Brown*, I previously wrote similarly in Matthew G. Washington, "Examining Interracial Civil Rights Activism in 1950s Pottstown, Pennsylvania," in *Contemporary Debates in Social Justice: An Interdisciplinary Approach to Exploring the Lives of Black and Brown Americans*, ed. Farrah G. Cambrice, William T. Hoston and Marco Robinson (Dubuque, IA: Kendall Hunt, 2021), 131.

15. Stanley Keith Arnold, *Building the Beloved Community: Philadelphia's Interracial Civil Rights Organizations and Race Relations, 1930–1970* (Jackson: University Press of Mississippi, 2014), 3, 51.

16. *Pottstown Plan*, 1955, FHPA-Temple. On national clout, see Marjorie Penney to William H. Gremley, June 23, 1955, Correspondence, [M.P.], 1955, Box 14/ folder 88, FHPA-Temple; Marjorie Penney to Roy Wilkins, February 23, 1955, Other Orgs: Pottstown Human Relations Council, 1955, Box 82/folder 84, FHPA-Temple.

17. Shandy Hill, *Dear Sir: You Cur* (Philadelphia: Whitmore Publishing, 1969), 17–19. For reporting samples, see Davis, "Beech St. Brews Trouble, Negro Worker States"; Frank J. Dostal, "Slum Razing Plan to Hit Borough's '*Forgotten Folk*,'" *Pottstown Mercury*, March 20, 1950; Normand Poirier, "Jim Crow, Yankee Style, Stalks Streets of Pottstown," *Pottstown Mercury*, June 28, 1954. Regarding the broad Great Depression time frame, see *Encyclopedia Britannica Online*, s.v., "Great Depression: Timeline," https://www.britannica.com/summary/Great-Depression -Timeline.

18. US Bureau of the Census, *Sixteenth Census of the United States, 1940*, vol. 2, *Characteristics of the Population*, part 6, *Pennsylvania–Texas* (Washington, DC: Government Printing Office, 1943), 161, https://www.census.gov/library/publications

/1943/dec/population-vol-2.html; US Bureau of the Census, *Seventeenth Census of the United States, 1950*, vol. 2, *Characteristics of the Population*, part 38, *Pennsylvania* (Washington, DC: Government Printing Office, 1952), 38-116, https://www.census.gov/library/publications/1953/dec/population-vol-02.html; US Bureau of the Census, *Eighteenth Census of the United States, 1960*, vol. 1, *Characteristics of the Population*, part 40, *Pennsylvania* (Washington, DC: Government Printing Office, 1963), 40-191, https://www.census.gov/library/publications/1961/dec/population-vol-01.html; US Bureau of the Census, *Nineteenth Census of the United States, 1970*, vol. 1, *Characteristics of the Population*, part 40, *Pennsylvania Section 1* (Washington DC: Government Printing Office, April 1973), 40-16, 40-147, https://www.census.gov/library/publications/1973/dec/population-volume-1.html.

19. Points will be demonstrated throughout this book.

20. Jeanne Theoharis, *A More Beautiful and Terrible History: The Uses and Misuses of Civil Rights History* (Boston: Beacon Press, 2018), 34. This book's interpretation of de facto segregation contrasts with Theoharis's assessment, as will be seen in the pages that follow. On the larger historical context of North, see Thomas J. Sugrue, *Sweet Land of Liberty: The Forgotten Struggle for Civil Rights in the North* (New York: Random House, 2008). For subhead quote, see "Pennsylvania Town Seeks Segregation Problem End," *Plainfield Courier-News*, February 22, 1955. For similar points I made in a previous work on de facto racism, see Washington, "Examining Interracial Civil Rights Activism in 1950s Pottstown, Pennsylvania," 133–34.

21. As will be captured throughout this study.

22. "Black Demands Place Emphasis on That Color," *Pottstown Mercury*, April 1, 1969. Also see "Phoenixville Classes Cancelled: Protest Halted with Arrest of 53," *Pottstown Mercury*, April 1, 1969. Again, I made similar arguments about de facto racism in Washington, "Examining Interracial Civil Rights Activism in 1950s Pottstown, Pennsylvania," 133–34.

23. "Pennsylvania Town Seeks Segregation Problem End." For de jure segregation, see Theoharis, *More Beautiful and Terrible History*, 34. Again, this book's interpretation contrasts from Theoharis's assessment. For a similar local juxtaposition about Jim Crow above and below the Mason-Dixon Line, see Normand Poirier, "Mister James P. Crow, Esq.—VII: A Plan of Action for Pottstown," *Pottstown Mercury*, July 5, 1954. Regarding southern Jim Crow, see, for example, Terry, *Struggle and the Urban South*. Overall, for points I have made previously about de facto and de jure oppression, see Washington, "Examining Interracial Civil Rights Activism in 1950s Pottstown, Pennsylvania," 133–34. On Mason-Dixon Line description, see Robert L. Boyd, "Southern Black Metropolis: Position, Place, and Population Below the Mason-Dixon Line," *Journal of African American Studies* 23, no. 3 (September 2019): 256–72, https://doi.org/10.1007/s12111-019-09441-x.

24. "Pennsylvania Town Seeks Segregation Problem End"; Poirier, "Mister James P. Crow, Esq.—VII." Overall, also see Washington, "Examining Interracial Civil Rights Activism in 1950s Pottstown, Pennsylvania," 133–34.

25. Chuck Treleven, "Story Stirs Memories of a Real Pro: Epilogue Prompts Prologue of Newspaper Casualty," *Prescott Courier*, March 1, 1981, https://news

.google.com/newspapers?id=mJ5OAAAAIBAJ&sjid=o0wDAAAAIBAJ&pg=3435 %2C2364194. For first article in reporting, see Poirier, "Jim Crow, Yankee Style, Stalks Streets of Pottstown." Overall, for points I have previously made about de facto racism, also see Washington, "Examining Interracial Civil Rights Activism in 1950s Pottstown, Pennsylvania," 133–34.

26. "Pennsylvania Town Seeks Segregation Problem End." On *Brown*, see Russo, Harris, and Sandidge, "*Brown v. Board of Education* at 40," 297–309. On Garden State term, see "Nickname: Origins of the Nickname," Official Site of the State of New Jersey, accessed September 6, 2023, https://www.state.nj.us/nj/about/facts/nickname/.

27. Lawrence Cohen, interview by Charles Stuart Kennedy, July 12, 2007 (Copyright 2008 ADST), transcript, Frontline Diplomacy: The Foreign Affairs Oral History Collection of the Association for Diplomatic Studies and Training, Manuscript Division, Library of Congress, Washington, DC, accessed November 15, 2022, https://www.loc.gov/item/mfdipbib001531/. For further information about Cohen, see Norman B. Cohen and Lawrence E. Cohen, *Chicken Hill Chronicle: Memoir of a Jewish Family* (Bloomington, IN: Xlibris Corporation, 2011).

28. "Pennsylvania Town Seeks Segregation Problem End"; Poirier, "Mister James P. Crow, Esq.—VII." Overall, for points I have made previously about de facto and de jure oppression, see Washington, "Examining Interracial Civil Rights Activism in 1950s Pottstown, Pennsylvania," 133–34.

29. Frances Young Williams, letter to the editor, *Pottstown Mercury*, July 17, 1954.

30. Poirier, "Jim Crow, Yankee Style, Stalks Streets of Pottstown." Overall, for points I have made previously about de facto oppression, see Washington, "Examining Interracial Civil Rights Activism in 1950s Pottstown, Pennsylvania," 133–34.

31. "Pennsylvania Town Seeks Segregation Problem End"; Poirier, "Jim Crow, Yankee Style, Stalks Streets of Pottstown."

32. Poirier, "Mister James P. Crow, Esq.—VII."

33. "Pottstown Plan Reprint Prompts Letter from GI," *Pottstown Mercury*, March 1, 1955. This evidence suggests, ostensibly, that the soldier from 1955 is the same David Chaplin. Specifically, the aforementioned piece of evidence and the following note Chaplin's Amherst connection. See "David Chaplin Obituary," *WMU News*, September 7, 2017, https://wmich.edu/news/2017/09/42352.

34. Theoharis, *More Beautiful and Terrible History*, 34. Again, for points I have made previously about de facto and de jure oppression, see Washington, "Examining Interracial Civil Rights Activism in 1950s Pottstown, Pennsylvania," 133–34.

35. Jason Sokol, *All Eyes Are upon Us: Race and Politics from Boston to Brooklyn* (New York: Basic Books, 2014), x.

36. Regarding the conventional comparative model, see Theoharis, *More Beautiful and Terrible History*, 34. Historian Todd E. Robinson also adds to the scholarly conversation about how pervasive and far-reaching Jim Crow in the North's lingering tentacles were. Specifically, Robinson's important work on Grand Rapids, Michigan, describes "managerial racism." See Todd E. Robinson, *A City within a City: The Black*

Freedom Struggle in Grand Rapids, Michigan (Philadelphia: Temple University Press, 2013), 22, 168.

37. All these phrases are terms already utilized within the scholarly literature on civil rights. For example, see Maurice C. Daniels, *Saving the Soul of Georgia: Donald L. Hollowell and the Struggle for Civil Rights* (Athens: University of Georgia Press, 2013), 151, 155, 188; Clarence Lang, *Grassroots at the Gateway: Class Politics and Black Freedom Struggle in St. Louis, 1936–75* (Ann Arbor: University of Michigan Press, 2009), 120, 221; Phillip Luke Sinitiere, "Religion and the Black Freedom Struggle for Sandra Bland," in *The Seedtime, the Work, and the Harvest: New Perspectives on the Black Freedom Struggle in America*, ed. Jeffrey L. Littlejohn, Reginald K. Ellis, and Peter B. Levy (Gainesville: University Press of Florida, 2018), 198; Martin L. Deppe, *Operation Breadbasket: An Untold Story of Civil Rights in Chicago, 1966–1971* (Athens: University of Georgia Press, 2017), 57; Jenny Carson, *A Matter of Moral Justice: Black Women Laundry Workers and the Fight for Justice*, The Working Class in American History (Urbana: University of Illinois Press, 2021), 7.

38. "Pennsylvania Town Seeks Segregation Problem End"; Poirier, "Mister James P. Crow, Esq.—VII."

39. Jeanne F. Theoharis and Komozi Woodard, eds., *Freedom North: Black Freedom Struggles Outside the South, 1940–1980* (New York: Palgrave Macmillan, 2003); Sugrue, *Sweet Land of Liberty*; Martha Biondi, *To Stand and Fight: The Struggle for Civil Rights in Postwar New York City* (Cambridge, MA: Harvard University Press, 2003); Randal Maurice Jelks, *African Americans in the Furniture City: The Struggle for Civil Rights in Grand Rapids* (Urbana: University of Illinois Press, 2006); Jack Dougherty, *More Than One Struggle: The Evolution of Black School Reform in Milwaukee* (Chapel Hill: University of North Carolina Press, 2004); Beth T. Bates, "'Double V for Victory' Mobilizes Black Detroit, 1941–1946," in Theoharis and Woodard, *Freedom North*, 17–39; Brian Purnell, *Fighting Jim Crow in the County of Kings: The Congress of Racial Equality in Brooklyn* (Lexington: University Press of Kentucky, 2013); Peter B. Levy, *The Great Uprising: Race Riots in Urban America During the 1960s* (Cambridge: Cambridge University Press, 2018); Sokol, *All Eyes Are upon Us*.

40. Purnell, *Fighting Jim Crow in the County of Kings*, 2–3; Jeanne Theoharis, introduction to Theoharis and Woodard, *Freedom North*, 2–3.

41. Levy, *Great Uprising*, 17–82; Timothy B. Tyson, *Radio Free Dixie: Robert F. Williams & the Roots of Black Power* (Chapel Hill: University of North Carolina Press, 1999). On Pottstown population data for the time frame, see US Bureau of the Census, *Sixteenth Census of the United States, 1940*, vol. 2, *Characteristics of the Population*, part 6, *Pennsylvania–Texas*, 161; US Bureau of the Census, *Seventeenth Census of the United States, 1950*, vol. 2, *Characteristics of the Population*, part 38, *Pennsylvania*, 38-116; US Bureau of the Census, *Eighteenth Census of the United States, 1960*, vol. 1, *Characteristics of the Population*, Part 40, *Pennsylvania*, 40-191; US Bureau of the Census, *Nineteenth Census of the United States, 1970*, vol. 1, *Characteristics of the Population*, Part 40, *Pennsylvania Section 1*, 40-16, 40-147.

42. Theoharis, introduction, 2.

43. Arnold, *Building the Beloved Community*; Bates, "'Double V for Victory' Mobilizes Black Detroit, 1941–1946," 17–39; Robert O. Self, *American Babylon: Race and the Struggle for Postwar Oakland* (Princeton, NJ: Princeton University Press, 2003); Quintard Taylor, "The Civil Rights Movement in the American West: Black Protest in Seattle, 1960–1970," *Journal of Negro History* 80, no. 1 (Winter 1995): 1–14, https://www.jstor.org/stable/2717703. I made similar arguments previously. See Washington, "Examining Interracial Civil Rights Activism in 1950s Pottstown, Pennsylvania," 132.

44. For scholarship, see, for instance, Bates, "'Double V for Victory' Mobilizes Black Detroit, 1941–1946," 17–39; Sugrue, *Sweet Land of Liberty*. This book uses historian Yohuru Williams's time frame: 1954–1968. Williams notes how "the dominant 1954 to 1968 paradigm" begins with the United States Supreme Court announcing *Brown v. Board of Education* in 1954. Dr. Martin Luther King Jr.'s 1968 killing, Williams continues, then concludes this same orthodox interpretation. See Yohuru Williams, *Rethinking the Black Freedom Movement* (New York: Routledge, 2016), xi–xii. Historians Jacquelyn Dowd Hall and Brian Purnell periodize the traditional time frame as 1954 to 1965. Although Williams's time frame is slightly lengthier than Hall and Purnell's, they both roughly align. At the same time, Williams's and Hall and Purnell's time periods emphasize the southern regional focus. Moreover, the three historians underscore the civil rights legislation enacted during 1964 and 1965 as significant initiatives when understood within the traditional time frame. See Williams, *Rethinking the Black Freedom Movement*, xi–xiv, xviii–xix; Jacquelyn Dowd Hall, "The Long Civil Rights Movement and the Political Uses of the Past," *Journal of American History* 91, no. 4 (March 2005), 1234–35, www.jstor.org/stable/3660172; Brian Purnell, *Fighting Jim Crow in the County of Kings*, 2–3.

45. Hall, "Long Civil Rights Movement and the Political Uses of the Past," 1233–63.

46. Hall, "Long Civil Rights Movement and the Political Uses of the Past," 1235.

47. Sugrue, *Sweet Land of Liberty*, 200–202, 211–12, 220–28, 230, 232–33, 243, 446; Levy, *Great Uprising*, 223–313; Jill Ogline Titus, *Gettysburg 1963: Civil Rights, Cold War Politics, and Historical Memory in America's Most Famous Small Town* (Chapel Hill: University of North Carolina Press, 2021). Also see Robinson, *City within a City*.

48. Sugrue, *Sweet Land of Liberty*, xxvii–xxviii.

49. Levy, *Great Uprising*, 251.

50. Titus, *Gettysburg 1963*, 9. Regarding Gettysburg's populace size, see Titus, *Gettysburg 1963*, 29. For similar historiographical points, also see Levy, *Great Uprising*, 228.

51. Purnell, *Fighting Jim Crow in the County of Kings*, 3. On the three scholars' influence, see Purnell, *Fighting Jim Crow in the County of Kings*, 300–301nn3–4.

52. Jeffrey Helgeson, "Essay Review II: Beyond a Long Civil Rights Movement," *Journal of African American History* 99, no. 4 (Fall 2014): 442–43, https://doi.org/10.5323/jafriamerhist.99.4.0442.

53. Irina Zhorov, "Explainer: Cities, Boroughs, and Townships, Oh My! Pa. Municipalities Clarified," WHYY, April 4, 2016, https://whyy.org/articles/explainer -cities-boroughs-and-townships-oh-my-pa-municipalities-clarified/.

54. Levy, *Great Uprising*, 228.

55. Levy, *Great Uprising*, 1, 228; Titus, *Gettysburg 1963*, 9.

56. Arnold, *Building the Beloved Community*; James Wolfinger, "'We Are in the Front Lines in the Battle for Democracy': Carolyn Moore and Black Activism in World War II Philadelphia," *Pennsylvania History: A Journal of Mid-Atlantic Studies* 72, no. 1 (Winter 2005): 1–23, https://www.jstor.org/stable/27778656. Purnell, *Fighting Jim Crow in the County of Kings*. I make similar arguments in Washington, "Examining Interracial Civil Rights Activism in 1950s Pottstown, Pennsylvania," 133.

57. Chancellor, *History of Pottstown Pennsylvania, 1752–1952*, 87. I made similar points previously in Washington, "Examining Interracial Civil Rights Activism in 1950s Pottstown, Pennsylvania," 133.

58. Chancellor, *History of Pottstown Pennsylvania, 1752–1952*, 94–120. Again, I made similar points previously in Washington, "Examining Interracial Civil Rights Activism in 1950s Pottstown, Pennsylvania," 133.

59. "Pottstown: Today and Tomorrow," in *Pottstown Sesqui-Centennial, 1965: 150th Anniversary of Formation of Borough*, ed. A. G. Strothers (Pottstown: Pottstown Sesquicentennial Committee, 1965), 5.

60. Michael T. Snyder, *Remembering Pottstown: Historic Tales from a Pennsylvania Borough* (Charleston, SC: History Press, 2010), 100.

61. Charles L. Blockson, "Blacks," in *Montgomery County: The Second Hundred Years*, vol. 2, ed. Jean Barth Toll and Michael J. Schwager (Norristown, PA: Montgomery County Federation of Historical Societies, 1983), 910. Regarding larger context, see Sugrue, *Sweet Land of Liberty*. For previous points I have made about Pottstown and the relocation of southern African Americans, see Washington, "Examining Interracial Civil Rights Activism in 1950s Pottstown, Pennsylvania," 133.

62. Blockson, "Blacks," 914–16.

63. Sokol, *All Eyes Are upon Us*, xxiv.

64. Jelks, *African Americans in the Furniture City*, xvi.

65. "Phoenixville Youths Riot Following School Skirmish," *Pottstown Mercury*, May 9, 1969. For historians on northern violence, see Levy, *Great Uprising*, 1–2, 253–78; Patrick D. Jones, *The Selma of the North: Civil Rights Insurgency in Milwaukee* (Cambridge, MA: Harvard University Press, 2009).

66. Sugrue, *Sweet Land of Liberty*, 6; Gordon P. Griffiths, "Beware Lest Teachers Defile Children, Is Klan Plea: KuKluxKlan," *Pottstown Mercury*, April 2, 1965. Regarding Pottstown KKK, also see Cohen and Cohen, *Chicken Hill Chronicle*, 187. For examples of other areas in the North where the KKK was active, see Robinson, *City within a City*, 2–3; Jones, *Selma of the North*, 55, 231. For a more comprehensive history of the KKK, see Wyn Craig Wade, *The Fiery Cross: The Ku Klux Klan in America* (New York: Oxford University Press, 1987).

67. Gordon P. Griffiths, "When Hooded Knights Reigned, KuKluxKlan: Cross Burning Here a 'Lark'; Pottstown Aims at 'Foreigners,'" *Pottstown Mercury*, March 31, 1965. On Hill, see Hill, *Dear Sir*, 50.

68. Griffiths, "When Hooded Knights Reigned, KuKluxKlan." On Hemlock Row, also see Dostal, "Slum Razing Plan to Hit Borough's '*Forgotten Folk*.'" Chap. 3 exams Hemlock Row further.

69. Gordon P. Griffiths, "The Night's Aglow and Klan Cross Brightens Chicken Hill: Afraid? No, Sight One of Beauty, Says White; KuKluxKlan," *Pottstown Mercury*, April 1, 1965.

70. Griffiths, "Beware Lest Teachers Defile Children, Is Klan Plea."

71. "Cross Burnings in Pottstown Blamed on Rowdies by Police," *Philadelphia Inquirer*, April 11, 1965.

72. Kirk, "NAACP Campaign for Teachers' Salary Equalization," 530.

73. Points will be demonstrated throughout this book.

74. Chancellor, *History of Pottstown Pennsylvania, 1752–1952*, v.

75. For equalization illustration, see Kirk, "NAACP Campaign for Teachers' Salary Equalization," 529–52. For examples of the orthodox interpretation, see Theoharis, *More Beautiful and Terrible History*, 102–3; Matthew F. Delmont, *Why Busing Failed: Race, Media, and the National Resistance to School Desegregation* (Oakland: University of California Press, 2016), 11.

76. On *Brown*, see Russo, Harris, and Sandidge, "*Brown v. Board of Education* at 40," 297–309.

77. Richard M. Dalfiume, "The 'Forgotten Years' of the Negro Revolution," *Journal of American History* 55, no. 1 (June 1968): 90, https://www.jstor.org/stable/1894253. I have made brief remarks previously about World War II's historiographical impact on Pottstown. See Washington, "Examining Interracial Civil Rights Activism in 1950s Pottstown, Pennsylvania," 133.

78. "Final Plans Made for Negro Center."

79. The phrase *white pushback* is already utilized within the scholarly literature as well. For example, see Hava Rachel Gordon, *This Is Our School! Race and Community Resistance to School Reform* (New York: NYU Press, 2021), 42.

80. On "massive resistance," see John A. Kirk, *Beyond Little Rock: The Origins and Legacies of the Central High Crisis* (Fayetteville: University of Arkansas Press, 2007), 94. For early examples on North, see Dougherty, *More Than One Struggle*, 34–50; Kristopher Bryan Burrell, "Black Women as Activist Intellectuals: Ella Baker and Mae Mallory Combat Northern Jim Crow in New York City's Public Schools during the 1950s," in *The Strange Careers of the Jim Crow North: Segregation and Struggle Outside of the South*, ed. Brian Purnell and Jeanne Theoharis, with Komozi Woodard (New York: NYU Press, 2019), 89–112.

81. Dougherty, *More Than One Struggle*, 34–50.

82. The Pottstown Committee on Human Relations, March 14, 1956, Other Orgs: Pottstown Human Relations Council, 1955, Box 82/folder 84, FHPA-Temple; Fellowship House Farm, *Cast Down Your Buckets Where You Are*, June 20–27, 1955, Correspondence, High Sch F-ship—Work Camp, 1953–55, Box 14/folder 79, FHPA-Temple.

83. In addition to Prince, Corum, and Marable, Randolph Henry briefly headed the Pottstown NAACP. On Henry's NAACP presidential tenure, see "Marable Named Head of NAACP." Henry is noted further in Chapter 6.

84. "Phoenixville Classes Cancelled."

85. Theoharis, *More Beautiful and Terrible History*, 34.

2. The Genesis of the Local Black Freedom Struggle in World War II–Era Pottstown

1. Hill, *Dear Sir*, 50; "Pennsylvania Town Seeks Segregation Problem End." For *Plessy v. Ferguson*, see Blair L. M. Kelley, *Right to Ride: Streetcar Boycotts and African American Citizenship in the Era of Plessy v. Ferguson*, John Hope Franklin Series in African American History and Culture (Chapel Hill: University of North Carolina Press, 2010).

2. Hill, *Dear Sir*, 50. On the local Black who made similar points, see Oscar Carter, letter to the editor, *Pottstown Mercury*, January 7, 1943. On larger historical context of Black experience, see Sugrue, *Sweet Land of Liberty*.

3. Carter, letter to the editor.

4. Kevin M. Kruse and Stephen Tuck, "Introduction: The Second World War and the Civil Rights Movement," in *Fog of War: The Second World War and the Civil Rights Movement*, ed. Kevin M. Kruse and Stephen Tuck (New York: Oxford University Press, 2014), 4–6.

5. Dalfiume, "'Forgotten Years' of the Negro Revolution," 90–91.

6. Williams, *Rethinking the Black Freedom Movement*, xi–xii.

7. Sugrue, *Sweet Land of Liberty*, xxi; Hettie V. Williams, "The Garden of Opportunity: Black Women Intellectuals and the Civil Rights Movement in New Jersey, 1912–1949" (PhD diss., Drew University, 2017).

8. Kruse and Tuck, "Introduction," 4–6; Bates, "'Double V for Victory' Mobilizes Black Detroit, 1941–1946," 17–39.

9. Biondi, *To Stand and Fight*; Self, *American Babylon*.

10. Hall, "Long Civil Rights Movement and the Political Uses of the Past," 1235. Regarding the historiography, also see Williams, *Rethinking the Black Freedom Movement*, xi–xii; Sugrue, *Sweet Land of Liberty*, xxi; Williams, "The Garden of Opportunity"; Kruse and Tuck, "Introduction," 4–6; Bates, "'Double V for Victory' Mobilizes Black Detroit, 1941–1946," 17–39; Biondi, *To Stand and Fight*; Self, *American Babylon*.

11. Regarding historical Black presence in Pottstown, see, for example, "History of Pottstown's Second Baptist Church"; Chancellor, *History of Pottstown, Pennsylvania, 1752–1952*, 63, 125–26. Concerning racism locally and throughout North, see Carter, letter to the editor; Hill, *Dear Sir*, 50, 58; Sugrue, *Sweet Land of Liberty*.

12. Carter, letter to the editor.

13. Points mentioned will be demonstrated throughout this chapter and in the chapters that follow.

14. Arnold, *Building the Beloved Community*, 20, 15–25; "Colored Girls Join white Y.W.C.A.," *Philadelphia Tribune*, April 17, 1930; Sallie Sims, "Happenings of the Colored Folks," *Pottstown Mercury*, August 30, 1938.

15. "History of Pottstown's Second Baptist Church"; Chancellor, *History of Pottstown Pennsylvania, 1752–1952*, 63; Sims, "Happenings of the Colored Folks"; Sallie Sims, "Worth While Happenings of the Colored Folks of Pottstown and Vicinity," *Pottstown Mercury*, April 16, 1935; M. D. Skerrett, "Pottstown," *Philadelphia Tribune*, January 24, 1935.

16. "Final Plans Made for Negro Center." This chapter discusses these civil rights initiatives at length.

17. Statistical data from these sources: US Bureau of Census, *Fifteenth Census of the United States, 1930*, vol. 3, part 2, *Montana–Wyoming* (Washington, DC: Government Printing Office, 1932), 690, https://www.census.gov/library/publications /1932/dec/1930a-vol-03-population.html; US Bureau of the Census, *Sixteenth Census of the United States, 1940*, vol. 2: *Characteristics of the Population*, part 6, *Pennsylvania–Texas*, 161; US Bureau of the Census, *Nineteenth Census of the United States, 1970*, vol. 1: *Characteristics of the Population*, part 40, *Pennsylvania Section 1*, 40-16, 40-147; US Department of Commerce Economics and Statistics Administration and US Bureau of Census, *We the Americans: Blacks*, by Claudette E. Bennett, Barbara M. Martin, and Kymberly DeBarros (Washington, DC: Government Printing Office, 1993), 2, https://www.census.gov/library/publications/1993/dec/we-01 .html; US Bureau of the Census, *Negro Population, 1790–1915*, part 7, *General Tables* (Washington, DC: Government Printing Office, 1918), 773, https://www.census .gov/library/publications/1918/dec/negro-population-1790-1915.html.

18. Pottstown Blacks resided in eight of Pottstown's ten wards. Within Montgomery County, Pennsylvania, the enumeration districts where African Americans are noted in the census records include 46-167, 46-169, 46-170, 46-171, 46-173, 46-174, 46-177, 46-180B, 46-181, and 46-183. For the enumeration districts online, see "1940 Census—Pennsylvania—Montgomery County," National Archive Catalog, accessed January 9, 2023, https://catalog.archives.gov/id/57228654.

19. Merl E. Reed, "Black Workers, Defense Industries, and Federal Agencies in Pennsylvania, 1941–1945," in *African Americans in Pennsylvania: Shifting Historical Perspectives*, ed. Joe William Trotter Jr. and Eric Ledell Smith (Harrisburg: Pennsylvania State University Press, 1997), 367.

20. Chancellor, *History of Pottstown Pennsylvania, 1752–1952*, 94–120. I made similar points previously in Washington, "Examining Interracial Civil Rights Activism in 1950s Pottstown, Pennsylvania," 133. For brief essay on the larger historical context surrounding the federal government's wartime production efforts, see Thomas D. Morgan, "The Industrial Mobilization of World War II: America Goes to War," *Army History*, no. 30 (Spring 1994): 31–35, http://www.jstor.org/stable/26304207.

21. Davis, "Beech St. Brews Trouble, Negro Worker States."

22. "NAACP Group Gives to Recreation Fund," *Pottstown Mercury*, February 29, 1944. For a brief description of the World War II theaters, see "World War II Dates and Timeline," Holocaust Encyclopedia, United States Holocaust Memorial Museum, accessed September 9, 2023, https://encyclopedia.ushmm.org/content/en/article /world-war-ii-key-dates.

23. "The Courier's Double 'V' for a Double Victory Campaign Gets Country-Wide Support," *Pittsburgh Courier*, February 14, 1942; "President Franklin Roosevelt's Annual Message (Four Freedoms) to Congress (1941)," Milestone Documents, National Archives, accessed December 13, 2022, https://www.archives.gov/milestone -documents/president-franklin-roosevelts-annual-message-to-congress. For a brief background on the *Pittsburgh Courier*, see Nico Slate, "America's Best Weekly:

A Century of the *Pittsburgh Courier*," *Journal of American History* 99, no. 1 (June 2012): 272–75, https://doi.org/10.1093/jahist/jas104.

24. "Courier's Double 'V' for a Double Victory Campaign Gets Country-Wide Support"; Dalfiume, "'Forgotten Years' of the Negro Revolution," 95. Locally, these points are further noted in this chapter.

25. "Courier's Double 'V' for a Double Victory Campaign Gets Country-Wide Support." Regarding Black Americans overall, see Neil A. Wynn, *The African American Experience during World War II* (Lanham, MD: Rowman & Littlefield, 2010), 39. For general history of World War II, see Bradley Lightbody, *The Second World War: Ambitions to Nemesis* (London: Routledge, 2004).

26. "Courier's Double 'V' for a Double Victory Campaign Gets Country-Wide Support"; Dalfiume, "'Forgotten Years' of the Negro Revolution," 95; H. C. W., letter to the editor, *Pottstown Mercury*, July 19, 1943; Bates, "'Double V for Victory' Mobilizes Black Detroit, 1941–1946," 31. For similar local piece, see Mrs. Dorothy Gibson, letter to the editor, *Pottstown Mercury*, July 14, 1943.

27. Mary Ellen Means, letter to the editor, *Pottstown Mercury*, July 20, 1943.

28. A Proud Negro, letter to the editor, *Pottstown Mercury*, July 15, 1943; H. C. W., letter to the editor.

29. "Courier's Double 'V' for a Double Victory Campaign Gets Country-Wide Support"; Gibson, letter to the editor.

30. Carter, letter to the editor.

31. "Courier's Double 'V' for a Double Victory Campaign Gets Country-Wide Support"; H. C. W., letter to the editor.

32. "Courier's Double 'V' for a Double Victory Campaign Gets Country-Wide Support"; H. C. W., letter to the editor. For a sample of the *Pottstown Mercury* capturing names of local Blacks, see "War in the Distance," *Pottstown Mercury*, January 23, 1941; "Next Selectee Group Expected to Number More Than a Hundred: Half Married Men," *Pottstown Mercury*, July 10, 1943; "29 Selectees Leave Today for 2 Camps," *Pottstown Mercury*, February 9, 1944.

33. "Simms, Milton," Fields of Honor Database, accessed March 21, 2019, https://www.fieldsofhonor-database.com/index.php/en/american-war-cemetery -margraten-s/65258-simms-milton; Milton Simms, enlisted December 19, 1942, Allentown, Pennsylvania, United States, United States World War II Army Enlistment Records, 1938–1946, December 5, 2014, FamilySearch database, https://familysearch .org/ark:/61903/1:1:K8T4-Z7S, citing "Electronic Army Serial Number Merged File, ca. 1938–1946," National Archives: Access to Archival Databases (AAD), National Archives and Records Administration, NARA NAID 1263923, National Archives at College Park, Maryland, 2002, http://aad.archives.gov; "Pottstown Negro, Limerick Man Die on Warfronts, Relatives Told," *Pottstown Mercury*, April 20, 1945; "Milton Simms Post Arranges Campaign to Build New Home," *Pottstown Mercury*, January 27, 1948; "Montgomery County Lost 654 Men in World War II; 90 from This Area," *Pottstown Mercury*, June 28, 1946.

34. "Club Pays Tribute to Late Pvt. Simms," *Pottstown Mercury*, May 1, 1945.

35. "Charter Given Milton Simms Legion Post: Commander G.C. Jones Presented Colors at Official Ceremonies," *Pottstown Mercury*, January 19, 1948.

36. Frank J. Dostal, "Veterans, Masonic Groups Joins Fight for Hemlock Row: Ministers Ask Congregations to Aid Families; Heavy Support Expected at Meeting to Protest Order for Razing Homes," *Pottstown Mercury*, March 27, 1950.

37. Poirier, "Jim Crow, Yankee Style, Stalks Streets of Pottstown."

38. Paul F. Levy, "Mr. James P. Crow, Esquire. . . . A Sequel: Same Old Fellow? No, He's Plain Jim Crow Now," *Pottstown Mercury*, June 11, 1963.

39. "Negroes Here Plan Cemetery." On Pearl Harbor and other important dates from World War II, see "World War II Dates and Timeline."

40. Angelika Krüger-Kahloula, "On the Wrong Side of the Fence: Racial Segregation in American Cemeteries," in *History & Memory in African-American Culture*, ed. Geneviève Fabre and Robert O'Meally (New York: Oxford University Press, 1994), 133.

41. Krüger-Kahloula, "On the Wrong Side of the Fence," 131–33.

42. Krüger-Kahloula, "On the Wrong Side of the Fence," 131–33. For a northern civil rights scholarship example, see Theoharis and Woodard, *Freedom North*.

43. Krüger-Kahloula, "On the Wrong Side of the Fence," 133–34.

44. Mary V. Reid, letter to the editor, *Pottstown Mercury*, July 10, 1954.

45. "Negroes Here Plan Cemetery." On Second Baptist and Edgewood, see "History of Pottstown's Second Baptist Church"; Michael Snyder, "Edgewood Cemetery: Buried History Tells Pottstown Stories," *Mercury*, August 1, 2014, 10:13 p.m. EST (updated September 24, 2021, 4:31 a.m. EST), https://www.pottsmerc.com /2014/08/01/edgewood-cemetery-buried-history-tells-pottstown-stories/. On Pearl Harbor, see "World War II Dates and Timeline."

46. "History of Pottstown's Second Baptist Church."

47. "Negroes Here Plan Cemetery."

48. "Long Time Hill Employe [*sic*] Found Dead: Willis H. Strawther Became Legend in Own Time; Served School for 54 Years," *Pottstown Mercury*, October 31, 1962; Willis Strawther; Burial, Pottstown, Montgomery, Pennsylvania, United States of America, Edgewood Cemetery, Find a Grave Index, record ID 205578848, FamilySearch database, August 6, 2020, https://www.familysearch.org/ark:/61903 /1:1:CV6M-7MMM. For Great Migration, see Alexander et al., "Second-Generation Outcomes of the Great Migration," 2249–71.

49. Judy Jennings, "Monday Morning Gossip of the Nation," *Philadelphia Inquirer*, October 13, 1952.

50. "Long Time Hill Employe [*sic*] Found Dead."

51. "Long Time Hill Employe [*sic*] Found Dead"; "Deaths and Funerals: John William Strawther," *Pottstown Mercury*, July 28, 1941; John W Strothers, Burial, Pottstown, Montgomery, Pennsylvania, United States of America, Edgewood Cemetery, Find a Grave Index, record ID 205579183, FamilySearch database, August 6, 2020, https://www.familysearch.org/ark:/61903/1:1:CV6M-W52M. As of January 7, 2023, Find a Grave has a copy of Strawther's death certificate. See memorial page for John W Strothers (1858–26 Jul 1941), Memorial ID 205579183, citing

Edgewood Cemetery, Pottstown, Montgomery County, Pennsylvania, USA, maintained by KFenstermacher (contributor 48730451), Find a Grave, database and images, accessed January 7, 2023, https://www.findagrave.com/memorial/205579183 /john-w-strothers.

52. "Deaths and Funerals: John William Strawther."

53. Chancellor, *History of Pottstown Pennsylvania, 1752–1952*, 45; Linda McCurdy, "The Potts Family Iron Industry in the Schuylkill Valley" (PhD diss., Pennsylvania State University, 1974), 57, 147.

54. Cohen, interview.

55. "Deaths and Funerals: John William Strawther."

56. Brian Purnell and Jeanne Theoharis, "Histories of Racism and Resistance, Seen and Unseen: How and Why to Think about the Jim Crow North," in Purnell and Theoharis, with Woodard, *Strange Careers of the Jim Crow North*, 4. For biographical data on Parks, see "Rosa Louise McCauley Parks," *Journal of Blacks in Higher Education*, no. 6 (Winter 1994): 18, https://doi.org/10.2307/2962437.

57. Poirier, "Jim Crow, Yankee Style, Stalks Streets of Pottstown."

58. Poirier, "Jim Crow, Yankee Style, Stalks Streets of Pottstown"; "Pennsylvania Town Seeks Segregation Problem End"; Levy, "Mr. James P. Crow, Esquire. . . . A Sequel." On *Brown*, see "Supreme Court Rules Public School Segregation Must End"; "NAACP Hails Move as 'Vindication' of 45-Year Battle"; Russo, Harris, and Sandidge, "*Brown v. Board of Education* at 40," 297–309.

59. Poirier, "Jim Crow, Yankee Style, Stalks Streets of Pottstown"; Levy, "Mr. James P. Crow, Esquire. . . . A Sequel."

60. "Deaths and Funerals: John William Strawther"; Fred C. Selby, "Hill's Whistling Butler: Job Was His Dream, He's Had It 50 Years," *Pottstown Mercury*, October 4, 1950; "History of Pottstown's Second Baptist Church."

61. "Long Time Hill Employe [*sic*] Found Dead"; "Negroes Here Plan Cemetery."

62. "Rev. Heywood L. Butler, Ecumenical Force Dies," *Pottstown Mercury*, December 14, 1971; "Man of God," *Pottstown Mercury*, December 17, 1971; "Rev. Butler Is Awarded for Service," *Pottstown Mercury*, June 23, 1952; "Church Goes into Business for Financing New Edifice," *Pottstown Mercury*, July 16, 1949; "Negroes Here Plan Cemetery"; W. Phillips Jones, "Frankford," *Philadelphia Tribune*, October 17, 1935. For background on Storer College, see Stephanie Shapiro, "A Black College Closed in 1955, but Its Fading Alumni Fight to Pass on a Legacy," *Washington Post*, October 22, 2015, https://www.washingtonpost.com/lifestyle/magazine/a -black-college-closed-in-1955-but-its-fading-alumni-fight-to-pass-on-a-legacy/2015/10 /21/1a1a379c-67d1-11e5-9223-70cb36460919_story.html.

63. "Church Goes into Business for Financing New Edifice"; "Rev. Heywood L. Butler, Ecumenical Force Dies."

64. "Rev. Heywood L. Butler, Ecumenical Force Dies."

65. "Negroes Here Plan Cemetery"; "Thomas Carter, Church Deacon, Dies at Age 70," *Pottstown Mercury*, December 28, 1959. On Old Dominion State phrase, see Patricia Keppel Anderson, "Virginia's Top Scenic Golf Courses for Fall," Virginia, accessed September 9, 2023, https://www.virginia.org/blog/post/scenic-golf-courses -fall/.

66. "Negroes Organize Group in Pottstown"; "Negroes Here Plan Cemetery."

67. On "accommodation," see Brian Kelley, "Sentinels for New South Industry: Booker T. Washington, Industrial Accommodation and Black Workers in the Jim Crow South," *Labor History* 44, no. 3(2003): 338–39. On illustrations of racial oppression in Virginia and the South more broadly, see "Welcome," Racial Terror: Lynching in Virginia, accessed September 9, 2023, https://sites.lib.jmu.edu/valynchings/; Jonathan Scott Holloway, *The Cause of Freedom: A Concise History of African Americans* (New York: Oxford University Press, 2021), 53–61. On interracialist strategy, see Ryan, "Catholic Liberal Interracialism in the Archdiocese of Chicago in the 1960s and 1970s." On Old Dominion State, see Anderson, "Virginia's Top Scenic Golf Courses for Fall."

68. Kirk, "NAACP Campaign for Teachers' Salary Equalization," 530–31, 534, 536–37; Kelley, "Sentinels for New South Industry," 338–39. On majority Black populace, see Glenda Elizabeth Gilmore, "'Somewhere' in the Nadir of African American History, 1890–1920," Freedom's Story: Teaching African American Literature and History, TeacherServe, National Humanities Center, accessed December 14, 2022, http://nationalhumanitiescenter.org/tserve/freedom/1865-1917/essays/nadir.htm.

69. "Church Goes into Business for Financing New Edifice."

70. Hill, *Dear Sir*, 50. Also see "Church Goes into Business for Financing New Edifice" for where congregation business was geographically situated. Regarding Chicken Hill and its geographical landscape, see Cohen and Cohen, *Chicken Hill Chronicle*, 37–38. Finally, the following illuminates present-day location of where the Second Baptist congregation business was. See "591 Jefferson Ave, Pottstown, PA 19464," Google Maps, accessed December 14, 2022, https://www.google.com/search?client=firefox-b-1-d&q=591+jefferson+avenue+pottstown.

71. "Church Goes into Business for Financing New Edifice."

72. "Business and Professional Week Inaugurated in Pottstown," *Pottstown Mercury*, June 25, 1949.

73. "Norristown Attorney Urges Audience to Seize Opportunities," *Pottstown Mercury*, June 29, 1949; "Business and Professional Week Inaugurated in Pottstown"; Keith Phucas, "Peers Reflect on County's First Black Assistant DA," *Times Herald*, February 12, 2012, 8:09 p.m. EST (updated September 24, 2021, 12:46 p.m. EST), https://www.timesherald.com/news/peers-reflect-on-countys-first-black-assistant-da/article_e881c0e9-45a8-5fe8-b50d-a827fd3f6f1c.html.

74. "Church Goes into Business for Financing New Edifice"; Jones, "Frankford."

75. Commonwealth of Pennsylvania, *Final Report of the Pennsylvania State Temporary Commission on the Conditions of the Urban Colored Population to the General Assembly of the State of Pennsylvania* (Harrisburg: Pennsylvania General Assembly of the State of Pennsylvania, January 1943), 114–15, https://archive.org/details/finalreportofpen00penn_0.

76. Levy, *Great Uprising*, 231. For York's population, see Levy, *Great Uprising*, 234.

77. "Church Goes into Business for Financing New Edifice."

78. Mjagkij, *Light in the Darkness*; "History of Pottstown's Second Baptist Church." Also see "Negroes Here Plan Cemetery"; "Church Goes into Business for Financing New Edifice."

79. Kirk, "NAACP Campaign for Teachers' Salary Equalization," 530, 534, 536–37; "Negroes Here Plan Cemetery."

80. "Negroes Here Plan Cemetery."

81. "Church Goes into Business for Financing New Edifice."

82. "Negroes Here Plan Cemetery."

83. "Church Goes into Business for Financing New Edifice."

84. "Negro Program Is Formulated: YMCA Council to Plan Recreational Activities Under Boys' Department," *Pottstown Mercury*, January 4, 1945; Mjagkij, *Light in the Darkness*, 8–23. For subtitle, see "Final Plans Made for Negro Center."

85. For "Colored YMCA" see Tim Prudente, "A Century of Swimming: Y in Druid Hill turns 100," *Baltimore Sun*, June 4, 2016; "Colored Y.M.C.A. Expects Twenty-Five Thousand," *Washington Times*, May 1, 1911. Regarding the Black YMCA's expansion around the mid-1920s see Mjagkij, *Light in the Darkness*, 5, 66, 79.

86. "Final Plans Made for Negro Center."

87. "Plans for Finance Campaign Completed at Meeting in YMCA," *Pottstown Mercury*, January 8, 1946; "Negro Activity Plans Pushed: Committee to Recruit Leaders for Groups to Be Sponsored by Local YMCA," *Pottstown Mercury*, January 11, 1945.

88. Chancellor, *History of Pottstown Pennsylvania, 1752–1952*, 170.

89. "Pottstown 'Y' Lowers Race, Religious Bars," *Philadelphia Tribune*, February 1, 1949.

90. Sugrue, *Sweet Land of Liberty*, 8.

91. "Full-Time Extension Director Appointed for Local YMCA," *Pottstown Mercury*, December 31, 1946. For Pottstown Recreation Commission, also see Chancellor, *History of Pottstown Pennsylvania, 1752–1952*, 181.

92. "Full-Time Extension Director Appointed for Local YMCA"; "Extension Work among Negro Youth Explained to Rotary," *Pottstown Mercury*, January 4, 1946; "Extension Program Activities Increasing," *Pottstown Mercury*, January 12, 1946; "Activities of YMCA for Negro Children Draw 378 in One Week," *Pottstown Mercury*, February 20, 1946; "Activity Participation in 'Y' Work Totals 459," *Pottstown Mercury*, February 26, 1946; "Teen-Age Boys, Girls Stage Summer Dance," *Pottstown Mercury*, July 18, 1946; "Give Report on Work of 'Y' Extension Unit," *Pottstown Mercury*, August 2, 1946; "'Y' Extension Attracted 1092 in September," *Pottstown Mercury*, October 2, 1946; "Christmas Laughter Fills Bethany Center," *Pottstown Mercury*, December 25, 1946; "A Sign of Progress," *Pottstown Mercury*, January 6, 1947.

93. "Rev. William Corum Accepts Charge at Bethlehem Church."

94. William Corum, March 1976, United States Social Security Death Index, FamilySearch database, US Social Security Administration, Death Master File database, National Technical Information Service, Alexandria, VA, ongoing, January 8, 2021, https://familysearch.org/ark:/61903/1:1:VM5Q-PZS; "Obituaries: William Corum, 60, Dies in Bryn Mawr," *Mercury*, March 29, 1976.

95. "Neville's Club Awaits Opening Baseball Tilt: All-Stars Will Start Campaign April 16; Jim Corum Is Business Manager," *Pottstown Mercury*, March 30, 1933;

"Colored All-Stars Meet Franklin in Opener," *Pottstown Mercury*, April 4, 1934; "Pine Forge Defeats Colored All-Stars: Schaeffer Smacks Two Doubles in 7-2 Victory," *Pottstown Mercury*, July 12, 1934; "Colored All-Stars Nose Out Emaus, 3-2," *Pottstown Mercury*, June 26, 1934. William also went by "Bill," as demonstrated, for instance, in the following article: "New Junior League to Open Saturday," *Pottstown Mercury*, December 16, 1946.

96. "Bethel Books Two Tilts," *Pottstown Mercury*, May 4, 1937; Paul Lucas, "Eureka Meets First Baptist in Church Loop Game: Colored Nine Seeks 3d Straight Win," *Pottstown Mercury*, May 29, 1939; "Sultans Want Games," *Pottstown Mercury*, January 9, 1940; Sims, "Happenings of the Colored Folks," *Pottstown Mercury*, August 18, 1937.

97. Sims, "Happenings of the Colored Folks," *Pottstown Mercury*, October 25, 1938; "Zion's Young People to Hear Talk."

98. As of January 7, 2023, Find a Grave has Benjamin F. Corum's death certificate. See memorial page for Benjamin Franklin Corum (11 Mar 1868–13 Jan 1928), Memorial ID 202691819, citing Edgewood Cemetery, Pottstown, Montgomery County, Pennsylvania, USA, maintained by KFenstermacher (contributor 48730451), Find a Grave, database and images, accessed January 7, 2023, https://www.findagrave.com/memorial/202691819/benjamin-franklin-corum; Benjamin F Corum, United States Census, 1920, database with images, FamilySearch, February 3, 2021, https://www.familysearch.org/ark:/61903/1:1:MF19-BJG; Montgomery > Marriage license applications, 1894, vol. 16, no 5560-6058 > image 127 of 557, county courthouses, Pennsylvania, County Marriages, 1885–1950, database with images, FamilySearch, July 27, 2020, https://familysearch.org/ark:/61903/3:1:33S7-9P6B-C27?cc=1589502&wc=Q6VB-1DW%3A1590263109%2C1590263104.

99. R. R. Wright, "The Migration of Negroes to the North," *Annals of the American Academy of Political and Social Science* 27 (May 1906): 97–98, http://www.jstor.org/stable/1010513.

100. Wright, "Migration of Negroes to the North," 104. For further background data on Wright, see "Bishop R.R. Wright, Jr.; AME Church Leader," *Philadelphia Daily News*, December 13, 1967.

101. Wright, "Migration of Negroes to the North," 97, 104.

102. For similar arguments, see James N. Gregory, *The Southern Diaspora: How the Great Migrations of Black and White Southerners Transformed America* (Chapel Hill: University of North Carolina Press, 2005), especially 237–82.

103. Isaiah E Glenn in household of David W Glenn, Accomack, Virginia, United States, United States Census, 1920, database with images, FamilySearch, accessed January 8, 2023, https://www.familysearch.org/ark:/61903/1:1:MJNM-KYR, citing, sheet, line, family, NARA microfilm publication T625 (Washington, DC: National Archives and Records Administration, 1992), roll, FHL microfilm; Isaiah Glenn, December 1985, United States Social Security Death Index, US Social Security Administration, Death Master File database, National Technical Information Service, Alexandria, VA, ongoing, FamilySearch database, January 8, 2021, https://familysearch.org/ark:/61903/1:1:JY77-5ZK; "Edith Louise Glenn: June 20, 1909—June 10,

2003," DeBaptiste Funeral Homes, West Chester, accessed January 7, 2023, https://www.debaptiste.com/obituary/6300712. On Old Dominion State, see Anderson, "Virginia's Top Scenic Golf Courses for Fall."

104. Isaiah E Glenn, Pottstown, Montgomery, Pennsylvania, United States, United States Census, 1940, database with images, FamilySearch, January 7, 2021, https://www.familysearch.org/ark:/61903/1:1:KQC6-841, citing enumeration district (ED) 46-177, sheet 10B, line 74, family 184, Sixteenth Census of the United States, 1940, NARA digital publication T627, Records of the Bureau of the Census, 1790–2007, RG 29 (Washington, DC: National Archives and Records Administration, 2012), roll 3583; "Rev. and Mrs. Glenn Note 50th Anniversary," *Mercury*, August 29, 1975; "Second Baptist Church Elects Officials," *Pottstown Mercury*, January 15, 1934; "Deaths and Funerals: Mrs. Marie Scott White," *Pottstown Mercury*, January 24, 1940; "Banquet Marks Close of Anniversary Program," *Pottstown Mercury*, November 27, 1945; "Negroes Organize Group in Pottstown."

105. "Negro Club Work to Start Tuesday," *Pottstown Mercury*, February 15, 1945; "'Y' Club Work Starts in Negro Community," *Pottstown Mercury*, February 1, 1945; "Century Club Activities Program Drafted; Fall and Winter Schedule Announced," *Pottstown Mercury*, September 17, 1946; "Senior High School Class Holds Class Night Exercises," *Pottstown Mercury*, June 7, 1945; Frances Young in household of Joseph Young, Pottstown, Montgomery, Pennsylvania, United States, United States Census, 1940, database with images, FamilySearch January 7, 2021, https://www.familysearch.org/ark:/61903/1:1:KQC6-MN8, citing enumeration district (ED) 46-171, sheet 8B, line 68, family 155, Sixteenth Census of the United States, 1940, NARA digital publication T627, Records of the Bureau of the Census, 1790–2007, RG 29 (Washington, DC: National Archives and Records Administration, 2012), roll 3583.

106. *The Troiad 1945: A Publication Presented Annually by the Graduating Class of Pottstown High School* (Boyertown, PA: Boyertown Times Publishing Company, 1945), 35, https://www.pottstownschools.org/AlumniYearbooks.aspx.

107. *Troiad 1945*, 82.

108. "Baptist Sunday School Elects Officers at Session," *Pottstown Mercury*, January 20, 1942.

109. Williams, letter to the editor. Frances uses her married name but still has her maiden name. On this point and further biographical data about Joseph and Geraldine, see "Obituaries: Joseph Young Dies in Hospital," *Pottstown Mercury*, May 18, 1966; Joseph Young in household of Joseph Young, Pottstown, Montgomery, Pennsylvania, United States, United States Census, 1940, database with images, FamilySearch, January 7, 2021 (https://www.familysearch.org/ark:/61903/1:1:KQC6-MNZ:), citing enumeration district (ED) 46-171, sheet 8B, line 67, family 155, Sixteenth Census of the United States, 1940, NARA digital publication T627, Records of the Bureau of the Census, 1790–2007, RG 29 (Washington, DC: National Archives and Records Administration, 2012), roll 3583; "Obituaries: Geraldine Young Dies at Age 62," *Pottstown Mercury*, July 1, 1969. Frances's remarks from the letter are further assessed in chap. 5.

110. "Greatest Problem Faced by Adult 'Y' Club Is Need of a Building to Conduct Programs," *Pottstown Mercury*, May 3, 1946.

111. "Extension Work among Negro Youth Explained to Rotary," *Pottstown Mercury*, January 4, 1946; "Wilke Elected President of the Lions Club: Race Relationships Discussed by YMCA Extension Workers," *Pottstown Mercury*, June 5, 1946; "William Corum Speaks at Meeting of ABC," *Pottstown Mercury*, April 11, 1946.

112. "William D. Corum Is Renamed Head of YMCA Council," *Pottstown Mercury*, April 23, 1946.

113. "Six to Be Elected to Extension Work Council of YMCA," *Pottstown Mercury*, April 1, 1946; "Negro Activity Plans Pushed"; "Programs for 100 Children Set Up," *Pottstown Mercury*, March 2, 1945; "176 Negro Boys, Girls Signed For YMCA Club Work Here," *Pottstown Mercury*, February 9, 1945; "Full-Time Extension Director Appointed for Local YMCA"; "Negro Youth Work Is Discussed," *Pottstown Mercury*, March 6, 1945; "Extension Work among Negro Youth Explained to Rotary," *Pottstown Mercury*, January 6, 1946; "Summer Membership Drive is Planned by YMCA Movement," *Pottstown Mercury*, May 14, 1946; "Plans for Finance Campaign Completed at Meeting in YMCA"; "Army Leading Navy in Campaign for Negro YMCA Work," *Pottstown Mercury*, January 29, 1946.

114. "William D. Corum Is Renamed Head of YMCA Council."

115. "Negro Activity Plans Pushed"; "'Y' Council Votes $200 to Aid Work at Center," *Pottstown Mercury*, November 19, 1946; "Progress Is Shown Under YMCA's New Extension Director," *Pottstown Mercury*, February 18, 1947; "William D. Corum Is Renamed Head of YMCA Council."

116. "Negro Club Work to Start Tuesday," *Pottstown Mercury*, February 15, 1945.

117. "Klinger to Address Negro Adult 'Y' Club Wednesday, Nov. 7," *Pottstown Mercury*, November 1, 1945; "Stresses Good Books to Further Education," *Pottstown Mercury*, November 9, 1945.

118. "Banquet Marks Close of Anniversary Program," *Pottstown Mercury*, November 27, 1945.

119. "Negro Club Work to Start Tuesday"; "'Y' Club Work Starts in Negro Community."

120. "Tri-Hi-Y Club Holds Season's First Meeting," *Pottstown Mercury*, September 17, 1946.

121. "Century Club Activities Program Drafted." On athletic background, see *Troiad 1945*, 35.

122. "'Y' Extension Attracted 1092 in September."

123. "YMCA Extension Leader Gives December Report," *Pottstown Mercury*, January 2, 1947.

124. "Full-Time Extension Director Appointed for Local YMCA."

125. "'Y' Extension Attracted 1092 in September."

126. "Full-Time Extension Director Appointed for Local YMCA." For census data, see US Bureau of the Census, *Sixteenth Census of the United States, 1940*, vol. 2, *Characteristics of the Population*, part 6, *Pennsylvania–Texas*, 161; US Bureau of the

Census, *Seventeenth Census of the United States, 1950*, vol. 2, *Characteristics of the Population*, part 38, *Pennsylvania*, 38-116.

127. "Pottstown 'Y' Lowers Race, Religious Bars"; "Extension Division Work at 'Y' Ends as Economy Step," *Pottstown Mercury*, July 29, 1949.

128. Mjagkij, *Light in the Darkness*, 124, also see 123–24.

129. Mjagkij, *Light in the Darkness*, 123–24.

130. Mjagkij, *Light in the Darkness*, 125–27, 8–23.

131. Mjagkij, *Light in the Darkness*, 124, 121.

132. Sugrue, *Sweet Land of Liberty*, 8. For general points concerning Black Pottstown YMCA programming and larger themes noted, see "Programs for 100 Children Set Up"; "176 Negro Boys, Girls Signed for YMCA Club Work Here"; "Full-Time Extension Director Appointed for Local YMCA." For an equalization example, see Kirk, "NAACP Campaign for Teachers' Salary Equalization," 530. On Black YMCAs, see Mjagkij, *Light in the Darkness*, 5, 66, 79; Prudente, "Century of Swimming."

133. "Race Relations Discussed by Council," *Pottstown Mercury*, February 12, 1946.

134. "Rev. H.H. Goeringer to Deliver Address at Mass Meeting," *Pottstown Mercury*, February 23, 1946.

135. "Inter-Racial Commission Organized in the Borough," *Pottstown Mercury*, January 31, 1946.

136. "Rotary Speaker Issues Plea for 'Christian Brotherhood,'" *Pottstown Mercury*, March 8, 1946.

137. "Negroes Organize Group in Pottstown"; "Our History," NAACP, accessed December 15, 2022, https://naacp.org/about/our-history.

138. "Negro Organization Is Given Charter," *Pottstown Mercury*, January 18, 1943.

139. Charles Radford Lawrence, "Negro Organizations in Crisis: Depression, New Deal, World War II" (PhD diss., Columbia University, 1952), 41–47, 102–4.

140. Lawrence, "Negro Organizations in Crisis," 104.

141. Lawrence, "Negro Organizations in Crisis," 102–3.

142. "N.Y.A. Survey," *Crisis*, June 1941, 201, https://books.google.com/books?id=xloEAAAAMBAJ.

143. Lucille Black to James Corum Sr., November 13, 1942, "Pottstown, PA., 1942–43," Box II:C172, folder 2, Branch File, Manuscript Division, Group II, Records of the National Association for the Advancement of Colored People, Library of Congress, Washington, DC, [hereinafter, NAACP-LOC]. For a brief background of Lucille Black, see "Lucille Black, Former Aide of the N.A.A.C.P., 66, Dies," *New York Times*, May 22, 1975.

144. Lucille Black to James Corum Sr., December 23, 1942, "Pottstown, PA., 1942–43," Box II: C172, folder 2, NAACP-LOC. On being brothers, see "Rev. William Corum Accepts Charge at Bethlehem Church."

145. "NAACP Chapter Receives Charter, Elects New Officers," *Pottstown Mercury*, October 8, 1951.

146. James H. Corum, 1902, Pennsylvania Births and Christenings, 1709–1950, FamilySearch database, January 27, 2020, https://familysearch.org/ark:/61903/1:1:HFJT-X1PZ; James Corum, December 1978, United States Social Security Death Index, US Social Security Administration, Death Master File database, National Technical Information Service, Alexandria, VA, ongoing, FamilySearch database, January 8, 2021, https://familysearch.org/ark:/61903/1:1:J2SM-N24.

147. Dunphy, "They Make Unions Tick"; "Corum Elected by Flagg Union: Wins His Fourth Term by Defeating Kochel in Biennial USW Voting," *Pottstown Mercury*, June 23, 1950; "2 Flagg Workers Retire After 94 Years of Service," *Pottstown Mercury*, April 28, 1967.

148. Norman B. Reed, "Pottstown Portraits: A Quick Look at Your Neighbor; James H. Corum," *Pottstown Mercury*, February 15, 1955. On Flagg and Corum, also see Dunphy, "They Make Unions Tick"; "Corum Elected by Flagg Union."

149. "Negroes Here Plan Cemetery"; "Second Baptist Church Elects Its Officers," *Pottstown Mercury*, January 14, 1942.

150. "Neville's Club Awaits Opening Baseball Tilt"; "Colored All-Stars Flay Spicer Crew, 7-3: Timely Bingles Enable Negro Nine to Win; Bill Corum Socks Home Run in Tri-County League Game; Victors Play Well," *Pottstown Mercury*, May 7, 1936. James Corum also utilized the nickname "Jim." See Dunphy, "They Make Unions Tick." On the Boy Scouts, see "Pottstown News," *Philadelphia Tribune*, April 26, 1928; Sallie Sims, "Happenings of the Colored Folks," November 30, 1938.

151. Frank Thomas in household of Bertha Thomas, Pottstown, Montgomery, Pennsylvania, United States, United States Census, 1940, database with images, FamilySearch, January 7, 2021, https://www.familysearch.org/ark:/61903/1:1:KQC6-WCR, citing enumeration district (ED) 46-177, sheet 13A, line 30, family 229, Sixteenth Census of the United States, 1940, NARA digital publication T627 Records of the Bureau of the Census, 1790–2007, RG 29 (Washington, DC: National Archives and Records Administration, 2012), roll 3583. For letter, see Frank W. Thomas Sr. to the Board of Directors N.A.A.C.P., December 1, 1942, "Pottstown, PA., 1942–43," Box II: C172, folder 2, NAACP-LOC.

152. "950 Deferments Here; Additional Names Published," *Pottstown Mercury*, March 13, 1944.

153. "110 Defense Police Enter Local Corps: New Class Inducted in Impressive Ceremony; 230 Now Belong; County, Borough Officials Attend," *Pottstown Mercury*, February 5, 1943.

154. "Senior Ushers: Second Baptist Church Held Their Anniversary May 20; Those Contributing Are as Follows," *Pottstown Mercury*, June 5, 1945.

155. Wolfinger, "We Are in the Front Lines in the Battle for Democracy," 1–23. For larger leadership role of Black men in the NAACP across United States, see Kevern Verney, Lee Sartain, and Adam Fairclough, eds., *Long Is the Way and Hard: One Hundred Years of the NAACP* (Fayetteville: University of Arkansas Press, 2009).

156. "Negroes Organize Group in Pottstown."

157. Jennie Green in entry for Jacob Green, 1900, United States Census, 1900, database with images, FamilySearch, January 13, 2022, https://www.familysearch

.org/ark:/61903/1:1:M3QP-GGD. On Jacob, see "Obituary: Jacob Green," *Pottstown Mercury*, November 28, 1935. On Jennie's familial connection to Jacob, see "Obituaries: Jennie Thornton, Active Church Member, Dies," *Pottstown Mercury*, July 3, 1970.

158. On Jennie's occupation, see Jennie Thornton in household of Richard Thornton, Pottstown, Montgomery, Pennsylvania, United States, United States Census, 1940, database with images, FamilySearch, January 7, 2021, https://www.familysearch.org/ark:/61903/1:1:KQC6-VGP, citing enumeration district (ED) 46-183, sheet 9A, line 6, family 187, Sixteenth Census of the United States, 1940, NARA digital publication T627 Records of the Bureau of the Census, 1790–2007, RG 29 (Washington, DC: National Archives and Records Administration, 2012), roll 3583. On the larger historical context, see John S. Portlock, "In the 'Fabled Land of Make-Believe': Charlotta Bass and Jim Crow Los Angeles," in Purnell and Theoharis, with Woodard, *Strange Careers of the Jim Crow North*, 71; Sugrue, *Sweet Land of Liberty*, 27–28, 66.

159. For Richard's connection to the graveyard, see "Negroes Here Plan Cemetery." For biographical data on the Thorntons, see "Obituaries: Jennie Thornton, Active Church Member, Dies"; "Obituaries: Richard T. Thornton," *Pottstown Mercury*, February 15, 1949. For a chronology of World War I, see "Timeline (1914–1921)," Collection Stars and Stripes: The American Soldiers' Newspaper of World War I, 1918 to 1919, accessed December 15, 2022, https://www.loc.gov/collections/stars-and-stripes/articles-and-essays/a-world-at-war/timeline-1914-1921/.

160. "Obituaries: Jennie Thornton, Active Church Member, Dies." For further data on Richard and Second Baptist, see "Obituaries: Richard T. Thornton."

161. James Corum to [recipient not identified], [unknown date], "Pottstown, PA., 1942–43," Box II:C172, folder 2, NAACP-LOC (penciled-in date of November 4, 1942, on this document); Thomas to the Board of Directors N.A.A.C.P., December 1, 1942, NAACP-LOC.

162. "Five Join Group," *Pottstown Mercury*, December 29, 1942; "NAACP to Discuss Anti-Poll Tax Bill," *Pottstown Mercury*, March 22, 1943; "Local Negro Organization Discusses Discrimination," *Pottstown Mercury*, March 23, 1943; Frank Thomas Sr. to [recipient not identified], January 15, 1943, "Pottstown, PA., 1942–43," Box II:C172, folder 2, NAACP-LOC; "Negroes Revive Advancement Assn.," *Pottstown Mercury*, July 31, 1944; "Association to Meet," *Pottstown Mercury*, November 25, 1944; "Negroes Plan Increased Part in Public Affairs," *Pottstown Mercury*, October 30, 1944.

163. James Corum to [recipient not identified], November 25, 1942, "Pottstown, PA., 1942–43," Box II: C172, folder 2, NAACP-LOC. On Philadelphia and Detroit, see Wolfinger, "We Are in the Front Lines in the Battle for Democracy," 6; Lawrence, "Negro Organizations in Crisis," 92, 375.

164. "Negro Organization is Given Charter," *Pottstown Mercury*, January 18, 1943. The increase of Pottstown NAACP members is documented in the following sources: James Corum Sr. to [recipient not identified], November 9, 1942, "Pottstown, PA., 1942–43," Box II: C172, folder 2, NAACP-LOC; "Negroes Organize

Group in Pottstown"; "Branch News," *Crisis*, January 1943, 28, https://books
.google.com/books?id=yloEAAAAMBAJ&rview=1&lr=; Corum to [recipient not
identified], November 25, 1942, NAACP-LOC; Thomas to the Board of Directors
N.A.A.C.P., December 1, 1942, NAACP-LOC; "Five Join Group"; "Local Colored
Group Plans Mass Meeting," *Pottstown Mercury*, January 15, 1943; "Negro Organization Is Given Charter."

165. Corum to [recipient not identified], November 25, 1942, NAACP-LOC;
"Negro Organization Is Given Charter"; Lawrence, "Negro Organizations in Crisis," 375.

166. On Black communities in highly industrialized zones, see Reed, "Black
Workers, Defense Industries, and the Federal Agencies in Pennsylvania," 363–87;
Bates, "'Double V for Victory' Mobilizes Black Detroit, 1941–1946," 17–39. Regard-
ing Philadelphia and Detroit, see "McClendon Reelected Detroit NAACP Pres.,"
Philadelphia Tribune, January 9, 1943; Wolfinger, "We Are in the Front Lines in the
Battle for Democracy," 1–23; Karl Ellis Johnson, "Black Philadelphia in Transition:
The African-American Struggle on the Home Front during World War II and the
Cold War Period, 1941–1963" (PhD diss., Temple University, 2001), 99, 127.

167. Lawrence, "Negro Organizations in Crisis," 102–3.

168. Corum to [recipient not identified], November 25, 1942, NAACP-LOC.

169. See biographical descriptions of local activists in this chapter. When comparing Pottstown to other larger northern areas, see Karen R. Miller, "'We Cannot Wait
for Understanding to Come to Us': Community Activists Respond to Violence at
Detroit's Northwestern High School, 1940–1941," in *Groundwork: Local Black Freedom Movements in America*, ed. Jeanne Theoharis and Komozi Woodard (New York:
New York University Press, 2005), 240–41; Patrick Flack, "Tensions in the Relationship between Local and National NAACP Branches: The Example of Detroit, 1919–
41," in Verney, Sartain, and Fairclough, *Long Is the Way and Hard*, 156, 162–64;
"McClendon Reelected Detroit NAACP Pres."; Wolfinger, "We Are in the Front
Lines in the Battle for Democracy," 1–23; Johnson, "Black Philadelphia in Transition," 99, 127.

170. Robinson, *City within a City*, 15.

171. Corum to [recipient not identified], November 9, 1942, NAACP-LOC.

172. Thomas to the Board of Directors N.A.A.C.P., December 1, 1942,
NAACP-LOC.

173. Thomas to [recipient not identified], January 15, 1943, NAACP-LOC.

174. Frank W. Thomas to [recipient not identified], [unknown date], "Pottstown, PA., 1942–43," Box II:C172, folder 2, "Pottstown, PA., 1942–43," NAACP-
LOC (source has stamped date of June 17, 1943, on it).

175. "Report Given on Recreation Activity Here: Stage Production and Tennis
Registration Reports; Community Center Will Open on July, 13," *Pottstown Mercury*,
June 8, 1943. For Pottstown Recreation Commission, also see Chancellor, *History of
Pottstown Pennsylvania, 1752–1952*, 181.

176. "NAACP Group Gives to Recreation Fund."

177. "Council Votes to Take Over Bethany Chapel: Group Approves Paving of
8th St.," *Pottstown Mercury*, November 5, 1942. For further background on the

structure, see "Bethany Chapel Deed Presented to the Borough," *Pottstown Mercury*, February 9, 1943. "Bethany Recreation Center" and "Bethany Chapel" are essentially the same place. See the following sources: "Council Votes to Take Over Bethany Chapel"; "Bethany Chapel Deed Presented to the Borough"; "Old Bethany Center Topples to Make Way for Playground," *Pottstown Mercury*, September 20, 1971.

178. "Notice! Members of Bethany Recreation Center—Fall Schedule," *Pottstown Mercury*, September 1, 1944.

179. "Bethany Recreation Center," *Pottstown Mercury*, October 12, 1943.

180. "Bethany Chapel Deed Presented to the Borough." Also see "Notice!," September 1, 1944; "Bethany Recreation Center."

181. "Council Votes to Take Over Bethany Chapel"; "Report Given on Recreation Activity Here."

182. Local civil rights economic assessments essentially suggested and gleaned from the following sources: "Negroes Here Plan Cemetery"; "Extension Work among Negro Youth Explained to Rotary," *Pottstown Mercury*, January 4, 1946; "Plans for Finance Campaign Completed at Meeting in YMCA"; Frank J. Dostal, "Hemlock Row Defies Threat to Raze Homes: Strong Aid Pledged: Decision Rests with County Housing Unit," *Pottstown Mercury*, March 30, 1950.

183. For similar tax monies points, see Julia Rabig, "'The Laboratory of Democracy': Construction Industry Racism in Newark and the Limits of Liberalism," in *Black Power at Work: Community Control, Affirmative Action, and the Construction Industry*, ed. David Goldberg and Trevor Griffey (Ithaca, NY: ILR Press, 2010), 49. On local YMCA generalization points, see "Extension Work among Negro Youth Explained to Rotary," *Pottstown Mercury*, January 4, 1946; "Plans for Finance Campaign Completed at Meeting in YMCA."

184. "Full-Time Extension Director Appointed for Local YMCA"; "William D. Corum Is Renamed Head of YMCA Council"; Mjagkij, *Light in the Darkness*, 124–27; "Sign of Progress"; "Progress Is Shown Under YMCA's New Extension Director"; "Extension Division Work at 'Y' Ends as Economy Step."

185. "Pottstown 'Y' Lowers Race, Religious Bars."

186. "City Couple at Post in Pottsville," *Philadelphia Tribune*, August 6, 1949.

187. "William D. Corum Is Renamed Head of YMCA Council"; "Negro Youth Work Is Discussed"; "Extension Work among Negro Youth Explained to Rotary," *Pottstown Mercury*, January 4, 1946; "Summer Membership Drive Is Planned by YMCA Movement"; "Plans for Finance Campaign Completed at Meeting in YMCA"; "Army Leading Navy in Campaign for Negro YMCA Work."

188. Corum's tenure as NAACP president officially began in late November 1942. See "Negroes Organize Group in Pottstown." The *Pottstown Mercury* identifies James Corum as NAACP president up until July 29, 1944. See F. Thomas and J. Corum, "Notice!," *Pottstown Mercury*, July 29, 1944. Two days later, it identifies him as "retiring president." See "Negroes Revive Advancement Assn."

189. Thomas to [recipient not identified], January 15, 1943, NAACP-LOC.

190. Corum to [recipient not identified], [unknown date], NAACP-LOC (penciled-in date of November 4, 1942, on this document). Concerning revenues to New York, see Corum to [recipient not identified], November 9, 1942, NAACP-LOC;

Thomas to the Board of Directors N.A.A.C.P., December 1, 1942, NAACP-LOC.

191. Flack, "Tensions in the Relationship between Local and National NAACP Branches," 156, 155–56. On Motor City description, see Thomas J. Sugrue, "Motor City: The Story of Detroit," AP US History Study Guide, Gilder Lehrman Institute of American History, accessed September 18, 2023, https://ap.gilderlehrman .org/history-by-era/politics-reform/essays/motor-city-story-detroit.

192. Black to Corum, November 13, 1942, NAACP-LOC.

193. "Negroes Organize Group in Pottstown"; "Dead or Inactive Branches in Eastern Pennsylvania," July 31, 1951, "Flamer, John W. Nov. 1–Dec. 26, 1951," Box II: C354, folder 6, NAACP-LOC; "NAACP Group to Be Formally Organized Here," *Pottstown Mercury*, October 5, 1951; "NAACP Chapter Receives Charter, Elects New Officers."

194. Thomas to [recipient not identified], January 15, 1943, NAACP-LOC.

195. Bates, "'Double V for Victory' Mobilizes Black Detroit, 1941–1946," 17.

196. William H. McCabe, "Pottstown," in *Montgomery County: The Second Hundred Years*, vol. 1, ed. Jean Barth Toll and Michael J. Schwager (Norristown, PA: Montgomery County Federation of Historical Societies, 1983), 533.

197. Dostal, "Hemlock Row Defies Threat to Raze Homes."

198. "Family Welfare Society Reports Increase in Cases," *Pottstown Mercury*, October 10, 1945. Also see McCabe, "Pottstown," 534.

199. Dostal, "Hemlock Row Defies Threat to Raze Homes."

200. Dostal, "Hemlock Row Defies Threat to Raze Homes." For when Pottstown NAACP disbanded, see "NAACP Group to Be Formally Organized Here."

201. Doug Rossinow, *Visions of Progress: The Left-Liberal Tradition in America* (Philadelphia: University of Pennsylvania Press, 2008), 195. On African Americans, especially see 212–32.

202. Mary L. Dudziak, *Cold War Civil Rights: Race and the Image of American Democracy* (Princeton, NJ: Princeton University Press, 2000), 12–13.

203. Rossinow, *Visions of Progress*; Dudziak, *Cold War Civil Rights*; Kirk, "NAACP Campaign for Teachers' Salary Equalization," 529–52.

204. "Negroes Organize Group in Pottstown"; Dostal, "Hemlock Row Defies Threat to Raze Homes"; "NAACP Chapter Receives Charter, Elects New Officers."

205. Reed, "Pottstown Portraits: A Quick Look at Your Neighbor; James H. Corum"; Dunphy, "They Make Unions Tick"; "Corum Elected by Flagg Union"; "Rev. William Corum Accepts Charge at Bethlehem Church."

206. Robert Korstad and Nelson Lichtenstein, "Opportunities Found and Lost: Labor, Radicals, and the Early Civil Rights Movement," *Journal of American History* 75, no. 3 (December 1988), 787, https://doi.org/10.2307/1901530.

207. Dunphy, "They Make Unions Tick"; "Corum Elected by Flagg Union"; "2 Flagg Workers Retire after 94 Years of Service."

208. Korstad and Lichtenstein, "Opportunities Found and Lost," 787; "The Week's Newsmakers," *Afro-American*, May 12, 1962, https://news.google.com /newspapers?nid=UBnQDr5gPskC.

209. "Week's Newsmakers."

210. Dunphy, "They Make Unions Tick."

211. "James Corum Is Honored as He Leaves Union Post," *Pottstown Mercury*, July 25, 1962.

212. "Corum Elected by Flagg Union."

213. Reed, "Pottstown Portraits: A Quick Look at Your Neighbor; James H. Corum."

214. Dunphy, "They Make Unions Tick."

215. "FEPC Supported by Steel Workers," *Philadelphia Tribune*, May 21, 1946.

3. The *Pottstown Mercury* and the World War II Origins of Civil Rights Advocacy Work

1. Hill, *Dear Sir*, 2, 17–19, 50–63.

2. "Obituary: Shandy Hill, 91, Journalist," *Philadelphia Inquirer*, October 3, 1992.

3. Hill, *Dear Sir*, 50–64.

4. Hill, *Dear Sir*, 62–63.

5. Sims, "Happenings of the Colored Folks," *Pottstown Mercury*, August 18, 1937. Sims's name appears as "Sally" and "Sallie." Nonetheless, US census records, corroborated by evidence from the *Pottstown Mercury*, suggest that although sources spelled her first name differently, it is the same local Black woman. Also, both sources demonstrate that her spouse was Otis Sims. See Sallie Sims in household of Otis Sims, Pottstown, Montgomery, Pennsylvania, United States, United States Census, 1940, database with images, FamilySearch, January 7, 2021, https://www.family search.org/ark:/61903/1:1:KQC6-N6D, citing enumeration district (ED) 46-183, sheet 19B, line 68, family 410, Sixteenth Census of the United States, 1940, NARA digital publication T627, Records of the Bureau of the Census, 1790–2007, RG 29 (Washington, DC: National Archives and Records Administration, 2012), roll 3583; "Obituaries: 'Mom' Sims Dies at Age of 72," *Pottstown Mercury*, March 3, 1962. For a sample of the column, see Sims, "Happenings of the Colored Folks," *Pottstown Mercury*, July 21, 1936; Sims, "Happenings of the Colored Folks," *Pottstown Mercury*, May 24, 1938; Sims, "Happenings of the Colored Folks," *Pottstown Mercury*, April 29, 1941.

6. Hill, *Dear Sir*, 62; Sims, "Happenings of the Colored Folks," *Pottstown Mercury*, July 21, 1936; Sims, "Happenings of the Colored Folks," *Pottstown Mercury*, April 29, 1941.

7. "Price of the Pottstown Mercury," newspaper advertisement, *Pottstown Mercury*, May 7, 1938.

8. Hill, *Dear Sir*, 50.

9. "Hostesses Are Named," *Pottstown Mercury*, May 3, 1939; "Club Stages Yule Party," *Pottstown Mercury*, January 4, 1941; "YWCA Forum Speaker Asks for Even Chance," *Pottstown Mercury*, February 13, 1946; "School Board Members Hear Dr. Weber Speak," *Pottstown Mercury*, June 12, 1943.

10. Chancellor, *History of Pottstown Pennsylvania, 1752–1952*, 171.

11. "School Board Members Hear Dr. Weber Speak."

12. "Report Given on Recreation Activity Here." For Pottstown Recreation Commission, also see Chancellor, *History of Pottstown Pennsylvania, 1752–1952*, 181.

13. Again, for column sample, see Sims, "Happenings of the Colored Folks," *Pottstown Mercury*, July 21, 1936; Sims, "Happenings of the Colored Folks," *Pottstown Mercury*, May 24, 1938; Sims, "Happenings of the Colored Folks," *Pottstown Mercury*, April 29, 1941.

14. Hill, *Dear Sir*, 2, 17; "Obituary: Shandy Hill, 91, Journalist." For subhead quote, see Hill, *Dear Sir*, 37.

15. "United States Social Security Death Index," database, FamilySearch (https://familysearch.org/ark:/61903/1:1:J2SB-W28: 8 January 2021), Shandy Hill, 30 Sep 1992; citing U.S. Social Security Administration, Death Master File, database, Alexandria, Virginia: National Technical Information Service, ongoing; "Obituary: Shandy Hill, 91, Journalist"; Hill, *Dear Sir*, 17–19.

16. Hill, *Dear Sir*, 17.

17. Hill, *Dear Sir*, 37.

18. Hill, *Dear Sir*, 2.

19. Hill, *Dear Sir*, 189.

20. Aurora Wallace, *Newspapers and the Making of Modern America: A History* (Westport, CT: Greenwood Press, 2005), 2.

21. "Obituary: Shandy Hill, 91, Journalist."

22. "The Courier's Double 'V' for a Double Victory Campaign Gets Country-Wide Support." For historiography, see Wallace, *Newspapers and the Making of Modern America*, 53–75; John C. Walter and Malina Iida, "The State of New York and the Legal Struggle to Desegregate the American Bowling Congress, 1944–1950," *Afro-Americans in New York Life & History* 35, no. 4 (January 2011): 7–32; Gene Roberts and Hank Klibanoff, *The Race Beat: The Press, the Civil Rights Struggle, and the Awakening of a Nation* (New York: First Vintage Books Edition, 2007); Theoharis, *More Beautiful and Terrible History*, 102–4.

23. Hall, "Long Civil Rights Movement and the Political Uses of the Past," 1234; Charlotte G. O'Kelly, "Black Newspapers and the Black Protest Movement, 1946–1972," *Phylon* 41, no. 4 (Winter 1980): 313–24, https://www.jstor.org/stable/274856. The time frame, 1954–1965, aligns with this book's 1954–1968 time frame. See chap. 1 of this book for further explanation.

24. Roberts and Klibanoff, *Race Beat*; Theoharis, *More Beautiful and Terrible History*, 102–4.

25. Theoharis, *More Beautiful and Terrible History*, 102–5; Mark Speltz, *North of Dixie: Civil Rights Photography Beyond the South* (Los Angeles: J. Paul Getty Museum, 2016), 3.

26. Theoharis, *More Beautiful and Terrible History*, 102.

27. Theoharis, *More Beautiful and Terrible History*, 103.

28. Delmont, *Why Busing Failed*, 11.

29. Davis, "Beech St. Brews Trouble, Negro Worker States." For articles relating to the series, also see Larry Davis, "Extra Policing Is Volunteered in Beech Street,"

Pottstown Mercury, June 30, 1944; Larry Davis, "Burgess, 7 Councilmen O.K. Negro Policeman to Check Delinquency," *Pottstown Mercury*, July 1, 1944. On D-day, see Thomas D. Morgan, "D-Day at Normandy Revisited," *Army History* no. 36 (Winter 1996): 30–35, https://www.jstor.org/stable/26304560. For larger context, see Charles L. Chute, "The Facts on War-Time Delinquency and Their Significance," *Marriage and Family Living* 5, no. 2 (May 1943): 25–26, https://www.jstor.org/stable/347706.

30. Davis, "Beech St. Brews Trouble, Negro Worker States"; Davis, "Extra Policing Is Volunteered in Beech Street"; Davis, "Burgess, 7 Councilmen O.K. Negro Policeman to Check Delinquency." For Corums being brothers, see "Bad Heart Cause of Corum Death."

31. Clarence Taylor, *Fight the Power: African Americans and the Long History of Police Brutality in New York City* (New York: New York University Press, 2018); Leonard N. Moore, *Black Rage in New Orleans: Police Brutality and African American Activism from World War II to Hurricane Katrina* (Baton Rouge: Louisiana State University Press, 2010).

32. Arthur Browne, *One Righteous Man: Samuel Battle and the Shattering of the Color Line in New York* (Boston: Beacon Press, 2015), 75.

33. Thomas Corum, 1906, Pennsylvania Births and Christenings, 1709–1950, FamilySearch database, January 27, 2020, https://familysearch.org/ark:/61903/1:1:HFKN-JYZM; Pottstown Police/Citizens Crime Check Committee, "In Memoriam: Officer Thomas W. Corum, Nov. 6. 1906–Jan. 20, 1964; Died in the Service of His Community; National Peace Officer's Memorial Day, May 15, 1969," *Pottstown Mercury*, May 15, 1969. On Thomas Corum's job and union activism, also see Davis, "Beech St. Brews Trouble, Negro Worker States"; "Flagg Union Gives Way to SWOC Branch: 420 Men Are Reported Signed for Membership in CIO Affiliate," *Pottstown Mercury*, April 20, 1938.

34. "Neville's Club Awaits Opening Baseball Tilt"; Don Rigg, "That's My Story," *Pottstown Mercury*, August 17, 1935. Thomas Corum also went by "Tom." See, for example, Davis, "Beech St. Brews Trouble, Negro Worker States."

35. "Scout Forum: Troop 17—Bethel A.M.E"; Sallie Sims, "Happenings of the Colored Folks," *Pottstown Mercury*, February 10, 1938.

36. Sims, "Happenings of the Colored Folks," *Pottstown Mercury*, September 29, 1936.

37. Sims, "Happenings of the Colored Folks," *Pottstown Mercury*, October 25, 1938.

38. "Negroes Plan Increased Part in Public Affairs." See chap. 2 for the comparison points on James and William Corum.

39. Davis, "Beech St. Brews Trouble, Negro Worker States"; Davis, "Extra Policing Is Volunteered in Beech Street"; Davis, "Burgess, 7 Councilmen O.K. Negro Policeman to Check Delinquency." For background on Davis, see "Army Hospital Public Relations Officer Dies," *Mercury*, July 24, 1973.

40. Davis, "Beech St. Brews Trouble, Negro Worker States."

41. Sitkoff, "Racial Militancy and Interracial Violence in the Second World War," 671.

42. Karen R. Miller, "'We Cannot Wait for Understanding to Come to Us': Community Activists Respond to Violence at Detroit's Northwestern High School, 1940–1941," in *Groundwork: Local Black Freedom Movements in America*, ed. Jeanne Theoharis and Komozi Woodard (New York: New York University Press, 2005), 235–57. Regarding rioting more broadly during World War II, see Stacey Close, "Fire in the Bones: Hartford's NAACP, Civil Rights and Militancy, 1943–1969," *Journal of Negro History* 86, no. 3 (Summer 2001): 228, http://www.jstor.org/stable/1562446.

43. Davis, "Beech St. Brews Trouble, Negro Worker States"; Taylor, *Fight the Power*, 26.

44. For politics of respectability, see Sugrue, *Sweet Land of Liberty*, 8. For local sphere, see Davis, "Extra Policing Is Volunteered in Beech Street."

45. Davis, "Beech St. Brews Trouble, Negro Worker States."

46. "The Negro Seeks to Solve a Problem," *Pottstown Mercury*, June 30, 1944; "The Courier's Double 'V' for a Double Victory Campaign Gets Country-Wide Support." For general history of World War II and main belligerents, the Allied and Axis powers, see, for example, Lightbody, *Second World War*.

47. "Corum Gets Council OK as Officer: Negro Special Policeman Begins Duties at Once," *Pottstown Mercury*, July 18, 1944.

48. "Badge for Mr. Corum," *Pottstown Mercury*, July 20, 1944.

49. "More Than Police Needed," *Pottstown Mercury*, July 18, 1944. For Merchant, see "Lincoln Community Center Dedicated at Pottsville By Interracial Commission," *New York Age*, June 29, 1935; Commonwealth of Pennsylvania, *Final Report of the Pennsylvania State Temporary Commission on the Conditions of the Urban Colored Population*, 115–16.

50. "Corum Gets Council OK as Officer"; "Corum Finds AWOL Lad," *Pottstown Mercury*, October 4, 1944; "Borough Yet Lacks Negro Special Police Officer Applications," *Pottstown Mercury*, July 17, 1944; Nick Cammero, "Flaggsmen Whip Patriots, 4–2: Zezenski Hurls Three-Hitter," *Pottstown Mercury*, July 22, 1944.

51. "Water Company Committee Agrees to Recommend Sale: Stockholders Will Be Asked to Approve Deal: Ordinance on Garage Referred to Sanitary Committee of Council," *Pottstown Mercury*, June 6, 1945; "Local Policeman Dies While Making Arrest," *Pottstown Mercury*, January 21, 1964. The June 6, 1945, article misspells Corum's name as "Thomas H. Corum"—it should be "Thomas W. Corum." See "Boro Council Will Discuss Garbage Law: Manager Sears Receives Proposed Ordinances from United Workers Council," *Pottstown Mercury*, June 5, 1945; "Two Men Pass Police Exams: Commission Will Ask for Their Appointment; Three Fail to Appear," *Pottstown Mercury*, May 15, 1945.

52. Blockson, "Blacks," 915.

53. "In Line of Duty?," *Pottstown Mercury*, January 23, 1964; "Pottstown Borough Officer Thomas W. Corum E.O.W. 1/20/1964," Montgomery County, Pennsylvania, accessed December 19, 2022, https://www.montcopa.org/Document Center/View/9422/WebpageTextCORUM?bidId=.

54. Hill, *Dear Sir*, 2; "Obituary: Shandy Hill, 91, Journalist." On how the press advocated for local Blacks, see, for example, Hill, *Dear Sir*, 50–59, 62–63, 103.

55. "Pottstown Borough Officer Thomas W. Corum E.O.W. 1/20/1964." For biographical data on Ferman, see "Risa Vetri Ferman, C'87," Netter Center for Community Partnerships, University of Pennsylvania, accessed December 19, 2022, https://www.nettercenter.upenn.edu/about-center/alumni-profiles/risa-vetri -ferman.

56. "Local Policeman Dies While Making Arrest."

57. "Bad Heart Cause of Corum Death."

58. "Local Policeman Dies While Making Arrest."

59. Pennsylvania Historic and Museum Commission, Pennsylvania (State) Death Certificates, 1906–1966, Box Number: 2374, Certificate Number Range: 005701-008550, Ancestry.com (Lehi, UT: Ancestry.com Operations, Inc., 2014).

60. "In Line of Duty?" Also see "Obituaries: 200 Attend Funeral Services for Policeman Thomas W. Corum," *Pottstown Mercury*, January 25, 1964.

61. J. H. Wagner, "Allegheny: News from the President," *Columbia Union Visitor*, December 27, 1945, Office of Archives, Statistics, and Research, General Conference of Seventh-day Adventists, Silver Spring, Maryland [hereinafter, ASTR-GCSDA], http://documents.adventistarchives.org/Periodicals/CUV/CUV19451227-V50-52 .pdf. On Pacific Theater ending, see "World War II Dates and Timeline." This chapter discusses all three themes at length. On Snyder, see Hill, *Dear Sir*, 51; Harper Photo, "Historic Site Bought for School," *Philadelphia Tribune*, April 6, 1946; "Historic Rutter-Bailey Premises May Be Converted into School," *Pottstown Mercury*, January 9, 1946.

62. Hill, *Dear Sir*, 51; US Bureau of the Census, *Seventeenth Census of the United States, 1950*, vol. 2, *Characteristics of the Population*, part 38, *Pennsylvania* (Washington, DC: Government Printing Office, 1952), 38-17, https://www.census.gov/library /publications/1953/dec/population-vol-02.html.

63. William J. Switala, *Underground Railroad in Pennsylvania* (Mechanicsburg, PA: Stackpole Books, 2001), 155.

64. Chancellor, *History of Pottstown Pennsylvania, 1752–1952*, 125–26.

65. W. Edmunds Claussen, "All around the Town: Sympathetic People Aid Runaway Slaves," *Pottstown Mercury*, April 25, 1973.

66. Hill, *Dear Sir*, 51.

67. Douglas Morgan, "Allegheny Conference (1944–1967)," ESDA: Encyclopedia of Seventh-day Adventists, accessed December 19, 2022, https://encyclopedia .adventist.org/article?id=CCDO; Samuel G. London Jr., *Seventh-day Adventists and the Civil Rights Movement* (Jackson: University Press of Mississippi, 2009), 145; H. D. Singleton, "Journey's End," *North American Informant*, November/December 1962, 5, ASTR-GCSDA, http://documents.adventistarchives.org/Periodicals/NAI /NAI19621101-V16-85.pdf; memorial page for Elder John Henry Wagner Sr. (31 Dec 1902–11 Aug 1962), Memorial ID 209103611, citing South View Cemetery, Atlanta, Fulton County, Georgia, maintained by Janet Nadol (contributor 47170277), Find a Grave, database and images, accessed November 12, 2021, https://www .findagrave.com/memorial/209103611/john-henry-wagner.

68. Jacob Justiss, *Angels in Ebony* (Toledo, OH: Jet Printing Service, 1975), 54. For birth and further biographical data on Wagner, see Singleton, "Journey's End," 5; "Allegheny Conference," in *A Star Gives Light: Seventh-day Adventist African-American*

Heritage Teacher's Resource Guide, ed. Norwida A. Marshall and R. Steven Norman III (Decatur, IL: Office of Education Southern Union Conference of Seventh-day Adventists, 1989), 49–50, ASTR-GCSDA, https://documents.adventistarchives .org/Books/ASGL1989.pdf; Charles D. Brooks, "Founding of Pine Forge Academy," unpublished and undated, 3, https://assets.documentcloud.org/documents /2722235/Pine-Forge-History.pdf.

69. Singleton, "Journey's End," 5, ASTR-GCSDA. For college, see "Mission & History," Oakwood University, accessed December 19, 2022, https://oakwood .edu/our-story/mission-history/.

70. Singleton, "Journey's End," 5, ASTR-GCSDA.

71. London, *Seventh-day Adventists and the Civil Rights Movement*, 144–45. For Pinkney, see Samuel London and Kiera Dixon, "Pinkney, Addison Vastapha (1903– 1981)," ESDA: Encyclopedia of Seventh-day Adventists, accessed December 19, 2022, https://encyclopedia.adventist.org/article?id=7FW4.

72. Singleton, "Journey's End," 5, ASTR-GCSDA; "Obituaries: Ex-Pine Forge Institute Principal, Founder Dies," *Pottstown Mercury*, August 15, 1962.

73. Justiss, *Angels in Ebony*, 55. On Justiss, see Melonie Gurley, "The Long-Awaited Republication of Angels in Ebony," February 18, 2020, Office of Regional Conferences Ministries, https://adventistregionalministries.org/the-long-awaited -republication-of-angels-in-ebony/.

74. Wagner, "Allegheny," December 27, 1945, ASTR-GCSDA.

75. Justiss, *Angels in Ebony*, 55; "Pine Forge Academy: The School in the North," in Marshall and Norman, *Star Gives Light*, 77–78, ASTR-GCSDA, http://documents .adventistarchives.org/Books/ASGL1989.pdf. On Kimbrough, also see Stephanie D. Johnson, "Cover Story: The Black SDA Woman: A Continuing Partnership with the Church," *North American Regional Voice*, November 1983, 2, ASTR-GCSDA, https://documents.adventistarchives.org/Periodicals/RV/RV19831101-V05-11.pdf.

76. J. H. Wagner, "Allegheny: A Reminder," *Columbia Union Visitor*, August 29, 1946, ASTR-GCSDA, http://documents.adventistarchives.org/Periodicals/CUV /CUV19460829-V51-35.pdf.

77. "Pine Forge Academy," 77.

78. J. H. Wagner, "Allegheny: Camp and School Site Purchase," *Columbia Union Visitor*, April 18, 1946, ASTR-GCSDA, http://documents.adventistarchives.org /Periodicals/CUV/CUV19460418-V51-16.pdf.

79. J. H. Wagner, "Allegheny: Workers' Meeting in Newark, New Jersey," *Columbia Union Visitor*, November 8, 1945, ASTR-GCSDA, http://documents.adventist archives.org/Periodicals/CUV/CUV19451108-V50-45.pdf.

80. Justiss, *Angels in Ebony*, 55; "Pine Forge Academy," 77–78; J. H. Wagner, "Allegheny: Special Dollar Day Offering, April 6, 1946," *Columbia Union Visitor*, March 21, 1946, ASTR-GCSDA, http://documents.adventistarchives.org/Periodicals /CUV/CUV19460321-V51-12.pdf.

81. Wagner, "Allegheny," December 27, 1945, ASTR-GCSDA.

82. "Adventists Buy Estate for Pennsylvania College Site," *Afro-American*, December 29, 1945, https://news.google.com/newspapers?nid=UBnQDr5gPskC.

83. "Church Group to Establish School Here," *Pottstown Mercury*, January 10, 1946.

84. J. H. Wagner, "Allegheny: Workers' Meeting," *Columbia Union Visitor*, March 14, 1946, ASTR-GCSDA, http://documents.adventistarchives.org/Periodicals /CUV/CUV19460314-V51-11.pdf.

85. J. H. Wagner, "Allegheny: Items from the President: Northern School," *Columbia Union Visitor*, January 31, 1946, ASTR-GCSDA, http://documents .adventistarchives.org/Periodicals/CUV/CUV19460131-V51-05.pdf; J. H. Wagner, "Allegheny: A Good Year," *Columbia Union Visitor*, January 17, 1946, ASTR-GCSDA, http://documents.adventistarchives.org/Periodicals/CUV/CUV194601 17-V51-03.pdf; Wagner, "Allegheny," March 14, 1946, ASTR-GCSDA.

86. Wagner, "Allegheny," January 17, 1946, ASTR-GCSDA.

87. Wagner, "Allegheny," January 31, 1946, ASTR-GCSDA.

88. J. H. Wagner, "Allegheny: Camp and School Site Purchase," *Columbia Union Visitor*, April 18, 1946, ASTR-GCSDA, http://documents.adventistarchives.org /Periodicals/CUV/CUV19460418-V51-16.pdf; J. L. Moran, "Allegheny: Good News," *Columbia Union Visitor*, April 11, 1946, ASTR-GCSDA, http://documents .adventistarchives.org/Periodicals/CUV/CUV19460411-V51-15.pdf; Harper Photo, "Historic Site Bought for School," *Philadelphia Tribune*, April 6, 1946.

89. Justiss, *Angels in Ebony*, 84; "Pine Forge Academy," 77–78; "Allegheny Conference," 49–50. For scholarship, see Theoharis, introduction, 5, 15n11.

90. Hill, *Dear Sir*, 51.

91. Kirk, *Beyond Little Rock*, 94.

92. "Association Taking Steps about School: Group Plans Meeting Tonight to Discuss Zoning Possibilities," *Pottstown Mercury*, January 24, 1946; "Local Residents Protest Rutter-Potts Land Sale," *Pottstown Mercury*, January 23, 1946; "Mass Meeting Is Held to Discuss School Site: Residents of Section Balk Project, Say School Would Cause Antagonism, Loss in Taxes; Church Group Represented," *Pottstown Mercury*, February 15, 1946.

93. "Local Residents Protest Rutter-Potts Land Sale." On populace, see Bureau of the Census, *Seventeenth Census of the United States, 1950*, vol. 2, *Characteristics of the Population*, part 38, *Pennsylvania*, 38-17.

94. "Historic Rutter-Bailey Premises May Be Converted into School"; "Church Group to Establish School Here."

95. "Local Residents Protest Rutter-Potts Land Sale."

96. "Association Taking Steps about School." For Diener, see Harper Diener, Douglass Township, Berks, Pennsylvania, United States, United States Census, 1940, database with images, FamilySearch, March 15, 2018, https://familysearch .org/ark:/61903/1:1:KQ87-1WK, citing enumeration district (ED) 6-28, sheet 15A, line 19, family 288, Sixteenth Census of the United States, 1940, NARA digital publication T627, Records of the Bureau of the Census, 1790–2007, RG 29 (Washington, DC: National Archives and Records Administration, 2012), roll 3433.

97. "Mass Meeting Is Held to Discuss School Site."

98. Robinson, *City within a City*, 74.

99. "Mass Meeting Is Held to Discuss School Site."

100. "Township Citizen Meeting Approves Working Program on Site Sale for School," *Pottstown Mercury*, March 27, 1946; "Victory for Democracy," *Pottstown Mercury*, March 28, 1946.

101. "Victory for Democracy."

102. Hill, *Dear Sir*, 52. For VIA, see "Association Taking Steps about School."

103. Mary McLeod Bethune, Letter to the editor, *Pottstown Mercury*, August 2, 1949; "Brotherhood at Home," *Pottstown Mercury*, July 9, 1949.

104. Maxine D. Jones, "'Without Compromise or Fear': Florida's African American Female Activists," *Florida Historical Quarterly* 77, no. 4, Women's Activism in Twentieth-Century Florida (Spring 1999): 483, https://www.jstor.org/stable/30150829.

105. Mary McLeod Bethune, letter to the editor; "Brotherhood at Home."

106. "Brotherhood at Home."

107. Mary McLeod Bethune to Shandy Hill, July 28, 1949, Bethune, Mary McLeod—Correspondence: General, 1943–1949, 88 pp., Folder: 001392-004-0001, *Mary McLeod Bethune Papers: The Bethune Foundation Collection*, part 3, *Subject Files, 1939–1955*, Mary McLeod Bethune Foundation Archive, Bethune-Cookman University, Daytona Beach, FL, 2011.

108. Bethune, letter to the editor.

109. Shandy Hill to Mary McLeod Bethune, August 3, 1949, Bethune, Mary McLeod—Correspondence: General, 1943–1949, 88 pp., Folder: 001392-004-0001, *Mary McLeod Bethune Papers: The Bethune Foundation Collection*, part 3: *Subject Files, 1939–1955*, Mary McLeod Bethune Foundation Archive, Bethune-Cookman University, Daytona Beach, FL, 2011.

110. J. H. Wagner, "Allegheny: An Ancient True Story," *Columbia Union Visitor*, February 7, 1946, ASTR-GCSDA, https://documents.adventistarchives.org/Periodicals/CUV/CUV19460207-V51-06.pdf. Can also see J. H. Wagner, "Allegheny: News from the President," *Columbia Union Visitor*, February 21, 1946, ASTR-GCSDA, http://documents.adventistarchives.org/Periodicals/CUV/CUV19460221-V51-08.pdf; J. H. Wagner, "Allegheny: It Is Almost Too Late," *Columbia Union Visitor*, March 28, 1946, ASTR-GCSDA, http://documents.adventistarchives.org/Periodicals/CUV/CUV19460328-V51-13.pdf.

111. Wagner, "Allegheny," December 27, 1945, ASTR-GCSDA; Wagner, "Allegheny," January 17, 1946, ASTR-GCSDA; "Allegheny: Historic Pine Forge to Become School Campus," *Columbia Union Visitor*, January 24, 1946, ASTR-GCSDA, http://documents.adventistarchives.org/Periodicals/CUV/CUV19460124-V51-04.pdf; John K. Binder, "Negro Pastors Wield Shovels and Hammers to Rush Opening of Pine Forge Institute," *Pottstown Mercury*, July 26, 1946; "Pine Forge Institute Opens; More Than 100 Are Registered," *Pottstown Mercury*, September 10, 1946; Ruth E. Mosby, "Allegheny: Highlights and Commencement Events at Pine Forge Institute," *Columbia Union Visitor*, July 10, 1947, ASTR-GCSDA, http://documents.adventistarchives.org/Periodicals/CUV/CUV19470710-V52-28.pdf.

112. A. V. Pinkney, "Allegheny: Camp Meeting Report," *Columbia Union Visitor*, July 28, 1949, ASTR-GCSDA, http://documents.adventistarchives.org/Periodicals/CUV/CUV19490728-V54-30.pdf.

113. Hill, *Dear Sir*, 52. For institute today, see Evan Brandt, "Black History Month: Pine Forge Academy Celebrating 70 Years of Learning," *Mercury*, February 27, 2016, 11:24 a.m. EST (updated September 24, 2021, 1:06 a.m. EST), https://www.pottsmerc.com/2016/02/27/black-history-month-pine-forge-academy-celebrating-70-years-of-learning/. For multiple Black Adventists, also see Hill, *Dear Sir*, 51–53.

114. Bethune, letter to the editor. For Black recreational issue, see "Bowlers Stew Over ABC Racial Clause, but No Action Is Taken," *Pottstown Mercury*, October 10, 1949.

115. William C. Kashatus, *Jackie & Campy: The Untold Story of Their Rocky Relationship and the Breaking of Baseball's Color Line* (Lincoln: University of Nebraska Press, 2014), 17, 2, 58.

116. "[Archived] City of Alexandria to Unveil Earl Francis Lloyd Statue at Virtual Ceremony," City of Alexandria Virginia, March 29, 2021, https://www.alexandriava.gov/recreation/info/default.aspx?id=121234.

117. Patricia L. Dooley, "Jim Crow Strikes Again: The African American Press Campaign against Segregation in Bowling during World War II," *Journal of African American History* 97, no. 3 (Summer 2012): 271–72, https://www.jstor.org/stable/10.5323/jafriamerhist.97.3.0270.

118. Walter and Iida, "State of New York and the Legal Struggle to Desegregate the American Bowling Congress, 1944–1950," 7–32.

119. Walter and Iida, "State of New York and the Legal Struggle to Desegregate the American Bowling Congress, 1944–1950," 7. On ABC, also see Dooley, "Jim Crow Strikes Again," 271–72. On Pottstown Bowling Association, see "Discrimination Here," *Pottstown Mercury*, October 7, 1949; "Bowlers Stew Over ABC Racial Clause, but No Action Is Taken."

120. Walter and Iida, "State of New York and the Legal Struggle to Desegregate the American Bowling Congress, 1944–1950," 7–32; Dooley, "Jim Crow Strikes Again," 280, 285–86.

121. Walter and Iida, "State of New York and the Legal Struggle to Desegregate the American Bowling Congress, 1944–1950," 7. For bowling popularity in Pottstown, see "In Retrospect: 50 Years Ago Dec. 21, 1903," *Pottstown Mercury*, December 21, 1953; Mary Neiburg, "Pottstown Did Its First Bowling in the Eighties: Teak Wood Balls; as Large as Basketballs Were Used, Binder Relates," *Pottstown Mercury*, February 3, 1938.

122. Chancellor, *History of Pottstown Pennsylvania, 1752–1952*, 179.

123. Chancellor, *History of Pottstown Pennsylvania, 1752–1952*, 171. I make this claim about Arrow Recreation Bowling Alleys because an advertisement mentioned how it was "Open to the Public." See "Arrow Bowling Alleys," newspaper advertisement, *Pottstown Mercury*, August 14, 1947. Moreover, in early August 1955, the *Pottstown Mercury* noted that Arrow Bowling Alley was Pottstown's biggest bowling establishment. See "Gerald Dietrich Announces Purchase of Pottstown's Arrow Bowling Alleys," *Pottstown Mercury*, August 3, 1955.

124. "System Is Changed for Collection of Bowling Alley Tax," *Pottstown Mercury*, February 5, 1949.

125. "Pottstown ABC Team Defeats North Penn: Local Keglers Rally to Cop Second Verdict: Glaes and Teammates Wind Up with 1102 to Total 2948," *Pottstown Mercury*, March 28, 1934; "Keck Bowls 600 in ABC Singles at Peoria: H.C. Creswell Hits 599; Local Doubles Teams Fail: Glaes Rolls 244 Then Slumps in Final Fray," *Pottstown Mercury*, April 10, 1934; "Retiree Keeps Hand in Selling Field; Now Prefers Shuffleboard to Bowling," *Pottstown Mercury*, April 23, 1962; "Hey, Hey Bowlers," *Pottstown Mercury*, January 22, 1934.

126. Don Rigg, "That's My Story," *Pottstown Mercury*, March 20, 1935; "Keglers Enter ABC Tourney in Detroit," *Pottstown Mercury*, April 23, 1948; "Discrimination Here."

127. "Discrimination Here."

128. "Bowlers Stew Over ABC Racial Clause, but No Action Is Taken."

129. "ABC Directors Retain 'White Man' Charter," *Pottstown Mercury*, March 10, 1949. Also see "Bowlers Advised to Keep 'Color' Ban: Directors Call on Convention of National Body to Vote against Liberalization," *New York Times*, March 10, 1949.

130. "ABC Reaffirms Ban on Negroes," *Pottstown Mercury*, March 12, 1949.

131. James H. Downing, letter to the editor, *Pottstown Mercury*, March 30, 1949. For Downing, see James Henry Downing, 1942, United States World War II Draft Registration Cards, 1942, database with images, FamilySearch, March 9, 2018, https://familysearch.org/ark:/61903/1:1:VQFJ-NDP, citing NARA microfilm publication M1936, M1937, M1939, M1951, M1962, M1964, M1986, M2090, and M2097 (Washington, DC: National Archives and Records Administration, n.d.).

132. James H. Downing, letter to the editor, *Pottstown Mercury*, September 16, 1948; Downing, letter to the editor, March 30, 1949; James H. Downing, letter to the editor, *Pottstown Mercury*, June 13, 1949; James H. Downing, letter to the editor, *Pottstown Mercury*, September 29, 1950.

133. Downing, letter to the editor, March 30, 1949.

134. Downing, letter to the editor, September 16, 1948.

135. Downing, letter to the editor, September 29, 1950.

136. Walter and Iida, "State of New York and the Legal Struggle to Desegregate the American Bowling Congress, 1944–1950," 9.

137. "Bowlers Stew Over ABC Racial Clause, but No Action Is Taken"; "ABC Sanction Sought by Spicer's Bowlers," *Pottstown Mercury*, November 23, 1949; "Discrimination Here."

138. "Discrimination Here"; "Pottstown 'Y' Lowers Race, Religious Bars."

139. "Discrimination Here." For ABC revamping discriminatory practice, see "True Test of Loyalty," *Pottstown Mercury*, December 15, 1950.

140. Hill, *Dear Sir*, 50.

141. "Discrimination Here"; "Bowlers Stew Over ABC Racial Clause, but No Action Is Taken"; "Attention: All Male Bowlers, Secretaries and Captains; Meeting of Pottstown Bowling Association; West End Fire Co., Stowe; Sunday, October 9—7:15 P.M.; Business Meeting & Election of Officers," *Pottstown Mercury*, October 8, 1949.

142. "Bowlers Stew Over ABC Racial Clause, but No Action Is Taken"; "ABC Sanction Sought by Spicer's Bowlers."

143. "ABC Sanction Sought by Spicer's Bowlers."

144. Special to the *New York Times*, "Bowling Congress Ends Color Bar Under Fire in Courts of 4 States," *New York Times*, May 13, 1950. For further data on the ABC gathering, also see Walter and Iida, "State of New York and the Legal Struggle to Desegregate the American Bowling Congress, 1944–1950," 8, 27n8; "American Bowling Congress Drops Restrictive 'White Male' Rule: 518 Delegates Take Only 27 Minutes to Oust Bias Clause," *Philadelphia Tribune*, May 16, 1950.

145. Dooley, "Jim Crow Strikes Again," 286. On the local and national spheres, see "Bowlers Stew Over ABC Racial Clause, but No Action Is Taken"; "ABC Sanction Sought by Spicer's Bowlers"; Walter and Iida, "State of New York and the Legal Struggle to Desegregate the American Bowling Congress, 1944–1950," 8, 27n8; special to the *New York Times*, "Bowling Congress Ends Color Bar Under Fire in Courts of 4 States"; "American Bowling Congress Drops Restrictive 'White Male' Rule."

146. Dostal, "Slum Razing Plan to Hit Borough's '*Forgotten Folk.*'" For other pieces in series and some subsequent articles by Dostal, see Frank J. Dostal, "Make 'Bad Citizen Out of You': 'Row' Families See Initiative Broken," *Pottstown Mercury*, March 21, 1950; Frank J. Dostal, "They'll Raze His Cottage Row 'Castle': Years of Saving, Toil Counted as Lost," *Pottstown Mercury*, March 22, 1950; Frank J. Dostal, "Loses Faith in Right to Own Home: 'If They Take This, God Help the Poor,'" *Pottstown Mercury*, March 23, 1950; Frank J. Dostal, "Decision on Saving Hemlock Row Asked of PHA by County Authority: Group Studies Plea for Other Project Sites: Mercury Executive Cites Other Possible Locations on Virgin Land in Area," *Pottstown Mercury*, March 24, 1950; Frank J. Dostal, "Pastor Enters Hemlock Row Fight: Calls Mass Meeting; Legal Aid Is Offered," *Pottstown Mercury*, March 25, 1950; Frank J. Dostal, "Veterans, Masonic Groups Joins Fight for Hemlock Row: Ministers Ask Congregations to Aid Families; Heavy Support Expected at Meeting to Protest Order for Razing Homes," *Pottstown Mercury*, March 27, 1950. For a picture of Dostal, see Hill, *Dear Sir*, 36.

147. Harry S. Truman, "Annual Message to the Congress on the State of the Union," January 5, 1949, online by Gerhard Peters and John T. Woolley, *American Presidency Project*, https://www.presidency.ucsb.edu/node/230007.

148. Harry S. Truman, "Statement by the President Upon Signing the Housing Act of 1949," July 15, 1949, online by Gerhard Peters and John T. Woolley, *American Presidency Project*, https://www.presidency.ucsb.edu/node/229714.

149. Sokol, *All Eyes Are upon Us*, 58.

150. "Pottstown Allotted 200 Federal Housing Units: Funds Reserved to Await Survey," *Pottstown Mercury*, September 30, 1949; *Final Report of the Pennsylvania State Temporary Commission on the Conditions of the Urban Colored Population to the General Assembly of the State of Pennsylvania*, 114–15; Carter, letter to the editor.

151. Mrs. C. K., letter to the editor, *Pottstown Mercury*, August 4, 1949.

152. Fred Selby, "300 Low Rent Homes to Be Sought for Pottstown Under U.S. Aid Plan: Housing Committee Asks Early Survey," *Pottstown Mercury*, August 25, 1949.

153. Dostal, "Pastor Enters Hemlock Row Fight." For the 1950 population, see Bureau of the Census, *Seventeenth Census of the United States, 1950*, vol. 2, *Characteristics of the Population*, Part 38, *Pennsylvania*, 38–116.

154. Selby, "300 Low Rent Homes to Be Sought for Pottstown Under U.S. Aid Plan." Also see "Small Towns Seen as First to Be Affected: Housing Expediter Reveals Plan to Cut One-Third Off Present Regulation List," *Pottstown Mercury*, August 18, 1949.

155. F. S., letter to the editor, *Pottstown Mercury*, February 1, 1950.

156. "Preview Asked on Census Data: Housing Agency Approves Agreement as Help in Plans for Local Project," *Pottstown Mercury*, March 8, 1950; Selby, "300 Low Rent Homes to Be Sought for Pottstown Under U.S. Aid Plan."

157. Dostal, "Slum Razing Plan to Hit Borough's '*Forgotten Folk*'"; Dostal, "Make 'Bad Citizen Out of You'"; Dostal, "Loses Faith in Right to Own Home."

158. Dostal, "Loses Faith in Right to Own Home." Also see Dostal, "Make 'Bad Citizen Out of You'"; Dostal, "They'll Raze His Cottage Row 'Castle.'"

159. Jones, *Selma of the North*, 171–72.

160. Dostal, "They'll Raze His Cottage Row 'Castle.'"

161. Dostal, "Slum Razing Plan to Hit Borough's '*Forgotten Folk*.'" For Corrine and Walter, see "Obituaries: Corrine (McMichael) Nixon," *Pottstown Mercury*, July 13, 1951; "Obituaries: Walter R. Nixon Dies at Center," *Mercury*, August 31, 1976.

162. Dostal, "Slum Razing Plan to Hit Borough's '*Forgotten Folk*.'"

163. Dostal, "Make 'Bad Citizen Out of You'"; Dostal, "They'll Raze His Cottage Row 'Castle'"; Dostal, "Loses Faith in Right to Own Home." Dostal initially identifies Columbus's last name as "Matthews." However, Dostal subsequently names it "Massey." For one subsequent article, see Dostal, "Veterans, Masonic Groups Joins Fight for Hemlock Row." For Columbus Massey's occupation and where he was originally from, see Columbus Massey, Line 23, Sheet 73, Enumeration District 46-319, Pottstown Township, Montgomery County, Pennsylvania; Seventeenth Census of the United States, 1950, Record Group 29, Records of the Bureau of the Census; National Archives and Records Administration, Washington DC, accessed July 16, 2022, https://1950census.archives.gov/.

164. Dostal, "Make 'Bad Citizen Out of You.'" Not surprisingly, I also change Elizabeth "Matthews" to "Massey." For Elizabeth Massey's occupation and where she was originally from, see Elizabeth Massey, Line 24, Sheet 73, Enumeration District 46-319, Pottstown Township, Montgomery County, Pennsylvania; Seventeenth Census of the United States, 1950, Record Group 29, Records of the Bureau of the Census, National Archives and Records Administration, Washington DC, accessed July 16, 2022, https://1950census.archives.gov/.

165. Dostal, "They'll Raze His Cottage Row 'Castle.'"

166. Dostal, "Make 'Bad Citizen Out of You'"; Dostal, "They'll Raze His Cottage Row 'Castle'"; Dostal, "Slum Razing Plan to Hit Borough's '*Forgotten Folk*.'"

167. "Preview Asked on Census Data." Also see "Pottstown Allotted 200 Federal Housing Units."

168. "Pottstown Allotted 200 Federal Housing Units."

169. "Preview Asked on Census Data."

170. "Fate of These Hemlock Row Homes Rests with County Housing Authority," *Pottstown Mercury*, March 24, 1950; "Hemlock Row Plans to Organize Pushed," *Pottstown Mercury*, March 31, 1950; Dostal, "Slum Razing Plan to Hit Borough's 'Forgotten Folk'"; "Preview Asked on Census Data."

171. Dostal, "Slum Razing Plan to Hit Borough's '*Forgotten Folk*.'"

172. Dostal, "Slum Razing Plan to Hit Borough's '*Forgotten Folk*'"; Dostal, "Pastor Enters Hemlock Row Fight"; Daniel Charles, West Pottsgrove Township, Montgomery, Pennsylvania, United States, United States Census, 1940, database with images, FamilySearch, March 15, 2018, https://familysearch.org/ark:/61903/1:1:KQ7H-H48, citing enumeration district (ED) 46-235, sheet 14A, line 8, family 257, Sixteenth Census of the United States, 1940, NARA digital publication T627, Records of the Bureau of the Census, 1790–2007, RG 29 (Washington, DC: National Archives and Records Administration, 2012), roll 3586.

173. Dostal, "Slum Razing Plan to Hit Borough's '*Forgotten Folk*.'"

174. Dostal, "Loses Faith In Right to Own Home"; John Harper in household of Alberta Harper, Pottsgrove Township, Montgomery, Pennsylvania, United States, United States Census, 1940, database with images, FamilySearch January 7, 2021, https://www.familysearch.org/ark:/61903/1:1:KQ7H-DRR, citing enumeration district (ED) 46-235, sheet 12B, line 70, family 235, Sixteenth Census of the United States, 1940, NARA digital publication T627, Records of the Bureau of the Census, 1790–2007, RG 29 (Washington, DC: National Archives and Records Administration, 2012), roll 3586. This census record is corroborated by two later obituaries, specifically revealing that Harper is indeed the same individual spotlighted in Dostal, "Loses Faith in Right to Own Home." For the obituaries, see "Obituaries: Albirta Harper Dies at Age 78," *Pottstown Mercury*, December 23, 1968; "Obituaries: Ida Harper, Mother of 2, Dies at 61," *Pottstown Mercury*, May 22, 1973.

175. Dostal, "Slum Razing Plan to Hit Borough's '*Forgotten Folk*.'"

176. Dostal, "Loses Faith in Right to Own Home."

177. Dostal, "Make 'Bad Citizen Out of You.'"

178. Dostal, "They'll Raze His Cottage Row 'Castle.'" For Neva Goffigon's occupation and where she was originally from, see Neva Goffigon, Line 3, Sheet 76, Enumeration District 46-319, Pottstown Township, Montgomery County, Pennsylvania; Seventeenth Census of the United States, 1950, Record Group 29, Records of the Bureau of the Census, National Archives and Records Administration, Washington DC, accessed July 16, 2022, https://1950census.archives.gov/.

179. "Surveying Job Begins on Site for New Homes: Housing Unit Secretary Tells Residents They Need Not Fear Eviction," *Pottstown Mercury*, March 18, 1950; Dostal, "Slum Razing Plan to Hit Borough's '*Forgotten Folk*.'"

180. Dostal, "Slum Razing Plan to Hit Borough's '*Forgotten Folk*.'"

181. "Penn Village Charges," *Pottstown Mercury*, April 26, 1950.

182. Dostal, "Slum Razing Plan to Hit Borough's '*Forgotten Folk*.'"

183. Dostal, "Make 'Bad Citizen Out of You.'"

184. Sugrue, *Sweet Land of Liberty*, 8; Dostal, "Loses Faith in Right to Own Home." Also see, for example, Dostal, "Slum Razing Plan to Hit Borough's '*Forgot-

ten Folk.'" On the YMCA, also see "Full-Time Extension Director Appointed for Local YMCA"; Mjagkij, *Light in the Darkness*, 5, 66, 79; Prudente, "Century of Swimming."

185. Dostal, "Slum Razing Plan to Hit Borough's '*Forgotten Folk.*'"

186. Dostal, "Make 'Bad Citizen Out of You.'" For similar points about Blacks seeking to ameliorate abodes, see Dostal, "Loses Faith in Right to Own Home"; "Slum Razing Plan to Hit Borough's '*Forgotten Folk.*'"

187. Dostal, "Decision on Saving Hemlock Row Asked of PHA by County Authority."

188. "Save Hemlock Row," *Pottstown Mercury*, March 24, 1950; "Hemlock Row—Pottstown's Sin," *Pottstown Mercury*, March 29, 1950.

189. Shandy Hill to Sirs, April 29, 1950, Group II, Series B, Legal Files, Housing, General [FHA Loan Policies; PHA Rental Policies; Government Housing Policies], January–June 1950, 88 pp., Folder: 001521-015-1034, *Papers of the NAACP*, part 5, *Campaign against Residential Segregation, 1914–1955*, Library of Congress, 2012, NAACP, ProQuest History Vault database. For article, see "Penn Village Charges." For Pottstown NAACP in the early 1950s reestablishing, see "NAACP Chapter Receives Charter, Elects New Officers."

190. Dostal, "Pastor Enters Hemlock Row Fight."

191. "Flagg Unionist Offer Funds to Aid Hemlock Row Battle," *Pottstown Mercury*, March 28, 1950. For Nixon, see Dostal, "Slum Razing Plan to Hit Borough's '*Forgotten Folk.*'"

192. Dostal, "Hemlock Row Defies Threat to Raze Homes."

193. "Flagg Unionist Offer Funds to Aid Hemlock Row Battle"; "Union Officially Backs Hemlock Row Families," *Pottstown Mercury*, April 6, 1950.

194. Dostal, "Veterans, Masonic Groups Joins Fight for Hemlock Row."

195. Dostal, "Pastor Enters Hemlock Row Fight"; Dostal, "Hemlock Row Defies Threat to Raze Homes." On Nelson, see "Realtor Makes Appeal for Fair Play," *Philadelphia Tribune*, June 27, 1942; "Main Line NAACP Drive Figures," *Philadelphia Tribune*, July 7, 1951.

196. Blockson, "Blacks," 917; "Realtor Makes Appeal for Fair Play." For Nelson, see further "Photo Standalone 4—No Title," *Philadelphia Tribune*, December 31, 1955; "Montco DA Quits, Enters Private Law: Herbert C. Nelson Was First Negro in Post," *Philadelphia Tribune*, May 26, 1962. Nelson is also briefly mentioned in chap. 2.

197. Dostal, "Hemlock Row Defies Threat to Raze Homes."

198. Frank J. Dostal, "Borough Is Charged with Neglect of Hemlock Row Home Facilities: Area Is Inspected by County Authority," *Pottstown Mercury*, March 29, 1950.

199. "Wood Takes Office as Lieut.-Governor," *Pottstown Mercury*, January 17, 1951. For Wood, see "Lloyd Wood Dies; Goes from Farming to 2d Highest State Office," *Pottstown Mercury*, February 17, 1964; "Governor John Sydney Fine," Pennsylvania Historical & Museum Commission, accessed December 26, 2022, https://archive.vn/20121214062741/http:/pa.gov/portal/server.pt/community/1951-present/4285/john_s__fine/471469.

200. Frank J. Dostal, "Hemlock Row Wins Fight for Homes; Project Site Shifted," *Pottstown Mercury*, April 7, 1950.

201. "Housing Agency Fails to Air Race Discrimination Charge: Negro Family Finally Gets Project Home: Move Made Few Days Before County Authority Was to Hear Accusations," *Pottstown Mercury*, April 29, 1950.

202. Hill, *Dear Sir*, 101–3.

203. Hill, *Dear Sir*, 103. For *Brown*, see Russo, Harris, and Sandidge, "*Brown v. Board of Education* at 40," 297–309. For periodization and geographical arguments, see Purnell, *Fighting Jim Crow in the County of Kings*, 2–3.

204. "Negro Leaders Form Pottstown Civic Group for Self-Improvement."

205. Larry Davis, "Understanding Is Urged for Better World: Closer Relations Pressed at Charter Presentation to Local Civic League," *Pottstown Mercury*, October 12, 1950.

206. Davis, "Understanding Is Urged for Better World"; "Negro Leaders Form Pottstown Civic Group for Self-Improvement."

207. Commonwealth of Pennsylvania, "Pottstown Group Organizes for Civic Rights," *Department of Internal Affairs* 18, no. 10 (September 1950): 24, https:// hdl.handle.net/2027/mdp.39015068488249.

208. "Negro Leaders Form Pottstown Civic Group for Self-Improvement"; Larry Davis, "Pottstown Portraits: A Quick Look at Your Neighbor; Dr. Daniel Lee," *Pottstown Mercury*, June 26, 1952; "Lee, Daniel," in *Who's Who among Black Americans*, 2nd ed., 1977–1978, vol. 1 (Northbrook, IL: Who's Who Among Black Americans, 1978), 544. On schools, see "Our History," Lincoln University, accessed October 14, 2023, https://www.lincoln.edu/about/history.html; "History," Howard University College of Medicine, accessed October 27, 2023, https://medicine.howard.edu /about/history.

209. "Nostalgia: 25 Years Ago; June 22, 1948; Receives Appointment," *Mercury*, June 22, 1973; "Lee, Daniel," 544; "Lions Day Campers Travel for Outing," *Pottstown Mercury*, July 14, 1948; "Education Director Presents Charter to NAACP Chapter," *Pottstown Mercury*, December 27, 1951; "100 Persons Hear Top Local Officials at Baptist's Meeting," *Pottstown Mercury*, July 1, 1949; "Negro Leaders Form Pottstown Civic Group for Self-Improvement"; Normand Poirier, "Borough Forms New Committee for Equality: Area Leaders Discuss Plans to Form Group," *Pottstown Mercury*, July 15, 1954. Chap. 5 of this book further illuminates Lee's involvement with the PCL as well as the PCHR more broadly.

210. "Dean Stresses Need for Help to Community," *Pottstown Mercury*, June 30, 1952; "Beech Street Girl Wins First Prize in Local Civic League's Spelling Bee," *Pottstown Mercury*, November 24, 1950; "Chestnut Street Girl Wins Spelling Bee, Presented with Cup," *Pottstown Mercury*, December 28, 1950; Julia Douglass, "Pottstown and Stowe News," *Philadelphia Tribune*, January 29, 1952; "Civic Unit Concert Clears $189 for Scholarship Fund," *Pottstown Mercury*, February 5, 1951; "Civic League Men Authorized to Buy House for Troop 17," *Pottstown Mercury*, February 11, 1952; "Scouts Plan New Activities for Fall, Winter Session," *Pottstown Mercury*, September 16, 1952; "Civic League Elects Dr. Lee New President," *Pottstown Mercury*, June 14, 1954; "League Celebrates First Anniversary; Dr. Gray Speaks," *Pottstown*

Mercury, July 2, 1951; "Civic League Holds Founders Day Fete," *Pottstown Mercury*, June 30, 1955.

211. Mjagkij, *Light in the Darkness*, 123–24; Arnold, *Building the Beloved Community*, 45–67.

212. For "Readers Say" pieces and other related articles, see One of the Majority, letter to the editor, *Pottstown Mercury*, May 22, 1954; Edgar S. Brown Jr. et al., letter to the editor, *Pottstown Mercury*, May 25, 1954; Methodist, letter to the editor, *Pottstown Mercury*, May 29, 1954; Jimmy, letter to the editor, *Pottstown Mercury*, May 28, 1954; Two June Graduates, letter to the editor, *Pottstown Mercury*, May 28, 1954; "Judge Outlines Values, Goals at Graduation: 200 Seniors Get Diplomas at Pottstown High Commencement," *Pottstown Mercury*, June 11, 1954; "Jessie Matthews Given Six Award Day Honors," *Pottstown Mercury*, June 9, 1954; Robert F. Hoyer, "Five Prizes, Scholarship Grant: Winning Awards Nothing New to Jessie," *Pottstown Mercury*, June 10, 1954; "The Same Opportunity?," *Pottstown Mercury*, June 11, 1954; June Graduate, letter to the editor, *Pottstown Mercury*, June 18, 1954. For *Brown* locally and larger historical context, see "Supreme Court Rules Public School Segregation Must End"; "NAACP Hails Move as 'Vindication' of 45-Year Battle"; Russo, Harris, and Sandidge, "*Brown v. Board of Education* at 40," 297–309.

4. Emerging Civil Rights Discourses and Pottstown Shortly after *Brown v. Board of Education*

1. Russo, Harris, and Sandidge, "*Brown v. Board of Education* at 40," 297–309; "Supreme Court Rules Public School Segregation Must End"; "NAACP Hails Move as 'Vindication' of 45-Year Battle." On *Brown*, I have made similar points previously. See Washington, "Examining Interracial Civil Rights Activism in 1950s Pottstown, Pennsylvania," 131.

2. For some "Readers Say" pieces, see One of the Majority, letter to the editor; Edgar S. Brown Jr. et al., letter to the editor; Methodist, letter to the editor; Jimmy, letter to the editor; Two June Graduates, letter to the editor; June Graduate, letter to the editor. For others across the nation, see Joseph Carroll, "Race and Education 50 Years after *Brown v. Board of Education*: Majority of Whites, Blacks Satisfied with Their Own Educations, but Blacks to a Lesser Extent," Gallup, May 14, 2004, https:// news.gallup.com/poll/11686/race-education-years-after-brown-board-education .aspx; "Nation's Press on Segregation Ruling—Some Editorial Excerpts," *Crisis*, June/ July 1954, 347–48, https://books.google.com/books?id=9VcEAAAAMBAJ&lr=. For local articles, see "Civic Leaders Hail Ruling by Supreme Court: Segregation Decision Lauded by Local Officials," *Pottstown Mercury*, May 20, 1954; "Judge Outlines Values, Goals at Graduation"; "Jessie Matthews Given Six Award Day Honors"; Hoyer, "Five Prizes, Scholarship Grant"; "Same Opportunity?"

3. Dougherty, *More Than One Struggle*, 34–50.

4. Poirier, "Mister James P. Crow, Esq.—IV"; Edward J. Price Jr., "School Segregation in Nineteenth-Century Pennsylvania," *Pennsylvania History: A Journal of Mid-Atlantic Studies* 43, no. 2 (April 1976): 134–37, https://journals.psu.edu/phj

/article/view/23908/23677. Also see Hill, *Dear Sir*, 56; "Darby Girl to Teach in Pottstown School," *Philadelphia Tribune*, August 21, 1956; Gertrude Tibbs, "Darby Doings: Cotton Club Debut," *Philadelphia Tribune*, September 15, 1956. For broader historical context, see, for example, Dougherty, *More Than One Struggle*, 34–50.

5. For some "Readers Say" pieces, see One of the Majority, letter to the editor; Edgar S. Brown Jr. et al., letter to the editor; Methodist, letter to the editor; Jimmy, letter to the editor; Two June Graduates, letter to the editor; June Graduate, letter to the editor. Chap. 5 of this book goes further in-depth in the local activism and its relationship to larger sphere. On one example of later activism, see, for example, "Pennsylvania Town Seeks Segregation Problem End." For *Brown*, see Russo, Harris, and Sandidge, "*Brown v. Board of Education* at 40," 297–309.

6. Brian J. Daugherity, *Keep On Keeping On: The NAACP and the Implementation of Brown v. Board of Education in Virginia*, Carter G. Woodson Institute Series (Charlottesville: University of Virginia Press, 2016), 22–25.

7. Carroll, "Race and Education 50 Years after *Brown v. Board of Education*."

8. "Nation's Press on Segregation Ruling—Some Editorial Excerpts," 348. On Garden State term, see "Nickname: Origins of the Nickname."

9. Daugherity, *Keep On Keeping On*, 22–23.

10. "Nation's Press on Segregation Ruling—Some Editorial Excerpts," 347.

11. For contrasting anti-desegregation arguments, see Gareth D. Pahowka, "Voices of Moderation: Southern Whites Respond to Brown v. Board of Education," *Gettysburg Historical Journal* 5, no. 6 (Fall 2006): 44–66, https://cupola.gettysburg .edu/ghj/vol5/iss1/6.

12. "Civic Leaders Hail Ruling by Supreme Court." In June 1954, Lee would reclaim the PCL presidency. See "Civic League Elects Dr. Lee New President."

13. "Civic Leaders Hail Ruling by Supreme Court."

14. Dudziak, *Cold War Civil Rights*, 110. For a brief background of the *Pittsburgh Courier*, see Slate, "America's Best Weekly," 272–75.

15. "NAACP Hails Move as 'Vindication' of 45-Year Battle."

16. "Civic Leaders Hail Ruling by Supreme Court."

17. "Civic Leaders Hail Ruling by Supreme Court"; "Southern Legislators Blast 'Tragic' Ruling, Claim It Won't Work," *Pottstown Mercury*, May 18, 1954. For further data on Eastland, see Daugherity, *Keep On Keeping On*, 23; "James Eastland: A Featured Biography," United States Senate, accessed December 27, 2022, https://www .senate.gov/senators/FeaturedBios/Featured_Bio_EastlandJames.htm.

18. Clive Webb, introduction to *Massive Resistance: Southern Opposition to the Second Reconstruction* (Oxford: Oxford University Press, 2005), 3–17.

19. On "massive resistance," see Kirk, *Beyond Little Rock*, 94. For white resistance too, see Waltraut Stein, "The White Citizens' Councils," *Negro History Bulletin* 20, no. 1 (October 1956): 21, https://www.jstor.org/stable/44215197; Webb, introduction, 3–17. For May 19, 1954, gathering, see "Civic Leaders Hail Ruling by Supreme Court."

20. For samples of "Readers Say" articles soon after *Brown*, see One of the Majority, letter to the editor; Brown Jr. et al., letter to the editor.

21. Kirk, *Beyond Little Rock*, 94. Can also see Webb, introduction, 3–17. For the subhead quote, see Two June Graduates, letter to the editor.

22. Stein, "White Citizens' Councils," 21; Paul Moke, *Earl Warren and the Struggle for Justice* (Lanham, MD: Lexington Books, 2015), 139.

23. Daugherity, *Keep On Keeping On*, 23.

24. "Nation's Press on Segregation Ruling—Some Editorial Excerpts," 347. On Old Dominion State, see Anderson, "Virginia's Top Scenic Golf Courses for Fall."

25. "Along the N.A.A.C.P. Battlefront: Atlanta Declaration," *Crisis*, June/July 1954, 358–59, https://books.google.com/books?id=9VcEAAAAMBAJ&lr=.

26. Sokol, *All Eyes Are upon Us*, 71–79.

27. For scholarship, see Dougherty, *More Than One Struggle*, 34–50. Also see Burrell, "Black Women as Activist Intellectuals," 89–112.

28. One of the Majority, letter to the editor. For Dubois similarity, see W. E. B. Dubois, *The Souls of Black Folk: Essays and Sketches*, 2nd ed. (Chicago: A. C. McClurg & Co., 1903), vii, accessed September 11, 2023, http://docsouth.unc.edu/church/duboissouls/dubois.html. I argue here that "One of the Majority" was white. I support this assertion from a population standpoint. Pottstown's overall 1954 populace was at around twenty-five thousand, with thirteen hundred of it being Black. Thus, population wise, the name "One of the Majority" suggests that he or she was a white resident of Pottstown. For population statistics, see "Pottstown Quietly Ending Jim Crow," *Afro-American*, March 5, 1955, https://news.google.com/newspapers?nid=UBnQDr5gPskC; US Bureau of the Census, *Seventeenth Census of the United States, 1950*, vol. 2, *Characteristics of the Population*, part 38, *Pennsylvania*, 38-116; US Bureau of the Census, *Eighteenth Census of the United States, 1960*, vol. 1, *Characteristics of the Population*, part 40, *Pennsylvania*, 40-191.

29. One of the Majority, letter to the editor. For church segregation above and below Mason-Dixon Line, see Stephen R. Haynes, *The Last Segregated Hour: The Memphis Kneel-Ins and the Campaign for Southern Church Desegregation* (Oxford: Oxford University Press, 2012); Peter C. Murray, *Methodists and the Crucible of Race, 1930–1975* (Columbia: University of Missouri Press, 2004).

30. Martin Luther King, "Advice for Living," *Ebony Magazine Archive*, February 1958, 84. Also see Haynes, *Last Segregated Hour*, 8, 252n8.

31. Edgar S. Brown Jr. et al., letter to the editor; One of the Majority, letter to the editor.

32. Methodist, letter to the editor.

33. Jimmy, letter to the editor.

34. Hill, *Dear Sir*, 53.

35. Two June Graduates, letter to the editor; Jimmy, letter to the editor.

36. "Jessie Matthews Given Six Award Day Honors"; Hoyer, "Five Prizes, Scholarship Grant." For subhead quote, see "Same Opportunity?"

37. Hoyer, "Five Prizes, Scholarship Grant." When Matthews graduated, see "Judge Outlines Values, Goals at Graduation"; "Jessie Matthews Given Six Award Day Honors"; Hoyer, "Five Prizes, Scholarship Grant"; "Same Opportunity?" On *Brown* spotlighting the pervasiveness of inequality, see Michael J. Klarman, *From Jim*

Crow to Civil Rights: The Supreme Court and the Struggle for Racial Equality (Oxford: Oxford University Press, 2004), 292–442.

38. *Troiad 1954* (Boyertown, PA: Boyertown Times Publishing Company, 1954), 31, https://www.pottstownschools.org/AlumniYearbooks.aspx.

39. *Troiad 1954*, 31; "Same Opportunity?" Eventually, Matthews obtained a Bachelor of Science in Library Science at Kutztown in 1958. See *Keystonia* (Kutztown, PA: Students of Kutztown State Teachers College, 1958), 107, 119, https://research.library.kutztown.edu/cgi/viewcontent.cgi?article=1007&context=yearbooks_1950-1959; "9 Area Students Receive Degrees," *Pottstown Mercury*, May 27, 1958. In 1959, Matthews completed graduate coursework in the same area of academic study, earning an MS at the University of Illinois at Urbana. See "Jessie L. Matthews—Received a Masters Degree in Library Science from the University of Illinois Library School, Urbana, Ill. Miss Matthews, Daughter of Mr. and Mrs. J.L. Hague, Boyertown RD 2, Was Graduated with Honors in 1958 from Kutztown State Teachers College, and in 1954 from Pottstown Senior High School," *Pottstown Mercury*, June 19, 1959.

40. Hoyer, "Five Prizes, Scholarship Grant." When Matthews graduated, see "Judge Outlines Values, Goals at Graduation"; "Jessie Matthews Given Six Award Day Honors"; "Same Opportunity?"

41. "Same Opportunity?" On Kutztown University, see "History," Kutztown University, accessed September 11, 2023, https://www.kutztown.edu/about-ku/history.html.

42. Herbert R. Northrup et al., *Negro Employment in Basic Industry: A Study of Racial Policies in Six Industries*, vol. 1, Studies of Negro Employment (Philadelphia: Trustees of the University of Pennsylvania, 1970), 28–29. For the *Pottstown Mercury* articles and "Readers Say" comparison, see "Same Opportunity?," Two June Graduates, letter to the editor, not only for comments on what the authors basically label clerical labor but also the sarcastic remarks. On de facto segregation points in Pottstown around the time, also see Jimmy, letter to the editor; Hill, *Dear Sir*, 53–56; "Same Opportunity?"

43. For "Readers Say" authors comparison, see Jimmy, letter to the editor; Two June Graduates, letter to the editor. For the larger historical Black experience of inequality, see Sugrue, *Sweet Land of Liberty*.

44. T. M. W., letter to the editor, *Pottstown Mercury*, June 15, 1954. For subhead quote, see June Graduate, letter to the editor.

45. Manning Johnson, *Color, Communism, and Common Sense* (New York: Alliance, 1958; Belmont, MA: American Opinion, 1963).

46. "Manning Johnson Dead; Led Turbulent Life," *Evening Star*, July 25, 1959.

47. "Obituary: Manning Johnson," *Daily News*, July 25, 1959. For FBI's anti-communism sentiment during early postwar, see William W. Keller, *The Liberals and J. Edgar Hoover: Rise and Fall of a Domestic Intelligence State*, Princeton Legacy Library (Princeton, NJ: Princeton University Press, 2014).

48. Johnson, *Color, Communism, and Common Sense*, 43–44.

49. US Congress, Senate, Committee on Commerce, *Civil Rights—Public Accommodations: Hearings before the Committee on Commerce on S. 1732, A Bill to Eliminate Discrimination in Public Accommodations Affecting Interstate Commerce*, 88th Cong., 1st sess., 1963, 1224–28, 1232–33, https://www.google.com/books/edition/Civil _Rights_public_Accomodations_Hearin/503ntajCb74C?hl=en&gbpv=0.

50. T. M. W., letter to the editor; Johnson, *Color, Communism, and Common Sense*, 43–44; Sokol, *All Eyes Are upon Us*, 73.

51. Purnell and Theoharis, "Histories of Racism and Resistance, Seen and Unseen," 7–8.

52. T. M. W., letter to the editor; Purnell and Theoharis, "Histories of Racism and Resistance, Seen and Unseen," 7–8.

53. June Graduate, letter to the editor. On Matthews, see "Jessie Matthews Given Six Award Day Honors."

54. For "series," see Poirier, "Jim Crow, Yankee Style, Stalks Streets of Pottstown"; Normand Poirier, "Officer Training, Yes—But What Job Chances?," *Pottstown Mercury*, June 29, 1954; Normand Poirier, "Mister James P. Crow, Esq.—III: Discrimination by 'Necessity,'" *Pottstown Mercury*, June 30, 1954; Normand Poirier, "Mister James P. Crow, Esq.—IV: With End of School Pottstown Divides into Two Worlds," *Pottstown Mercury*, July 1, 1954; Normand Poirier, "Mister James P. Crow, Esq.-V: They Learn Timidity, Fear," *Pottstown Mercury*, July 2, 1954; Normand Poirier, "Mister James P. Crow, Esq.—VI: Is The Negro Happy Here?," *Pottstown Mercury* July 3, 1954; Normand Poirier, "Mister James P. Crow, Esq.—VII: A Plan of Action for Pottstown," *Pottstown Mercury*, July 5, 1954. For a look behind the scenes, see Treleven, "Story Stirs Memories of a Real Pro"; Hill, *Dear Sir*, 53–54.

55. Klarman, *From Jim Crow to Civil Rights*, 292–343. For subhead quote, see Shandy Hill, letter to the editor, *Afro Magazine*, December 12, 1953, https://news .google.com/newspapers?nid=UBnQDr5gPskC.

56. "Robinson Opens School Argument: Thurgood follows Virginian; Merge Va.-S.C. Cases; South Fears New Chief Justice Warren, California Liberal, to Tip Scales against JC Schools," *Afro-American*, December 12, 1953, https://news .google.com/newspapers?nid=UBnQDr5gPskC. On the *Afro Magazine*, see Hill, letter to the editor; Chicago Tribune, letter to the editor, *Afro Magazine*, December 12, 1953, https://news.google.com/newspapers?nid=UBnQDr5gPskC; Roy Parker Jr., letter to the editor, *Afro Magazine*, December 12, 1953, https://news.google. com/newspapers?nid=UBnQDr5gPskC; James Kerney Jr., letter to the editor, *Afro Magazine*, December 12, 1953, https://news.google.com/newspapers?nid=UBnQD r5gPskC; Jack Kilpatrick, letter to the editor, *Afro Magazine*, December 12, 1953, https://news.google.com/newspapers?nid=UBnQDr5gPskC; Charles L. Reese Jr., letter to the editor, *Afro Magazine*, December 12, 1953, https://news.google.com /newspapers?nid=UBnQDr5gPskC; Bart Richards, letter to the editor, *Afro Magazine*, December 12, 1953, https://news.google.com/newspapers?nid=UBnQDr5gPskC.

57. "Letters: About the School Case," *Afro Magazine*, December 12, 1953, https://news.google.com/newspapers?nid=UBnQDr5gPskC.

58. Hill, letter to the editor; Chicago Tribune, letter to the editor; Parker, letter to the editor; Kerney, letter to the editor; Kilpatrick, letter to the editor; Reese, letter to the editor; Richards, letter to the editor.

59. Hill, letter to the editor.

60. For the early December 1953 article, see "Letters: About the School Case." For extensive analysis of "series," see chap. 5. For *Brown*, see Russo, Harris, and Sandidge, "*Brown v. Board of Education* at 40," 297–309.

5. The Pinnacle of Civil Rights Struggle in Pottstown and Beyond following *Brown v. Board*

1. Russo, Harris, and Sandidge, "*Brown v. Board of Education* at 40," 297–309; "Supreme Court Rules Public School Segregation Must End"; "NAACP Hails Move as 'Vindication' of 45-Year Battle."

2. Poirier, "Jim Crow, Yankee Style, Stalks Streets of Pottstown"; Poirier, "Officer Training, Yes—But What Job Chances?"; Poirier, "Mister James P. Crow, Esq.—III"; Poirier, "Mister James P. Crow, Esq.—IV"; Poirier, "Mister James P. Crow, Esq.—V"; Poirier, "Mister James P. Crow, Esq.—VI"; Poirier, "Mister James P. Crow, Esq.—VII." For national sphere, see, for example, "Project Attracts Attention of the Nation: Cities, Papers from Coast to Coast Show Interest in the Pottstown Plan," *Pottstown Mercury*, March 1, 1955.

3. Poirier, "Mister James P. Crow, Esq.—IV"; Price, "School Segregation in Nineteenth-Century Pennsylvania," 134–37; Sugrue, *Sweet Land of Liberty*, 174.

4. Sugrue, *Sweet Land of Liberty*; Davidson Douglas, *Jim Crow Moves North: The Battle over Northern School Segregation, 1865–1954* (New York: Cambridge University Press, 2005); Delmont, *Why Busing Failed*.

5. Poirier, "Jim Crow, Yankee Style, Stalks Streets of Pottstown"; "Pottstown Quietly Ending Jim Crow"; US Bureau of Census, *Seventeenth Census of the United States, 1950*, vol. 2, *Characteristics of the Population*, part 38, *Pennsylvania*, 38-116; US Bureau of the Census, *Eighteenth Census of the United States, 1960*, vol. 1, *Characteristics of the Population*, part 40, *Pennsylvania*, 40-191. Regarding the 5 percent populace, also see Washington, "Examining Interracial Civil Rights Activism in 1950s Pottstown, Pennsylvania," 133.

6. "Does Jim Crow Live in Pottstown?," *Pottstown Mercury*, June 26, 1954. For subhead quote, see Poirier, "Jim Crow, Yankee Style, Stalks Streets of Pottstown." For series, see Poirier, "Jim Crow, Yankee Style, Stalks Streets of Pottstown"; Poirier, "Officer Training, Yes—But What Job Chances?"; Poirier, "Mister James P. Crow, Esq.—III"; Poirier, "Mister James P. Crow, Esq.—IV"; Poirier, "Mister James P. Crow, Esq.—V"; Poirier, "Mister James P. Crow, Esq.—VI"; Poirier, "Mister James P. Crow, Esq.—VII."

7. Poirier, "Jim Crow, Yankee Style, Stalks Streets of Pottstown."

8. "Deaths and Funerals: Normand Poirier Is Dead; Wrote about Vietnam War," *Muncie Star*, February 2, 1981; "Obituaries: Normand Poirier, 53, Reporter, Editor,"

Newsday (Nassau Edition), February 2, 1981; "Truman Stacey Heads State AP Sports Scribes," *Alexandria Daily Town Talk*, August 18, 1952; "Louisiana Sportswriters Select Double-A Elevens," *Shreveport Times*, December 1, 1952.

9. "Deaths and Funerals: Normand Poirier Is Dead."

10. Treleven, "Story Stirs Memories of a Real Pro." For background on Treleven, see "Obituaries: Charles Treleven," *Daily Tribune*, June 1, 1995; Hill, *Dear Sir*, 36.

11. For their titles, see "*Pottstown Mercury* and *the Pottstown News*," *Pottstown Mercury*, July 5, 1954. For Treleven points, see Treleven, "Story Stirs Memories of a Real Pro."

12. "200 Hear Poirier Trace Pottstown Plan at Headliner Banquet," *Lincoln Clarion*, April 22, 1955, http://digital.shsmo.org/cdm/ref/collection/LUClarion/id/2426.

13. Treleven, "Story Stirs Memories of a Real Pro."

14. "200 Hear Poirier Trace Pottstown Plan at Headliner Banquet."

15. Treleven, "Story Stirs Memories of a Real Pro."

16. Poirier, "Jim Crow, Yankee Style, Stalks Streets of Pottstown."

17. "Pennsylvania Town Seeks Segregation Problem End"; Poirier, "Mister James P. Crow, Esq.—VII." For examples of papers, see "'Unaware of It': Pennsylvania Town Goes to Work on Non-Segregation," *Bryan Daily Eagle*, February 27, 1955; "Town Takes Steps to Erase Its Own Jim Crow System," *St. Cloud Daily Times*, February 23, 1955.

18. Poirier, "Jim Crow, Yankee Style, Stalks Streets of Pottstown."

19. "Does Jim Crow Live in Pottstown?" For example of subscriber numbers to the *Pottstown Mercury* around the time, see "The Standing Pat Has Only One Leg to Stand On—And Figures That's Enough!," newspaper advertisement, *Pottstown Mercury*, May 7, 1954.

20. Poirier, "Jim Crow, Yankee Style, Stalks Streets of Pottstown."

21. Poirier, "Mister James P. Crow, Esq.—VII."

22. Poirier, "Mister James P. Crow, Esq.—IV."

23. Poirier, "Mister James P. Crow, Esq.—III."

24. Poirier, "Mister James P. Crow, Esq.—VI." For "persecution complex," see T.M.W., letter to the editor.

25. Poirier, "Mister James P. Crow, Esq.—VI"; Poirier, "Jim Crow, Yankee Style, Stalks Streets of Pottstown."

26. Poirier, "Mister James P. Crow, Esq.—VI."

27. Poirier, "Mister James P. Crow, Esq.—VII"; "Civic League Elects Dr. Lee New President." I make similar point previously in Washington, "Examining Interracial Civil Rights Activism in 1950s Pottstown, Pennsylvania," 132. For examples of committees in the South, see Kirk, *Beyond Little Rock*, 116–38.

28. June Graduate, letter to the editor; One of the Majority, letter to the editor; Thinker, letter to the editor, *Pottstown Mercury*, June 30, 1954; Mrs. M. L. B., letter to the editor, *Pottstown Mercury*, July 7, 1954. For African American writers, see Shirley L. Jackson, letter to the editor, *Pottstown Mercury*, July 12, 1954; Williams, letter to the editor; Reid, letter to the editor.

29. Williams, letter to the editor; Reid, letter to the editor.

30. Williams, letter to the editor. For further biographical data on Williams, maiden name Young, see chap. 2.

31. Reid, letter to the editor. See Poirier, "Mister James P. Crow, Esq.—IV," for his argument. For Williams, see Williams, letter to the editor.

32. Raymond C. De Wald, letter to the editor, *Pottstown Mercury*, July 10, 1954.

33. "Letters: About the School Case." On Lee, see "League Celebrates First Anniversary; Dr. Gray Speaks." For *Brown*, see Russo, Harris, and Sandidge, "*Brown v. Board of Education* at 40," 297–309. On *Afro-American*, can see Hayward Farrar, *The Baltimore Afro-American, 1892–1950* (Westport, CT: Greenwood Press, 1998).

34. "Why We Print This Story," *Afro-American*, July 10, 1954, https://news .google.com/newspapers?nid=UBnQDr5gPskC. The *Afro-American* and the *Afro-Magazine* published Poirier's series during July and August 1954. For a sample of the articles, see Normand Poirier, "Meet JC—Yankee Style: Method Found More Subtle in Northern Areas; Series of Seven Articles will Prove Supreme Court's School Decision has Impact on American Action," *Afro-American*, July 10, 1954, https://news .google.com/newspapers?nid=UBnQDr5gPskC; Poirier, "Jim Crow—Yankee Style: They Learn Timidity, Fear," *Afro Magazine*, August 7, 1954, https://news.google .com/newspapers?nid=UBnQDr5gPskC.

35. (Mrs.) Portia Madison, letter to the editor, *Afro-American*, July 17, 1954, https://news.google.com/newspapers?nid=UBnQDr5gPskC; Phoebe Dudley, letter to the editor, *Afro-American*, July 17, 1954, https://news.google.com/newspapers? nid=UBnQDr5gPskC; Mal Jordan, letter to the editor, *Afro-American*, July 17, 1954, https://news.google.com/newspapers?nid=UBnQDr5gPskC; Jim Halperin, letter to the editor, *Afro-American*, July 17, 1954, https://news.google.com /newspapers?nid=UBnQDr5gPskC; Edward Evans, letter to the editor, *Afro-American*, July 17, 1954, https://news.google.com/newspapers?nid=UBnQDr5gPskC; Georgine Clark, letter to the editor, *Afro-American*, July 17, 1954, https://news.google.com /newspapers?nid=UBnQDr5gPskC; Ray Powell, letter to the editor, *Afro-American*, July 17, 1954, https://news.google.com/newspapers?nid=UBnQDr5gPskC; Joseph Daniels, letter to the editor, *Afro-American*, July 17, 1954, https://news.google .com/newspapers?nid=UBnQDr5gPskC.

36. Madison, letter to the editor; Evans, letter to the editor; Dudley, letter to the editor.

37. Jordan, letter to the editor; Halperin, letter to the editor. On Harrisburg, see *Encyclopedia Britannica Online*, s.v. "Harrisburg," September 30, 2023, https://www .britannica.com/place/Harrisburg-Pennsylvania.

38. Halperin, letter to the editor.

39. Clark, letter to the editor; Powell, letter to the editor. On Motor City description, see Sugrue, "Motor City."

40. Daniels, letter to the editor.

41. Normand Poirier, "Mister James P. Crow, Esq.—VII."

42. The *Pittsburgh Courier* published Poirier's series in July and August 1954 too. For sample of the articles, see Normand Poirier, "The Story of a Town 'Up North':

Jim Crow . . . Yankee Style!; Reporter Finds J-C Stalking Pottstown, Pa. Streets," *Pittsburgh Courier*, July 17, 1954; Normand Poirier, "Story of a Town 'Up North': Jim Crow . . . Yankee Style," *Pittsburgh Courier*, August 7, 1954. For a brief background about the *Pittsburgh Courier*, see Slate, "America's Best Weekly," 272–75.

43. "South Carolina Newspaper: First Southern Daily Reprints 'Jim Crow,'" *Pottstown Mercury*, August 2, 1954. On *Afro-American*, can see, for example, "Why We Print This Story." On editor Patrick, see "Veteran Newsman Talbot Patrick Dies," *Times and Democrat*, January 24, 1980. On the *News-Argus*, see "The Fight against Discrimination," *Pottstown Mercury*, August 19, 1954.

44. "The Fight against Discrimination," *Pottstown Mercury*, August 19, 1954. On editor, see "Henry Belk Dies at Age 74; Educator and News Editor," *Danville Register*, October 21, 1972. For two paper comparisons, see "South Carolina Newspaper"; "Why We Print This Story."

45. Hill, *Dear Sir*, 37; George W. Troxler, "Belk, Henry," NCpedia, accessed December 29, 2022, https://www.ncpedia.org/biography/belk-henry.

46. "No Negro Heaven," *Pottstown Mercury*, August 23, 1954; Hill, *Dear Sir*, 55.

47. William Loeb, letter to the editor, *Pottstown Mercury*, July 30, 1954. On editor, see Adolphe V. Bernotas, "Publisher Succumbs: William Loeb Dies of Cancer at 75," *Burlington Free Press*, September 14, 1981.

48. Hill, *Dear Sir*, 63. For Loeb comparison, see Loeb, letter to the editor. For Biblical illustration, see Matthew 7:3–5 (KJV).

49. A. V. Pinkney to Claude Barnett, July 1, 1954, Folder: 001599-010-0221, General and Miscellaneous Correspondence, 1945–1954, Box 142, Folder 4, *The Claude A. Barnett Papers: The Associated Negro Press, 1918–1967*, part 2: *Associated Negro Press Organizational Files, 1920–1966*, Personal Papers: Chicago Historical Society, Claude A. Barnett Papers, Copyright 2011: Chicago Historical Society. For Pinkney's activism, see London, *Seventh-day Adventists and the Civil Rights Movement*, 144–45; London and Dixon, "Pinkney, Addison Vastapha (1903–1981)."

50. For a brief overview of the "Red Summer," see Karen Grigsby Bates and Jason Fuller, "Red Summer in Chicago: 100 Years after the Race Riots," Code Sw!tch: Race. In Your Face, *NPR*, July 27, 2019, ET (6:00 a.m. ET), https://www.npr.org/sections/codeswitch/2019/07/27/744130358/red-summer-in-chicago-100-years-after-the-race-riots. For biographical data on Barnett, see Ryan Hurst, "Claude Albert Barnett (1889–1967)," BlackPast, accessed December 29, 2022, https://www.blackpast.org/african-american-history/barnett-claude-albert-1889-1967/.

51. A. V. Pinkney to Claude Barnett, July 1, 1954, Folder: 001599-010-0221, General and Miscellaneous Correspondence, 1945–1954, Box 142, Folder 4, *The Claude A. Barnett Papers: The Associated Negro Press, 1918–1967*, Part 2, *Associated Negro Press Organizational Files, 1920–1966*, Personal Papers: Chicago Historical Society, Claude A. Barnett Papers, Copyright, 2011: Chicago Historical Society. For Pinkney's activism, see London, *Seventh-day Adventists and the Civil Rights Movement*, 144–45; London and Dixon, "Pinkney, Addison Vastapha (1903–1981)."

52. Claude A. Barnett to Shandy Hill, July 2, 1954, Folder: 001599-010-0221, General and Miscellaneous Correspondence, 1945–1954, Box 142, Folder 4, *The

Claude A. Barnett Papers: The Associated Negro Press, 1918–1967, part 2, *Associated Negro Press Organizational Files, 1920–1966*, Personal Papers: Chicago Historical Society, Claude A. Barnett Papers, Copyright, 2011: Chicago Historical Society.

53. Shandy Hill to Claude A. Barnett, July 8, 1954, Folder: 001599-010-0221, General and Miscellaneous Correspondence, 1945–1954, Box 142, Folder 4, *The Claude A. Barnett Papers: The Associated Negro Press, 1918–1967*, part 2, *Associated Negro Press Organizational Files, 1920–1966*, Personal Papers: Chicago Historical Society, Claude A. Barnett Papers, Copyright, 2011: Chicago Historical Society.

54. Claude A. Barnett to Shandy Hill, July 10, 1954, Folder: 001599-010-0221, General and Miscellaneous Correspondence, 1945–1954, Box 142, Folder 4, *The Claude A. Barnett Papers: The Associated Negro Press, 1918–1967*, part 2, *Associated Negro Press Organizational Files, 1920–1966*, Personal Papers: Chicago Historical Society, Claude A. Barnett Papers, Copyright, 2011: Chicago Historical Society.

55. Poirier, "Mister James P. Crow, Esq.—VII"; "Human Relations Group Will Meet," *Pottstown Mercury*, July 14, 1954; "Civic League Elects Dr. Lee New President."

56. "Human Relations Group Will Meet Tonight," *Pottstown Mercury*, July 28, 1954.

57. The Pottstown Committee on Human Relations, March 14, 1956, FHPA-Temple.

58. Normand Poirier, "Borough Forms New Committee for Equality: Area Leaders Discuss Plans to Form Group," *Pottstown Mercury*, July 15, 1954.

59. [Recipient not identified] to Mae Gellman, June 16, 1955, Branches [MD] Baltimore, 1955, Box 78/folder 32, FHPA-Temple.

60. *The Pottstown Plan*, 1955, FHPA-Temple; *Pottstown Human Relations Council . . . For Equality*, 1955, FHPA-Temple; Pottstown Human Relations Council: The Council, Other Orgs: Pottstown Human Relations Council, 1955, Box 82/folder 84, FHPA-Temple; Arnold, *Building the Beloved Community*, 3, 51.

61. Arnold, *Building the Beloved Community*, 19–25, 31.

62. Fred C. Selby, "Center for Study of Human Relations: Fellowship House Buys Former Showplace," *Pottstown Mercury*, June 25, 1951; Arnold, *Building the Beloved Community*, 6.

63. *Fellowship House: An Approach in Human Relations*, November 1955, 7–8, 15, Fellowship House/Farm Human Resources, 1955, Box 2/folder 13, FHPA-Temple.

64. The Pottstown Committee on Human Relations, March 14, 1956, FHPA-Temple.

65. Helen Stark Tomkins, "Fellowship House Farm," in *Invisible Philadelphia: Community through Voluntary Organizations*, ed. Jean Barth Toll and Mildred S. Gilliam (Philadelphia: Atwater Kent Museum, 1995), 608.

66. [Recipient not identified] to Gellman, June 16, 1955, FHPA-Temple; Normand Poirier, "Plan Drafted Here in Fight on Prejudice: Every Person, Organization Asked to Take 'First Step'; Project to Attack 'All Forms of Bias,'" *Pottstown Mercury*, February 21, 1955; *Fellowship House: An Approach in Human Relations*, November 1955, 5, FHPA-Temple; Marjorie Penney to William Hastie, September 8, 1954, Correspondence, [M.P.], 1954, Box 14/folder 82, FHPA-Temple.

67. *The Pottstown Plan*, 1955, FHPA-Temple.

68. Penney to Hastie, September 8, 1954, FHPA-Temple; Fellowship Houses Development Committee, Report on Survey of Fellowship House, May 1955, 2, Fellowship House/Farm Committees Survey Reports, 1954–55, Box 3/folder 32, FHPA-Temple. For background on Hastie, see Samantha Kealoha, "William Henry Hastie (1904–1976)," BlackPast, accessed October 14, 2023, https://www.blackpast .org/african-american-history/hastie-william-henry-1904-1976/.

69. *The Pottstown Plan*, 1955, FHPA-Temple.

70. Arnold, *Building the Beloved Community*, 3; *The Pottstown Plan*, 1955, FHPA-Temple.

71. *The Pottstown Plan*, 1955, FHPA-Temple. On Fellowship House and Farm's inclusive message, see, for example, Tomkins, "Fellowship House Farm," 606–10.

72. "Anti-Bias Plan Gets Approval: Local Leaders Will Present Brochure Aimed at Discrimination," *Pottstown Mercury*, October 21, 1954.

73. For example, see Penney to Wilkins, February 23, 1955, FHPA-Temple; "The Pottstown Plan," *Fellowship House and Farm: Dedicated to the Proposition That All Men Are Created Equal*, March 1955, Branches: Fellowship House, 1955, Box 79/ folder 137, FHPA-Temple; Mitzi R. Jacoby to Cornell Hewson, May 12, 1955, Branches [MO] Kansas City, 1955, Box 78/folder 42, FHPA-Temple; Poirier, "Plan Drafted Here in Fight on Prejudice."

74. Poirier, "Plan Drafted Here in Fight on Prejudice."

75. A. Herbert Haslam, 1917–1918, United States World War I Draft Registration Cards, 1917–1918, database with images, FamilySearch, March 13, 2018, https://familysearch.org/ark:/61903/1:1:K6V3-1SW, citing Carbon County no 2, Pennsylvania, United States, NARA microfilm publication M1509 (Washington, DC: National Archives and Records Administration, n.d.), FHL microfilm 1,877,832; "Obituary: Dr. A.H. Haslam Dies at Age of 56," *Philadelphia Inquirer*, February 14, 1955; "Release: Dr. A. Herbert Haslam," Individuals: Haslam, A. Herbert, undated, Box 11/folder 120, FHPA-Temple.

76. "The Pottstown Plan," *Fellowship House and Farm*, March 1955, FHPA-Temple.

77. Poirier, "Plan Drafted Here in Fight on Prejudice"; "Dr. A. H. Haslam Died on Sunday," *Jim Thorpe Times-News*, February 17, 1955.

78. Marjorie Penney in household of Maurice Penney, Philadelphia Ward 15, Philadelphia, Pennsylvania, United States, United States Census, 1910, database with images, FamilySearch, accessed December 31, 2022, https://familysearch.org /ark:/61903/1:1:MGDR-YS3, citing enumeration district (ED) ED 235, sheet 10A, family 192, NARA microfilm publication T624 (Washington, DC: National Archives and Records Administration, 1982), roll 1391, FHL microfilm 1,375,404; John Woestendiek, "Obituaries: Marjorie P. Paschkis; Founded 2 Fellowship Houses in Phila," *Philadelphia Inquirer*, May 30, 1983; "Memory Stream: Historical Society of Pennsylvania; Growing Peace and Tolerance," *Philadelphia Inquirer*, July 13, 2014.

79. "Mitzi Rona Barnes: March 17, 1931–April 21, 2018," Monarch Society, accessed January 9, 2023, http://www.monarchsociety.com/obituary/mitzi-barnes.

80. "Comments Welcomed," *Pottstown Mercury*, February 21, 1955; Poirier, "Plan Drafted Here in Fight on Prejudice."

81. Mrs. Bessie M. James, letter to the editor, *Pottstown Mercury*, February 26, 1955. For further data on James, see Bessie James, Line 15, Sheet 2, Enumeration District 46-311, Pottstown Township, Montgomery County, Pennsylvania; Seventeenth Census of the United States, 1950; Record Group 29, Records of the Bureau of the Census; National Archives and Records Administration, Washington DC, accessed December 30, 2022, https://1950census.archives.gov/.

82. Bert Dobry, letter to the editor, *Pottstown Mercury*, March 1, 1955.

83. Club Member, letter to the editor, *Pottstown Mercury*, June 30, 1954.

84. *The Pottstown Plan*, 1955, FHPA-Temple; "Give Full Endorsement: 'Pottstown Plan' Gets YWCA, Grange Aid," *Pottstown Mercury*, February 25, 1955; "Kiwanis Members Vote Endorsement to Pottstown Plan," *Pottstown Mercury*, March 2, 1955; "Continuing Project Promised: Foreman, Girl Scouts Back 'Pottstown Plan,'" *Pottstown Mercury*, February 24, 1955.

85. "Anti-Bigotry Plan Gets Solid Backing," Newspaper clipping, Other Orgs: Pottstown Human Relations Council, 1955, Box 82/folder 84, FHPA-Temple. For background on Boden and Miller, see "W.J. Boden Is Named to County Post: Appointed Commercial Appraiser of Board; Pottstonian Held Office 8 Years," *Pottstown Mercury*, February 2, 1960; "Ex-Democratic Leader Maurice Miller Dies," *Pottstown Mercury*, March 30, 1971. Locals emphasized Pottstown as the "Community of Opportunity." For example, see "'Community of Opportunity': Housewife Wins $500 for Slogan," *Pottstown Mercury*, July 8, 1955; "Doehler's to Aid Slogan Publicizing," *Pottstown Mercury*, August 9, 1955.

86. Penney to Wilkins, February 23, 1955, FHPA-Temple. For Hastie letter, see Marjorie Penney to William Hastie, February 25, 1955, Other Orgs: Pottstown Human Relations Council, 1955, Box 82/folder 84, FHPA-Temple. For biographical data on Wilkins, see "Roy Wilkins, Civil Rights Leader, Dies in New York," *Philadelphia Inquirer*, September 9, 1981. The points relating to Jacoby are demonstrated later in this chapter.

87. Roy Wilkins to Marjorie Penney, March 7, 1955, Other Orgs: Pottstown Human Relations Council, 1955, Box 82/folder 84, FHPA-Temple.

88. Penney to Gremley, June 23, 1955, FHPA-Temple; Marjorie Penney to William Gremley, February 25, 1955, Other Orgs: Pottstown Human Relations Council, 1955, Box 82/folder 84, FHPA-Temple; Marjorie Penney to Marshall Bragdon, February 25, 1955, Other Orgs: Pottstown Human Relations Council, 1955, Box 82/folder 84, FHPA-Temple; Marjorie Penney to Marshall Bragdon, November 18, 1954, Correspondence, [M.P.], 1955, Box 14/folder 89, FHPA-Temple; Marjorie Penney to George Schirmer, February 26, 1955, Other Orgs: Pottstown Human Relations Council, 1955, Box 82/folder 84, FHPA-Temple. Penney spells George Schirmer's last name wrong; it should be Schermer. Names of the Ohio and Philadelphia organizations are also further clarified in following correspondences: Marshall Bragdon to Marjorie Penney, March 9, 1955, Correspondence: Speakers, 1951–58, Box 13/folder 73, FHPA-Temple; George Schermer to Marjorie Penney, April 7, 1955, Other Orgs: Pottstown Human Relations Council, 1955, Box 82/folder 84, FHPA-Temple. For brief data and photos of the three white activists, see

"Urban League to Mark Its 25th Anniversary," *Evening Independent*, May 17, 1961; "Relations Unit Warned Against Influx of Bigots," *Miami Daily News*, March 27, 1957; "Schermer Feted for Race Work," *Philadelphia Daily News*, June 13, 1963.

89. Bragdon to Penney, March 9, 1955, FHPA-Temple. On NAIRO, see Daryl Michael Scott, "Postwar Pluralism, Brown v. Board of Education, and the Origins of Multicultural Education," *Journal of American History* 91, no. 1 (June 2004): 73–74, https://www.jstor.org/stable/3659614.

90. Schermer to Penney, April 7, 1955, FHPA-Temple. For Robinson's observation, see Robinson, *A City within a City*, xi.

91. Marjorie Penney to Phillip Buskirk, June 4, 1956, Other Orgs: Pottstown Human Relations Council, 1955, Box 82/folder 84, FHPA-Temple; Marjorie Penney to Rabbi Arthur Gilbert, September 1, 1956, Correspondence, RE: "Count Me In," 1956, Box 14/folder 92, FHPA-Temple; Marjorie Penney to J. Oscar Lee, June 15, 1955, Other Orgs: Pottstown Human Relations Council, 1955, Box 82/folder 84, FHPA-Temple. For the response from NCCCUSA associate to the last letter, see J. Oscar Lee to Marjorie Penney, June 3, 1955, Correspondence, [M.P.], 1955, Box 14/folder 88, FHPA-Temple.

92. Penney to Gremley, June 23, 1955, FHPA-Temple.

93. Marjorie Penney to Lewis Stevens, November 3, 1955, Correspondence, [M.P.], 1955, Box 14/folder 89, FHPA-Temple; Marjorie Penney to Phil Buskirk, July 12, 1956, Other Orgs: Pottstown Human Relations Council, 1955, Box 82/folder 84, FHPA-Temple.

94. Marjorie Penney to William Rafsky, March 31, 1955, Correspondence, [M.P.], 1955, Box 14/folder 89, FHPA-Temple. For biographical data on Rafsky, see "Obituaries: William L. Rafsky, 81, Urban Planner," *Philadelphia Inquirer*, June 13, 2001.

95. *Fellowship House: An Approach in Human Relations*, November 1955, 5, FHPA-Temple.

96. Milton M. Gordon to Marjorie Penney, March 12, 1955, Other Orgs: Pottstown Human Relations Council, 1955, Box 82/folder 84, FHPA-Temple; Marjorie Penney to Milton Gordon, February 23, 1955, Other Orgs: Pottstown Human Relations Council, 1955, box 82, folder 84, FHPA-Temple; Milton M. Gordon, *Assimilation in American Life: The Role of Race, Religion, and National Origins* (New York: Oxford University Press, 1964). For biographical data on Gordon, see "Milton M. Gordon," John Simon Guggenheim Memorial Foundation, accessed December 31, 2022, https://www.gf.org/fellows/all-fellows/milton-m-gordon/.

97. Jacoby to Hewson, May 12, 1955, FHPA-Temple; Mitzi R. Jacoby to Henrietta C. Carry, April 12, 1955, Branches [NY] Brooklyn, 1955, Box 78/folder 57, FHPA-Temple; Mitzi R. Jacoby to Alberta Morris, April 12, 1955, Branches [OH] Columbus, 1955, Box 79/folder 77, FHPA-Temple; Mitzi R. Jacoby to Harold C. [last name not fully legible], March 25, 1955, Branches [Wash. D.C] Washington, 1955, Box 78/folder 12, FHPA-Temple. For Pennsylvania affiliations, see Mitzi R. Jacoby to Dorothy James, May 12, 1955, Branches [PA] Media, 1955, Box 79/folder 98, FHPA-Temple; Mitzi R. Jacoby to Joseph Fugett, May 18, 1955, Branches [PA] West Chester, 1955, Box 79/folder 118, FHPA-Temple; Mitzi R. Jacoby to Donald

Warrington, April 12, 1955, Branches [PA] Reading, 1955, Box 79/folder 113, FHPA-Temple.

98. Jacoby to James, May 12, 1955, FHPA-Temple.

99. "Proclamation: 'The Pottstown Plan' Day," Newspaper clipping, Other Orgs: Pottstown Human Relations Council, 1955, Box 82/folder 84, FHPA-Temple.

100. Poirier, "Plan Drafted Here in Fight on Prejudice."

101. "Project Attracts Attention of the Nation"; "Pottstown Plan Reprint Prompts Letter from GI."

102. "Project Attracts Attention of the Nation"; "Pennsylvania Town Is Jolted into Action by Series on Segregation: Yankee Style Jim Crow System Hit," *Lubbock Evening Journal*, February 22, 1955; "Unaware of It"; "In Pottstown, Pa.: Northern Town Tries to End 'Jim Crowism,'" *Daily Independent Journal*, February 22, 1955; "Small Town Launches Anti-Discrimination Plan," *Bakersfield Californian*, February 23, 1955; "Pottstown Seeks End of Informal 'Jim Crowism,'" *Great Bend Daily Tribune*, February 23, 1955; "Pottstown Launches Its Own Attack on Jim Crow," *Manhattan Mercury*, February 22, 1955; "Town Takes Steps to Erase Its Own Jim Crow System"; "City Launches Plan to Solve Discrimination: Quietly Starts Work to Eliminate Subtle Form of Segregation," *Moberly Monitor-Index and Moberly Evening Democrat*, February 22, 1955; "Desegregation Plan Starts in Pottstown," *St. Petersburg Times*, February 23, 1955; "Pennsylvania Town Tackles Race Problem," *Fort Lauderdale Daily News*, February 26, 1955; "James P. Crow, Esquire: City Launches Integration Plan," *Raleigh Register*, February 23, 1955; "Newspaper Series Sparks Pennsylvania City Crusade," *Rapid City Daily Journal*, February 23, 1955; "Pennsylvania Town Seeks Segregation Problem End."

103. "Pottstown Takes Action When It Finds Segregation Practiced at Home, Too," *Gazette and Daily*, February 24, 1955; "Program Launched Quietly: Pottstown Goal Is Eradication of North Style Jim Crow Plan," *Scranton Times*, February 22, 1955; "Pottstown Segregation Going Quietly," *Indiana Evening Gazette*, February 22, 1955; "Pottstown Launches Campaign to Correct Unsuspected Segregation," *Plain Speaker*, February 23, 1955.

104. Phil Buskirk to Marjorie Penney, June 26, 1956, Other Orgs: Pottstown Human Relations Council, 1955, Box 82/folder 84, FHPA-Temple.

105. Lee to Penney, June 3, 1955, FHPA-Temple. For an assessment of the Interracial News Service as well as brief biographical data on Lee, see David P. Cline, "Revolution and Reconciliation: The Student Interracial Ministry, Liberal Protestantism, and the Civil Rights Movement, 1960–1970" (PhD diss., University of North Carolina at Chapel Hill, 2010), 42–43.

106. Penney to Buskirk, July 12, 1956, FHPA-Temple; Penney to Lee, June 15, 1955, FHPA-Temple.

107. "Project Attracts Attention of the Nation."

108. "Pottstown Plan Prompts Letter from GI."

109. "Project Attracts Attention of the Nation."

110. "Pottstown Plan Wiping Out Prejudice," *Pittsburgh Courier Magazine Section*, April 30, 1955.

111. "Village Asks a Question," *Pottstown Mercury*, March 1, 1955.

112. "Goodwill Prizes to Be Given to 35: Winners in Mass Media Are Chosen by Conference of Christians and Jews," *New York Times*, February 13, 1955. Can also see "Be a Better Brother," *Pottstown Mercury*, February 19, 1955. Hill also talks about the National Conference of Christians and Jews journalistic distinction that the *Pottstown Mercury* obtained. See Hill, *Dear Sir*, 56. For reference to the month the Pottstown Plan pamphlets started circulating, see Poirier, "Plan Drafted Here in Fight on Prejudice." For Paton, see Herbert Mitgang, "Alan Paton, Author and Apartheid Foe, Dies of Cancer at 85," *New York Times*, April 12, 1988. For subhead quote, see Fellowship House Farm, *Cast Down Your Buckets Where You Are*, June 20–27, 1955, FHPA-Temple.

113. "Mercury Wins Acclaim of Church Council: 'Jim Crow' Series Lauded as Prophetic Venture," *Pottstown Mercury*, July 19, 1954.

114. Hill, *Dear Sir*, 57.

115. "200 Hear Poirier Trace Pottstown Plan at Headliner Banquet."

116. "Pottstown Plan to Highlight Headliner Banquet Address," *Lincoln Clarion*, April 15, 1955, http://digital.shsmo.org/cdm/ref/collection/LUClarion/id /2419. Also, see "Wins Lincoln U Award for Series on Jim Crow," *Philadelphia Tribune*, April 26, 1955; "Education Notes: Schools and Colleges; Lincoln University," *New York Age Defender*, April 23, 1955.

117. Hill, *Dear Sir*, 56. Also see "Pottstown Plan to Highlight Headliner Banquet Address."

118. Hill, *Dear Sir*, 56.

119. "Darby Girl to Teach in Pottstown School," *Philadelphia Tribune*, August 21, 1956; Gertrude Tibbs, "Darby Doings," *Philadelphia Tribune*, September 15, 1956.

120. "Hill-Molock, Elaine," *Press of Atlantic City*, January 5, 2016; *Encyclopedia Britannica Online*, s.v., "West Chester University of Pennsylvania," March 23, 2020, https://www.britannica.com/topic/West-Chester-University-of-Pennsylvania.

121. "Human Relations Council Conducts Election of Officer," *Pottstown Mercury*, May 5, 1958.

122. Hill, *Dear Sir*, 56.

123. *Pottstown Human Relations Council . . . For Equality*, 1955, FHPA-Temple; *The Pottstown Plan*, 1955, FHPA-Temple.

124. "Frank Thomas Named to Council: GOP Appoints First Negro to Position; Replaces Councilman Who Died in Accident; Nominee Cited for Party Service," *Pottstown Mercury*, September 26, 1961; Marjorie Penney to William Rafsky, August 25, 1955, Correspondences: Speakers, 1951–58, Box 13/folder 66, FHPA-Temple.

125. "William Barber Is Recipient of Fellowship," *Pottstown Mercury*, May 7, 1965; *Pottstown Human Relations Council . . . For Equality*, 1955, FHPA-Temple; *The Pottstown Plan*, 1955, FHPA-Temple; Levy, *Great Uprising*, 247–48.

126. Marjorie Penney to Whom It May Concern, November 28, 1955, Other Orgs: Pottstown Human Relations Council, 1955, Box 82/folder 84, FHPA-Temple; Penney to Rafsky, August 25, 1955, FHPA-Temple.

127. Penney to Rafsky, August 25, 1955, FHPA-Temple.

128. *Pottstown Human Relations Council . . . For Equality*, 1955, FHPA-Temple.

129. *The Pottstown Plan*, 1955, FHPA-Temple; *Pottstown Human Relations Council . . . For Equality*, 1955, FHPA-Temple.

130. *The Pottstown Plan*, 1955, FHPA-Temple.

131. The Pottstown Committee on Human Relations, March 14, 1956, FHPA-Temple.

132. The Pottstown Committee on Human Relations, March 14, 1956, FHPA-Temple. On networks, see Sugrue, *Sweet Land of Liberty*; Matthew J. Countryman, *Up South: Civil Rights and Black Power in Philadelphia* (Philadelphia: University of Pennsylvania Press, 2006).

133. The Pottstown Committee on Human Relations, March 14, 1956, FHPA-Temple.

134. "Pottstown Plan," *Crisis*, December 1955, 610–11, https://books.google.com/books?id=9VsEAAAAMBAJ. On the Pottstown Plan being initially conceptualized the previous October, see "Anti-Bias Plan Gets Approval."

135. *Pottstown Human Relations Council . . . For Equality*, 1955, FHPA-Temple. The second pamphlet notes that gathering occurred during November 1955; however, it was late October. See "Pottstown Plan," 610–11.

136. "Pottstown Plan," 610–11.

137. Fellowship House Farm, *Cast Down Your Buckets Where You Are*, June 20–27, 1955, FHPA-Temple.

138. "Pottstown Plan," 610–11; Fellowship House Farm, *Cast Down Your Buckets Where You Are*, June 20–27, 1955, FHPA-Temple.

139. Arnold, *Building the Beloved Community*, 48. Also see Janet Yamron, Sonya Garfinkle, and Amanda Bumgarner, "Elaine Brown: Breaking Down Barriers through Song," *Choral Journal* 58, no. 5 (December 2017): 24–32, https://www.jstor.org/stable/26412916.

140. Marjorie Penney to Rabbi Arthur Gilbert, October 10, 1956, Correspondence, RE: "Count Me In," 1956, Box 14/folder 92, FHPA-Temple; "Fellowship House Choir at JCC Tomorrow," *Standard Sentinel*, May 1, 1954; "Churches and Synagogue Sponsor Concert Featuring Fellowship House Choir Feb. 24," *Vineland Times Journal*, February 18, 1955; "Nettie Mae Merritt: Nettie Mae Merritt Wins Master's Degree," *Vineland Times Journal*, May 31, 1951; "Deaths and Funerals: Mrs. Nettie Hare," *Burlington Free Press*, February 16, 1965. For Elaine Brown, see "About Us," Singing City, accessed January 2, 2023, https://www.singingcity.org/about; Janet Yamron, Sonya Garfinkle, and Amanda Bumgarner, "Elaine Brown: Breaking Down Barriers through Songs," *Choral Journal* 58, no. 5 (December 2017): 24–32, https://www.jstor.org/stable/26412916; "Former Black Panthers Who Have Turned to Higher Education," *Journal of Blacks in Higher Education*, no. 21 (Autumn 1998): 63, https://doi.org/10.2307/2998992.

141. Fellowship House Farm, *Cast Down Your Buckets Where You Are*, June 20–27, 1955, 7, FHPA-Temple.

142. Fellowship House Farm, *Cast Down Your Buckets Where You Are*, June 20–27, 1955, 3, FHPA-Temple.

143. Mitzi R. Jacoby to Carol M. Gabler, January 23, 1956, Correspondence [Jacoby, Mitzi], 1956, Box 14/folder 94, FHPA-Temple; Mitzi R. Jacoby to Carol Gabler, February 14, 1956, Correspondence [Jacoby, Mitzi], 1956, Box 14/folder 94, FHPA-Temple; Arnold, *Building the Beloved Community*, 37.

144. Marjorie Penney to Dr. Oscar Lee, September 1, 1956, Correspondence, RE: "Count Me In," 1956, Box 14/folder 92, FHPA-Temple. On Belafonte's activism, see Colin Campbell, "Belafonte Reflects on Civil Rights, King at UB: 'He Wanted Much More Than Money,' Belafonte Said, 'He Wanted My Life,'" *Baltimore Sun*, May 7, 2014.

145. Penney to Lee, September 1, 1956, FHPA-Temple.

146. Marjorie Penney to Rabbi Arthur Gilbert, September 1, 1956, Correspondence, RE: "Count Me In," 1956, Box 14/folder 92, FHPA-Temple. For background on Gilbert, see "Rabbi Arthur Gilbert, 49, Dead; Promoted Interreligious Amity," *New York Times*, May 18, 1976.

147. Marjorie Penney to Robert A. Elfers, December 6, 1956, Correspondence, RE: "Count Me In," 1956, Box 14/folder 92, FHPA-Temple. For background on Elfers, see "Elfers Editor for Church Group," *Poughkeepsie New Yorker*, October 22, 1955.

148. Arthur Gilbert to Marjorie Penney, September 25, 1956, Correspondence, RE: "Count Me In," 1956, Box 14/folder 92, FHPA-Temple; Robert A. Elfers to Marjorie Penney, November 26, 1956, Correspondence, RE: "Count Me In," 1956, Box 14/folder 92, FHPA-Temple.

149. Library of Congress, *Catalog of Copyright Entries: Summer 1954 Series, Volume 13, Part 5, Number 2, Music* (Washington, DC: Copyright Office, the Library of Congress, July–December 1959), 1210, https://books.google.com/books?id=AD0h AQAAIAAJ.

150. The Staff of Fellowship House to Buyer of "Count Me In!," Proposed Preface Page to "Count Me In," Correspondence, RE: "Count Me In," 1956, Box 14/folder 92, FHPA-Temple. For two booklets, see *The Pottstown Plan*, 1955, FHPA-Temple; *Pottstown Human Relations Council . . . For Equality*, 1955, FHPA-Temple.

151. "Human Relations Council Conducts Election of Officer"; "Russell Barbour Speaks to Jewish Women's League: Human Relations Council Official Advises Facing Race Problems without Fear," *Pottstown Mercury*, April 6, 1967.

152. I make a comparable argument previously in Washington, "Examining Interracial Civil Rights Activism in 1950s Pottstown, Pennsylvania," 133.

153. "Pottstown Civic League Pays Honor to Dr. Daniel Lee at Farewell Fete," *Pottstown Mercury*, May 2, 1955; Anne L. Boles, "He Was 'Everybody's Doctor'—A Job That Has No Takers Now: An Era Ends with Dr. Lee," *Philadelphia Inquirer Metro*, March 1, 1993; Andy Wallace, "Dr. W.C. Atkinson, 97; Physician Founded a Coatesville Hospital," *Philadelphia Inquirer*, January 5, 1991; "Easton NAACP Installation, Speaker Listed," *Morning Call*, December 31, 1964. Other notables are Newstell Marable and William D. Barber. Chap. 6 covers Marable extensively. On Marable, see, for instance, "Community Icon Newstell Marable, Longtime Pottstown NAACP President, Dies at 84." On Barber, see Levy, *Great Uprising*, 247–48; "City Councilman Bid Observance of Freedom Day: Tribute Paid to Centennial of Emancipation Proclamation and to Civil Rights Movement," *Gazette and Daily*, August 19,

1963; *The Pottstown Plan*, 1955, FHPA-Temple; "Frank Thomas Named to Council."

154. Steven Lawson, "Freedom Then, Freedom Now: The Historiography of the Civil Rights Movement," *American Historical Review* 96, no. 2 (April 1991): 457, https://www.jstor.org/stable/2163219. Also see Thomas J. Sugrue, "Affirmative Action from below: Civil Rights, the Building Trades, and the Politics of Racial Equality in the Urban North, 1945–1969," *Journal of American History* 91, no. 1 (June 2004): 147, https://doi.org/10.2307/3659618.

155. Hall, "Long Civil Rights Movement and the Political Uses of the Past," 1235. For historiography further, see Williams, *Rethinking the Black Freedom Movement*, xi–xii; Purnell, *Fighting Jim Crow in the County of Kings*, 3. On the historiographical argument that "there was no long uninterrupted civil rights movement in the 20th century," see Helgeson, "Essay Review II," 443.

156. Chap. 6 of this book covers the postwar Pottstown NAACP extensively.

6. The Pottstown NAACP and the Postwar Industrial North

1. "Bold Prowler Alarms Stowe: 25 Armed Men Aiding Township Policeman in Effort to Nab Stranger," *Pottstown Mercury*, July 31, 1951. For background on Guadagno, see "James Guadagno Is Found Dead," *Pottstown Mercury*, March 11, 1967.

2. "Don't Take Law into Own Hands!," *Pottstown Mercury*, August 1, 1951.

3. On lynching in the South, see Campbell Robertson, "History of Lynchings in the South Documents Nearly 4,000 Names," *New York Times*, February 10, 2015, https://www.nytimes.com/2015/02/10/us/history-of-lynchings-in-the-south -documents-nearly-4000-names.html.

4. "The Lynching of Zachariah Walker Historical Marker," Explore PA History, accessed January 2, 2023, http://explorepahistory.com/hmarker.php?markerId =1-A-3DB.

5. "Don't Take Law into Own Hands!" On Guadagno's commentary, see "Bold Prowler Alarms Stowe."

6. "Armed Search in Stowe Gets NAACP Attention: Agent Ordered Here to Probe Hunt for Negro; Situation Is Termed 'Loaded with Dynamite'; Volunteer Posse Called Off," *Pottstown Mercury*, August 1, 1951. On Marshall, see Spencer R. Crew, *Thurgood Marshall: A Life in American History*, Black History Lives (Santa Barbara, California: ABC-CLIO, 2019). On Flamer, also see "Miscellaneous," *Crisis*, May 1951, 331, https://books.google.com/books?id=91cEAAAAMBAJ; "Negro Leader to Speak at Interracial Forum," *Journal-Every Evening*, April 4, 1952.

7. "Seek to Advert Violence in Pennsylvania Town," August 2, 1951, "Flamer, John W., Jan. 18–Oct. 10, 1951," Box II: C354, folder 5, NAACP-LOC.

8. "Stowe Police Nab Prowler Suspect: Man, 25, Held for Court, but Denies Charge; Defendant Is Identified at Hearing; Witness Says He Tossed Rock at Car," *Pottstown Mercury*, August 2, 1951. Also, can see "Keeps Eye on Terror Suspect," *Pottstown Mercury*, August 2, 1951.

9. "Freedom Is Granted to Prowler Suspect," *Pottstown Mercury*, September 7, 1951.

10. Kevern Verney and Lee Sartain, "The NAACP in Historiographical Perspective," in *Long Is the Way and Hard: One Hundred Years of the NAACP*, ed. Kevern Verney, Lee Sartain, Adam Fairclough (Fayetteville: University of Arkansas Press, 2009), xvii–xviii. For brief data on White, see *Encyclopedia Britannica Online*, s.v., "Walter White," June 27, 2023, https://www.britannica.com/biography/Walter -White-American-civil-rights-activist. For "Pottstown Plan" and Wilkins, see Wilkins to Penney, March 7, 1955, FHPA-Temple. For Wilkins era, see Yvonne Ryan, "Leading from the Back: Roy Wilkins's Leadership of the NAACP," in Verney, Sartain, and Fairclough, *Long Is the Way and Hard*, 43–58.

11. Verney and Sartain, "NAACP in Historiographical Perspective," xxi–xxii.

12. For other chapters' activism during the postwar, see Verney, Sartain, and Fairclough, *Long Is the Way and Hard*.

13. "NAACP Chapter Receives Charter, Elects New Officers."

14. "NAACP Chapter Receives Charter, Elects New Officers"; "Presentation of Scholarship to Highlight Youth Rally," *Pottstown Mercury*, August 27, 1951; "Dead or Inactive Branches in Eastern Pennsylvania," NAACP-LOC; "Field Schedule Pennsylvania & New Jersey, John Flamer, August 20th–October 20th," "Flamer, John W. Nov. 1–Dec. 26, 1951," Box II: C354, folder 6, NAACP-LOC; Memo to John W. Flamer, July 31, 1951, "Flamer, John W. Nov. 1–Dec. 26, 1951," Box II: C354, folder 6, NAACP-LOC.

15. Charles Prince to Sir, October 29, 1949, Pennsylvania State Conference, 1950. 109 pp, Folder: 001495-011-0575, *Papers of the NAACP*, part 26, *Selected Branch Files, 1940–1955*, series B, *The Northeast*, Library of Congress, 2014, NAACP. For NAACP response to Prince, see Gloster B. Current to Charles Prince, November 17, 1949, Pennsylvania State Conference, 1950, 109 pp, Folder: 001495-011-0575, *Papers of the NAACP*, part 26, *Selected Branch Files, 1940–1955*, series B, *The Northeast*, Library of Congress, 2014, NAACP. On Prince, see "NAACP Chapter Receives Charter, Elects New Officers"; "United States Census, 1940," database with images, Family Search (https://familysearch.org/ark:/61903/1:1:KQ7H-88K : 15 March 2018), Charles Prince, West Pottsgrove Township, Montgomery, Pennsylvania, United States; citing enumeration district (ED) 46-235, sheet 11A, line 24, family 206, Sixteenth Census of the United States, 1940, NARA digital publication T627, Records of the Bureau of the Census, 1790–2007, RG 29. Washington, D.C.: National Archives and Records Administration, 2012, roll 3586.

16. "Biographical Information: John W. Flamer, Assistant Field Secretary, National Association for the Advancement of Colored People"; "Flamer, John W. Nov. 1–Dec. 26, 1951," Box II: C354, folder 6, NAACP-LOC; "Miscellaneous," 331.

17. Memo to Flamer, July 31, 1951, NAACP-LOC.

18. "Dead or Inactive Branches in Eastern Pennsylvania," NAACP-LOC.

19. "Presentation of Scholarship to Highlight Youth Rally." Also see "Field Schedule Pennsylvania & New Jersey, John Flamer, August 20th–October 20th," Box II: C354, Folder 6, "Flamer, John W. Nov 1.-Dec. 26, 1951," Branch File, Manuscript Division, Group II, NAACP-LOC.

20. "Pottstown Bridge Named in Honor of Newstell Marable Sr."

21. Holly Herman, "Prominent Civil-Rights Leader in Pottstown Recalled," *Reading Eagle*, January 29, 2015, 12:00 a.m. EST (updated August 19, 2021, 6:19 a.m. EST), https://www.readingeagle.com/news/article/prominent-civil-rights -leader-in-pottstown-recalled. On further information regarding Ross, see Evan Brandt, "Rev. Ross leaves Bethel AME, Founds New Church in Synagogue," *Mercury*, May 4, 2015, 7:55 a.m. EST (updated September 24, 2021, 3:02 a.m. EST), https://www .pottsmerc.com/2015/05/04/rev-ross-leaves-bethel-ame-founds-new-church-in -synagogue/.

22. "Opportunity Board Names N. Marable: Pottstown Man Gets Fulltime Post as Organizer," *Pottstown Mercury*, March 9, 1967; "Pastor Says Men Must Rededicate Themselves to Preserve Civilization," *Pottstown Mercury*, November 17, 1958.

23. "Opportunity Board Names N. Marable."

24. "NAACP Executive Board Endorses Court Action," *Pottstown Mercury*, May 26, 1954; "NAACP Hears Delegates Report on Convention," *Pottstown Mercury*, June 10, 1963; "NAACP Hears Speech by Funeral Director," *Pottstown Mercury*, June 10, 1958; "Local NAACP Observes Desegregation Day," *Pottstown Mercury*, May 24, 1965. For subhead quote, see Paul F. Levy, "Mr. James P. Crow, Esquire. . . . A Sequel: Same Old Fellow? No, He's Plain Jim Crow Now," *Pottstown Mercury*, June 11, 1963.

25. "Education Director Presents Charter to NAACP Chapter," *Pottstown Mercury*, December 27, 1951; "Fellowship House Raises Funds," *Pottstown Mercury*, August 29, 1960.

26. Hill, *Dear Sir*, 59; M. C. F., letter to the editor, *Pottstown Mercury*, September 7, 1961; Tom Stie, letter to the editor, *Pottstown Mercury*, May 4, 1963; Mr. and Mrs. John H. Ivory, letter to the editor, *Pottstown Mercury*, January 25, 1963; LMM, letter to the editor, *Pottstown Mercury*, August 28, 1965. For civil rights legislation pertaining to the historiography, see Hall, "Long Civil Rights Movement and the Political Uses of the Past," 1234; Williams, *Rethinking the Black Freedom Movement*, xi–xii.

27. "Mercury Will Revisit James P. Crow, Esquire," *Pottstown Mercury*, June 10, 1963. For 1963 series, see Levy, "Mr. James P. Crow, Esquire. . . . A Sequel: Same Old Fellow"; Paul F. Levy, "Mr. James P. Crow, Esquire. . . . A Sequel: That Home's Rented, Just Few Minutes Ago!," *Pottstown Mercury*, June 12, 1963; Paul F. Levy, "Mr. James P. Crow, Esq.: Invisible Wall Separates Negroes from 'Friends'; They Can't Scale Barrier," *Pottstown Mercury*, June 13, 1963; Paul F. Levy, "Mr. James P. Crow Esquire: Not Even Tax Dollar Will Aid Him," *Pottstown Mercury*, June 14, 1963; Paul F. Levy, "Mr. James P. Crow Esquire: 'We Operate under the Constitution': Private Organizations, Public Funds; Still No Negroes in Fire Companies," *Pottstown Mercury*, June 15, 1963; Paul F. Levy, "Mister James P. Crow Esquire: Alone in the Crowd. . . . Not That No One Wants Him. . . . But Because He Doesn't Ask!. . . .," *Pottstown Mercury*, June 17, 1963; Paul F. Levy, "Mr. James P. Crow, Esq.: Education Salvation of Negro, but Few Here Take Advantage of It," *Pottstown Mercury*, June 18, 1963; Paul F. Levy, "Mr. James P. Crow, Esq.: Good Enough to Spend Money, but Not Good Enough for Job," *Pottstown Mercury*, June 19, 1963; Paul F. Levy, "Mr. James P. Crow, Esq.: Firms within Law, Must Just Make It," *Pottstown Mercury*, June 20, 1963; Paul F. Levy, "Mr. James P. Crow Esquire: Equal Opportu-

nity Leads to End of Discrimination," *Pottstown Mercury*, June 21, 1963. For 1954 series, see chap. 5.

28. Levy, "Mr. James P. Crow, Esquire. . . . A Sequel: That Home's Rented, Just Few Minutes Ago!" On ghettoization, see Jones, *Selma of the North*, 19. For the Black housing discrimination nationally and locally, see Theoharis, introduction, 9; Levy, *Great Uprising*, 231–33; Sugrue, *Sweet Land of Liberty*, 11, 16–17; Carter, letter to the editor.

29. Cohen and Cohen, *Chicken Hill Chronicle*, 98, 115, 178.

30. Griffiths, "Night's Aglow and Klan Cross Brightens Chicken Hill."

31. "Chicken Hill—This Is an Area in Pottstown, Pa., Known as 'Chicken Hill', Occupied Mainly by Negro Citizens. Pottstown, like Other Cities in the South and North, Deny Negroes the Right to Live in Certain Areas," *Pittsburgh Courier*, August 21, 1954.

32. Hill, *Dear Sir*, 50.

33. Timothy White, "Soul to Soul: Rock's Most Famous Duo Just Can't Seem to Break Up: The Continuing Saga of Hall & Oates," *Spin*, July 1988, 34, https:// books.google.com/books?id=gBfYiTJzzxEC. For background on Hall, see Mike Morsch, "40th Anniversary of Hall & Oates' 'Abandoned Luncheonette,'" *Mercury*, February 16, 2013, 10:19 p.m., EST (updated September 24, 2021, 10:51 a.m. EST), https://www.pottsmerc.com/2013/02/16/40th-anniversary-of-hall-oates -abandoned-luncheonette/.

34. Levy, "Mr. James P. Crow, Esq.: Invisible Wall Separates Negroes from 'Friends.'"

35. Ed Zumach, "Residents of Hemlock Row Will Take Petition to Council for Paving, Sewers, Lights," *Pottstown Mercury*, August 15, 1952.

36. "Hemlock Row Complaint to Bring Council Action," *Pottstown Mercury*, August 19, 1954.

37. Radford Crouse, "Junior High Boundary Line Decisions Are Postponed: Schoolmen Will Await Suggestions; NAACP Explains Segregation Charge; Fosnocht Denies Intentional Bias," *Pottstown Mercury*, March 7, 1961.

38. "Orphans Barred from Pine Forge, Pa., School," *Evening Sun*, September 22, 1960; "School Doors Open to Foster Children: State Reverses Board's Decision; Raps Reason for Banning Youngsters," *Pottstown Mercury*, October 28, 1960. See chap. 3 for an earlier civil rights struggle relating to African American education in early postwar America, particularly about Pine Forge.

39. "Berks School Denies Entry by 5 Negroes," *Morning Call*, September 22, 1960; "Status of Orphans Is in Dispute," *Gettysburg Times*, September 22, 1960; "School Argument Underway—: Are Orphans Legal Residents in Foster Parents' Community?," *Indiana Evening Gazette*, September 22, 1960.

40. "Race Issue Not Involved in Pine Forge School Ban," *Philadelphia Tribune*, September 24, 1960; "Ban Negro Children from School in Pa." (Special to the Courier), *Pittsburgh Courier*, October 8, 1960; "5 Foster Children Barred from Class," *Afro-American*, October 8, 1960, https://news.google.com/newspapers?nid=UBn QDr5gPskC. On *Philadelphia Tribune*, see V. P. Franklin, "'Voice of the Black Community': The *Philadelphia Tribune*, 1912–41," *Pennsylvania History: A Journal of Mid-Atlantic Studies* 51, no. 4 (1984): 261–84, http://www.jstor.org/stable /27773002.

41. William Randall, "Five Orphans Barred from Classes by Pine Forge School Board Order: No Room, Says Panel Solicitor; Children Missed Two Weeks of Studies; Ruling Miffs Foster Parents," *Pottstown Mercury*, September 22, 1960; "Status of Orphans Is in Dispute."

42. "Status of Orphans Is in Dispute."

43. "Segregation and Racism in Berks County," in *Woven with Words: A Collection of African American History in Berks County, Pennsylvania*, ed. Laurie Grobman and Gary Kunkelman (West Reading, PA: Rieck's Printing, 2006), 44. There is also a website about this piece of scholarship. See "(Re)Writing Local Histories: Racial, Ethnic, and Cultural Communities," Sites at Penn State, accessed January 4, 2023, https://sites.psu.edu/localhistories/woven-with-words/segregation-and-racism-in-berks-county/.

44. "5 Foster Children Barred from Class."

45. "No Room for Them," *Pottstown Mercury*, September 23, 1960. For coverage, see, for example, Randall, "Five Orphans Barred from Classes by Pine Forge School Board Order."

46. On Henry's NAACP presidential tenure, see "Marable Named Head of NAACP"; "Congressman to Be Guest at Banquet: George M. Rhodes Is Invited by NAACP," *Pottstown Mercury*, November 12, 1962. Henry is mentioned later in this chapter in relation to NAACP activism. For further data on Henry, also see Randolph Henry, personal communication, August 27, 1961, "Jim Gaut" Activities Programs, [Test Cases] Sunnybrook Swim Club, 1961–73, Box 28/folder 491, FHPA-Temple; Gaut, "Report of the Test of the Sunnybrook Swimming Club August 27, 1961 Pottstown, Pennsylvania," FHPA-Temple; Gaut to Boyer, September 5, 1961, FHPA-Temple.

47. "NAACP Group Pickets Club in Pottstown," *Pottstown Mercury*, November 8, 1965; "NAACP Seeks Boycott of Borough Club: Charges Discrimination by Die Casters Group," *Pottstown Mercury*, April 13, 1965; "NAACP Youths Bar Die Casters as Party Site," *Pottstown Mercury*, April, 15, 1965; Levy, "Mr. James P. Crow Esquire: Equal Opportunity Leads to End of Discrimination"; "NAACP Maps Drive to Upset Town's Discrimination: Will Wage Total Campaign to End Local Inequalities; Anti-James Crow Esq. Campaign Planned This Summer," *Pottstown Mercury*, April 14, 1965; "Area Swim Club Is Picketed by NAACP Group"; "Pickets Again Demonstrate at Swimming Pool," *Pottstown Mercury*, June 6, 1966; "Council Seeks Repeal of Pottsgrove Work Tax: School Levy Is Termed 'Big Mistake'; Councilman Proposes Similar Measure in Borough; Solution Is Asked for BB Menace," *Pottstown Mercury*, June 14, 1966. For subhead quote, see "Business on Wheels Irks Storeman; Seeks Council Help," *Pottstown Mercury*, July 12, 1966.

48. Poirier, "Jim Crow, Yankee Style, Stalks Streets of Pottstown."

49. "NAACP Seeks Boycott of Borough Club."

50. "'Tax Supported Fire Unit Never Private': NAACP," *Afro-American*, June 29, 1963, https://news.google.com/newspapers?nid=UBnQDr5gPskC. For Moser, see "Mayor: 'He Was a Dedicated Man': Fire Chief Moser Dies; Served in Post 19 years," *Mercury*, May 6, 1977.

51. Levy, "Mr. James P. Crow Esquire: 'We Operate under the Constitution.'"

52. "Tax Supported Fire Unit Never Private."

53. Levy, "Mr. James P. Crow Esquire: 'We Operate Under the Constitution'"; Levy, "Mr. James P. Crow Esquire: Equal Opportunity Leads to End of Discrimination."

54. "Area Swim Club Is Picketed by NAACP Group."

55. "Business on Wheels Irks Storeman."

56. Arnold, *Building the Beloved Community*, 60. On Mitzi, see "Mitzi Rona Barnes: March 17, 1931–April 21, 2018."

57. Gaut to Boyer, September 5, 1961, FHPA-Temple. For Gaut's activism during Marable's presidency, see, for example, "Business on Wheels Irks Storeman."

58. James E Gaut, 1974, United States Public Records, 1970–2009, Family-Search database December 18, 2019, https://familysearch.org/ark:/61903/1:1:KRYQ -PXB; "James Edwin Gaut: October 19, 1921–November 21, 2012; Obituary," Warker-Troutman Funeral Home, accessed November 16, 2022, https://memorials .kuhnfuneralhomes.com/james-gaut/4449769/index.php.

59. For Gaut's employment and unionism, see "Doehler Apprentices Awarded Diplomas," *Pottstown Mercury*, April 20, 1949; R.L. Polk & Co., *Polk's Pottstown (Montgomery County, PA.) City Directory Vol. 1961 XXXVI Including Kenilworth, Sanatoga, South Pottstown and Stowe and Boyertown Including Morysville* (Boston, MA: R.L. Polk & CO., 1961), 155, https://phspa.org/portfolio-item/city-directories/; R.L. Polk & Co., *Polk's Pottstown (Montgomery County, PA.) City Directory 1964 Including Kenilworth, Sanatoga, South Pottstown and Stowe and Boyertown Including Morysville* (Boston, MA: R.L. Polk & CO., 1964), 181, https://phspa.org/portfolio-item/city -directories/; "Union Delegates Go to Capital," *Pottstown Mercury*, February 22, 1960; "Nine Pottstown Unionists Hear Reuther Speak," *Pottstown Mercury*, March 21, 1960.

60. *Pottstown Human Relations Council . . . For Equality*, 1955, FHPA-Temple.

61. [Undated and Unidentified Document, "The record of John Henry . . ."], "Jim Gaut" Activities Programs, [Test Cases] Sunnybrook Swim Club, 1961–73, Box 28/folder 491, FHPA-Temple.

62. Gaut to Boyer, September 5, 1961, FHPA-Temple.

63. James Gaut, "Report of the Test of the Sunnybrook Swimming Club August 27, 1961 Pottstown, Pennsylvania," "Jim Gaut" Activities Programs, [Test Cases] Sunnybrook Swim Club, 1961–73, Box 28/folder 491, FHPA-Temple; "Corum to Head NAACP Chapter," *Pottstown Mercury*, December 12, 1960; Gaut to Boyer, September 5, 1961, FHPA-Temple; "Marable Named Head of NAACP."

64. Henry, personal communication, August 27, 1961, FHPA-Temple. Also, see Gaut, "Report of the Test of the Sunnybrook Swimming Club August 27, 1961 Pottstown, Pennsylvania," FHPA-Temple.

65. Gaut, "Report of the Test of the Sunnybrook Swimming Club August 27, 1961 Pottstown, Pennsylvania," FHPA-Temple; Gaut to Boyer, September 5, 1961, FHPA-Temple.

66. "Sunnybrook Founder R.C. Hartenstine, Dies," *Pottstown Mercury*, July 27, 1972.

67. Gaut, "Report of the Test of the Sunnybrook Swimming Club August 27, 1961 Pottstown, Pennsylvania," FHPA-Temple.

68. "Open Letter to People at Sunnybrook," "Jim Gaut" Activities Programs, [Test Cases] Sunnybrook Swim Club, 1961–73, Box 28/folder 491, FHPA-Temple.

69. Phillip H. Savage to Marjorie Penney, February 2, 1967, "Jim Gaut" Activities Programs, [Test Cases] Sunnybrook Swim Club, 1961–73, Box 28/folder 491, FHPA-Temple. For HRC's response, see Elliot M. Shirk to Phillip H. Savage, February 9, 1967, "Jim Gaut" Activities Programs, [Test Cases] Sunnybrook Swim Club, 1961–73, Box 28/folder 491, FHPA-Temple. For an image of Savage, see "Pumping Iron, a Streaker and Perfection: 24 Iconic Images That Were Taken on July 23; 1963: Civil Rights Churches," *St. Louis Post-Dispatch*, July 23, 2023, https://www.stltoday .com/news/archives/iconic-images-that-were-taken-on-july/collection_b8688d53 -4c7b-5fbf-b13e-d620f91facf8.html#15.

70. *The Troiad 1949* (Boyertown, PA: Boyertown Times Publishing Company, 1949), 18, https://www.pottstownschools.org/AlumniYearbooks.aspx. On Millicent's familial connection to James H. Corum as well as from where, see Millicent E. Corum, Line 24, Sheet 8, Enumeration District 46-312, Pottstown Township, Montgomery County, Pennsylvania, Seventeenth Census of the United States, 1950, Record Group 29, Records of the Bureau of the Census, National Archives and Records Administration, Washington, DC, accessed August 4, 2022, https:// 1950census.archives.gov/.

71. On Millicent's familial connection to James H. Corum, see Millicent E. Corum, Line 24, Sheet 8, Enumeration District 46-312, Pottstown Township, Montgomery County, Pennsylvania, Seventeenth Census of the United States, 1950, Record Group 29, Records of the Bureau of the Census, National Archives and Records Administration, Washington, DC, accessed August 4, 2022, https://1950census.archives.gov/. For further familial connection, see "Bad Heart Cause of Corum Death."

72. "Community Icon Newstell Marable, Longtime Pottstown NAACP President, Dies at 84."

73. "NAACP Plans Citation for James Corum: Union President to Be Honored At Banquet," *Pottstown Mercury*, May 17, 1960.

74. "Women's Excelsior Class to Present Fashion Show," *Pottstown Mercury*, June 26, 1951; "Baby Queen Is Crowned at Circus Bazaar Sponsored by Girl Scout Troop in Center," *Pottstown Mercury*, May 1, 1950; "Scout Troop 13 Entertains at Leaders' Club Meeting," *Pottstown Mercury*, March 4, 1952.

75. Evan Brandt, "Evan Brandt: Reporter Sees History of Civil Rights Era Come Alive," *Mercury*, February 13, 2015, 2:04 p.m. EST (updated September 24, 2021, 3:19 a.m. EST), https://www.pottsmerc.com/2015/02/13/evan-brandt-reporter -sees-history-of-civil-rights-era-come-alive/.

76. "Community Icon Newstell Marable, Longtime Pottstown NAACP President, Dies at 84."

77. Evan Brandt, "Millicent Marable, Widow of NAACP President Newstell Marable, on Protesting Black Exclusion from Sunnybrook Pool," *Mercury*, February 15, 2015, YouTube video, 0:56, https://www.youtube.com/watch?v=VDjQRpSuMXA.

78. Brandt, "Millicent Marable, Widow of NAACP President Newstell Marable, on Protesting Black Exclusion from Sunnybrook Pool."

79. Brandt, "Evan Brandt: Reporter Sees History of Civil Rights Era Come Alive"; "Community Icon Newstell Marable, Longtime Pottstown NAACP President, Dies at 84"; Brandt, "Millicent Marable, Widow of NAACP President Newstell Marable, on Protesting Black Exclusion from Sunnybrook Pool."

80. Thomas Sephakis, *The Sunnybrook Ballroom*, Images of America (Charleston, SC: Arcadia Publishing, 2007), 7; "NAACP Seeks Boycott Of Borough Club."

81. "Open Letter to People at Sunnybrook," FHPA-Temple.

82. "Council Seeks Repeal of Pottsgrove Work Tax"; Poirier, "Jim Crow, Yankee Style, Stalks Streets of Pottstown"; Levy, "Mr. James P. Crow Esquire: 'We Operate under the Constitution.'"

83. "Business on Wheels Irks Storeman."

84. Levy, "Mr. James P. Crow, Esq.: Firms within Law, Must Just Make It." For 1954 series, see chap. 5. While Randolph Henry also headed the Pottstown NAACP, there is not much data on his presidency. Thus, I only compare and contrast Marable to Corum's and Prince's NAACP presidencies in the analyses for the remainder of this chapter.

85. "Unionists' Help Seen for NAACP: Campaign for Equality Is Aimed at Local Companies; Meany Gives Support to Equal Employment," *Pottstown Mercury*, April 15, 1965.

86. "NAACP Asks Fireman to Change Show: Objects to Minstrel Performance in Collegeville," *Pottstown Mercury*, January 23, 1963.

87. Levy, *Great Uprising*, 1. For subhead quote, see "Phoenixville Classes Cancelled," *Pottstown Mercury*, April 1, 1969.

88. "Local NAACP Organizes Unit to Combat Rioters," *Pottstown Mercury*, July 27, 1967.

89. "NAACP Eyes 'Preventive' Riot Program," *Afro-American*, July 1, 1967; "Local NAACP Organizes Unit to Combat Rioters."

90. "Local NAACP Organizes Unit to Combat Rioters."

91. "Traffic Controls Approved as Plea for Sign Is Made," *Pottstown Mercury*, April 11, 1967.

92. "Safety and Riots Don't Mix," *Pottstown Mercury*, April 14, 1967; "Traffic Controls Approved as Plea for Sign Is Made."

93. Martin Kirby, "'Clean Up Penn Village': A Teen Evaluates Pottstown," *Philadelphia Inquirer*, March 17, 1968. On Brown, see Levy, *Great Uprising*, 66–116.

94. Kirby, "Clean Up Penn Village."

95. "An Editorial: Okay Kids, Cool It," *Pottstown Mercury*, April 11, 1968.

96. Levy, *Great Uprising*, 153.

97. "Phoenixville Classes Cancelled." On Pottstown-Phoenixville NAACP name, also see James E. Shapiro, "Local Negroes Sure There'll Be No Riot," *Pottstown Mercury*, August 7, 1967.

98. "Phoenixville Classes Cancelled"; Al Haas, "53 Arrests End School Sit-In at Phoenixville," *Philadelphia Inquirer*, April 1, 1969; "53 Arrested in Sit-in At Phoe-

nixville High," *Hazelton Standard-Speaker*, April 1, 1969; "50 Students Arrested at Sit-In," *Indiana Evening Gazette*, April 1, 1969.

99. Lemberg Center for the Study of Violence, *U.S. Race-Related Civil Disorders, January–June, 1969* (Waltham, MA: Civil Disorder Clearinghouse, Brandeis University, 1969), 47; National Association for the Advancement of Colored People, *Annual Report 1969*, New York, June, 1970, 47.

100. "53 Freed in Bail after School Sit-In at Phoenixville," *Philadelphia Daily News*, April 1, 1969.

101. For example, see Levy, *Great Uprising*, 82, 222, 262, 265.

102. "Black Demands Place Emphasis on That Color," *Pottstown Mercury*, April 1, 1969.

103. "Phoenixville Classes Cancelled." For Ramsey using name Virginia too, see "Phoenixville Situation Stays Tense," *Pottstown Mercury*, May 12, 1969.

104. "Phoenixville Situation Stays Tense"; "Phoenixville Classes Cancelled."

105. Haas, "53 Arrests End School Sit-In at Phoenixville"; "Phoenixville Classes Cancelled."

106. Peniel E. Joseph, "Dashikis and Democracy: Black Studies, Student Activism, and the Black Power Movement," *Journal of African American History* 88, no. 2 (Spring 2003): 182–203, www.jstor.org/stable/3559065; "Phoenixville Classes Cancelled."

107. Robinson, *City within a City*, 112; "Phoenixville Classes Cancelled."

108. "Phoenixville Youths Riot Following School Skirmish," *Pottstown Mercury*, May 9, 1969. On comparison, see "Phoenixville Classes Cancelled."

109. "4 Phoenixville Students Hurt in Racial Clash over Parade," *Philadelphia Daily News*, May 9, 1969. For larger comparison, see Levy, *Great Uprising*.

110. "Phoenixville Youths Riot Following School Skirmish."

111. "Phoenixville Situation Stays Tense." For other areas, see Levy, *Great Uprising*, 17–116, 225–313.

112. "Two Sink in Mud: Downpour Opens Trap for Trucks," *Pottstown Mercury*, August 12, 1955. For Pottstown NAACP activism over time, see, for instance, Zumach, "Residents of Hemlock Row Will Take Petition to Council for Paving, Sewers, Lights"; "Prince Re-Elected President of NAACP in Baptist Church," *Pottstown Mercury*, November 26, 1952; "Hemlock Row Complaint to Bring Council Action"; "Two Are Appointed to NAACP Committee," *Pottstown Mercury*, June 15, 1955.

113. "School Doors Open to Foster Children"; "New Order for School," *Evening Standard*, October 29, 1960; "5 Foster Children Start Classes at Pine Forge," *Pottstown Mercury*, November 1, 1960. On Pottstown NAACP involvement, see "5 Foster Children Barred from Class."

114. Radford Crouse, "School Boundary Praised by Minister," *Pottstown Mercury*, October 3, 1961. For previous activism, see Crouse, "Junior High Boundary Line Decisions Are Postponed."

115. "NAACP Group Pickets Club in Pottstown"; "NAACP Seeks Boycott of Borough Club"; "NAACP Youths Bar Die Casters as Party Site"; Levy, "Mr. James P.

Crow Esquire: Not Even Tax Dollar Will Aid Him"; Levy, "Mr. James P. Crow Esquire: Equal Opportunity Leads to End of Discrimination"; "NAACP Maps Drive to Upset Town's Discrimination"; "Area Swim Club Is Picketed by NAACP Group"; "Pickets Again Demonstrate at Swimming Pool"; "Council Seeks Repeal of Pottsgrove Work Tax"; "Business on Wheels Irks Storeman"; "Negro Joins North End; Not Glenn: Rejected Applicant Plans Fight for Membership," *Pottstown Mercury*, November 30, 1966.

116. "Sunnybrook Swim Club Ruled 'Private' by State Commission" (Pottstown Mercury penned in on document), December 9, 1966, newspaper clipping, "Jim Gaut" Activities Programs, [Test Cases] Sunnybrook Swim Club, 1961–73, Box 28/folder 491, FHPA-Temple; "Open Letter to People at Sunnybrook," FHPA-Temple. For further historical context, see Phillip H. Savage to Lou Gaut, Marjorie Penney, C. Delores Tucker, Henry R. Smith and Newstell Marable, 31 March 1967, "Jim Gaut" Activities Programs, [Test Cases] Sunnybrook Swim Club, 1961–73, Box 28/folder 491, FHPA-Temple.

117. Savage to Penney, February 2, 1967, FHPA-Temple. To see the Pennsylvania HRC's response, see Shirk to Savage, February 9, 1967, FHPA-Temple.

118. James E. Shapiro, "Racial Violence: Is Pottstown Kindled for a Spark?," *Pottstown Mercury*, August 5, 1967.

119. "An Editorial: End All Injustices," *Pottstown Mercury*, August 7, 1967.

120. Shapiro, "Racial Violence."

121. Stephen R. Allen, "Firemen Give Minstrel but Keep Off Blackface," *Pottstown Mercury*, January 26, 1963; "NAACP Asks Fireman to Change Show."

122. "Collegeville Minstrel Keeps Blackface Ban," *Philadelphia Inquirer*, January 26, 1964.

123. "Phoenixville Youths Riot Following School Skirmish"; "Phoenixville Situation Stays Tense."

124. "Cited for Civil Rights Achievements," *Philadelphia Tribune*, November 2, 1965; "Opportunity Board Names N. Marable."

125. See earlier in this chapter for the three NAACP civil rights initiatives under Marable. For other examples of white pushback, see Hill, *Dear Sir*, 59; M. C. F., letter to the editor; Stie, letter to the editor; Ivory, letter to the editor; LMM, letter to the editor.

126. Levy, "Mr. James P. Crow, Esquire. . . . A Sequel: Same Old Fellow?" See chap. 5 for the 1954 series.

127. Hill, *Dear Sir*, 59, 58.

128. M. C. F., letter to the editor.

129. Stie, letter to the editor.

130. Ivory, letter to the editor. For local NAACP activism, see "NAACP Asks Fireman to Change Show."

131. LMM does not identify Watts specifically, but the time coincides with Watts. See LMM, letter to the editor. For Watts, see Gerald Horne, *Fire This Time: The Watts Uprising and the 1960s* (Charlottesville: University Press of Virginia, 1995). On CORE, see Purnell, *Fighting Jim Crow in the County of Kings*, 31.

132. "Local NAACP Protests Death of Fla. Leader," *Pottstown Mercury*, January 24, 1952. On the Moores, see "Harry T. and Harriette Moore," Civil Rights Leaders, NAACP, accessed January 6, 2023, https://naacp.org/find-resources/history -explained/civil-rights-leaders/harry-t-and-hariette-moore.

133. "33 Join NAACP March as Tribute to Slain Evers," *Pottstown Mercury*, June 24, 1963. For background on Evers, see Michael Vinson Williams, *Medgar Evers: Mississippi Martyr* (Fayetteville: University of Arkansas Press, 2011).

134. "Local Rights Marchers Are Elated at Success," *Pottstown Mercury*, August 29, 1963. On March, see *Encyclopedia Britannica Online*, s.v., "March on Washington," August 28, 2023, https://www.britannica.com/event/March-on-Washington.

135. For King, see "Martin Luther King, Jr.," National Archives at New York City, National Archive's Website, accessed January 9, 2023, https://www.archives .gov/nyc/exhibit/mlk. For Millicent's remarks, see Evan Brandt, "Millicent Marable, Widow of Pottstown NAACP Chapter President Newstell Marable, Recalls the March on Washington," *Mercury*, February 15, 2015, YouTube video, 1:00, https://www .youtube.com/watch?v=knRygnJjYTI.

136. "Fellowship House Raises Funds"; "Pottstown Coed Arrested in Mass Sitdown Dispute: College Student Fights Racial Bias," *Pottstown Mercury*, April 22, 1960. On iconic sit-ins, see William H. Chafe, *Civilities and Civil Rights: Greensboro, North Carolina, and the Black Struggle for Freedom* (New York: Oxford University Press, 1981), 71. On Prince being president during this time, see "Local NAACP Chapter Will Meet Tonight," *Pottstown Mercury*, July 23, 1960; "Corum to Head NAACP Chapter."

137. Deidre B. Flowers, "The Launching of the Student Sit-in Movement: The Role of Black Women at Bennett College," *Journal of African American History* 90, no. 1/2, *Brown v. Board of Education: Fifty Years of Educational Change in the United States, 1954–2004* (Winter 2005): 59, https://www.jstor.org/stable/20063975.

138. United Press International, "Mixing Attempt Starts Brawl: Biloxi Has Rioting at Gulf Beach," *Greenville News*, April 25, 1960. On the initial four Black activists, see Jaime Huaman, "Greensboro Four: David Richmond, Franklin McCain, Ezell Blair Jr. (Jibreel Khazan), Joe McNeil; Civil Rights Sit-Ins at Woolworth," NCpedia, accessed January 6, 2023, https://www.ncpedia.org/greensboro-four. On Bennett and North Carolina A&T, see Chafe, *Civilities and Civil Rights*, 20–21.

139. United Press International, "Sitdown Starters Charged," *Times Recorder*, April 25, 1960; "2 White Girls Held in Sitdown Incident," *Scranton Times*, April 22, 1960; "Mixing Attempt Starts Brawl"; "Leonia Girl Is Arrested: Aided Negro Sit-Down in Greensboro," *Bergen Evening Record*, April 22, 1960; "45 Arrested in Sitdowns, Greensboro," *High Point Enterprise*, April 22, 1960; "Indictment Action Delayed on Sitdowns," *Sun*, June 14, 1960; Special to the *New York Times*, "45 Students Seized in Greensboro Sit-In," *New York Times*, April 22, 1960.

140. "Margaret Jean Neff, 20, of Pottstown, PA, White Student at Bennett College, Greensboro, N.C., Confers with Unidentified Negro Student at Lunch Counter of Chain Store before Telling R.L. Bland (at Her Right), an Official of the Store, That

She Wouldn't Leave Counter. She and 44 Other Students Were Arrested," *Philadel-phia Inquirer*, April 23, 1960.

141. "Pottstown Coed Arrested in Mass Sitdown Dispute."

142. M. F. D., letter to the editor, *Pottstown Mercury*, April 26, 1960.

143. "Fellowship House Raises Funds."

144. "NAACP Sends Clothes to Sharecroppers," *Pottstown Mercury*, February 21, 1961; "NAACP Names Three Delegates," *Pottstown Mercury*, April 15, 1963; "Local NAACP Group Conducts March," *Pottstown Mercury*, March 8, 1965; "Local NAACP Protests Death of Fla. Leader"; "33 Join NAACP March as Tribute to Slain Evers."

145. "1200 at Memorial Service Mourn Death of Dr. King," *Pottstown Mercury*, April 8, 1968.

146. Herman, "Prominent Civil-Rights Leader in Pottstown Recalled."

7. Lessons Learned from Pottstown's Black Freedom Struggle

1. "Final Plans Made for Negro Center."

2. On Great Migration, see Alexander et al., "Second-Generation Outcomes of the Great Migration," 2250–71.

3. Theoharis, *More Beautiful and Terrible History*, 103.

4. Theoharis, *More Beautiful and Terrible History*, 102.

5. "How George Floyd Died, and What Happened Next: Mr. Floyd, a Black Man, Died in May 2020 after Being Handcuffed and Pinned to the Ground by Minneapolis Police Officers in an Episode That Was Captured on Video, Touching Off Nationwide Protests," *New York Times*, July 29, 2022, https://www.nytimes.com/article /george-floyd.html; Richard Fausset, "Before Breonna Taylor and George Floyd, There Was Ahmaud Arbery: A Year after His Killing in Georgia, His Death Has Sparked a Bipartisan Effort to Remake the State's 158-Year-Old Citizen's Arrest Law. But a Potentially Divisive Trial Awaits," *New York Times*, February 28, 2021 (updated November 3, 2021), https://www.nytimes.com/2021/02/28/us/ahmaud-arbery -anniversary.html; Washington, "Examining Interracial Civil Rights Activism in 1950s Pottstown, Pennsylvania," 137.

6. Karen Dolan, "The Movement for Black Lives Is a Small-Town Movement, Too: Turns Out a Whole Lot of Americans Don't Like Racism or Police Brutality—Even in Conservative, White, Rural, or Southern Towns," Institute for Policy Studies, June 16, 2020, https://ips-dc.org/movement-for-black-lives-small-town-movement-too/.

7. Maggie Astor, "Census Updates: Survey Shows Which Cities Gained and Lost Population: Here Are the States and Cities That Grew the Most," *New York Times*, August 12, 2021 (updated August 19, 2021), https://www.nytimes.com/live/2021/08 /12/us/census-results-data.

8. "Census Updates"; Dolan, "Movement for Black Lives Is a Small-Town Move-ment, Too."

9. "Pottstown NAACP: Hope Can, and Will, Heal the World," Pottstown NAACP, accessed January 6, 2023, https://www.pottstownnaacp.org/.

10. Evan Brandt, "Thousands March in Pottstown for Racial Justice," *Digital Notebook: All the News That Doesn't Fit in Print* (blog), June 7, 2020, http:// evan-brandt.blogspot.com/2020/06/thousands-march-in-pottstown-for-racial.html.

11. Pottstown Area Health & Wealth Foundation, accessed January 6, 2023, https://pottstownfoundation.org/.

12. Brandt, "Thousands March in Pottstown for Racial Justice." For some other examples in which *Mercury* reporting illuminates the tradition cultivated by Hill's civil rights advocacy work, see "Pottstown Bridge Named in Honor of Newstell Marable Sr."; "Community Icon Newstell Marable, Longtime Pottstown NAACP President, Dies at 84." Throughout this book, there are many more examples captured by the *Mercury* and cited as well. For illustrations relating to the civil rights advocacy tradition Hill cultivated, see Hill, *Dear Sir*, 50–63.

13. For "usable past" conceptualization, see Robert Cook, "'The Glory of the Nation': Black Soldier-Historians and the Continuing African American Struggle for a Usable Past," *Acta Universitatis Carolinae Studia Territorialia* 20, no. 2 (2020): 15, https://doi.org/10.14712/23363231.2021.2. On "de facto" and "de jure," see Theoharis, *More Beautiful and Terrible History*, 34. On analogous modern-day points, also see Washington, "Examining Interracial Civil Rights Activism in 1950s Pottstown, Pennsylvania," 133–34, 137–38. For an article that makes similar points on "de facto" and "de jure" exclusions, see Robert Longley, "What Is De Facto Segregation? Definition and Current Examples," ThoughtCo., February 28, 2021, https:// www.thoughtco.com/de-facto-segregation-definition-4692596.

14. For local Blacks and scholarship, see McCurdy, "Potts Family Iron Industry in the Schuylkill Valley," 57, 147; Chancellor, *History of Pottstown Pennsylvania, 1752–1952*, 58, 60, 63, 125–26; Blockson, "Blacks," 910, 913–15, 917; Snyder, *Remembering Pottstown*, 69, 107–11.

15. Sugrue, *Sweet Land of Liberty*, 200–202, 211–12, 220–28, 230, 232–33, 243; Levy, *Great Uprising*, 223–313.

16. Poirier, "Jim Crow, Yankee Style, Stalks Streets of Pottstown."

Selected Bibliography

Primary Sources

Archival Collections

Fellowship House (Philadelphia, Pennsylvania) Records. Special Collections Research Center, Temple University Libraries, Philadelphia, PA.

Records of the National Association for the Advancement of Colored People. Manuscript Division, Library of Congress, Washington, DC.

Interviews and Miscellaneous Printed Materials

Brandt, Evan. "Millicent Marable, Widow of NAACP President Newstell Marable, on Protesting Black Exclusion from Sunnybrook Pool." *Mercury*, February 15, 2015. YouTube video, 0:56. https://www.youtube.com/watch?v=VDjQRpSuMXA.

———. "Millicent Marable, Widow of Pottstown NAACP Chapter President Newstell Marable, Recalls the March on Washington." *Mercury*, February 15, 2015. YouTube video, 1:00. https://www.youtube.com/watch?v=knRygnJjYTI.

The Claude A. Barnett Papers: The Associated Negro Press, 1918–1967. Part 2, *Associated Negro Press Organizational Files, 1920–1966*. Personal Papers: Chicago Historical Society. Claude A. Barnett Papers, 2011.

Cohen, Lawrence. Interview by Charles Stuart Kennedy. July 12, 2007 (Copyright 2008 ADST). Transcript, Frontline Diplomacy: The Foreign Affairs Oral History Collection of the Association for Diplomatic Studies and Training. Manuscript Division, Library of Congress, Washington, DC. Accessed November 15, 2022. https://www.loc.gov/item/mfdipbib001531/.

Cohen, Norman B., and Lawrence E. Cohen. *Chicken Hill Chronicle: Memoir of a Jewish Family*. Bloomington, IN: Xlibris Corporation, 2011.

Hill, Shandy. *Dear Sir: You Cur*. Philadelphia: Whitmore Publishing, 1969.

Lemberg Center for the Study of Violence. *U.S. Race-Related Civil Disorders, January–June, 1969*. Waltham, MA: Brandeis University, 1969.

Mary McLeod Bethune Papers: The Bethune Foundation Collection. Part 3, *Subject Files, 1939–1955*. Mary McLeod Bethune Foundation Archive. Bethune-Cookman University, Daytona Beach, FL, 2011.

National Association for the Advancement of Colored People. *Annual Report 1969*. New York, June 1970.

The Troiad 1945: A Publication Presented Annually by the Graduating Class of Pottstown High School. Boyertown, PA: Boyertown Times Publishing, 1945. https://www.pottstownschools.org/AlumniYearbooks.aspx.

The Troiad 1949. Boyertown, PA: Boyertown Times Publishing, 1949. https://www.pottstownschools.org/AlumniYearbooks.aspx.

The Troiad 1954. Boyertown, PA: Boyertown Times Publishing, 1954. https://www.pottstownschools.org/AlumniYearbooks.aspx.

Government Documents

Commonwealth of Pennsylvania. *Final Report of the Pennsylvania State Temporary Commission on the Conditions of the Urban Colored Population to the General Assembly of the State of Pennsylvania.* Harrisburg: General Assembly of the State of Pennsylvania, January 1943. https://archive.org/details/finalreportofpen00penn_0.

United States Bureau of the Census. *Eighteenth Census of the United States, 1960.* Vol. 1, *Characteristics of the Population.* Part 40, *Pennsylvania.* Washington, DC: Government Printing Office, 1961. https://www.census.gov/library/publications/1961/dec/population-vol-01.html.

United States Bureau of the Census. *Negro Population, 1790–1915.* Part 7, *General Tables.* Washington, DC: Government Printing Office, 1918. https://www.census.gov/library/publications/1918/dec/negro-population-1790-1915.html.

United States Bureau of the Census. *Nineteenth Census of the United States, 1970.* Vol. 1, *Characteristics of the Population.* Part 40, *Pennsylvania Section 1.* Washington, DC: Government Printing Office, April 1973. https://www.census.gov/library/publications/1973/dec/population-volume-1.html.

United States Bureau of the Census. *Seventeenth Census of the United States, 1950.* Vol. 2, *Characteristics of the Population.* Part 38, *Pennsylvania.* Washington, DC: Government Printing Office, 1952. https://www.census.gov/library/publications/1953/dec/population-vol-02.html.

United States Bureau of the Census. *Sixteenth Census of the United States, 1940.* Vol. 2, *Characteristics of the Population.* Part 6, *Pennsylvania–Texas.* Washington, DC: Government Printing Office, 1943. https://www.census.gov/library/publications/1943/dec/population-vol-2.html.

United States Department of Commerce Economics and Statistics Administration and United States Bureau of the Census. *We the Americans: Blacks.* By Claudette E. Bennett, Barbara M. Martin, and Kymberly DeBarros. Washington, DC: Government Printing Office, 1993. https://www.census.gov/library/publications/1993/dec/we-01.html.

Books and Articles

Alexander, J. Trent, Christine Leibbrand, Catherine Massey, and Stewart Tolnay. "Second-Generation Outcomes of the Great Migration." *Demography* 54, no. 6 (December 2017): 2249–71. http://www.jstor.org/stable/45047340.

"Allegheny Conference." In *A Star Gives Light: Seventh-day Adventist African-American Heritage Teacher's Resource Guide*, edited by Norwida A. Marshall and R. Steven Norman III, 49–50. Decatur, GA: Office of Education Southern Union Conference of Seventh-day Adventists, 1989. http://documents.adventist archives.org/Books/ASGL1989.pdf.

Arnold, Stanley Keith. *Building the Beloved Community: Philadelphia's Interracial Civil Rights Organizations and Race Relations, 1930–1970*. Jackson: University Press of Mississippi, 2014.

Bates, Beth T. "'Double V for Victory' Mobilizes Black Detroit, 1941–1946." In *Freedom North: Black Freedom Struggles outside the South, 1940–1980*, edited by Jeanne Theoharis and Komozi Woodard, 17–39. New York: Palgrave Macmillan, 2003.

Biondi, Martha. *To Stand and Fight: The Struggle for Civil Rights in Postwar New York City*. Cambridge, MA: Harvard University Press, 2003.

Blockson, Charles L. "Blacks." In *Montgomery County: The Second Hundred Years*, vol. 2, edited by Jean Barth Toll and Michael J. Schwager, 910–18. Norristown, PA: Montgomery County Federation of Historical Societies, 1983.

Browne, Arthur. *One Righteous Man: Samuel Battle and the Shattering of the Color Line in New York*. Boston: Beacon Press, 2015.

Burrell, Kristopher Bryan. "Black Women as Activist Intellectuals: Ella Baker and Mae Mallory Combat Northern Jim Crow in New York City's Public Schools during the 1950s." In *The Strange Careers of the Jim Crow North: Segregation and Struggle Outside of the South*, edited by Brian Purnell and Jeanne Theoharis, with Komozi Woodard, 89–112. New York: NYU Press, 2019.

Chancellor, Paul. *A History of Pottstown Pennsylvania, 1752–1952*. Pottstown, PA: Historical Society of Pottstown, 1953.

Commonwealth of Pennsylvania. "Pottstown Group Organizes for Civic Rights." *Department of Internal Affairs* 18, no. 10 (September 1950): 24. https://hdl .handle.net/2027/mdp.39015068488249.

Countryman, Matthew J. *Up South: Civil Rights and Black Power in Philadelphia*. Philadelphia: University of Pennsylvania Press, 2006.

Dalfiume, Richard M. "The 'Forgotten Years' of the Negro Revolution." *Journal of American History*, 55, no. 1 (June 1968): 90–106. https://www.jstor.org /stable/1894253.

Delmont, Matthew F. *Why Busing Failed: Race, Media, and the National Resistance to School Desegregation*. Oakland: University of California Press, 2016.

Dooley, Patricia L. "Jim Crow Strikes Again: The African American Press Campaign against Segregation in Bowling during World War II." *Journal of African American History* 97, no. 3 (Summer 2012): 270–90. https://www.jstor.org/stable /10.5323/jafriamerhist.97.3.0270.

Dougherty, Jack. *More Than One Struggle: The Evolution of Black School Reform in Milwaukee*. Chapel Hill: University of North Carolina Press, 2004.

Douglas, Davidson. *Jim Crow Moves North: The Battle over Northern School Segregation, 1865–1954*. New York: Cambridge University Press, 2005.

Dudziak. Mary L. *Cold War Civil Rights: Race and the Image of American Democracy*. Princeton, NJ: Princeton University Press, 2000.

Hall, Jacquelyn Dowd. "The Long Civil Rights Movement and the Political Uses of the Past." *Journal of American History* 91, no. 4 (March 2005): 1233–63. https://www.jstor.org/stable/3660172.

Jelks, Randal Maurice. *African Americans in the Furniture City: The Struggle for Civil Rights in Grand Rapids.* Urbana: University of Illinois Press, 2006.

Jones, Maxine D. "'Without Compromise or Fear': Florida's African American Female Activists." *Florida Historical Quarterly* 77, no. 4 (Spring 1999): 475–502. https://www.jstor.org/stable/30150829.

Jones, Patrick D. *The Selma of the North: Civil Rights Insurgency in Milwaukee.* Cambridge, MA: Harvard University Press, 2009.

Joseph, Peniel E. "Dashikis and Democracy: Black Studies, Student Activism, and the Black Power Movement." *Journal of African American History* 88, no. 2 (Spring 2003): 182–203. https://www.jstor.org/stable/3559065.

Justiss, Jacob. *Angels in Ebony.* Toledo, OH: Jet Printing Service, 1975. https://www.blacksdahistory.org/_files/ugd/dc5cd6_794e69ae1d1e45acb7f5194b61c3d0a2.pdf.

Kirk, John A. "The NAACP Campaign for Teachers' Salary Equalization: African American Women Educators and the Early Civil Rights Struggle." *Journal of African American History* 94, no. 4, Special Issue: "Documenting the NAACP's First Century" (Fall 2009): 529–52. http://www.jstor.org/stable/25653977.

Korstad, Robert, and Nelson Lichtenstein. "Opportunities Found and Lost: Labor, Radicals, and the Early Civil Rights Movement." *Journal of American History* 75, no. 3 (December 1988): 786–811. https://doi.org/10.2307/1901530.

Kruse, Kevin M., and Stephen Tuck. "Introduction: The Second World War and the Civil Rights Movement." In *Fog of War: The Second World War and the Civil Rights Movement,* edited by Kevin M. Kruse and Stephen Tuck, 3–14. New York: Oxford University Press, 2014.

Lawrence, Charles Radford. "Negro Organizations in Crisis: Depression, New Deal, World War II." PhD diss., Columbia University, 1952.

"Lee, Daniel." In *Who's Who Among Black Americans, 2nd Edition 1977–1978,* vol. 1, 544–45. Northbrook, IL: Who's Who Among Black Americans, 1978.

Levy, Peter B. *The Great Uprising: Race Riots in Urban America during the 1960s.* New York: Cambridge University Press, 2018.

London, Samuel G., Jr. *Seventh-day Adventists and the Civil Rights Movement.* Jackson: University Press of Mississippi, 2009.

McCabe, William H. "Pottstown." In *Montgomery County: The Second Hundred Years,* vol. 1, edited by Jean Barth Toll and Michael J. Schwager, 528–48. Norristown, PA: Montgomery County Federation of Historical Societies, 1983.

McCurdy, Linda. "The Potts Family Iron Industry in the Schuylkill Valley." PhD diss., Pennsylvania State University, 1974.

Miller, Karen R. "'We Cannot Wait for Understanding to Come to Us': Community Activists Respond to Violence at Detroit's Northwestern High School, 1940–1941." In *Groundwork: Local Black Freedom Movements in America,* edited by

Jeanne Theoharis and Komozi Woodard, 235–57. New York: New York University Press, 2005.

Mjagkij, Nina. *Light in the Darkness: African Americans and the YMCA, 1852–1946.* Lexington: University Press of Kentucky, 1994.

Moore, Leonard N. *Black Rage in New Orleans: Police Brutality and African American Activism from World War II to Hurricane Katrina.* Baton Rouge: Louisiana State University Press, 2010.

"Pine Forge Academy: The School in the North." In *A Star Gives Light: Seventh-day Adventist African-American Heritage Teacher's Resource Guide,* edited by Norwida A. Marshall and R. Steven Norman III, 77–79. Decatur, GA: Office of Education Southern Union Conference of Seventh-day Adventists, 1989. http://documents.adventistarchives.org/Books/ASGL1989.pdf.

"Pottstown-Today and Tomorrow." In *Pottstown Sesqui-Centennial, 1965: 150th Anniversary of Formation of Borough,* edited by A. G. Strothers, 5–7. Pottstown, PA: Pottstown Sesquicentennial Committee, 1965.

Purnell, Brian. *Fighting Jim Crow in the County of Kings: The Congress of Racial Equality in Brooklyn.* Lexington: University Press of Kentucky, 2013.

Reed, Merl E. "Black Workers, Defense Industries, and Federal Agencies in Pennsylvania, 1941–1945." In *African Americans in Pennsylvania: Shifting Historical Perspectives,* edited by Joe William Trotter Jr. and Eric Ledell Smith, 363–87. Harrisburg: Pennsylvania State University Press, 1997.

Roberts, Gene, and Hank Klibanoff. *The Race Beat: The Press, the Civil Rights Struggle, and the Awakening of a Nation.* New York: First Vintage Books Edition, 2007.

Robinson, Todd E. *A City within a City: The Black Freedom Struggle in Grand Rapids, Michigan.* Philadelphia, PA: Temple University Press, 2013.

Rossinow, Doug. *Visions of Progress: The Left-Liberal Tradition in America.* Philadelphia: University of Pennsylvania Press, 2008.

Russo, Charles J., J. John Harris III, and Rosetta F. Sandidge. *"Brown v. Board of Education* at 40: A Legal History of Equal Educational Opportunities in American Public Education." *Journal of Negro Education* 63, no. 3 (Summer 1994): 297–309. https://www.jstor.org/stable/2967182.

Self, Robert O. *American Babylon: Race and the Struggle for Postwar Oakland.* Princeton, NJ: Princeton University Press, 2003.

Sephakis, Thomas. *The Sunnybrook Ballroom.* Images of America. Charleston, SC: Arcadia Publishing, 2007.

Sitkoff, Harvard. "Racial Militancy and Interracial Violence in the Second World War." *Journal of American History* 58, no. 3 (December 1971): 661–81. https://www.jstor.org/stable/1893729.

Snyder, Michael T. *Remembering Pottstown: Historic Tales from a Pennsylvania Borough.* Charleston, SC: History Press, 2010.

Sokol, Jason. *All Eyes Are upon Us: Race and Politics from Boston to Brooklyn.* New York: Basic Books, 2014.

Speltz, Mark. *North of Dixie: Civil Rights Photography beyond the South*. Los Angeles: J. Paul Getty Museum, 2016.

Sugrue, Thomas J. *Sweet Land of Liberty: The Forgotten Struggle for Civil Rights in the North*. New York: Random House, 2008.

Switala, William J. *Underground Railroad in Pennsylvania*. Mechanicsburg, PA: Stackpole Books, 2001.

Taylor, Clarence. *Fight the Power: African Americans and the Long History of Police Brutality in New York City*. New York: New York University Press, 2018.

Taylor, Quintard. "The Civil Rights Movement in the American West: Black Protest in Seattle, 1960–1970." *Journal of Negro History* 80, no. 1 (Winter 1995): 1–14. https://www.jstor.org/stable/2717703.

Terry, David Taft. *The Struggle and the Urban South: Confronting Jim Crow in Baltimore before the Movement*. Politics and Culture in the Twentieth-Century South. Athens: University of Georgia Press, 2019.

Theoharis, Jeanne. Introduction to *Freedom North: Black Freedom Struggles outside the South, 1940–1980*, edited by Jeanne Theoharis and Komozi Woodard, 1–15. New York: Palgrave Macmillan, 2003.

———. *A More Beautiful and Terrible History: The Uses and Misuses of Civil Rights History*. Boston: Beacon Press, 2018.

Theoharis, Jeanne, and Brian Purnell. "Histories of Racism and Resistance, Seen and Unseen: How and Why to Think about the Jim Crow North." In *The Strange Careers of the Jim Crow North: Segregation and Struggle Outside of the South*, edited by Brian Purnell and Jeanne Theoharis, with Komozi Woodard, 1–42. New York: NYU Press, 2019.

Theoharis, Jeanne F., and Komozi Woodard, eds. *Freedom North: Black Freedom Struggles Outside the South, 1940–1980*. New York: Palgrave Macmillan, 2003.

Titus, Jill Ogline. *Gettysburg 1963: Civil Rights, Cold War Politics, and Historical Memory in America's Most Famous Small Town*. Chapel Hill: University of North Carolina Press, 2021.

Tomkins, Helen Stark. "Fellowship House Farm." In *Invisible Philadelphia: Community through Voluntary Organizations*, edited by Jean Barth Toll and Mildred S. Gilliam, 606–10. Philadelphia: Atwater Kent Museum, 1995.

Verney, Kevern, Lee Sartain, and Adam Fairclough, eds. *Long Is the Way and Hard: One Hundred Years of the NAACP*. Fayetteville: University of Arkansas Press, 2009.

Wallace, Aurora. *Newspapers and the Making of Modern America: A History*. Westport, CT: Greenwood Press, 2005.

Walter, John C., and Malina Iida. "The State of New York and the Legal Struggle to Desegregate the American Bowling Congress, 1944–1950." *Afro-Americans in New York Life & History* 35, no. 4 (January 2011): 7–32.

Washington, Matthew G. "Examining Interracial Civil Rights Activism in 1950s Pottstown, Pennsylvania." In *Contemporary Debates in Social Justice: An Interdisciplinary Approach to Exploring the Lives of Black and Brown Americans*, edited by

Farrah G. Cambrice, William T. Hoston and Marco Robinson, 131–41. Dubuque, IA: Kendall Hunt Publishing Company, 2021.

Williams, Hettie V. "The Garden of Opportunity: Black Women Intellectuals and the Civil Rights Movement in New Jersey, 1912–1949." PhD diss., Drew University, 2017.

Williams, Yohuru. *Rethinking the Black Freedom Movement.* New York: Routledge, 2016.

Wolfinger, James. "'We Are in the Front Lines in the Battle for Democracy': Carolyn Moore and Black Activism in World War II in Philadelphia." *Pennsylvania History: A Journal of Mid-Atlantic Studies* 72, no. 1 (Winter 2005): 1–23. https://www.jstor.org/stable/27778656.

Yamron, Janet, Sonya Garfinkle, and Amanda Bumgarner. "Elaine Brown: Breaking Down Barriers through Songs." *Choral Journal* 58, no. 5 (December 2017): 24–50. https://www.jstor.org/stable/26412916.

Index

About the Author

Matthew George Washington is an assistant professor of history at Prairie View A&M University. A historian who specializes in the twentieth-century civil rights movement of the American North, he obtained his PhD in history from Morgan State University. Washington has also contributed to the edited compilations *Contemporary Debates in Social Justice: An Interdisciplinary Approach to Exploring the Lives of Black and Brown Americans* (Dubuque, IA: Kendall Hunt Publishing Company, 2021) and *For the Sake of Peace: Africana Perspectives on Racism, Justice, and Peace in America* (Lanham, MD: Rowman & Littlefield Publishers, 2020).